Managing the President's Program

PRINCETON STUDIES IN AMERICAN POLITICS:
HISTORICAL, INTERNATIONAL, AND COMPARATIVE
PERSPECTIVES

SERIES EDITORS
Ira Katznelson, Martin Shefter, Theda Skocpol

A list of titles
in this series appears
at the back of
the book

Managing the President's Program

PRESIDENTIAL LEADERSHIP
AND LEGISLATIVE POLICY FORMULATION

Andrew Rudalevige

PRINCETON UNIVERSITY PRESS
PRINCETON AND OXFORD

Copyright © 2002 by Princeton University Press
Published by Princeton University Press, 41 William Street,
Princeton, New Jersey 08540
In the United Kingdom: Princeton University Press, 3 Market Place,
Woodstock, Oxfordshire OX20 1SY

LIBRARY OF CONGRESS CATALOGING-IN-PUBLICATION DATA

Rudalevige, Andrew, 1968–
Managing the President's program : presidential leadership and legislative policy
formulation / Andrew Rudalevige.
p. cm. — (Princeton studies in American politics)
Includes bibliographical references and index.
ISBN 0-691-09071-8 (alk. paper) — ISBN 0-691-09501-9 (pbk. : alk. paper)
1. Presidents — United States.   2. Political leadership — United States.   3. Political
planning — United States.   4. United States. Congress.   I. Title.   II. Series.

JK585 .R83 2002
352.25'6'0973 — dc21   2001051038

British Library Cataloging-in-Publication Data is available

This book has been composed in Sabon

Printed on acid-free paper. ∞

www.pup.princeton.edu

Printed in the United States of America

1   3   5   7   9   10   8   6   4   2

1   3   5   7   9   10   8   6   4   2
(Pbk.)

TO CHRISTINE, OWEN, AND ELIZA, WITH LOVE

~~~~~~

Enough, if something from our hands have power
To live, and act, and serve the future hour

CONTENTS

List of Tables and Figures   ix

Preface   xi

CHAPTER ONE
Managing the President's Program: Necessary and
    Contingent Truths   1

CHAPTER TWO
Bargaining, Transaction Costs, and Contingent Centralization   18

CHAPTER THREE
The President's Program: History and Conventional Wisdom   41

CHAPTER FOUR
The President's Program: An Empirical Overview   63

CHAPTER FIVE
Putting Centralization to the Test   86

CHAPTER SIX
Congress Is a Whiskey Drinker: Centralization and
    Legislative Success   113

CHAPTER SEVEN
The Odds Are with the House: The Limits of Centralization   134

CHAPTER EIGHT
Hard Choices   152

Appendix: Additional Data and Alternate Specifications   165

Notes   187

References   245

Index   265

LIST OF TABLES AND FIGURES

Table 4.1   Legislative Messages and Proposals, by President   72
Table 4.2   Characteristics, Universe, and Sample of Presidential
             Legislative Proposals   73
Table 4.3   Policy Formulation Strategies, 1949–1996   81
Table 4.4   Level of Centralization, by President, 1949–1996   82
Table 4.5   Source of Legislative Proposals, by Period   82
Table 5.1   Summary of Independent Variables: Centralization   100
Table 5.2   The Context of Centralization (ordered probit)   103
Table 5.3   Impact of Independent Variables on the Likelihood
             of Centralization   105
Table 7.1   Presidential Success in Congress (on presidential
             initiatives)   137
Table 7.2   Mean Success, by President, 1949–1996   138
Table 7.3   Summary of Independent Variables: Success in
             Congress   142
Table 7.4   Determinants of Presidential Success in Congress
             (ordered probit)   144

Figure 3.1   Growth in Government, 1949–2000   48
Figure 3.2   "Thickening" Government, 1952–1992   48
Figure 3.3   White House Office Staff Size, 1949–1996   52
Figure 4.1   Presidential Messages and Proposals, 1949–1996   71
Figure 4.2   Mean Level of Centralization, by Congress   81
Figure 4.3   Processes of Program Formulation, 1949–1996   83
Figure 4.4   Department- and EOP-led Program Formulation   84
Figure 4.5   The Use of Mixed Formulation Strategies   84
Figure 5.1   Determinants of Centralization   106
Figure 5.2   Determinants of Decentralization   107
Figure 7.1   Impact of Centralization on Success in Congress   146
Figure 7.2   Determinants of Success in Congress   147
Figure 7.3   Determinants of Failure in Congress   148

PREFACE

THIS book is about presidential management. That may seem an odd subject: in recent years, after all, the phrase has come to be considered an oxymoron. For while the president is chief executive, his control over the executive branch often seems tenuous at best.

Indeed, this research sprang originally from a desire to pay the compliment of empirical scrutiny to a near-truism of presidency studies: that presidents, responding to an ever larger and less-responsive bureaucracy, have moved inexorably to shift policy formulation into the White House. This theory of centralization seemed plausible, and it was one of the things we actually seemed to "know" about the presidency. However, I made two discoveries. First, while centralization was solidly grounded in the new institutionalism, few scholars had pushed its theoretical logic very far. Second, to my short-term dismay, the systematic data needed to test it had not been collected. Has centralization truly occurred? Does it help presidents? How?

In this book the proving ground for those questions is the president's legislative program. By its very nature, the program provides a useful vantage for helping us to understand not just White House–Cabinet relations but also presidential dealings with Congress. As a recent institution — an expectation of presidents only since the 1940s — the legislative program fits neatly into the time frame associated with centralization. And it is important in its own right, both to presidents and to the polity, as evaluations of presidential leadership itself become tied up in assessments of his legislative success.

Centralization, I will argue, is indeed a reality of modern presidential management. But it is not the only reality. Instead, across the postwar period, presidents have been flexible managers, drawing on a wide range of staff resources as they formulate their legislative programs. They have sought out the least expensive source of reliable information, whether it be centralized in the White House, out in the departments, or somewhere in between. And because the transaction costs associated with different sources of information vary systematically with factors ranging from policy complexity to a president's ideological compatibility with Congress, we can learn about the workings of the institutional presidency by developing a model of contingent centralization that explains why presidents make the choices they do.

Those choices invariably have costs. Although centralization is supposed to be a way for presidents to control their own destiny, proposals formulated via centralized processes do worse in Congress, all else equal, than those produced by a decentralized or mixed process. Presidents must centralize to bargain with the executive branch—but this undercuts their efforts to sway the legislative branch. Such is presidents' delicate balancing act in the midst of a separated system—and such are the managerial challenges that underlie presidential leadership in the twenty-first century.

The first year of George W. Bush's presidency provided a reminder of the centrality of presidents to the policy stage. Bush's legislative program dominated the national agenda in the spring of 2001, bringing discussion of tax cuts, education reform, and fast-track trade authority to the fore. The tragic events of September 11 necessitated the replacement of the pending agenda by presidential requests aimed at fighting terrorism and boosting the domestic economy, from disaster relief and military funding to the enhancement of law enforcement agencies' surveillance and information-sharing capacities.

As the program was launched, attention was also drawn to the means by which it was formulated—to the new president's management style and the advice he received from his White House staff and Cabinet departments. Some observers saw in the Bush Cabinet a reversal of centralization; no less an authority than retired New York senator Daniel Patrick Moynihan declared that "it's going back to a Cabinet government." Yet at the same time others commented on "another truism about the Bush administration: White House aides' dominance over domestic Cabinet agencies."[1]

Which is true? In fact both are likely to be true at different times and under different conditions. The answer is—as usual—"it depends." This book, I hope, will help readers gain a better understanding about what it depends upon. It provides a new theory about presidents and their management environment; it provides a new data source for scholars to use; and it utilizes the systematic tests needed to reveal the patterns underlying presidential behavior. It is a first step, one that seeks to provide a useful signpost for those interested in the role of institutions and information in the presidency.

This book has been a long time in the making, and along the way I have incurred many debts. I am happy to acknowledge them here. My thanks go to Dickinson College, the Mellon Foundation, Harvard University's Center for American Political Studies, and the Lyndon B. Johnson and Gerald R. Ford foundations, for research support. No less help was provided by the people who work in all those places and many others: I am particularly grateful to the staffs of the seven presidential libraries in which I conducted research, as well as those who assisted me at the National Archives in College Park, Maryland, and the Pennsylvania State Library. I am grateful too to all the "real world" political actors who gave me the benefit of their time and their extensive experience, and to all my colleagues at Harvard and Dickinson who provided support, feedback, and ideas.

A number of people deserve special mention. I begin with those who pointed the way to sources of data, often their own, outside my own research. Thanks on this front are due to Sarah Binder, Matt Dickinson, George Krause, Dan Ponder, Lyn Ragsdale, and Charles Stewart. Michael Malbin's kindness in letting me work with his legislative proposals project is especially acknowledged. Various others who gave me feedback, will, I trust, see their input reflected in the pages that follow; thanks to Jeff Cohen, Bob Durant, John Gilmour, Charles Glaser, Sam Hoff, Paul Light, Mark Peterson, Russ Renka, Ken Scheve, Theda Skocpol, Andy Solomon, Wayne Steger, Rob Van Houweling, and several thoughtful anonymous reviewers. Special acknowledgment must go to Dan, Ken, and Rob, as well as to Ted Brader, Mike Tomz, and Josh Tucker, especially but hardly exclusively for their reasoned responses to questions of all stripes; the remaining shortcomings of this book are my fault, not theirs. Thanks too to Dickinson departmental secretary Vickie Kuhn and to Princeton's Chuck Myers and Elizabeth Gilbert, for different reasons but for the same traits of patience and good humor.

I was fortunate to begin my research with the guidance of four special individuals: Matt Dickinson, Richard Neustadt, Paul Peterson, and Paul Pierson. Matt especially gave me a stunning amount of time, data, commentary (on my work and on the state of Red Sox Nation), and overpriced whisky. Paul Peterson's broad knowledge and common sense and Paul Pierson's imaginative puzzling about the institutions of governance guided my thinking at crucial points. And I am honored to have had the chance to exploit Dick Neustadt's astonishing grasp of the nuances of presidential history and bureaucratic politics.

As thousands of acknowledgments sections have pointed out before me, it is impossible to adequately thank my family for their role in this book and beyond it. I concede failure on this score, and only hope I repay my debt in the ways my life reflects your guidance. To all of you — and above all to Christine — I will always be grateful. You made this work possible, in many different ways — not least by putting it in needed perspective. Thank you.

Carlisle, Pennsylvania
October 2001

Managing the President's Program

CHAPTER ONE

Managing the President's Program: Necessary and Contingent Truths

ON the evening of June 11, 1963, President John F. Kennedy announced that he would ask Congress to pass comprehensive civil rights legislation. "We face . . . a moral crisis as a country and as a people," said the president. "A great change is at hand, and our task, our obligation, is to make that revolution . . . peaceful and constructive for all."

Kennedy spoke from the heart and without a completed text. Yet the substance behind the speech, if not its peroration, had been long discussed. The president had sent Congress a package of civil rights legislation on February 28, 1963 — broad in scope, but relatively weak. Then, as the protest movement grew through the spring and was met with armed resistance, Kennedy met in long sessions with his advisers to hash out tougher measures.[1] Quickly jotted notes by JFK's special counsel, Ted Sorensen, open a window onto the wide range of choices that had to be made.

First came "questions of tactics," Sorensen observed. Should the "President deliver message in person? How great a price to pay for Dirksen co-sponsorship? Can any Southerner be persuaded to be a 'Vandenberg'? One bill or several? Should bi-partisan leaders and Mansfield staff review Message?"

Then there were "questions of substance," and closely related "questions of drafting." How might the president's staffers craft the proposed bill's public accommodations provisions and the power of the Justice Department to enforce the various aspects of the law? Should the bill be omnibus — combining multiple provisions — or would members of Congress only support a number of more discrete measures? Melding presidential preferences with legislative realities was proving a tricky business.[2]

And so it remains. Though particularly fraught in this instance, the questions facing Kennedy — questions of substance, tactics, and detail — were the choices that go into every presidential decision about his legislative program. "That we cannot have everything is a necessary, not a contingent, truth," wrote Isaiah Berlin.[3] Presidents know this better than anyone.

But if choice is inevitable, the basis for choice is contingent. This

book examines presidents' legislative programs over the past half century and the institutional circumstances that help dictate presidents'
managerial choices in formulating those programs. I will argue that
presidents are flexible managers, rather than reflexive, seeking to obtain
reliable information about the political and substantive ramifications of
their legislative proposals at minimal cost and utilizing their staff and
extra-staff resources accordingly. But these choices are hard, because
they are far from unconstrained — and because the stakes are so high.
These choices are hard, because they help determine the success or failure of the presidential program, and in so doing the president's very
place in history.

The following chapters theorize about the institution of the presidency on the basis of a new dataset compiling nearly five decades of
information about presidential relations with the executive branch and
with Congress. Rigorous hypothesis, qualitative research, and quantitative analysis are combined in a way that seeks to systematically extend
what we know about presidential management. The approach also provides a new lens for examining other aspects of presidential decision
making, highlighting the informational economics at the heart of presidential bargaining.

THE PRESIDENT'S PROGRAM

Why study the president's legislative program? In part, certainly, because it is important in its own right for contemporary governance.
Although the idea of a legislative program is outlined in the Constitution, it is only in the past half century that presidents have transformed
invitation into institution. The "president's program," conceived as a
bounded set of legislative requests, comprehensive in subject matter
and specific in detail, dates just to the late 1940s and the Truman
administration.

Within a few years, however, the legislative program had become a
cornerstone of presidential-congressional relations, part of the definition
of the "modern" presidency. "From a state of affairs in which there was
at best a somewhat grudging acceptance that the President would be
'interested' in the doings of Congress," Fred Greenstein has written, "it
has come to be taken for granted that he *should* regularly initiate and
seek to win support for legislative action as part of his continuing responsibilities."[4] Congress may not always be inclined to dispose, but
presidents are now very much expected to propose. John Kennedy observed in 1962 that "it is a responsibility of the President of the United
States to have a program and to fight for it."[5]

Four decades later this point seems too obvious to require presidential utterance. Candidates on the campaign trail tout their legislative

proposals; presidents defending their performance turn, nearly automatically, to a recitation of their statutory achievements. In late 1997, for example, Bill Clinton was asked if he was already a lame duck. Hardly, said Clinton; after all, his administration had been very successful in Congress that year. "We passed. . . . a score of . . . things," the president boasted, listing the Balanced Budget Act, increases in education funding, NATO expansion, the Chemical Weapons Convention, and "sweeping reform" of adoption and drug approval laws—and pledging that 1998 would be more vigorous yet.[6]

This shift in the burden of legislative agenda setting matters to students of American politics in at least three related ways. First, of course, it matters for the nation's public policy agenda more broadly: the president has more influence here than any other individual actor. John Kingdon found that "the president can single-handedly set the agendas, not only of people in the executive branch, but also of people in Congress."[7] This should not be read to forecast presidents' success in achieving their policy preferences, or even to say, given the empirical evidence to date, that the president's role in agenda setting is either necessary or sufficient.[8] It seems clear, however, that the president's legislative initiatives almost invariably receive congressional attention and agenda space—and that the scope and content of the president's program will frequently form the backbone of national policy debate.[9]

Second, the shift in the burden of legislative agenda setting matters for presidential-congressional relations, in part because it elevates the importance of the legislative aspect of the presidency. Presidents have found that their capacity for leadership, even their competence, is assessed on the basis of their program and its reception by the Congress. Nixon budget director Roy Ash argued in a memo to his boss that "legislating is perceived as governing and governing is perceived as legislating. Legislation—conceiving it, proposing it, fighting over it, winning or losing, making the proper proclamation when passed or signed—not only is the main 'action' seen in Washington but is the key political currency in dealing with the voting public. . . . [T]he President must necessarily consider legislative initiatives and actions as central to his own interest and his own leadership efforts." A top adviser to a very different president, Jimmy Carter, agreed: "People judge strong presidents versus weak presidents on the basis of whether they perceive that the president is able to get the Congress to do what he wants. And brother, if you have the perception that you cannot, then regardless of how competent you may be you are not going to be judged competent in the office."[10] One academic review of the topic concludes that "since [Franklin] Roosevelt, presidents have been judged more by their legislative success than by their executive ability."[11]

Yet the third key implication of the rise of the presidential program—

as Kennedy's deliberation over civil rights makes clear—is that legislative success and executive ability are not so readily separable. It is here that the program grants a panoramic vantage over the terrain of presidential management and decision making. By its very nature, the president's legislative program gets at the heart of both the relationship between the White House and the departments and that between the president and Congress. Because legislating is crucial to presidents, managing the creation of that legislation becomes crucial too. After all, as Paul Quirk puts it, "a president's legislative success often will depend on the ability to design winning proposals that serve his objectives and yet provide the basis for winning coalitions in Congress. In view of the typical indeterminacy of majority preferences, there presumably is often a wide scope for shaping the outcome through the appropriate design of the proposal."[12] This, in turn, focuses attention on presidential management of policy formulation.

Despite the importance of this topic, we know surprisingly little about it. A frequent complaint about the academic literature on the American presidency is that it produces rich empirical detail but little in the way of theoretical heft.[13] The reverse is true, however, with regard to the president's program. True, much scholarly attention has been focused on the spotlighted side of the policy stage, on the congressional votes that delineate legislative success; gauging this endgame has engendered intense study and debate.[14] At the same time, though, the curtain drawn across backstage—the White House side of that process—remains mostly opaque. Two decades after Stephen Wayne delineated the "legislative presidency" and Paul Light's seminal work brought the president's agenda to scholarly consciousness, we know little about either the broad makeup of the president's program, year to year, or how it is drafted and specified for public and congressional consumption.[15]

Yet we do have a body of work springing from the "new institutionalism" (more specifically, from that part of it derived from rational choice theory in economics, strategic management, and political economy) that makes strong predictions about the development of presidential staff management.[16] It posits that development as a series of rational responses to the opportunities and constraints put in place by the broader political setting; thus, given a defined environment, we can predict presidential action across a range of individual presidents. Terry Moe goes so far as to argue that "the institutional presidency is destined to develop in a particular way over time," namely, in accord with a linear increase in presidential centralizing strategies.[17] In the case of the legislative program, this argument implies that presidents have centralized policy formulation resources over time, away from the wider executive branch bureaucracy and into organizations and staffers more directly under their command and responsive to their wishes. Thus an increasing proportion of policy will be made in the White House.

The present work aims to extend our understanding of both the theoretical and the empirical sides of the above equation. It takes the tenets of new institutionalism seriously: the overall analysis is clearly institutional, not personal. Concepts and insights from transaction cost theory in economics and public choice work will be used here frequently, though for the most part heuristically; though presidential styles and personalities clearly matter to American politics, the office shapes the occupant as much as the reverse.[18] As Charles Cameron has written, "savoring details and celebrating complexity require no models. Understanding the order beneath the details does."[19] This orientation may miss details that would allow a deeper understanding of a particular presidential decision. But it allows broader generalizations about what all presidents face with regard to their bargaining contexts within the White House, across the executive branch, and at the other end of Pennsylvania Avenue.

I will argue that environmental incentives and constraints matter very much for presidential behavior. Still, complexity will rarely be absent from the narrative. Building on the same basic notions of institutionally derived motivations that drive current theory, but tied into a new information-centered model of presidential bargaining needs, the chapters that follow show that centralization is not itself "destiny" or destined to increase over time. Instead, presidents over the entire era of the presidential program have chosen centralizing strategies according to predictable conditions governing White House–Cabinet relations and presidential information needs. A detailed look at the creation of the president's program over the past five decades shows that, when brought to bear on the president's program, those contexts point in a different direction: not toward linear centralization, but to what might be called "contingent" centralization.

CONTINGENT CENTRALIZATION

How a president chooses to distribute policymaking resources within his administration outlines agenda-setting power not simply with regard to Congress but within the administration itself. Richard Neustadt, himself a Truman staffer, reflected that legislative proposals "are not merely vehicles for *expressing* policy, they are devices for getting policy *decided*" and thus how that process is worked affects "not only the power that goes with choosing the words but also the power that goes with presenting the issues for decision."[20] Organizational choice, and the informational flow it promotes (or prevents), is wound up tightly in this process. It should be stressed that this *is* a choice: presidents have a good deal of discretion in structuring their staffs and channels of advice as well as their programmatic proposals.[21]

Seen in this light, the president's program has special relevance to arguments regarding the growth of the White House staff in size and importance (in both absolute and relative terms) and to presidential relations with the wider bureaucracy. That is, here the "institutional presidency" meets the "administrative presidency."[22]

The conceptual ground on which they intersect is that of centralization, which links presidential staff management decisions and White House–Cabinet relations. Again, centralization refers simply to the shift of duties and functions from the wider executive branch to the White House staff. Rational choice scholars lay out its logic in straightforward terms. If expectations of presidential performance have risen far above the capacities of the office to respond satisfactorily, presidents must attempt to expand their capacity to have an impact on policy. Since presidents' reach is institutionally (and constitutionally) limited, they act to build and shape what is within their grasp, namely the executive offices and the White House.[23]

That the history of White House–Cabinet interaction follows this path is the academic conventional wisdom, shared by scholars of widely varying methodological persuasions. One leading student of presidential management, for example, concludes that "the reality of the modern presidency is that the White House staff dominates the administration, and cabinet secretaries inevitably play a secondary role. . . . The most important reason . . . is that the White House has taken over a number of functions that used to be performed by cabinet departments and political parties."[24]

Still, given the potential importance of centralization as a tool for studying presidential management, the literature to date falls short on two key measures. First, with few exceptions the concept has not been paid the compliment of empirical scrutiny. Has centralization even occurred? The evidence gathered to date is largely anecdotal and even on those terms rather ambivalent. Second, and perhaps relatedly, theory building on the subject, while making strong predictions about presidential behavior, has not been pushed much beyond the broad notion already outlined. Rational choice centralization has thus not explored the subtleties inherent in its own assumptions.

I turn first to the latter problem, to provide a theoretical grounding for the hypotheses to be tested using the data gathered for this project. It is worth considering the argument briefly here.

Centralization posits that while presidents, driven by electoral incentives (plus the siren call of a "legacy") that reward coherent executive management, must show they are in control, they have a hard time gaining that control. The main culprit is the separated system they survey, stretching even to the departmental bureaucracy they nominally head. Given these institutional realities, a rational president brings as much as possible under his direct control. Centralization is the key result.[25]

A quick glance shows this to be a plausible, even a linear, trend. After all, the Executive Office of the President (EOP) has grown dramatically in size and functional specialization since its creation in 1939. The government does more and spends more: the federal budget more than quintupled, in real terms, between 1949 and 2000. The Cabinet has grown from eight to fourteen departments, bringing new constituencies and their claims to the table, while at the same time each department has added new layers of internal management.[26] In short, presidents overlook a bureaucratic establishment larger and more unwieldy than ever. In these circumstances presidents might well find responsiveness elusive, with people, people everywhere but none to do his will. A president thus afloat should be a perfect candidate to import policymaking into the White House.

A pair of narratives helps to illustrate the conventional wisdom in substantive terms. The first comes from 1954. On January 14 of that year, President Dwight D. Eisenhower sent Congress a Special Message on Old Age and Survivors Insurance (OASI) and Federal Grants-in-Aid for Public Assistance Programs. In the message, Eisenhower urged that the OASI program (better known today simply as Social Security) be broadened to cover ten million more people, including dentists, clergymen, and self-employed farmers. To this he added five new proposals, including a general increase in OASI benefits (then averaging $50 per month) and new formulae for computing various aspects of those benefits.

The substance of Eisenhower's message had been formulated by staff in the Department of Health, Education, and Welfare (HEW) in the classic style of "Cabinet government." The previous October, HEW undersecretary Nelson Rockefeller had written to the president suggesting that the upcoming State of the Union message include a programmatic statement in favor of expanding OASI. At a November 20, 1953, meeting of the Cabinet, Secretary Oveta Hobby presented the departmentally prepared program for such an expansion. It was favorably received by the assembled secretaries, and approved by Eisenhower. Early in the new year the proposals were briefly mentioned in the State of the Union address and the president's Economic Report, then transmitted to Congress via the January 14 special message. On September 1, 1954, Eisenhower signed most of them into law.[27]

Nearly forty years later, in September 1993, President Bill Clinton stood before a joint session of Congress and presented his mammoth plan for reforming the American health care system. In his address, and in the subsequent message transmitting the text of the Health Security Act, Clinton urged nearly thirty broad proposals within a framework of "managed competition" in the $800 billion health care industry. "[A]fter decades of false starts," the president said, "we must make this our most urgent priority, giving every American health security, health care that can never be taken away, health care that is always there."

The Clinton plan was designed to ensure that every citizen was covered by a comprehensive insurance package covering all medically necessary care, including preventative treatment, prescription drugs, and, eventually, long-term care. Utilizing a series of competing regional health alliances, employers would either provide insurance directly or contribute toward pooled coverage; more people were to be insured, against a wider range of illnesses, while the cost of the overall system declined.[28]

Clinton's process of policy formulation bore little resemblance to Eisenhower's. It was centralized in the President's Task Force on Health Care Reform, led by Clinton's wife, Hillary Rodham Clinton, and coordinated by White House aide Ira Magaziner. This group contained a number of working groups organized in "clusters" and in charge of preparing options and recommendations for specific areas of health policy. A wide range of people (some five hundred in all) were involved. Although many of these were departmental employees, they were present as individuals rather than as departmental representatives, and Magaziner tightly controlled the working groups' output through grueling "tollgate" sessions. Departments were not even trusted to conduct technical analysis; this was handled inside the White House, as Magaziner insisted on controlling "what the Cabinet knew."[29] After the full task force disbanded in May, smaller White House teams continued to work on the issue, translating final decisions into legislative language. Clinton aide George Stephanopoulos later called health care a "wholly owned subsidiary within the White House," with its own staff, its own schedule, and even its own "war room."[30]

The tale so far is one oft-told and as such rather comforting. But what if the story had started another way? Shift back to the Eisenhower administration. This time the subject is space science and exploration, centered on the 1958 creation of a National Aeronautics and Space Administration (NASA). The Soviet launching of the Sputnik satellite the previous fall had made a new effort on this front a political necessity.

NASA was to take over management of the space program from the

Department of Defense and the outdated National Advisory Committee for Aeronautics (NACA, created in 1915). Though a major purpose of space exploration was, Eisenhower said, "the need to assure that full advantage is taken of the military potential of space," it was not the president's only interest. He wanted to ensure the wide dissemination of any scientific benefits accruing from associated research, and urged that the effort be placed firmly under civilian control.[31] In part this was a reaction to the military services' inability to work with one another, or anyone else, in developing missile or satellite technology. Their squabbling (and that of each branch's congressional allies) had resulted in an embarrassing lack of progress, and while Eisenhower grumbled privately that a moon shot would be "useless," he knew, as his message noted, that "the effect on national prestige" of the space program's success was of no small importance. Thus he decided to push the program forward.[32]

The Defense Department, NACA, the National Science Foundation, and other agencies interested in international relations generally all had a stake in the shape and scope of the new agency. But in the months after Sputnik, science advising had been consolidated in the White House, and in November 1957 Eisenhower chose to formulate the NASA proposal in the office of his special assistant for science and technology, James R. Killian, with assistance from the president's Science Advisory Council, a standing task force made up of scientists in industry and academia. The outline in place, in late January the legislative draft was sent to the Bureau of the Budget for fine-tuning. Only then was it more widely circulated.[33] Lyndon Johnson, then Senate majority leader, marveled that "Ike must have carried it through the Pentagon on a motorcycle," so little chance did Defense have to comment.[34]

Again, fast forward. In late 1995, President Clinton urged Congress to pass his Employee Retirement Income Security Act (ERISA) Enforcement Improvement Act, which beefed up the auditing of fraud or irregularities in 401(k) retirement accounts and increased the penalties for misuse of 401(k) funds. Twenty-two million American workers rely on 401(k) investments to supplement Social Security payments in retirement, Clinton noted: "We need to make certain the government has the tools to assure American workers they can put their savings — and their trust — into a system that will be there when they need it most."[35]

This proposal had been formulated in the Labor Department under Secretary of Labor Robert Reich and the department's Pension and Welfare Benefits Administration and ERISA Advisory Council, in conjunction with the Pension Benefit Guaranty Corporation. Senator Paul Simon, who introduced the Clinton legislation, noted that "recent investigations by Secretary Reich of 401(k) plans further demonstrate the need for Congress to act promptly on this measure. . . . I want to commend Secretary Reich for the Department's substantial work and effort."[36]

All of these items were part of their president's programs. But they diverge on many other dimensions. Both Eisenhower proposals became law; neither of Clinton's did. In two cases (1954 and 1993) both Congress and the presidency were led by the same party; in the other two divided government held sway. The proposals are of different scopes on different subjects with differently oriented solutions.

If centralization is inevitable, why this variation? Although these cases in themselves are not "proof" of anything, they should give us pause nonetheless, sufficient at least to motivate new theoretical thinking about presidents' management of their staffs, broadly conceived. And, as detailed in Chapter Three, empirically it is far from clear that centralization has followed a linear course. There are unsatisfying ambiguities in the extant accounts of administration-by-administration policy formulation. It is worth noting, as above, that many of these questions come at the start of the process, presumably "decentralized" but in fact replete with Executive Office involvement in program production. The implication is that centralization may have been an arrow in the president's managerial quiver as early as there was a presidential program.

I am not arguing, then, that presidents do not centralize. Frequently they do — and they seem to have realized far earlier than did political scientists the virtue of the strategy. Variation in presidential centralizing strategy, however, is not a simple matter of chronology that can be summarized by noting "once there was Cabinet government, now there is centralization." For I am arguing that centralization is an instrument, not a mandate: it has costs as well as benefits, and even contemporary presidents do not *have* to centralize. If we look to the environment surrounding presidential choice of management strategies — as public choice theory itself urges — we do not see a unidirectional shift in its elements over time. Instead we find that environment fluctuating across a range of relevant dimensions, from the number of agencies interested in a given policy to the availability of extra-departmental sources of expertise. These changes are Congress to Congress and even issue to issue. The backdrop of presidential choice shifts regularly, even within a single presidency.

This does not mean, however, that the resultant choices are ad hoc. For there is common ground across the institutional environment presidents face, as it relates to the formulation of policy: namely, a continuous need for information. That the president and the executive branch he heads often feel at cross-purposes is at the heart of the centralization strategy, since its analytic thrust presumes that presidents have an interest in where policy is formulated. And the source of policy formulation does matter, for it has a bearing on the information the president receives concerning issues and options. For example, departments bring to the table expert substantive knowledge usually unmatched in the White House staff; the president's personal staffers offer political expertise and a single-minded devotion to the president's interest. Both of these, in varying combination, may be of value to the president on a given piece of policy. His choice of how to structure the policy formulation process thus affects the scope and quality of the information he receives.[37]

Recast in these terms, centralization provides a link from the new institutionalism to the old. After all, in order to gain power, in Neustadt's classic sense of effective influence over governmental outcomes, presidents need information about the likely result of their policy choices.[38] This information is both political and substantive, to the extent those are separable. Presidents need to know what potential solutions exist to given problems, what likely real-world effect those solutions will have, what prospect each option has for attracting the support of various constituencies, and how to blend these dimensions into one or several pieces of draft legislation. For different issues, one or another of these considerations may be paramount; in combination, they add up to the president's gain from offering a legislative proposal to Congress. To calculate this—an exercise akin to solving a set of multiple equations—presidents must choose where to place their resources for policy formulation. They must choose, most simply, whether to centralize and to what degree.

If so, centralization is better seen as a matter less of evolution than of expedience. As such it remains a deeply institutional effect; presidents are still seeking responsiveness within a given environment's incentives and constraints. But this vantage suggests that presidents have been able to traverse that environment with a lighter tread than we tend to presume, shifting staffing strategies for policy formulation as the situation dictates.

The model used here posits that presidents will choose the source of that information which provides the optimal combination of reliability and cost. The "cheaper" (in a managerial sense) the information is, the better, providing that it is trustworthy. Minimizing costs will not always dictate drawing on centralized staff resources. Departments, after all, have their own legislative production line, and often a program, already in place. Thus, like firms in economics, presidents must choose whether to "make or buy" their policy, and, if the former, where within their organization to make it. Different choices have different transaction costs associated with them. The creation of a centralized staff for spe-

cialized, substantive policymaking has advantages, when bargains requiring high management costs are made frequently in a given area. But
it has costs, too — in time, in the personal outlay of management effort,
and sometimes in quality.[39]

When will presidents centralize? Chapter Two develops detailed hypotheses in accordance with the tenets above. Previewing that argument, I suggest that at least five sets of conditions will be taken into
consideration. The first four increase the benefits of some form of centralized strategy; the last lowers the cost of pursuing alternative
strategies.

First, centralization is more likely when the president wants quick
action or when an issue is new to the president's program. Second, management needs dictate centralization when the policy area under consideration cuts across several different departmental jurisdictions. Third,
and similar, are proposals that seek to reorganize one or more agencies
or reorient the management of the executive branch itself. Fourth, the
scope of the presidential agenda will affect the cost-benefit analysis. The
more technical is any one proposal, the more departmental expertise is
necessary — but the more concerned a president is likely to be about
getting "rolled" by the department. A formulation process mixing EOP
and department staff is most likely here. The larger the overall workload of messages and proposals, however, the more the president will
find it necessary to institutionalize a staff to support those repeated
tasks and the more likely any one item will be centralized. And having
created that staff, presidents will use it more frequently than presidents
without staff resources in place.

Finally, to the extent that the costs of extra–White House information are lowered, centralization will decline. One source of such information is, of course, the departments; another is the expert personal
and committee staffs of relevant members of Congress. The extent to
which presidential preferences are congruent with those of the bureaucracy and of Congress is the key variable of interest here. The former is
tied in part to whether presidents have successfully "politicized" the
departments and in part to the majority status of the president's party in
Congress. In a situation of divided government, presidents will be more
suspicious of departmental expertise, responsive as it must be to its alternate principals in Congress. Control of Congress — more specifically,
the congruence of presidential and congressional policy preferences —
should make presidential use of legislative expertise more likely.

These considerations form the framework of "contingent centralization." Do they hold true in reality? The approach is compatible with
recent work finding evidence for contextual shifts in presidential policy
formulation in individual presidencies. For example, Matthew Dickin-

son found that Franklin Roosevelt used a variety of staffing techniques to ensure that he had sufficient informational resources in his dealings with various bargaining audiences. Daniel Ponder found that President Carter employed a similarly flexible "staff shift" to best balance his dueling needs for responsiveness and competence.[40] However, there has been no systematic analysis of contingent centralization's observable implications across administrations. A broader view is needed to get around the "$n = 1$" problem that results from studying presidents as unique units of analysis.

Plugging the Gap: New Data, Systematic Analysis

Such a view has been difficult to achieve, in part because until now there has been no unified, comprehensive set of presidential proposals available to scholars. Most researchers have relied instead on the items highlighted in the State of the Union address, sometimes screened in some way; others utilize the Boxscore listings compiled by Congressional Quarterly (CQ) from 1953 through 1975 or variants thereof.[41] Rarely do two sources have the same count of proposals from year to year.

This is not necessarily the fault of academe. When figures can be obtained from archival sources, they rarely match other tallies. Indeed, one Nixon staffer, assigned to the task of comparing his boss's legislative success with JFK's over each man's first two years in office, replied that "it will take more study to determine what they included in their figures. . . . we could be accused of comparing apples and avocados." He had reason to worry about the Kennedy count — a 1962 memo from JFK counsel Ted Sorensen on the legislative program suggests to the president that "other bills we expect to pass could be added to fatten our 'batting average.' "[42]

Even in the qualitative literature on the presidency, there is little comprehensive assessment of how presidential policy is formulated. A number of scholars, certainly, have made important contributions in this area. Stephen J. Wayne's 1978 book, *The Legislative Presidency*, for example, brought together oral history and primary research in tracing the origins and development of the EOP role in policy preparation. Paul C. Light's 1982 study, *The President's Agenda*, sought to highlight presidents' domestic priorities and trace the decision-making process that led to items' inclusion therein. My work owes much to these and other efforts.[43]

In general, though, evaluations of presidential policymaking processes have been most frequent in "president as chief legislator" chapters in textbooks on the presidency, traditional soup-to-nuts legislative case studies,[44] or chapters on the topic in works devoted to the summary of one[45] or several[46] presidencies. Through this research, as Chapter Three details, one can trace an aggregate conventional wisdom through the ensuing administrations; indeed, there is a sense of how each president has organized for policymaking and which staff had what broad roles (indeed, the analysis may be limited to the White House staff organization nominally in charge of policy production). But this compilation is far from systematic and is often circumscribed by the substantive area of interest to the author.

Fortunately, the current question admits of a more comprehensive analysis. After all, there is no logical reason why one could not look at every presidential legislative proposal, determine its source, and calculate methodically the number and nature of those sources. Within the more limited bounds of statistical sampling and with the sometimes problematic constraints of available data, this has been my approach.

The *Public Papers of the Presidents* across the postwar period (1949 through 1996) were used to conduct two counts of the president's program. First, I tabulated the messages sent to Congress by each president. These included any communications from the president that made specific legislative proposals, whether transmitting an energy bill, a reorganization plan, or suggested joint resolution. Since messages vary in their complexity, the number of specific proposals contained in each message was also calculated. This second count incorporates an expansion and correction of the CQ Boxscore data, as adjusted for my needs.[47] (Chapter Four describes the data in depth.)

Using these criteria, a total of 2,796 messages comprising 6,926 proposals were identified across the forty-eight-year period. These vary widely by subject, scope, and substantive importance, ranging from the first item in the database (Truman's State of the Union call to strengthen antitrust laws, in January 1949) to the last (Clinton's plea in September 1996 to increase funding for NASA's "Globe" education program).

From this universe of proposals, a random sample of nearly four hundred legislative messages was drawn, stratified by administration. A legislative "prehistory" was generated for each, using a wide array of primary and secondary research resources, in order to determine its level of centralization. Each item's preponderant source within the executive branch was categorized along an index from least to most centralized: as the product of the Cabinet departments and executive agencies, of the White House, or some mix of the two. The term "preponderant" is used purposefully: it is a useful way to acknowledge that most proposals have many sires but that responsibility for the final, overall form and content of the presidential proposal can generally be assigned. This notion is borrowed from Lawrence Chamberlain, who used it in his

1946 book, *The President, Congress, and Legislation,* to evaluate whether a bill was mainly a legislative or executive product.[48] I ask the same basic question here. But the branches in question have shifted — from the executive and legislative to the executive and the presidential.

With these data and an array of control variables in hand, I used ordered probit analysis to test the hypotheses of contingent centralization developed above against those of a simpler linear centralization model. Controlling for more finely tuned managerial factors, there is little evidence for increased centralization over time. But the results strongly support contingent centralization. Whether a policy is old or new, is of a cross-cutting nature, or has a heavy reorganizational impact are the three strongest predictors of centralization. Centralization also rises with the president's in-house capacity for policymaking — and declines with the complexity of a given item or as the level of trustworthy expertise available to presidents outside the White House increases, as in times of unified government.

This last finding brings us back to the broader implications of centralization. Does it help presidents to design proposals that will meet legislative muster? Although the literature on presidential success in Congress is rich and vibrant, it tends to examine roll-call votes in something of a vacuum, without considering the process that went into formulating the policy in the first place. By contrast, the key question of interest here is whether a presidential centralizing strategy in formulating a given policy proposal increases the probability of its passage through Congress.

The findings of contingent centralization predict that it should not. Indeed, since centralization seems adopted in the main to coordinate complex policy areas encompassing a variety of departmental jurisdictions, it is likely that Congress — whose committee system, despite sporadic efforts at reform, is still extremely decentralized and turf conscious — finds it hard to deal with just those items linked to presidential centralization. Congress has long resisted efforts at comprehensive executive reorganization; and the rise of deficit politics in the postwar era has made any sort of large-scale change difficult. The extraordinary measures needed to expedite complex legislation make those processes vulnerable to hijack by small minorities in either chamber, especially the Senate.

Further, White House staff find it difficult to view the world through legislative lenses. A centralized process by its nature is less inclusive and consultative, with the established networks between congressional committee and departmental policy staff disrupted.

This implication of contingent centralization is once again tested using ordered probit analysis, this time with the measure of centralization developed above as an independent variable. A number of control variables common in models of presidential-congressional relations are also utilized, including measures of co-partisanship and ideological proximity; the type of policy proposed (foreign or domestic, complex or simple); presidential popularity; the time in the term during which the policy was proposed; whether the request is in response to an external crisis or other focusing event; the fiscal climate; and the overall congressional workload.

The "usual suspects" do, indeed, play a strong role as predictors of legislative success; most prominently, presidents succeed as the number of seats held by their party increases and their ideological distance from legislators declines. However, as predicted, centralization undercuts presidents in the legislative arena — even controlling for the other factors known to matter for success, a centralizing strategy hurts presidential proposals. What helps in bargaining with the executive branch, hurts in relating to the legislative.

This is probabilistic, of course: all else is unlikely to be equal, and presidents may feel that the managerial exigencies of the executive branch make the strategy worth the risk. Nonetheless, this finding highlights the delicate position of presidents within America's separated system of governance.

Limits

It is no wonder that presidents try to short-circuit that system by the use of unilateral administrative strategies.[49] Legislative policymaking is a critical subset of policy, but it is not the entire set; thus, while it serves as a vital test of linear centralization, I make no claim here that it is the only test. Just as centralization is contingent in presidents' legislative management decisions, so is it likely contingent in other areas of presidential policymaking where the management environment may have evolved in different ways. Indeed, the concluding chapter explores how models centered on informational economics can help explicate presidential choices between divergent policymaking arenas.

Still, in the end, the president's program is a robust institution. Presidents' legislative roles are not likely to fade away. Presidential efforts to act unilaterally will continue to supplement the presidential legislative program, but will not replace it. The limelight of the congressional stage brings benefits internal redirection cannot, along with the authority and legitimacy needed to cement policy change. Congress and the public continue to expect presidential programmatic leadership. Short-term electoral credit, the desire to have a lasting impact on the American polity, and the related drive toward one's ultimate place in history mean that presidents will continue to comply.

THE STRUCTURE OF THE BOOK

The following chapters move from theory, to data and testing, to import. They move from what and why to "so what?" and "when?" Chapter Two develops in more detail the theory of contingent centralization. Chapter Three traces the history of the presidential legislative program and the conventional wisdom surrounding policy formulation, then raises additional questions about that conventional wisdom.

Chapter Four presents the presidential program database and explains the sampling and coding processes used in Chapter Five, which tests contingent centralization against other hypotheses. Chapters Six and Seven then trace the presidential program down Pennsylvania Avenue to assess theoretically and quantitatively whether, and how, management matters for legislative success. Chapter Eight concludes with reflections on presidential bargaining, institutions, and information. It argues that presidential leadership is wrapped up in how presidents manage the sequential bargains inherent in the legislative program — first with the executive branch, then with the legislative.

The answers are important to our assessment of executive governance over time — and to larger scholarly claims about the nature of the presidential quest for "responsive competence." This book aims to show systematically, with regard to centralization and the president's program, exactly upon what presidential decisions depend — and why this matters.

If the demands on the president leave him, in Neustadt's famous formulation, with the capacity only to be a clerk, how does he become a leader instead? One way is through the structuring of action-forcing processes in ways that benefit him — each president must submit a legislative program, but the shaping and formulation of that program is discretionary. Statesmen have long known that "events which cannot be avoided must be directed."[50] If the presidential power to command is limited, then the ability to bargain becomes key, and with it the ability to structure a situation. This book examines how presidents bargain with their executive branch, the better to bargain with Congress, and the better to exercise presidential power.

CHAPTER TWO

~~~~~~

Bargaining, Transaction Costs, and Contingent Centralization

CENTRALIZATION is the strongest theory we have of presidential management, but it paints presidential behavior with a broad brush. Its own logic dictates finer lines of inquiry. This is not to say that presidents do not centralize; indeed, they do, and in the modern era always have. But even the most modern of presidents is not bound to centralize: the key is not chronological but managerial. Presidents are proactive within their institutional constraints, placing their resources for policy formulation in patterns consistent with the informational environment in which they work.

This chapter focuses on the theory behind presidential management decisions surrounding legislative policy formulation, building a more powerful model of "contingent centralization" grounded in the transaction costs that attend presidents' informational and bargaining needs. The subsequent historical and quantitative analysis will build on this framework.

CENTRALIZATION AND ITS DISCONTENTS

Theory building is a cumulative exercise. Thus before turning to a discussion of contingent centralization, this chapter must accomplish two things. First, it must explain what centralization itself is, and why it matters to presidents or polity — that is, why it matters where in the executive branch the president's program is formulated. This may seem self-evident, given the wealth of research on White House–Cabinet relations in the presidency literature.[1] Still, the analytic thrust of centralization rests heavily upon the importance of this distinction, and it is worth unpacking here.

Second, this chapter must demonstrate that the standard theory of centralization — what might be called "linear" centralization — needs to be refined. These tasks are undertaken in turn, followed by a discussion of contingent centralization.

Working Definitions

As noted earlier, there is general consensus as to what centralization encompasses. Centralization occurs when there is a shift in functions from the wider executive bureaucracy to the Executive Office of the President, particularly the White House Office (WHO) itself. Walter Williams writes, "centralization generally refers to the division of power over major decisions, both in making them and advising on them, as distributed among the president's inner circle, EOP staff, and the Cabinet secretaries."[2] As this intimates, the standard usage of the term in the literature draws a dividing line between the Cabinet departments and independent agencies, on the one hand, and the president's personal staff located in the WHO and EOP, on the other: the former are considered decentralized, the latter centralized. Even within the EOP, some staffs are closer to the president than others.[3]

The definition used here builds on these foundations. By "centralized" staff, I mean staff whose only constituent (whether in statute or in practice) is the president himself, and which is organizationally (and normally, physically) proximate to him. A centralized policy proposal is one produced by a centralized staff or staff member; a decentralized proposal is one produced by someone else.

In the main, this follows the departmental/White House divide. The first part of this definition means, however, that not every staff located in the EOP should be considered centralized. The office of the U.S. Trade Representative (USTR) is effectively an operating agency, with outside clients, as was, during its lifetime (1964–1975), the Office of Economic Opportunity (OEO). As Budget Bureau director and Council of Economic Advisers chair Charles L. Schultze commented on the latter, "nobody ever considered it in the Executive Office, even though the law says it is. But simply sticking an operating agency in the table of organization in the Executive Office doesn't really mean it is a presidential outfit."[4] Similarly, other policy formulation mechanisms such as presidential commissions or task forces are too varied to classify under a single term: they may be placed along a continuum of centralization depending on their congruence with the definition above. (Coding rules along these lines are discussed in Chapter Four.)

The White House/Departmental Divide

The literature is rife with presidential comment, most of it defamatory, on the bureaucracy: Richard Nixon's denunciation of the "striped pants f— —s in Foggy Bottom" is notable only in tastelessness, not in kind.[5] Efforts to reform or "reinvent" government aim not to energize bureaucracies, but to rein them in.[6] At the same time, though no recent president has used his collective Cabinet as a policymaking board—and many scholars argue this cannot be done—nearly all swear fealty to the notion of Cabinet government. By some accounts President Clinton's transition report did not even include a section on the White House staff.[7]

Why does it matter where policy is formulated? The flippant answer is that it clearly matters to presidents; but this only shifts the question laterally. Why do presidents care? At the heart of the answer is the old adage, "where you stand depends on where you sit,"[8] tempered with an understanding of how and why those seats differ. That understanding must be grounded in the institutions that make up the White House and Cabinet and the subsequent institutional behavior prompted in their inhabitants. Leslie Gelb, who served in the State and Defense departments, commented, "I have generally found that staffers from the Department of State or Defense or from the Central Intelligence Agency behave very differently if they are moved to the White House. They become far more conscious of Presidential stakes and interests."[9]

As Gelb suggests, the key variable is less the individual than the institution in which she serves. The two sets of staffs are centered around different goals, missions, and relationships, and as a result have different preferences, skills, and resources. Each has a different task; and as James Q. Wilson has observed, "people matter, but organization matters more and tasks most of all."[10] In the aggregate these institutional differences imply differences in the kind of information each staff gives the president on policy matters; each set of advice will have advantages and disadvantages to the president.

James MacGregor Burns has noted that the creation of the EOP was prompted by executive desires for "a personal presidential staff that would be given a privileged sanctuary under the President's wing against the kinds of political and organizational pressures that played on the more conspicuous men around the President. These aides would be appointed solely by the President . . . they would serve wholly at the President's discretion . . . their responsibility and loyalty would be wholly and only to the President."[11] The White House staff's very existence is tied up in serving the president: Clinton adviser Stephanopoulos writes that "doing the president's bidding was my reason for being; his favor was my fuel."[12] Such staff are physically close to the president, and managers in both the public and the private sectors know that proximity matters.[13] Closeness breeds personal intimacy and trust, and team camaraderie. Some scholars have noted distinctions between presidential staff who are "inside" and those "outside," that is, those who deal with external audiences (for example, the Office of Public Liaison or of Legislative Affairs). The former staffs tend to distrust the latter, and this *within* the White House — the gap between White House and department is much greater.[14]

But in organizational relationships, the psychological sense of "trust" is trumped by two factors: shared preferences and the competence to bring them about.[15] On the first, at least, the White House staff wins hands down over the bureaus. Presidents can be fairly confident that White House aides share presidential priorities and points of view, given that their behavioral incentives are under the president's control. The growth of presidential staffs has engendered its own management problems; the more people who can plausibly invoke the president's name, the more likely that the principal-agent problems usually associated with presidential-bureaucratic relationships will replicate themselves within the EOP.[16] Still, as scandals ranging from the Iran-*contra* affair to "Filegate" indicate, these are rarely problems of too little loyalty, but too much. White House aides are the agents of one principal, the president. If the president cannot always control them, at least no one else does, or even has a claim to.

By contrast, the collective preferences of the civil service are under much looser constraint. They have often diverged from those of the president, and tend to change only slowly over time.[17] Further, Cabinet departments and executive agencies serve multiple masters. Presidents fear that once a bureaucrat puts the White House out of sight, she puts it out of mind as well; as Nixon staffer John Ehrlichman famously opined, departmental appointees go off and "marry the natives."[18] There is a divide here between principle and principal: while the president is titular head of the executive branch, he is not the only actor with a claim to that branch. The structure of American government demands that Cabinet members participate in what Richard Fenno termed a "great multiplicity of external relationships" not directly related to the president — with legislators, interest groups, members of the public, and even other levels of government.[19]

Part of the reason for this is that bureaus have their own independent standing; they are created by statute, with mandates and missions assigned by law. Eisenhower's deputy secretary of agriculture, True Morse, pointed out, "It's Congress that enacts the laws, and [when] you come into office . . . you take an oath of office to administer the laws of the United States. And until . . . Congress changes those laws, there is a definite limit as to how far you can go as part of the [presidential] arm of the government."[20] Bureaus thus serve not just as agents but as principals in their own right. A large portion of the research devoted to political control of the bureaucracy concludes that such control is quite limited.[21]

As distinct entities, departments may see their interests diverge from the presidential vantage; yet they are mandated to seek policy competence on the issues within their given jurisdiction. This expertise contrasts with a White House populated with staff drawn largely from the president's campaign and enhanced by the creation of units with interest group liaison and communications responsibilities. The result is a staff with a certain kind of political skills — but not necessarily one that is skilled in the technical complexities of public policy.[22] The departments, though, house large staffs of professionals tied into experts both in and out of government. Further, while the White House rewards generalists, departments' substantive assignments tend to be quite specialized, segmenting the government organizationally around particular policy areas.

Congress, of course, doesn't just pass laws and leave the agencies to operate in isolation. The legislative branch remains the favored answer to the academic literature's disentanglement of the question of bureaucratic control.[23] But one need not posit "control" to agree that bureau chiefs are careful to heed congressional preferences. After all, Congress created their agency, authorizes (and sometimes micromanages) its activities, and funds it year to year; congressional committees hold oversight hearings and members have multiple means of publicizing what they see as agency missteps. Herbert Kaufman argues that members of Congress have an "awesome arsenal" of tools for influencing bureaucratic views.[24]

Departments and agencies must also respond to constituency pressures, both as those pressures are channeled through Congress and directly. Some government departments, indeed, were formed as organizational means of responsiveness to groups such as farmers, teachers, unions, or business leaders. The "iron triangle" model of interest group influence contains just groups, agencies, and congressional committees; there is little room here for the president qua president. Later, perhaps more realistic, models of influence posit multiple "issue networks" populating a more open and conflictual universe of policymaking. But groups still matter — indeed, issue networks suggest a framework for policy not far removed from the pluralist theories of the 1950s.[25]

In short, "each bureau [is] surrounded by constellations of groups telling its leaders what they wanted it to do, criticizing its operations (or, more rarely, commending them), and seeking information about its actions and its plans for the future."[26] Those external preferences likely go some way toward shaping agency preferences. Gardner Ackley, chair of Lyndon Johnson's Council of Economic Advisers (CEA), was once asked whether there was "a discount applied to some of the depart-

ments' offerings on the grounds that they represented constituencies."
Ackley replied, "Oh, no question. Yes, [LBJ] very much believed that,
and I think it's true. I think it's undeniable and unavoidable and perhaps
not even undesirable. But the president does need a staff that has no
constituency other than himself."[27]

The planning documents for the "counsellor" or "supersecretary" reorganization of the second Nixon administration provide a telling summary of this point. Nixon wanted the departments to report to him
through counsellors assigned along broad functional lines, some of
whom were already departmental secretaries. How could this best be
done organizationally?

The answer, Nixon's White House argued, was that if the president
wanted to ensure a counsellor was "his man," the counsellors must be
"'organizationally recognized' as part of the [Executive Office of the
President]." In contrast

> the appointment by the President of an agency head does not necessarily
> mean that he partakes of the President's complete philosophy in discharging
> his duties. He is soon immersed in the day-to-day problems of administer-
> ing his own agency, makes compromises with Congressional pressures,
> takes on the biases of his department's constituencies and bureaucracy, and
> soon begins a life of his own. . . . As part of the [Executive Office], the
> Counsellor may be expected to view prospective policy actions and evaluate
> policy more objectively than he would if he did not really feel he was a part
> of the President's office. . . . [and since] success of the plan depends on how
> the bureaucracy reacts every effort should be made to clearly delineate the
> direction he gives as coming from the President.[28]

The net effect of these organizational distinctions between White
House staff and the departments and agencies is to give the two staffs
different preferences, missions, and skills. Thus they have different resources on which the president can draw.

A theoretical means of organizing these observations, and for hypoth-
esizing about their specific implications for staff use, will be presented
below. For the moment it is enough to say that the decision of where to
turn for policy formulation matters for governance. White House advice
will differ from departmental advice, and one can expect a different
process—grounded in different information and expertise, weighted by
diverging preferences—when resources for policy formulation are channeled to one place rather than the other. The informational dimension
to presidential bargaining has, oddly, been slow to surface in the presidency literature, especially when compared with other subfields; but it is
this dimension that will prove critical in the discussion below.[29]

Linear Centralization

Much of the "institutional presidency" literature springs from one of the basic tenets of contemporary presidency studies: namely, that expectations of presidential performance have risen far above the capacities of the office to respond satisfactorily. Presidential payoffs are for bold leadership and decisive action, but their operational reality reveals a dense thicket of organization and expectation. As the United States government has grown larger and more complex, starting especially with the New Deal, its institutions have become less responsive to presidential leadership. At the same time, public expectations of the capacities of that leadership have grown at a heady rate, partly inflated by presidents themselves.[30]

The key to the usual theory of centralization is grounded in presidents' rational response to this growing disconnect between demands and actual powers. It posits that if expected presidential capabilities far outstrip real resources, presidents must respond by attempting to expand their ability to have an impact on policy. Since presidents have limited reach, they act to build and shape what is within their grasp, namely the executive office agencies and the White House. Hence they move functions into Schultze's "presidential outfits" instead of relying on departmental or agency staff who have other people to please. What presidents want, according to this view, is not the classic governmental virtue of "neutral competence" but rather "responsive competence," with the accent on "responsive." They want the staff described by LBJ aide Bill Moyers: "You aren't a man in your own right when you are working for a president. To be most effective you have to have an umbilical cord right to his character, nature, and personality."[31] Terry Moe sums it up this way in his seminal essay on the topic: "Whatever his particular policy objectives, whatever his personality and style, the modern president is driven by these formidable expectations to seek control over the structures of government. . . . He is not interested in efficiency or effectiveness or competence per se. . . . What he wants is an institutional system responsive to his needs as a political leader."[32]

Despite the broad acceptance of centralization by scholars of widely diverging methodological persuasions, Moe's hypothesis should make it clear that the theoretic logic of centralization has a firm footing in the scholarly branch of the new institutionalism derived from economic theories of organizations and strategic choice. In this view, individual behavior is strongly conditioned by that individual's strategic interaction with her institutional environment, because the environment affects the costs and benefits — the constraints and incentives — associated with a given course of action.[33] Political actors will seek to maximize their utility (however defined) while minimizing the costs of doing so, within the bounds of available information.

The new institutionalist vantage helps students of the presidency see the office beyond the person who holds it. Put in its strongest terms, "whatever their personalities and ideologies, they are presidents and they behave presidentially. Because they do, we can know reasonably well what to expect from them."[34]

In this case, given the linked dimensions of time, presidential capacity, and the dense American institutional environment, we expect presidents to incrementally centralize their resources for policy formulation. Moe notes that existing institutional structures are modified over time to fit incentives and resources; centralization simply brings the former into congruence with the latter. Time matters in part because future patterns of behavior are predicated on past actions: the latter generate expectations for future actors to consider. Centralization in this sense builds on itself; as a result, "the institutionalized presidency is destined to develop in a particular way over time, owing to the nature and degree of the underlying incongruence, serious constraints on presidential resources, and the consequent channeling of presidential effort into areas of greatest flexibility," namely, the White House staff and EOP.[35]

This argument is appealing in several ways. In part, it offers a means of escaping reliance on the analysis of aspects of presidential personalities, whose distinctiveness make systematic argument difficult, if not impossible.[36] Even more appealing, the argument lays out in clear terms its assumptions and its expectations. As a result, it can be tested — and built upon.

While an empirical test, examining the historical record of presidential policymaking over time, is reserved to the chapters to come, the Eisenhower and Clinton cases presented earlier give a sense of the unsatisfying ambiguities involved.

Yet theory should precede tests. And there are reasons based in the institutional logic of centralization itself to think that a linear evolution is not the most satisfying theory in which to ground a detailed explanation of presidential management of legislative policy formulation.

Linear Centralization and the Management Environment

If presidents seek to make structures compatible with incentives, it is important to specify the structures and incentives relevant to a given presidential task. The broad theory of centralization simply posits that as the presidential workload increases and the bureaucracy becomes more fragmented — proxies for as time goes by, more or less — presidents will seek to bring more functions into the orbit of the White House.

Policy formulation is clearly one of those functions (though, to be sure, not the only one).[37]

An observable implication of this should be that a larger proportion of the president's program is formulated in a centralized manner over time. That is, more proposals will be centralized in the 1990s than in the 1940s.

This prediction can be tested. But we should expect it to hold true only if the "macro" institutional environment Moe describes is the appropriate determinant of presidential incentives in policy formulation. There is a levels of analysis question here, analogous to that faced in transaction cost economics. Scholars there, most prominently Oliver Williamson, have argued that rather than the composite output of goods and services, the appropriate unit of analysis is the transaction and the governance thereof. Williamson adapts an example from Adam Smith's *Wealth of Nations* to shift the object of analysis to "how to organize (more generally, how to govern)" pin making from "how many pins to make and at what price." As a result, Williamson argues elsewhere, we should "treat the institutional environment as a set of shift parameters, which change the relative cost of alternative modes of governance."[38]

The president's perspective on legislative policymaking is likewise transaction-based and cost-oriented. Consider that the president has two related sets of incentives when it comes to policy formulation. First is a substantive dimension: he wants his policy proposals to reflect his own policy preferences. Second, because he cares about outcomes, there is a political dimension: in most cases, at least, he wants the proposal to garner support — ideally from a majority of Congress but at a minimum from public constituencies important to his administration.

Two points follow. First, presidents' key need is for information. In order to gain effective influence over governmental outcomes,[39] presidents need information about the likely outcome of their policy choices. They need to know what potential solutions exist to given problems, what likely real-world effect those solutions will have, and what prospect each option has for attracting the support of various constituencies. For different issues, one or another of these considerations may be paramount; in combination, they add up to the president's expected utility with regard to the proffer of legislation to Congress.[40]

Second, while we talk of "the president's program" as a bounded whole, this is true only in retrospect. The program is not formulated as such. It is an accretion of individual proposals, each representing its own transaction between the president and his staff.[41] Information on the formulation of each program item can only be gathered bill by bill (at most, by type of bill). And each transaction takes place along different dimensions and, potentially, in a different political environment.

The key variable is policy *type*, in several senses. What is a proposal's substantive content? How technically complex is it? Is it a repeat of an earlier proposal, or new? What departments might logically be involved?

If the primary dimension is informational, then the specific environment within which that calculation is made is tied to the departments — and political context — relevant to the bill at hand. Again, which departments are involved? How many? How much does he trust them? Further: how large is the president's agenda? How many seats in Congress does his party control? How close, ideologically or preference-wise, is he to those co-partisans? All of these variables might be thought to matter to presidential decisions surrounding the placement of resources for policy formulation. These types of things we might consider the relevant "shift parameters." But none of them vary simply over time. Further, while the size of government (and its cost) *have* risen in a near linear way in the period under study, not all legislative proposals involve multiple departments; not all departmental budgets have gone up or changed at the same rate; nor are all legislative proposals money bills.

Thus what we might call the *management* environment does not always equate to the broader, macro-environment; it varies much more, and does not evolve in so monolithic a manner (that is, ever upward). Within the larger framework, the elements of the management environment may shift quite frequently — not unlike a children's toy with small balls, inside a larger plastic sphere, that bounce wildly even as the overall vessel calmly rolls forward. The environment shifts, and the relative costs of modes of governance shift with it. Presidents' "political time," as Stephen Skowronek has written in a somewhat different context, changes in predictable ways, while the "secular time" on which it is overlain steadily marches on.[42]

Given this interrelationship, we should expect a "phase shift" of sorts: that a new threshold level of centralization will occur as a new part of the macro-environment is institutionalized — in this case, as the president's program becomes an annual expectation, and organizational support allowing presidents the capacity for more centralized choice is put in place. Whether they choose to use that capacity then depends on the prevailing management environment. This suggests one way, discussed more fully in the concluding chapter, that the micro- and macro-vantages can be synthesized to gain even more leverage over a wider range of presidential activity.

Note that the logic of this model remains that of the new institutionalism: presidents are still seeking responsiveness within a given institutional environment, attempting to minimize their management costs. Indeed, the transaction approach is drawn directly from the work in organizational economics that motivates new institutionalism in political science generally.[43] But as the president chooses from where among his staff he will get his information — in Moe's terms, matching his structure to his incentives, or in the language of institutional economics, choosing among governance structures — he might find himself able to traverse his institutional environment more nimbly than we tend to presume. Centralization becomes a question of expedience rather than evolution, contingent on presidential information needs related to the bargain at hand.

It is critical that "contingent" not mean "ad hoc." And it need not: we can make systematic predictions about the effects of the above variables on presidential choices. To do so, we need to elaborate a theory of presidential informational bargaining, and the specifications of "contingent centralization."

INFORMATION AND CONTINGENT CENTRALIZATION: TRANSACTION COST BARGAINING

Four claims have been made:

- that information is the crucial element to understanding presidential decision making about legislative policy formulation;
- that the appropriate way to study the president's program, from the president's vantage, is as an aggregation of decisions about specific policy items — as a series of transactions;
- that there are different governance structures within the wider macro-institutional environment (in this case, most simply, centralized, decentralized, and different sorts of mixed structures), and that the president can make a choice between them, but that
- there are bases for making that choice that go beyond presidential personality. Instead, underlying that choice is the relative cost of each option: that is, the president will choose the cheapest source of information that he trusts.

These claims bring the discussion full circle, and highlight a means of testing a theory of contingent centralization. While in determining "cost" it is difficult to assign numerical values, one can instead calculate relative cost, and link it to systemic hypotheses about information.

The Centrality of Information

That information is the currency of presidential power is not a new assertion. Our conception of a persuading, bargaining president, stressed by Richard Neustadt more than forty years ago, rests upon it.

After all, what do presidents need in order to bargain effectively? Neustadt himself provides the answer: "A President is helped by what he gets into his mind. His first essential need is for information."[44] The historian Barry Karl comments, "The problem of information [is] the central problem of the presidency, given the essential isolation and singularity of its constitutional responsibility."[45]

The centrality of information to choice is key not just for the "old" institutionalists but for the new ones as well. Peter Hall and Rosemary Taylor note in their review of the strands of new institutionalism, "Members of this school emphasize that political action involves the management of uncertainty, long one of the most central and neglected features of politics, and they demonstrate the importance that flows of information have for power relations and political outcomes."[46]

One need not accept Neustadt's bargaining paradigm to accept the primacy of information — presidents who rely on executive command, or who "go public" to avoid bargaining,[47] still need to know the likely outcomes of their decisions and actions. But the bargaining framework is particularly apt in the arena of legislative policy formulation. As I have argued, the president's program is properly seen as an aggregation of individual proposals, in part because it is constructed that way: the program is designed to cover the range of problems the president sees facing the country, but is presented in temporally — and substantively — distinct messages over the course of the year.[48] Further, presidents seek information on a bill-by-bill basis, because the appropriate dimensions of the management environment vary bill by bill. Each policy proposal within the program is best seen as a transaction — a bargain — between the president and his staff (located either in the EOP or in the wider bureaucracy), and can be analyzed as such. The transaction becomes the basic unit of analysis.

The "Make or Buy" Analogy

The choice of how to manage each transaction links directly to institutional choices. In institutional economics, the distinction is broken down by a firm's decision to "make or buy." That is, should a company manufacture a good or purchase it on the open market? Firms choose to make some inputs and buy others.[49] As a heuristic, though not an exact analogue, we might consider this question from the president's vantage. He, too, can choose to formulate policy within the Executive Office or delegate its formation to the wider bureaucracy.

Other subfields have been quicker to make the link between institutional choice and information — Keith Krehbiel's work on the informational dimensions of congressional committees is a prominent example.[50]

Certainly presidency scholars have accepted the connection; Norman Thomas observed in 1970 that the primary job of presidential staff "is to furnish [the president] with sufficient information and analysis to permit him to make decisions with an awareness of the available alternatives and their probable consequences."[51] Still, an explicit accounting of the informational role of institutions is lacking in most approaches to presidential studies.[52] The preceding discussion of the White House/departmental divide shows that centralization provides a theoretic means of bridging this gap. In itself, though, it doesn't answer the crucial question: which staff to use, and when? More formally, if different governing structures exist, under what conditions will the president choose a given structure? The answer returns to institutional economics: the president will utilize the source of information with the lowest overall transaction costs.

Transaction cost theory comes from a question plaguing students of the firm: why, if markets are the most efficient way to allocate prices and goods, have firms created a hierarchy devoted to internalizing market transactions? As early as 1937, Ronald Coase pointed out that one answer lay in the fact that market bargains bore their own transaction costs.[53] Economic theory to that time (and thereafter, until transaction cost economics was reborn in the 1970s) had presumed that transactions were costless and resources allocated exactly efficiently as a result. But in the real world, all transactions have friction attached — they have costs. The problem might be one of time to negotiate a contract, or of information, or of preferences (or, more accurately, of information about preferences). It might be one of "asset specificity" — that specialized knowledge or equipment is needed to use the asset in question. Depending on the nature of the bargain, the costs associated with the acquisition of a given commodity will vary.[54]

Transaction cost theories have been used in political science mainly as ways to get leverage on questions of interbranch delegation. That is, when and how does Congress delegate powers to the executive branch?[55] This delegation question differs somewhat from that facing presidents, and is probably a cleaner application of the transaction cost framework. For one thing, the transaction cost focus on contracts includes a presumption that a third party can enforce those contracts. The courts can interpret congressional delegations of authority, written into statute; but while presidents seeking policy formulation can turn to another "supplier" they cannot sue to get better information. For another, it goes too far to see the bureaus as firms independent of the president: the distinction between "market" and "hierarchy" is necessarily less defined when the market option is itself part of the executive branch hierarchy.

Still, the important question is not whether the executive branch of the United States government is the exact equivalent of a private corporation — clearly it is not. Rather, the test is whether this perspective gives us any leverage over the question of centralization. And that it clearly does. As a heuristic, the "make or buy" question serves to highlight some of the conditions under which presidents might choose one source of policy formulation over another. After all, on the one hand, bureaus might well be seen as producers of legislation; they have their own legislative production line, and often a program, already in place. When will a president choose to "buy" part of that and make it his own? On the other hand, when bargains requiring high management costs are made frequently in a specific area, the creation of a centralized staff for specialized, substantive policymaking has advantages. Yet this too may have its own costs — in time, in the personal outlay of management effort, and sometimes in quality.[56] The arrow doesn't have to point in only one direction, as suggested by models of linear centralization.

What is meant by "cost" in this informational context? I presume that presidents will choose the source of policy information that provides the optimal combination of reliability and managerial effort. The "cheaper" (in this managerial sense) the information the better, provided that it is trustworthy. One analogue here is the decision to buy a car. One considers the sticker price, but discounts that by the projected budget for repair and maintenance for the model in question — the true cost of an initially cheap vehicle could turn out to be rather high. The cost of policy formulation to the president, then, is a similar combination of price and a consideration of reliability. The latter hinges on whether the president trusts the information he is given, with trust, in turn, seen as an assessment of the expertise of the giver, weighted by the degree to which she shares presidential preferences. Roy Ash, who was budget director under Presidents Nixon and Ford, described presidential decision making in just these terms. Describing Ford, Ash recalled that "when an issue would arise, he would attempt to get the views of a number of people given to him directly. He would obviously have in his own mind some weighting that he would give to these different people, and their views. Then, after applying that weighting he would have a pretty good leg up on what his decision was going to be. . . . And I sensed, as I watched it at work, the importance of applying different weights, from subject to subject, to the views of the people whom he consulted."[57] This is not to say that the president will never seek "biased" information, merely that he must also take care to calculate the direction and scope of that bias, so that he can correct for it in determining its relationship to his own preferences.[58]

Clearly the calculation of presidential transaction costs will not translate into dollars and cents or, for that matter, into any exact unit of measurement. We can instead aim to define shift parameters—to get a sense of which options are more costly than others under what circumstances, and thus to make predictions about the effects, in direction and intensity, of different management environments on presidents' choices regarding centralization and policy formulation.

Synthesis and Hypothesis

The two discussions above—of the White House/departmental divide and of the role of transaction costs in decision making—can be synthesized, suggesting five interwoven areas in which to ground a model of contingent centralization. These either raise the relative benefits to the president of centralization or lower the cost of alternate strategies.

RESPONSIVENESS

The physical location of the White House staff matters because it is tied to—or is perceived to be tied to—responsiveness, immediacy, and a willingness to look at things in new ways. By contrast, presidents see bureaus as balky and hidebound. Organization trumps location, perhaps, for since the departments are mainly staffed by career civil servants, they have established organizational routines whose time horizons diverge from those of the EOP.

"What [presidents] want, they want now," argue Harold Seidman and Robert Gilmour.[59] A four-year term goes by at lightning speed, its effective half-life shortened by midterm elections and presidential primaries; thus "from the perspective of the White House, even minor delays or objections in the departments are commonly viewed as monstrous insubordination."[60] But civil servants' time horizons are much longer. They have a long-term interest in good policy, but no reason to prefer an approach to a problem that will effect a solution in twenty months rather than fifty. Presidents do. If presidents want to move quickly, or in response to crisis, they may look to White House aides rather than to the departments. While not legislative formulation per se, Bill Clinton's 1995 process of developing an affirmative action policy was centered in the White House for just this reason. As Harvard Law School professor Christopher Edley, who directed the effort, later noted, "this decision had to move at a pace . . . simply inconsistent with the ordinary pace of agency decisionmaking. It was being driven at a pace that was determined by the president. It's just unthinkable that you could turn it out to a bunch of agencies and say, 'We'd like you to study affirmative action and come back to us as soon you can.' They just wouldn't—that would not work."[61]

Bureaus' statutory grounding has another effect as well. Because bureaus have extant agendas and duties, they may have little organizational interest in producing "new" policy, especially when that policy would undercut existing programs or constituencies.[62] Lyndon Johnson's use of task forces and the White House staff to create policy was, he said, a reaction to his judgment that the agencies "did not encourage enough fresh or creative ideas. The bureaucracy of the government is too preoccupied with day-to-day operations, and there is a strong bureaucratic inertia dedicated to preserving the status quo."[63] Likewise, Jimmy Carter recounted that "I can't recall a single exciting or innovative idea that ever came out of the State Department during the four years that I was President. That's the nature of the State Department — it's an anchor. [National Security Adviser Zbigniew] Brzezinski and his staff, on the other hand, would come every week with several innovative, bright ideas."[64]

POLICY SCOPE

"New" proposals are generally thought of as "big" proposals, but "big" problems tend to cut across more than one departmental jurisdiction. Indeed, one feature of the postwar era as a whole has been the prominence of issue-areas that cut across multiple departmental lines. This is true in two senses: segments of broad topics (for example, job training or pollution control) are assigned to more than one agency, and broad problems are the synthesis of smaller (though rarely small) interlocking elements.

It is hard to reconcile these types of policies with the very targeted nature of departmental jurisdictions. "Cabinet officers," Clinton labor secretary Robert Reich noted, "have nothing in common except for the first word in our titles."[65]

And so coordination is needed. Since cross-cutting policies affect a wide array of constituencies, the calculation of these measures' substantive and especially their political impact is more difficult for parochial agencies to manage. The wider the scope of the policy, the less likely are presidents to trust departmental assessments. Presidents fear that the bureaucratic response to such issues will be a lowest-common-denominator solution. Johnson's top domestic staffer Joe Califano complained that the bureaucracy had an "inability to think big — I don't mean big in the sense that I'm a big spender . . . but presidentially global. Just couldn't see that Johnson had a picture of educating the world, the whole country. Food was part of it and health care was part of it, consumer education was part of it all, but not quite [all]."[66]

Thus since "almost nothing about the bureaucratic ethos makes it hospitable to interagency collaboration," it falls to the White House staff to bring those disparate planks of a functional platform together.[67]

Ford staffer (and George W. Bush Cabinet secretary) Don Rumsfeld comments, "The way our world works, it's rare when you find an issue that is the jurisdiction of only one cabinet officer. . . . [Y]ou have all these threads, and the White House staff's function is to see that those threads get through the needle's eye in a reasonably coherent way."[68]

Here the frequency of cross-cutting issues, the low reliability of departmental information on such matters, and the generalist nature of the EOP staff come together (ironically, the "asset specificity" at issue here is one of breadth). Centralization is more likely when the policy area under consideration cuts across several different departmental jurisdictions.

Further, the larger the overall workload of messages and proposals, the higher the frequency of related transactions, and the more coordination is required between them as a whole. Repeated transactions along the same lines imply advantages to "making" advice: as repeated bargains are struck, a staff to support those needs will be institutionalized. This does not necessarily imply more staff, though it could, but rather a staff used to performing programmatic tasks. Once in place, they are likely to stay part of the process, raising the likelihood of any individual program item's being more centralized.[69] Thus staff size itself is in fact likely to be associated with centralization, even if the causal arrow is somewhat muddled: staffs, once in place, tend to be used.[70]

REORGANIZATION

One answer to jurisdictional balkanization might be to reorganize the structure of government — Johnson domestic aide Jim Gaither suggested that "in the long run we probably have to be thinking about super-departments on [the] domestic side, one on human resources . . . probably one on natural resources."[71]

President Nixon proposed just that. Over time, presidents have been fond of these sorts of solutions, as the wide range of efforts to "reinvent" government testifies.[72] They are components of most presidents' programs, and considered important: as William Carey of the Budget Bureau wrote to Kennedy congressional liaison Larry O'Brien, "The prestige of the President often rides more on the fate of his reorganization proposals than on his [other] legislative proposals."[73] Further, even legislation that is not in the form of an official "reorganization plan" may well contain reorganizational aspects, creating new departments or subdepartments and shifting components of one bureau to another.[74]

This repeated transaction is another that fits poorly with departmental policy formulation, for agencies (and often legislators) are less enamored of this approach. Departments protect their turf fiercely and even fight over the institutional scraps of discarded agencies. President

Ronald Reagan's 1982 proposal to dismantle the Department of Energy, for example, represented a triumph for Commerce Secretary Malcolm Baldridge over Interior Secretary James Watt in the battle over who would add Energy's nuclear power functions to his departments.[75]

Peri Arnold comments, "Reorganization episodes [originate] in a president's distrust of the permanent government, combined with his assumption that innovative solutions could be supplied only by those who were not wedded to government."[76] Something similar could be said about issues of personnel management, such as civil service changes. Presidents do not find departmental advice on these matters reliable: the result is that centralization is more likely when reorganization or management issues are concerned.

EXPERTISE AND TECHNICAL KNOWLEDGE

As we have seen, one measure of the scope of an issue is its cross-cutting nature. But another is its complexity. What are a proposal's substantive ramifications, its technical complications? These are not always the same thing—an issue falling within the purview of a single agency may yet be difficult to formulate correctly so that the proposal, if passed, will achieve in the real world what it is advertised to achieve. "Complexity" here, refers to the technical expertise necessary to write the statute needed to implement the president's policy preferences in a given area. If, as Clinton aide W. Bowman Cutter notes, "it is a law that the economics of an issue always run exactly counter to the politics,"[77] then advice on both dimensions is needed. Expert advice on the first must often come from departments. Discussing welfare policy in the late 1970s, for example, Laurence Lynn and David Whitman point out that "Carter's decision to have the welfare reform issue handled chiefly in the cabinet agencies had some potential advantages: the experts were in the agencies, and they would readily respond to the call."[78]

Advice on the political front, one might think, would automatically come from the White House. After all, the members of the White House staff are selected largely on the grounds of their campaign background and political skills. But while those staffers bring to bear formidable experience in electoral politics, campaign skills generally differ from those needed to govern. Nixon staffer John Whitaker argued that the president's "political cronies that have just come to town with him, many of [them] don't know the first damn thing about government. That's the nature of campaigns, they just come that way."[79] White House staffers are often new to Washington; they are often young (President Clinton complained to his political consultant, Dick Morris, that his staff comprised "the children who got me elected");[80] and they are frequently unversed in the history of the politics of a given issue. That

assessment—the institutional memory of past efforts and their results—
may also need to come from outside the White House.[81] Once again this
depends on issue type, and on its congruence with organizational
boundaries.

The more complex and technical is any one proposal, the more departmental expertise is necessary. This fact, however, is unlikely to mean
unalloyed decentralization. Because presidents worry about departmental control of the shadings of legislative language, they will want to
maintain some central involvement in the overall formulation process.
As Carter found out to his chagrin on welfare reform, pure decentralization has its own limitations when technical issues are allowed to mo-
nopolize the debate: instead of providing useful political summary or
particular examples, one staffer complained, "all HEW talked about
was norms and medians."[82]

Although policy complexity is thus a predictor of decreased centralization, a mixed strategy is its most probable empirical result. The Aviation Act of 1975 provides a good example. While the Department of
Transportation was charged with drafting the legislation, members of
the EOP staff watched closely. Indeed, in his letter conveying the department's proposal to the administration's task force, Deputy Undersecretary of Transportation John Snow took a downright defensive posture:
"Herewith is a revised version of the air bill which we drafted in accordance with the understandings reached at yesterday's meeting at OMB.
Again I would invite your close attention to the language to assure that
we have been faithful to these understandings."[83]

PRINCIPAL CONGRUENCE: "BUREAUCRACY AND BUREAUCRACY"

"There was bureaucracy and bureaucracy," CEA chair Art Okun once
commented. "[HEW Secretary] Wilbur Cohen could get almost anything he wanted out of Johnson and knew exactly how to approach the
president. Califano would have these carefully constructed task forces,
but before the task force report was on the President's desk, you would
hear that Cohen had gotten a commitment from the President to do
thus and so in the January budget. . . . Califano would tear his hair
out."[84]

Cohen was a skilled bureaucratic operator, a player in the field of
health and human services since the New Deal. But Okun's observation
is not *sui generis*; there is clear variation in the relations between the
president and the various bureaus of the executive branch.

This issue might be addressed more systematically by returning to the
principal-agent question. That is, presidents' fear that departmental expertise may be biased derives in part from the fact that each bureau has
multiple principals and its own organizational dynamic, with the result

that its outputs do not mirror presidential preferences. The corollary is that we should expect presidents to be more trusting of bureaus' advice when the preferences of the various principals align. Congressional ties are especially important here, as these can be considered additionally as proxies, albeit imperfect ones, for relevant interest groups.[85]

The idea is that to the extent that costs of extra–White House information are lowered (and its reliability increased), centralization will decline. One source is, of course, the departments; another is the expert personal and committee staffs of relevant members of Congress. Both of these are tied to the majority status of the president's party in Congress. In a situation of divided government, presidents may well be more suspicious of departmental expertise, responsive as it must be to its alternate principals in Congress. Further, committee staffs are selected by committee chairs, who in turn are of the majority party.[86] If the president can rely on congressional expertise, he can afford to centralize less.

Sharing party affiliation does not, of course, guarantee cooperation: northern and southern Democrats had little in common on many issues for much of the period under study. It can be supplemented by examining the congruence of presidential and congressional ideology and policy preferences. This strategy highlights the importance of the median voter to legislative outputs, a notion crucial to recent spatial models of Congress. It also takes into account the declining importance of the party platform as an external constraint on presidential legislative leadership and the concurrent rise of partisanship as "preferenceship."[87] Indeed, in theory, ideology can be disaggregated to the committee level. That is, since proposals are sent to committees, and committees are tied to particular bureaus, we might expect the formulation decision to reflect not the general proximity of presidential-congressional preferences but of that obtaining between the president and the relevant committee.

Presidents are more likely to trust bureaus, then, when Congress shares the president's party affiliation and policy preferences. What other factors specific to the bureaus might be relevant?

One key lies in the appointment power. Terry Moe has suggested that a presidential strategy complementary to centralization is "politicization," in which presidents stock the bureaus and agencies with ideologically like-minded and loyal appointees. Other scholars similarly stress presidents' administrative strategies.[88] The idea is that responsive appointees can curb presidents' fears of secretarial intermarriage with "the natives."

As such, the question of politicization is linked closely to centralization: it is an additional managerial context for presidents to consider. If appointments are sufficiently politicized, the distinction traced above might be irrelevant—for if a president can place enough of "his" people in the bureaucracy, he should be able to trust its policy outputs. Nixon chief of staff H. R. Haldeman's handwritten notes of a November 1972 meeting with the president capture the essence in an almost poetic shorthand:

> loyalty up is the most impt thing
> as we dismantle [EOP] offices use the *loyal* people out thru agencies
> follow Harlow's rule — control the key posts
> press, legal, personnel, Congl, Deputy
> loyalty much more impt than competence[89]

This implies that the more politicized an agency, in this sense, the less centralized policy proposals relating to it should be. Departments headed by someone close to the president, for example, someone who once served on the White House staff, should be deemed more trustworthy as they go about policy formulation. Examples here might include the Treasury under George Shultz (Nixon), James Baker (Reagan), or Robert Rubin (Clinton). The Kennedy Justice Department under Robert Kennedy is a parallel case.

Although this hypothesis is tested in Chapter Five, there is some evidence to think that being sure of the secretary him- or herself is insufficient. Consider this conversation from a January 1975 Cabinet meeting about enforcing President Gerald Ford's decision to propose block grants instead of categorical grants:

> *Undersecretary of Agriculture Campbell*: A very realistic problem . . . is dealing with the second layer of bureaucracy, because regardless of what kind of leadership we offer the departments, that second layer of bureaucracy wants to see categorical grants continued.
> *Interior Secretary Morton*: You are right, Mr. Campbell, it is a real problem. I have got 70,000 people under me and 35,000 of them today are up on the Hill talking with the Congressmen about categorical grants. Every time I talk to a Congressman, they seemed to have talked to somebody in the parks department or some other area below that second level of bureaucracy [who is] making important policy decisions.[90]

A wider attempt to politicize, perhaps by increasing the number of presidential appointments across the executive branch, might therefore be more plausible. The higher the proportion of employees with civil service protection, the less likely a president will trust departments to act in his interest. Note that this views administrative strategies as a *substitute* for, not a *complement* to, centralization. Given that both have costs, presidents might choose to pursue one, but rarely both at once.[91]

It should also be noted that presidents might choose strategies short of all-out politicization. One tactic might be to rely more heavily on what Thomas Cronin deems the "inner cabinet" of State, Defense, Justice, and Treasury. Because these departments tend to stress counsel over advocacy, Cronin argues, their heads often have "close and collaborative relationships with presidents and their top staffs."[92] Presidents might also choose the heads of these departments with more care (and with less pressure from constituent groups to name one of their own). Either way, inner Cabinet departments are likely more reliable sources of information on policy formulation than the "outer" departments.

SUMMARY AND CONCLUSION

The logic of models of linear centralization can be extended to propose a more subtle, yet more powerful, contingent theory of centralization. Incorporating insights from theories of bureaucratic politics and transaction cost economics, I have hypothesized a number of relationships important to presidential choices about strategies of legislative policy formulation. These can be restated in conditional terms to outline when a policy proposal will be formulated in a more or less centralized manner.

More centralization is expected when:

- a policy proposal deals with cross-cutting jurisdictions;
- a policy proposal incorporates reorganization of government or reorientation of its management;
- the president has institutionalized greater capacity for formulation within the EOP (as a result of a large overall agenda, for example);
- the proposal requires speedy formulation (for example, it represents a response to an external focusing event or crisis); or
- the policy represents a new approach or an entirely new issue.

Less centralization is expected when:

- the complexity of a policy proposal rises;
- a majority of Congress is of the same party as the president; and/or
- Congress (and especially the roster of the committee relevant to the policy proposal) is close ideologically to the president; or
- the bureau responsible for the policy area in question is closer to the president, because it is headed by a former White House staffer, or is part of the inner Cabinet, or is part of a politicized executive branch.

These considerations form the framework of "contingent centralization." Do they hold true empirically? This theory is compatible with recent work finding evidence for contextual shifts in presidential policy formulation in individual presidencies, but there has been no systematic analysis of its observable implications across administrations. The remainder of this book takes a first step toward filling that gap. Chapter Three begins by analyzing the qualitative record. It provides both the history of the presidential program and a sense of the ambiguities that make that record insufficient to test the predictive power of contingent centralization. This account prepares the field for the more systematic approach of Chapters Four and Five.

CHAPTER THREE

The President's Program:
History and Conventional Wisdom

We challenge any member of Congress to point to any
instance in the past history of our Republic where a bill was
submitted to a committee of the Congress, drawn at the
instance and aid of the President of the United States and
declared to be the President's bill, and should be made a
law. — House Commerce Committee, 1910[1]

[Mr. President,] you will recall that at a Leadership meeting
with you in early March, it was reported that the
Committee Chairmen were concerned by the delays in the
Departments in submitting draft legislation to Congress to
carry out your program. . . . The result is that time is now
being lost, when Committees could be working on
significant parts of your program. . . . It would be very
helpful, therefore, if you would prevail upon the
Departments to get the relevant draft legislation to the
Senate as soon as possible. — Senate majority leader Mike
Mansfield to President Lyndon Johnson, 1965[2]

WHAT role should presidents play in the formulation of legislation? Although Article II of the Constitution invites the president to recommend
for congressional consideration "such measures as he shall judge necessary and expedient," the legislative prerogative was long and fiercely
guarded by Congress. Strong presidents throughout American history
had a "program," in the sense that they were identified with controversial issues of their time; not until the twentieth century, however, did
presidents supplement broad policy recommendations with specific legislative draft language. And not until after World War II did a comprehensive, annual presidential program become expectation and substance. Only then did invitation become institution.

This chapter discusses the origins of the presidential program, then
evaluates what we know about the policy formulation processes of the
presidents since 1949 with an eye toward the theories of centralization
laid out in Chapter Two. The answer, in brief, is "not enough" — in

large part because there has been little systematic work to date analyzing, or even collating, the president's program.

FROM INSULT TO INSTITUTION: THE PRESIDENT'S PROGRAM

As William McKinley prepared to take office after his landslide win in 1896, one contemporary observer noted that the shorthand of referring to the president's party as the "administration party" in Congress had vanished. After all, "the President has . . . so slight a share in initiating the legislative policy. His message to Congress is really an address to the country and has no direct influence upon Congress." Members of the legislature, in fact, found presidential presumption in this area rather insulting.[3]

But this state of affairs would not last long into the new century. The first shift came relatively quickly, with Theodore Roosevelt's accession to the Oval Office in 1901. As governor of New York, Roosevelt wrote, he had learned that "a good Executive under present conditions of American life must take a very active interest in getting the right kind of legislation in addition to performing his Executive duties with an eye single to the public welfare."[4] Roosevelt brought this "active interest" into the presidency, though he was somewhat cautious in his recommendation of detailed measures to Congress. While he occasionally provided drafts to legislative allies, in this area, as Louis Koenig has put it, he was uncharacteristically "a trifle sheepish and clandestine."[5] It was left to TR's successor, William Howard Taft, to be the first to formally present draft legislation to Congress—inciting the first, furious epigraph to this chapter. Woodrow Wilson, given his approach to presidential party leadership, positively delighted in expanding his office's involvement in policy formulation, appearing in person before Congress several times to demand new legislation.[6]

Since Wilson's time all presidents have forwarded draft bills designed to enact their messages into law.[7] Indeed, it did not take long for presidential initiation of specific legislative proposals to become common practice; in the wake of Franklin Roosevelt's tidal wave of New Deal bills, the president was dubbed "chief legislator" and the Congress deemed a very junior partner in the initiation of public policy.

The Roosevelt legend arises from the dark Depression days of 1933—notably from the emergency banking measure sent by Roosevelt to a special session of Congress soon after his inauguration in March. It was passed in hours (after just forty minutes of debate in the House), without having even been formally printed. A stream of successful proposals followed, making FDR's "Hundred Days" a symbol of executive activity presidents still try—and generally fail—to emulate.

Even in this period, Congress was rarely a simple rubber stamp.[8] Indeed, Lawrence Chamberlain felt it necessary as early as 1946 to point out, through a detailed analysis of major laws, that the legislative branch was perhaps not irrelevant to the legislative process.[9]

The key point here, though, is that by the time Harry Truman took office, the president's involvement in the legislative process had become a given. Indeed, Congress had given him structural opportunities to do so extending beyond the State of the Union address. The Employment Act of 1946 demanded governmental action across the breadth of the economy, and required the president to prepare an Economic Report each year presenting "a program for carrying out [such a] policy."[10] The Bureau of the Budget (BoB) had been shifted from the Treasury Department into the new Executive Office of the President in 1939, bringing with it the chance to shape the annual budget message into a truly presidential document. As the postwar order developed, even foreign policy—the Marshall Plan, Point IV, Korea—was increasingly tied to legislation.[11]

Herein lay a golden opportunity for presidential leadership. Wracked by transition and reconversion pains—and then by the shock of the 1946 midterm elections, which brought Republicans into the majority in both chambers for the first time since 1931—the Truman administration did not immediately seize the legislative initiative. But by the end of 1947 a presidential strategy was beginning to take shape: if a "do nothing" Congress was to be an issue in the 1948 campaign, the administration needed an affirmative and comprehensive record of its own. At least, the marker needed to be laid down. And throughout 1948, it was; Truman's annual messages (the State of the Union, Budget Message, and Economic Report) were broad in their coverage and specific in their content. Special messages rounded out the president's recommendations in each subject area; Truman aide Charlie Murphy later noted that in 1948 "we wanted to have a special message ready to go to Congress every Monday morning."[12]

The aggregate result—even more notably in 1949 after Truman's surprise reelection—was to replace sporadic recommendations with a systematic agenda. This is the genesis of the president's program as we know it today, a package of recommendations comprehensive in subject matter, specific in prescription, and bounded in scope.

That definition of the program highlights two important factors: that it is presidential (that is, not a simple compilation of departmental wishes, foisted upon him) and that a president's choices are important for what they leave out as well as for what they include (that is, the program is an exercise in agenda setting rather than a blanket set of solutions to all potential societal ills).[13] As Neustadt puts it, the program serves as "a comprehensive and coordinated inventory of the nation's current legislative needs, reflecting the President's own judgements, choices, and priorities in every major area of Federal action . . . an entity distinctive and defined, its coverage and omissions, both, delimiting his stand across the board."[14]

The clear distinction between the president's program and the summation of departmental initiatives should be emphasized. As early as 1948, programmatic planning documents indicate a divide between "special presidential programs," that is to say "high priority items of direct interest to the president," and administration proposals "below th[at] level."[15] A 1959 letter from budget director Maurice Stans to HEW Secretary Arthur Flemming expands on this theme:

> Generally speaking, legislative proposals originating within the Executive Branch and submitted to the Congress for consideration are classified either as 'Presidential' proposals or 'Departmental' proposals. Presidential proposals are those to which the President gives specific endorsement, generally through one of the State messages or a special message. . . .
>
> There are some important reasons for maintaining the clearest possible distinction between Departmental and Presidential proposals. First of all, many of the legislative proposals of Executive agencies are of such minor importance or of concern within so narrow a spectrum that it is clearly inappropriate to burden either the President or his principal staff assistants with considering them. . . . Secondly, the use of the President's title and prestige on all Executive agency legislative proposals would reduce the effectiveness of his support in the relatively few situations where proposals are of such importance or of such personal interest to the President that they are mentioned in [a presidential message]. . . . You may not know that whereas the number of items endorsed in messages is of the magnitude of one hundred, the number of legislative proposals originating in Executive agencies is of the magnitude of one thousand during a single Congress.
>
> With respect to situations in which you are asked whether a proposal . . . is 'in accord with the President's program,' . . . your response should take cognizance of the fact that the words 'in accord with the President's program' have been used only to identify items specifically endorsed by him.[16]

The presentation of this elaborated program became an institution in its own right with remarkable speed. The political reasons for this were augmented by policy reasons: the end of World War II (with new hostilities, both Cold and Korean, soon to start) demanded continuous legislative action on the social, economic, military, and diplomatic fronts. Further, "policy and politics aside, perpetuation of the practice during Truman's second term owe[d] much to the fast rise of institutional stakes in the game."[17] Simply put, the program met not only presidential needs but the organizational demands of other Washingtonians as well.

By the time Dwight Eisenhower took office, Congress no less than the executive agencies anticipated and demanded a presidential legislative agenda. When in 1953 the new administration was slow in complying, a House committee chair admonished it in no uncertain terms: "Don't expect us to start from scratch on what you people want. That's not the way we do things here — *you* draft the bills and *we* work them over."[18] By 1965 the sentiments of this chapter's second epigraph, taken from a letter from Senate majority leader Mike Mansfield to Lyndon Johnson, were seen not as vacating congressional prerogative but as a routine part of interbranch business. (Indeed, by the late 1970s, presidential aides were almost fatalistic about it: "Since we must propose legislation which will be the embodiment of our governmental programs, we cannot avoid sending up draft legislation," wrote one.)[19] What scholar Stephen Wayne would later dub "the legislative presidency" had arrived, and was here to stay.[20]

As a result, the president's program serves as an excellent proving ground for hypotheses about presidential management and centralization. It is a regular and expected task — an "action-forcing process."[21] It is of importance to the president personally. And by its substantive nature it gets at the heart of the White House/departmental relationship discussed in Chapter Two, as well as the ties between president and Congress. The sections that follow therefore assess the organizational origins of presidential program management, then trace the ambiguities of the academic conventional wisdom surrounding how presidents have developed that new capacity for centralized control.

EARLY COORDINATING MECHANISMS

As noted in Chapter Two, for there to be a real choice of management styles — a real choice of governance structures, in the terminology of transaction cost studies — the president must have at least the capacity for centralized policy formulation. This came early on in the legislative clearance functions centered in the Bureau of the Budget.

The BoB had been created by the Budget and Accounting Act of 1921 and placed in the Treasury Department, though reporting directly to the president, who himself was charged with annual presentation of a consolidated executive budget. At the suggestion of congressional leaders who feared departmental end-runs around the new act's provisions, the bureau quickly gained clearance powers over agency submissions to and comments on matters before Congress, where those had an impact on the budget; under the Republican administrations of the 1920s, this process was utilized mainly as a way of keeping down expenditures.[22] In the mid-1930s, Franklin Roosevelt expanded the process to include both the cost and the substance of all legislation, first through the mechanism of the National Emergency Council and then back through the BoB.[23] In 1939, as already noted, the BoB became part of the new Executive Office of the President.

By 1945, when the Legislative Reference Division (later called the Office of Legislative Reference, only to return to its original name still later) was created within the bureau, a three-part process of central clearance was in place.[24] This required that Legislative Reference review ("clear") all administration-proposed legislation to determine its relationship to the president's agenda;[25] that departmental testimony on any matter pending before Congress be similarly cleared; and that enrolled bills (those approved by Congress and awaiting presidential action) be reviewed, with relevant agencies commenting on their disposition.

When legislative activity returned to center stage after World War II, it was natural—though not inevitable—for Legislative Reference to undertake the task of sifting departmental proposals for inclusion in the new presidential program. Under budget director James Webb, this became standard practice: in the summer of 1948 the BoB requested for the first time that agencies include recommendations for proposed legislation in their budget estimates. Four days after his election President Truman reinforced this with a written request to all agencies asking them to submit legislative proposals for the upcoming 81st Congress. In 1949, bureaus were asked both for a preliminary legislative program (along with their budget estimates) and for a "final" program in conjunction with the president's annual messages.[26] With this a call for legislative proposals for the president's program became an annual ritual. Budget Bureau Circular A-19, most recently revised in 1979 and entitled "Legislative Coordination and Clearance," lays out clearance procedures for pending, proposed, and enrolled legislation.[27]

Yet despite its longevity, the process always operated at the president's discretion. The Budget Bureau summed up:

> In general terms the procedure described in Circular A-19 makes the Office of Legislative Reference a clearing-house and what might be termed an 'honest broker' among the Executive agencies and the Congress on draft legislation originating within the Executive branch. . . .
>
> [T]he clearance procedure . . . is essentially a staff service performed for the President, and in accordance with his wishes. It rests basically on the President's constitutional powers and hence upon his personal support. . . . [as] reflected in the issuance of Circular A-19 'by direction of the President.'[28]

There is a clear nod here to the president's ability to choose different policy formulation processes as they served his needs. What the memo does not point out, but might have, is that the clearance process — while an important way to bring new policy proposals to the president's attention, and clearly a crucial management mechanism *after* the fact — has never been the only means that presidents have utilized for program formulation. The decentralized formulation process that A-19 clearance implies — the welling up of departmental proposals to be selected for presidential elevation — is merely part of the whole. From the outset, other avenues were also utilized. For example, the BoB played its own affirmative role in making policy, with Legislative Reference playing a key role in giving White House staff control over the budget examiners. Not only that, programmatic staff burgeoned within the White House Office; budgeting merged with policymaking; task forces, commissions, and Cabinet Councils were organized; and Congress played its own role in placing demands on presidents and providing incentives to meet those demands in particular ways.

TRACKING THE CONVENTIONAL WISDOM

The scholarly conventional wisdom surrounding policy formulation reads these developments, collectively, as coherent evolution toward increased centralization. In part this rests on a glance at the president's broader environment. While responsiveness is a difficult concept to assess quantitatively, we can think of proxies that might represent, at least, "unresponsiveness." Certainly the federal government has grown larger and, by extension, more unwieldy. From fiscal years 1949 through 2000, federal spending (in 1996 dollars) went from $293 billion to over $1.6 trillion at a near-linear rate of expansion. Growth in federal regulations over the same period, as measured somewhat crudely by the annual pages of the *Federal Register*, has been immense.[29] These measures are presented in figure 3.1. Figure 3.2 adapts Paul Light's work on "thickening government" to give a sense of the accumulating layers of management in the executive branch. His listings of the "total departments adopting new layers" calculated from the quadrennial "plum book" of political appointments are presented here in graphical form, accreted over time.[30] Given the constant rate of increase in "thickening" over time, a linear model seems to fit nicely.

As noted in Chapter One, a variety of studies provide discrete or sequential views, if little comprehensive assessment, of policymaking processes over the course of one or several presidencies.[31] Amalgamating this work reveals a standard narrative through ensuing administrations that serves to accompany the figures above. It goes something like this.

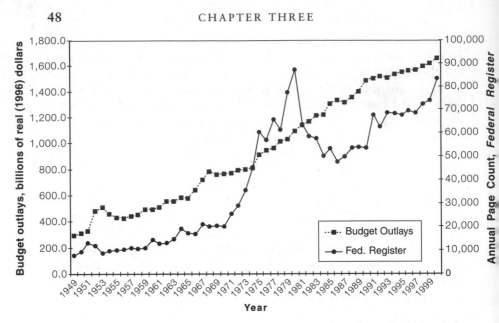

Figure 3.1   Growth in Government, 1949–2000 (data from *Budget of the United States, FY2002* and Office of the *Federal Register*)

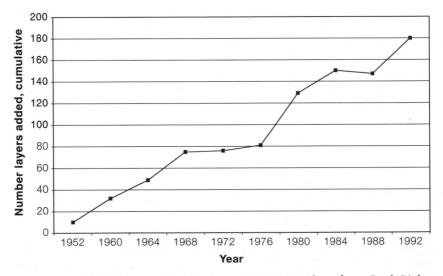

Figure 3.2   "Thickening" Government, 1952–1992 (data from Paul Light, *Thickening Government*, Washington, D.C.: Brookings Institution, 1995)

Early on Congress itself expanded presidential capabilities with the imposition of the Council of Economic Advisers (1946) and the National Security Council (1947). Harry Truman ignored this structure for the most part, though, at least until the onset of the Korean War. Instead he had a small White House staff, and relied for program development on the BoB-centered processes already described. The BoB in those prepoliticized days served the institution of the presidency rather than the person of the president and was itself not a truly centralized organization.[32] In any case, policy formulation was a departmental task, if only because the EOP lacked the capacity to take it on.[33]

Dwight Eisenhower, in turn, expanded the EOP and greatly formalized its structure, putting in place a formal chief of staff and a variety of consultative machinery. However, he was a true proponent of "Cabinet government" and had little in the way of a legislative agenda in any case. The difficulty of positive policy formulation capacity remained: "The presidency . . . was exceptionally well-equipped to reject or modify departmental initiatives, but not to seize the policy initiative on its own where agency timidity or the need for a multidepartmental approach made this necessary."[34]

John F. Kennedy undid much of Eisenhower's formal organization but kept a good deal of responsibility in the White House, the better to codify and market the pent-up Democratic program, as well as to control international affairs. "He expected his [White House] staff to cover every significant sector of federal activity — to know everything that was going on. . . . He wanted the staff to get into substance. He constantly called for new ideas and programs."[35]

Lyndon Johnson, even hungrier for legislative success, took Kennedy's pre-inaugural idea of task forces and made them a regular source of policy proposals, creating a White House–based domestic policy staff to coordinate the task forces and compile their output.[36] So important was this to the Great Society that Johnson staffer Joseph Califano later claimed that "in new areas, I don't think a hell of a lot came out of the federal bureaucracy as such. We got most of our stuff from academics and quite frankly, a lot of stuff we just did and handed it to the department concerned."[37]

The story continues with Richard Nixon, who formalized these trends with the creation in 1970 of both a successor agency to the BoB and a Domestic Council within the White House Office.[38] The new Office of Management and Budget (OMB) was, as its name suggested, to stress the management of the wider executive branch. To aid in this, the reorganization widened the layer of political appointees ("PADs") above the agency's career employees. With less success, Nixon also tried to install loyalists across the bureaucracy so as to better control governmental operations.[39] The Domestic Council was, like the National Security Council, made up of Cabinet members, but again like the NSC—which had itself grown more prominent as a policymaking unit under McGeorge Bundy, Walt Rostow, and now Henry Kissinger[40]—its staffers eclipsed their formally subsidiary roles. The Domestic Council and OMB overlapped in many ways, working together on some issues and competing on others, either way producing a merger of politically controlled policy development and implementation functions.[41]

The executive excesses of the Watergate era induced what Moe calls a "pause in the modern presidency" under Gerald Ford and Jimmy Carter, both outspoken advocates of Cabinet governance.[42] Ford gave his Domestic Council little support: indeed, he "kept his pledge of a Cabinet-based government."[43]

Carter's pledge on that front was even stronger—at his Cabinet swearing-in ceremony he vowed that secretaries would play a major role in policymaking, would choose their own staffs, and would generally serve as his first-line circle of advisers in both domestic and foreign policy.[44] Chester Newland concludes that Carter's "Cabinet departments were endlessly involved in policy formulation."[45] Over time, though, Carter grew dissatisfied with this system. While he had originally sworn fealty to a "spokes-of-the-wheel" staff model, without a chief of staff, Carter shifted gears on this point in most dramatic fashion.[46] His decision in July 1979 to formally elevate Hamilton Jordan to staff chief, while at the same time replacing five Cabinet secretaries, marked a wrenching public shift in the perception of the focus of policymaking in his administration. But in practice it only underscored an ongoing reality, that the centralized policy staffs—in Zbigniew Brzezinski's NSC and Stu Eizenstat's Domestic Policy Staff—had already been dominant for some time.[47]

The Carter experience presaged an onslaught of centralization under Ronald Reagan. Reagan instituted a series of seven Cabinet Councils under the thumbs of his White House "troika,"[48] consolidating the councils to just two in his second term. He established in the White House an Office of Policy Development and a powerful, though informal, Legislative Strategy Group. Further, he was more aggressive, and more successful, in politicizing lower-level appointments than any president to date.[49] He installed bright ideologue David Stockman as OMB director, politicizing that agency even further—and using the need for urgent budget (and then deficit) reductions to firm up central control of budgeting and give all new policy initiatives a fiscal tinge. The Circular A-19 process for handling legislation continued, but was effectively derailed as budgetary decisions became a necessary prerequisite to programmatic ones and reduced agency requests to "wish lists."

The second-term Iran-*contra* scandal, brought on by an overeager and undersupervised NSC staff, reactivated the alarm bells surrounding White House staff power. But despite this the Reagan lessons of centralization became touchstones for his successors. White House control over program development remained the norm under George Bush (under whom the "loop" actually narrowed, yanked tight by chief of staff John Sununu and OMB director Richard Darman)[50] and even under Democrat Bill Clinton. Indeed, Clinton added a National Economic Council — once more, crucially, with a staff to support it — within the White House to supplement the Domestic Policy Council and the NSC.[51] A leading textbook account notes simply that Clinton "centered political and policy decisions in his White House staff."[52]

The standard account thus begins with a tiny presidential staff and ends with an extensive White House counterbureaucracy creating policy through the efforts of the politicized OMB, ongoing variants of the Domestic Council, the NSC, and various ad hoc working groups. As a result academic summaries of the topic comment matter-of-factly on a "larger movement toward centralization of executive-branch policy-making in the White House. In recent years, presidents have devoted more of their own and their staff's time to the process of policy development — to the assembling of ideas for policies, to the discussion of those ideas in the White House, and to the drafting and ultimate submission of legislative proposals embodying those ideas to Congress."[53]

This conclusion is not all wrong. But it is not the whole story. It takes a bird's-eye view of the programmatic process without ever really defining the president's program or examining its component parts, except for illustrative purposes. That is, it presumes that the proper level of analysis, to study presidential decisions about policy formulation, is the macro-environment and not the management environment discussed earlier.

Further, the narrative suggests not just a high level of centralization in contemporary administrations, but a very low level in earlier ones. This progression can be questioned in two ways. First, even at a "macro" level, scholars studying the institutionalization of the presidency have argued that centralization (more accurately, the organizational structure that facilitates centralization) cannot continue indefinitely. They note rapid growth in the EOP in early years but suggest that something of a plateau was reached in the 1970s as institutional space was filled to capacity.[54] Supporting this view, the size of the White House staff itself shows no constant upward linear trend but rather shifts up and down (see figure 3.3).[55]

Second, and more important for my purposes, the narrative above does not consider the "phase shift" posited in Chapter Two. If that hypothesis

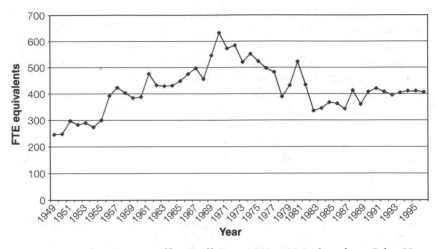

Figure 3.3   White House Office Staff Size, 1949–1996 (data from John Hart, *The Presidential Branch,* 2d ed., Chatham, N.J.: Chatham House, 1995; updated by author)

is correct, the baseline level of centralization should have increased to reflect the newly institutionalized presidential program, giving presidents the capacity needed for choice — but this level should have remained more or less constant, with variation explained by proposal-by-proposal contextual factors. A closer look shows that the institutional shift toward making centralization a viable formulation option occurs as early as the Truman administration. And, as Warshaw notes, "the degree to which the domestic policy office interacts with the departments and the process used for that interaction is the least institutionalized [that is, least consistent] part of the domestic policy process."[56]

Indeed, the qualitative record as a whole itself yields ambiguities sufficient to warrant uncertainty about the narrative just presented. Without trying to be comprehensive, the next section presents a complicating view of the postwar policy formulation process. It is not in itself dispositive, but it reinforces the need for a more systematic view of the making of the president's program.

Wrinkles in Time

The conventional wisdom has suggested that in the early years of the presidential program, the formulation of legislative proposals was centered in the departments and agencies — that the process moved in a steadily more centralized fashion over time.

There are wrinkles across the expanse of this relatively unruffled fab-

ric. But these are particularly noticeable in examining the early formulation process. I do not argue that centralization has never occurred,
but rather that it occurred very early indeed. As Johnson aide Jack Valenti insisted, LBJ's use of staff was nothing new: "It is true that the
White House became more involved but that was true since the time of
Roosevelt."[57]

Certainly it was true by the time Truman began his second term. Two
points should be stressed in this regard. First, as noted, departmental
submissions were only a part of the Truman legislative program. A
good number came from outside advisory commissions, especially the
first Hoover Commission, which Truman effectively co-opted.[58] But in
the office of his special counsels, Truman also built his own staff devoted to legislative drafting and the formulation of policy proposals;
aides like Clark Clifford, George Elsey, David Bell, and Charles Murphy
(who had previously worked in the Senate Legislative Counsel's office)
were key to this process.[59] "The most important function . . . of the
special counsel," Murphy recalled later, "was built around the staff
work on messages and speeches. The way it worked during the Truman
administration meant that the special counsel was involved in the formulation of policy."[60]

The Budget Bureau added to this capacity, serving not just to vet
proposals but to suggest its own. A BoB document from late 1948 gives
a good sense of the developing Truman policy process. It suggests an
operation that shifted from centralized to agency-centered depending on
presidential needs. The agencies might, but well might not, participate
in policy formulation or receive a given drafting assignment:

> [W]ork of this sort was frequently performed during the last session by
> Executive Office working groups . . . with selected agency participation. In
> the majority of cases the groups were oriented to the preparation of special
> messages, and organized around Mr. Murphy. . . . It is recommended that
> the working group technique be continued, with increased emphasis on
> more advance action than was possible last session. The Bureau of the Bud-
> get will expect to contribute technical staff, official views, or leadership to
> working groups where appropriate to its established functions. Because of
> its regular responsibility for legislative clearance, it will maintain contact
> with all working groups. . . .
>
> Once the president's decision is obtained, there follows the translation of
> Presidential policies into (1) concrete drafts of legislation; (2) assignment of
> responsibility for Executive presentation and justification; (3) development
> of supporting materials. These steps usually are accomplished by assigning
> the lead to one agency (or a group of agencies) to develop specific pro-
> posals, and by coordinating these specifics with the interests and views of

all other parts of the Executive branch and with all other interests which the President desires be taken into consideration (including Congressional interests). In those selected cases of programs developed under White House leadership directly for the president, he presumably will wish White House staff to participate, or to take the leadership in performing these functions, as a follow-up to development of the policies on which the legislative specifics are based. Indeed, last spring, policy development and the working out of the specific legislation were conducted simultaneously on several occasions with excellent results.[61]

The Truman White House itself could be kept small because of a second important point. That is, rather than serving as the purely "institutional" staff discussed above, the legislative side of the Budget Bureau under Truman was already an extension of the president's personal staff. At the edges the two were nearly interchangeable: indeed, a fair number of Budget staffers would become members of the White House Office staff proper. This was no accident. Budget director James Webb saw it as key to cementing BoB influence with the president, and Budget staffers gave serious thought to how to make the agency most useful to the White House.[62] As a result, the BoB and other EOP staffs — such as the Council of Economic Advisers — could serve effectively as backup staff for the Special Counsel's office.

Thus the 1970 reorganization into OMB highlighted a shift to political management (in the sense of responsiveness to presidential desires) that had, in truth, long since occurred.[63] The BoB archives make quite clear that the Truman bureau was to place a tight rein on the agencies on the president's behalf and that it tried to take the president's political outlook into consideration in its planning. One memo reviewing the 1949 program notes, for example, that "it is our distinct impression that reciprocal trade agreements enjoy popular support and are desired by the people of the Middle West."[64] Richard Neustadt, commenting on his role as a BoB staffer in the late 1940s, noted that the review of departmental proposals was "not meant to be exclusive but supplemental. . . . [W]e created a system that both defined the program and gave the White House staff — the personal staff — as much control as they wanted over the formulation of its contents."[65]

The counternarrative does not end there. Consider, for example, Dwight Eisenhower, often seen as the exemplar of departmental delegation. At times this was certainly true. But Eisenhower also created a large number of functionally specific posts in the White House that doubled Cabinet portfolios — including White House offices for Airways Modernization, Disarmament, Cold War Planning, International Understanding and Cooperation, Public Works Planning, Agricultural Surpluses, Foreign Economic Policy, Science and Technology, and Atomic Energy.[66] He strengthened his control over the NSC by downgrading its statutory executive secretary and placing a personal staffer, the newly created assistant for national security affairs, in charge of NSC staff work. He was also the first to appoint someone from the private sector as budget director.

Eisenhower commonly sought extradepartmental advice and utilized a variety of advisory commissions, kept on a tight presidential leash.[67] One such, the President's Advisory Commission on Government Organization, was headed by Milton Eisenhower — the President's brother. Robert C. Wood, who later became secretary of housing and urban development, noted, "The first basic contribution of Eisenhower was to enhance the capacity of the executive office and the President and it was not only a professional in the Budget Bureau . . . [or a] chief of staff, it was Jim Killian as Presidential Science Advisor, it was the restoration of the Council of Economic Advisors. These steps made it possible to 'do' domestic policy."[68]

While Eisenhower did, indeed, frequently use the departments for program formulation — more, probably, than Truman did — he also used the BoB to limit departmental autonomy on both the budget and the policy fronts. The budget process was aimed at reducing spending and was quite centralized in a way that presaged the 1980s' twinning of public policy with fiscal policy.[69] Likewise, an interesting exchange highlights Eisenhower's desire to keep policy formulation within the EOP's purview. On March 1, 1954, then budget director Joseph Dodge wrote to White House chief of staff Sherman Adams and special counsel Bernard Shanley, complaining that the Department of Agriculture was repeatedly allowing constituency groups to draft presidential legislation, then introducing it directly without consultation with the BoB or the White House:

> Last Friday at the Cabinet meeting, Mr. Benson [the secretary of Agriculture] told me he had a bill to cover the President's agriculture program which had been worked out by the Department of Agriculture and the Congressional Committee staffs, and which Senator [George] Aiken intended to introduce immediately. . . . Here again, apparently the specific bill had been drawn without prior consultation or review by the White House staff or the Bureau and without clearance with other departments at interest.

This can't go on, Dodge continued, since

> general discussion of principles is converted into legislation without final consideration of the specific bill to be introduced. The terms of the bill are learned either after it has been introduced, at the time, or just before it is

introduced. This can create and has created substantial difficulties, particularly in relation to projects that are directly connected with the President's program.[70]

Alarmed, Adams wrote sharply to Benson: "We are concerned about recurring difficulties in connection with the preparation and introduction of legislation related to the President's agricultural program. Some of this appears to arise from a practice of drafting legislation with more emphasis on consultation with elements outside the Executive Branch of the Government than within it. . . . [I]t is of the utmost importance that all legislation so drafted shall be finalized in conjunction with existing procedures for review and clearance."[71]

A month later Deputy Secretary True Morse finally replied. The bill, he offered, "was worked out in cooperation with the various wool interests, and Congressional leaders, who were vitally interested in the matter. The Secretary, who as you know has wide personal acquaintance with this leadership, kept closely in touch with the development of the bill. . . . At the very last, apparently there was White House clearance on the major points involved without the knowledge of the Bureau of the Budget." "Apparent" clearance or not, this explanation didn't fly. A handwritten note appended to the exchange sums up the EOP reaction: "They have missed the point obviously and completely."[72]

The point is that even in the 1950s the capacity for centralized program formulation was in place. Further, if the earlier process tended to involve more centralized efforts than generally recognized, it is fair to say that the later process involved fewer. Or, to be more exact, that the process continued to allow for a good deal of presidential flexibility in choosing how to formulate his program.

As figure 3.3 indicates, if one counts consistently over the years (including detailees, off-budget consultants, and the like), it is not clear that the oft-posited logarithmic expansion in employees defined here as centralized has in fact taken place. Where staff growth has been explosive, it has often been in the areas of outreach (media relations, and so on) and presidential "care and feeding" as opposed to core policy areas.[73] These areas are also inherent to the postwar modern presidency of which the president's program is a defining element. But growth in policy areas has been much more sporadic, more contingent. Even examining the trend as a whole, it is evident that White House staff numbers have leveled off at about four hundred full-time equivalent employees after peaking at more than six hundred in the early 1970s.

Thus, executive staffs have shifted in size over time (both up and down); further, presidents have shifted around their policy formulation resources within the formal elements of the EOP itself. Although the

Kennedy administration continued to lean heavily on the BoB for man-power,[74] soon the White House proper was taking over an increasing amount of legislative formulation. The Budget Bureau found its individ-ual staffers utilized for discrete tasks, but over the 1960s "policy staff functions were increasingly separated out of the BoB."[75] In part this reflected the emphasis placed on large, new programs by the New Fron-tier (and later, Great Society) agendas.

While this indicated a shift in the balance of staffing *within* the EOP, it did not in itself mean a drastic increase in centralized policymaking, given the long-standing permeability between the BoB and the White House on legislative affairs. The focus on novelty in policymaking, however, arguably did mean that. This was especially true of the task force approach tried by Kennedy over the 1960–61 transition period and implemented systematically by Lyndon Johnson.[76] The idea, as bud-get director Charles Schultze put it, was that the president "decided that this time it would be much better to exercise a direct and heavy White House initiative rather than just getting what bubbled up. Because what bubbled up tended to be relatively marginal. . . . [T]he key thing that it was not just *a* task force but looking across the board, breaking the whole area of domestic economic policy up into meaningful chunks and assigning a task force to each."[77]

As we have seen, Johnson aides later argued that little of this work was carried out by the departments. But task force membership (and, vitally, the follow-up needed to translate task force proposals into presi-dential program items) seems to have varied quite significantly. Early Johnson task forces tended to be made up of people outside govern-ment, later ones were mainly "in-house." In the latter case, obviously, departments had a fair amount of input into their outputs: the in-teragency team that formulated the Education Professions Develop-ment Act of 1967 was chaired by Secretary of HEW John Gardner — Commissioner Harold Howe of the Office of Education did much of the program development — with nine of fourteen members coming from the departments.[78]

Interestingly, though, even the more highly touted early task forces often required departmental support — probably more than Johnson wanted. This was not a case of simple dictation. As Califano later con-ceded, the 1964 task forces (preparing the 1965 legislative program) proved "really superficial in terms of government policy-making."[79] Task forces handed rough ideas to departments; the Cabinet was called upon to do much of the policy formulation work. (Note along these lines that Senator Mansfield, in this chapter's second epigraph, fully ex-pected the departments to be working out the president's policies.) Sim-ilarly, "for the most part, with very few exceptions in 1965 — in terms of the program that went up in January of 1966 — the ideas came from individuals outside the government. But the kind of task force work was done mainly by groups of people within the government, although sometimes we'd [the White House] have one or two people. Part of that was sheerly a function of time. When I got there in July of 1965, zero had been done in terms of the 1966 legislative program, aside from whatever the Bureau of the Budget was doing."[80] Until new White House staff were added in the spring of 1967, the White House simply couldn't get deeply involved in the substance of new programs.[81] Thus after campaigning against the supposedly bloated Kennedy/Johnson executive office, Richard Nixon's immediate staff was "startl[ed] . . . to understand that there literally had never been any kind of formal structure to deal with this kind of thing."[82]

The Nixon administration generally seems marked by something of a U-curve in terms of decentralization. Early on, hewing to his campaign theme of Cabinet government, the president did give his departments a good deal of authority in formulating legislation.[83] This also occurred later in his administration as the departments moved into the policy-making void created by Watergate.[84] In between, of course, Nixon is best remembered as a compulsive centralizer, creator of the Domestic Council and its staff, which all presidents since have utilized under some name.

Still, even at the height of the Domestic Council staff's influence, its ability to initiate programmatic proposals and its capacity to develop them have been questioned. Robert Gilmour commented in 1971, "In the public mind, line bureaucrats appear to have been eclipsed as legislative innovators by presidential task forces and other outsiders to the traditional process. Nonetheless, in the business of elevating ideas as serious proposals and issues, bureaus remain well situated and prolific."[85] Richard Pious, after reviewing the official functions of the Domestic Council, concluded that "no one believes that the council does any of these things to a significant degree. . . . It had plumbers but not policy analysts."[86] Council staffers tended to tread heavily on the operating, rather than on the formulation, side of the ledger and to get involved in time-sensitive casework issues.[87] For policy preparation the departments still mattered greatly (though so did OMB, returning the EOP balance closer to the pre-Johnson era). And by the end of his first term Nixon had rejected the strong White House model and turned, with his "super-secretary" scheme, to an administrative strategy stressing appointment politicization (in Moe's sense), not centralization.[88]

Suddenly succeeding to the presidency in August 1974, Gerald Ford was quick to promise a return to the old Nixon, believer in Cabinet governance; as we have seen, Ford is generally given credit for keeping this pledge. Yet Ford also appointed a plethora of counsellors to the

president; one of them (Jack Marsh) was assigned "supervisory responsibility for the preparation of legislation."[89] Further, he elevated the stat-
ure of the Domestic Council by naming Vice President Nelson Rockefeller as its head and granting it explicit input into the legislative clearance
process.[90] In late 1975, after Rockefeller was pressured to remove himself from the 1976 ticket, the Domestic Council found itself under-
staffed and without much in the way of political or policy influence.[91]
But one of the key mechanisms that helped to supplant the Council's
role was the Economic Policy Board (EPB), an interagency group run
largely by its active Executive Committee, whose members were heavily
tilted in favor of the "presidential outfits": the director of OMB, the
chair of the CEA, the assistant to the president for economic affairs (Bill
Seidman, who directed the EPB's staff), and the executive director of the
Council on International Economic Policy (yet another EOP agency),
along with the Treasury secretary.[92] OMB was also active in producing
the nineteen budget rescission messages Ford sent to Congress through
1976.

Jimmy Carter's about-face with regard to Cabinet government has
already been mentioned. It suffices to say here that scholarly opinion
traces Carter's own ambivalence. Some argue the Domestic Policy Staff
(DPS) — Carter abolished the Domestic Council itself — was never dor-
mant, and oft-dominant, in policy formulation; others differ.[93] Certainly
with regard to politicizing appointments Carter is viewed as a reluctant
centralizer.[94]

This is hardly the case for Ronald Reagan. Even so, some argue that,
given his prefabricated — even lifelong — agenda, the White House played
a far greater role in selling legislation than in its formulation.[95] The
Office of Policy Development (OPD), which succeeded Carter's DPS, is
given little credit for living up to its name.[96] This does not in itself imply
decentralization, since troika member Edwin Meese took responsibility
for an array of domestic policymaking and since the OMB took up any
slack under the energetic leadership of director Stockman. But some
question whether the Cabinet Councils effectively enforced presidential
preferences. OPD staffer John McClaughry argued that the councils created a "pernicious process" by which "the policy agenda [was] in large
measure transferred from the Reagan White House to the departments.
Instead of informing the departments that the president believes so-
and-so, and wants such-and-such done about it . . . the Reagan White
House . . . instituted itself as an arbitration forum for disagreements
brought up to it by its department heads."[97] Certainly some Cabinet
members, including Meese after his move to the Justice Department,
were able to bypass the councils or shape their outputs to departmental
ends.[98]

One development of the mid-1980s is worth a brief digression, since the centrality of budgeting to policymaking might affect the nature, if less consistently the source, of presidential legislative policy over time. After all, during the Reagan years budgetary and deficit issues trumped all others. Does this matter for policy formulation?

It is true that budgeting and programming have never been wholly distinct. Truman observed as early as 1946 that "it is clear that the budgetary program and the general program of the government are actually inseparable"; the very purpose of the 1921 Budget Act creating the BoB was to give the president the capacity for centralized control over the process.[99] Still, beginning in fiscal year 1970 the national budget was in deficit for thirty years. Fifteen years in the 1980s and 1990s were marked by the "fiscalization" of American politics.[100] Until a balanced budget was restored in fiscal year 1998, budgeting became the driving force of American policymaking—"both an obsession and a weapon," as Aaron Wildavsky wrote.[101] With regard to lawmaking the deficit was at once a result, a cause, and a constraint: a result of legislation (notably the Reagan budget package of 1981, P.L. 97–35), the cause of much other remedial legislation (for example, Gramm-Rudman-Hollings I and II, the Budget Enforcement Act of 1990, the Omnibus Budget Reconciliation Act of 1993), and a constraint on yet other legislation, notably on large program initiatives.

Deficit politics, arguably, gave OMB—though also Treasury—an organizational boost. If more items are budgetary, then this might be reflected in more programmatic "action" for OMB and thus a higher level of centralization. This hypothesis will be addressed in Chapter Five. Still, a parallel development also reinforced OMB power: the first Reagan term saw the peak of the use of rescission legislation, noted above under the Ford years. Responding to unilateral presidential impoundment of appropriated funds by the Nixon administration, Congress had changed the rules of the game in 1974.[102] Now, spending cuts had to be carried out via budget rescission messages submitted for legislative approval—in short, rescissions had to be made part of the presidential program. Ford and Carter sent forty such messages; Reagan sent nineteen in 1981 and 1982 alone, thirty-three in all.[103]

The use of rescissions has tailed off (only twenty-two messages were sent in the twelve years from 1989 to 2000). But they make clear how Congress itself can shape the presidential decision-making environment, realigning the incentives for presidential action. As it had previously through the granting of broad reorganization authority, which tends to breed reorganization proposals, in the rescission case Congress effectively empowered OMB.

But Congress can strengthen the hand of decentralization as well. Reorganization authority expired in 1981 and was not renewed. Further, congressional delegation of power to the executive branch can be crafted to add to the presidential program while substantively bypassing the White House. The Nuclear Nonproliferation Act of 1978 (P.L. 95-242) is a good example. It requires the president to negotiate bilateral agreements concerning the peaceful use of nuclear equipment, material, and technology, and to submit these agreements directly to Congress. But the statute dictates exactly how the management of these agreements is to be conducted:

> Any proposed agreement for cooperation shall be negotiated by the Secretary of State, with the technical assistance and concurrence of the Secretary of Energy . . . ; and after consultation with the [Nuclear Regulatory] Commission shall be submitted to the President jointly by the Secretary of State and the Secretary of Energy accompanied by the views and recommendations of the Secretary of State, the Secretary of Energy, [and] the Nuclear Regulatory Commission.[104]

Likewise, the Fishery Conservation and Management Act of 1976 (P.L. 94-265) requires the secretary of state, in cooperation with the secretary of commerce, to renegotiate bilateral international agreements governing fishing rights. The president is required to transmit the agreement to Congress directly, but the State Department is given the statutory authority to craft it.[105] These are relatively routine agreements. But by writing the statutes in this manner, Congress has elevated them to components of the presidential program while at the same time structuring their formulation in a way that requires departmental involvement and limits presidential discretion.

The narrative peters out somewhat at this point, since the literature on presidential staffing thins after Reagan. George H. W. Bush and even Bill Clinton are treated as organizational appendices to the Reagan model. The passage of time will expand our knowledge here. Still, at the moment, commentary on the senior Bush administration tends to focus on foreign policy and use the administration's minimal legislative agenda as a foil.[106] Studies of the Clinton administration highlight staff shakeups and the roles of the first lady and consultant Dick Morris.

Ambiguities nonetheless abound. Was George H. W. Bush a team player, with respect for the bureaucracy and in search of policy ideas "in a systematic, if uninspired way"[107]—or a purveyor of that airtight White House loop? While the phrase "Cabinet government" was not at issue in the 1988 election, Bush's pledge for a "new leadership style" promised much the same thing.[108] Bush had a fair amount of one-on-one interaction with Cabinet members. And while the Office of Policy Development remained in place, it provided mainly a synthesis of departmental views, without adding options of its own or providing political comment. Not until late in the administration, some analysts argue, did "the White House . . . tak[e] control of the domestic policy agenda" and even then did so without much success.[109]

The Clinton administration has been accused of having been too confused in its first half term even to centralize.[110] Selection of a Cabinet that "look[ed] like America" consumed Clinton's time.[111] Teamwork was the watchword for the administration, with a real effort made at the outset to include both White House and departmental staff in policy formulation.[112] This began to shift in 1994 with the arrival of Leon Panetta as the new White House chief of staff; but at the same time, control over sub-Cabinet appointments began to flow back to the departments.[113] The picture overall is perhaps best described, in the words of one Clinton appointee, as "organizationally untidy."[114]

Next Steps

"Untidy," in fact, might be the prevailing adjective for the qualitative evidence presented here. Just as Harry Truman never found a one-armed economist, so is the literature marshaled on behalf of a thesis of linear centralization unable to shake off the nagging suspicions of "the other hand."

It is not that we know nothing about presidential policymaking; we know a great deal. Still, the approach to date has been tied to individual presidents and to rather broad generalization. The results are unsatisfying, with little rationale for choosing between competing versions of history.

Even so, the literature viewed as a whole leaves the sense of multifaceted presidential options — in short, of contingency. This does not mean presidents have not managed programmatic formulation in coherent ways, merely that these have not been consistently measured, controlling for the management contexts that condition presidential choices on this front. We are not only unsure about presidential programmatic direction, but, without consistent points of comparison, even unsure of *how* unsure we should be.[115]

The chapters that follow step into the breach. They detail the breadth of the president's program over time and present a methodology for drawing more incisive generalizations about presidential management strategies — and their implications for interbranch relations.

In Chapter Four, the problem of how to define the program in practice is addressed, and a new database of presidential legislative proposals is presented. Chapters Five through Seven then test the theories proposed earlier — and assess the fruits of centralization.

CHAPTER FOUR

The President's Program:
An Empirical Overview

GIVEN the salience of the president's legislative program to the public, the media, and, not least, other political actors, the lack of an "industry standard" measure of that program is somewhat surprising. After all, presidents are compared, and compare themselves, on a programmatic basis. At the end of 1962, for instance, the Kennedy White House produced a report indicating that JFK was far ahead of Dwight Eisenhower's pace in terms of the number of policies proposed and passed into law.[1] In mid-1977 Jimmy Carter's congressional relations staff complained instead that looking at Lyndon Johnson's 1965 achievements set an unfair standard. The first-year records of Harry Truman — and, for that matter, of John Kennedy — were thought to be better reference points, presumably because "by this more normal bench mark President Carter has done exceedingly well with the Congress to date."[2]

Solid, systematic comparisons are hard to come by. Each administration naturally uses a counting method that boosts its figures — LBJ managed to claim a 91 percent success rate in the 89th Congress, and Bill Clinton avowed that during the 103d Congress (1993–94) he had "substantially or partially accomplished" more than three-quarters of his 1992 campaign promises.[3] As a result even presidents have a hard time figuring out what, exactly, constituted their predecessors' programs. The plight of Nixon staffer Jim Keogh was mentioned in Chapter One: asked to compare Nixon's legislative success to JFK's, he could only reply that "it will take more study to determine what they included in their figures." He mused, "They must have counted more items as 'bills' than we have. . . . We could use the percentage comparison, I suppose, since ours is better, but since we are not yet sure how they counted theirs, we could be accused of comparing apples and avocados." Of course, the Kennedy count was a moving target, since the New Frontiersmen had reserved the option of listing as part of the program "other bills we expect to pass," explicitly to "fatten our 'batting average.' "[4]

Nonetheless, with hindsight — or, more precisely, with the benefit of the archival record — the question does admit of systematic analysis. Most broadly, one might try to look at every presidential legislative proposal, determine its formulation process, and then calculate methodically the number and nature of those processes. Within the bounds of statistical sampling and available data, this is the approach taken here.

This chapter thus does three things. It presents a dataset comprising the president's program as a whole, and compares this accounting with others used in the literature. It discusses the random sample on which the book's subsequent analysis will rely. And it presents some analytic first steps suggesting a fairly constant level of centralization over the postwar period with regard to legislative policy formulation. These findings lay the groundwork for the tests of contingent centralization to follow.

PRESIDENTIAL LEGISLATIVE PROPOSALS, 1949–1996

The first step in tracing the source of the elements of the president's program is determining what the program as a whole actually contains. But like many first steps, it has proven rather wobbly. Ideally, the program could be compiled from sources within each administration. The Legislative Reference Division in OMB is the checkpoint for almost all administration legislation, after all; why not utilize the internal records of the legislative clearance process?

Though appealing, this approach is problematic. It is far from clear, for example, that every bill approved by OMB's central clearance process deserves attention as part of the president's program. Paul Light's study of the president's agenda found that in 1977 alone more than 550 draft bills were considered by OMB for clearance. Many of these initiatives, while by their definition sponsored by the administration, are not necessarily important to the president.[5] This distinction is clear to OMB itself, as discussed in Chapter Three, but is hard to get at systematically. Light was able to gain access to more discriminating internal reports generated by the Legislative Reference Division; I have replicated these data from the copies available in the National Archives and presidential libraries. Still, while very useful, these are slightly inconsistent between administrations. Nor are they available for each year under study, most notably the Reagan years.[6]

To date, therefore, scholars interested in the study of presidential legislation have tended to use one of two public sources of data: presidential State of the Union messages[7] and the presidential legislative Boxscores compiled by Congressional Quarterly until 1975.[8] Each has advantages, but also some critical limits.

The State of the Union

In Article II, Section 3, the Constitution requires that the president "from time to time give Congress information of the State of the

Union." In modern times this has usually taken the form of a personal address in front of a joint session assembled in the House chamber. There the president lists a number of items for congressional consideration; much executive infighting goes into the placement of these recommendations and the emphasis accorded each. The usual result is a rhetorical logroll. Bush communications director David Demarest commented that "everyone wants his or her issue mentioned in the State of the Union address so as not to feel insignificant. Every State of the Union address is the same, however. They are initially thematic speeches, but they become much more inclusive."[9]

This in itself, of course, is not necessarily a problem for our purposes — the longer the laundry list, the better the tally of the overall load. But there are reasons to think that the State of the Union address is not an adequate measure of the president's program as a whole.

The main difficulty is that this speech is not invariably the platform for the president's program. At times presidents have made this point quite explicit: the Truman Budget Bureau, for example, wrote to a senator noting that "since the State of the Union message did not contain all the legislative proposals made by the President, we have broadened your questions to include other legislative proposals made by the President." Similarly, in his fiscal 1958 Budget Message, Eisenhower stated that "this year I discussed only a few of the administration's legislative recommendations in the State of the Union message."[10] Of the presidential messages described below, only about a third were included in the State of the Union, and even fewer were presented there exclusively.

There are a number of other vehicles presidents may utilize for presenting legislative proposals. Presidents Nixon, Carter, and Reagan, for example, decided to transmit to the Congress a supplementary written State of the Union message detailing legislative priorities and the preferred means for their achievement. These presidents' corresponding State of the Union addresses were designed for oral (and televised) presentation, but not as a comprehensive expression of the president's legislative program.[11] In 1973 President Nixon sent *four* topical messages, all entitled "State of the Union" — on human services, law enforcement, foreign affairs, and natural resources. Presidents have also used wide-ranging messages at different points in the year to put forth legislative proposals, for example, Kennedy's May 1961 message on "urgent national needs" — deemed the "second State of the Union" by his staff — or Ford's twin messages on legislative priorities in the fall of 1974.[12] Presidents in their first year may not give a formal State of the Union address at all, though they usually give some type of early speech laying out their priorities.[13]

Despite (or perhaps because of) the bargaining that shapes its text, the State of the Union address is usually seen as a good indicator of presidential priorities. Focusing only on high-priority items, however, might serve to bias the analysis. For example, what if important items, however defined, are more likely to be handled within the White House as opposed to the departments? Using State of the Union data alone would then find more centralized legislative policy formulation than might actually exist, a hypothesis put to the test in Chapter Five.

Finally, the State of the Union message is not itself discretionary and thus says less about presidential choice than do other communications. As an annual address given at roughly the same time each year, it is rarely an appropriate vehicle for responding to immediate needs. The *Public Papers of the President* are filled with accounts of, and reaction to, nonroutine (but quite regular) events such as labor disputes, natural disasters, and international disruption. If Neustadt is right in noting that in the postwar era crises have become business as usual,[14] this should be taken into account in studying how the executive works to prepare legislative proposals. Items that seemed timely in January might be supplanted by June.

None of this is to say that using State of the Union data is never appropriate. Jeffrey Cohen utilizes State of the Union proposals in his study of presidential responsiveness to public opinion precisely because the speech focuses on presidential priorities and is a "scarce resource."[15] Likewise Light, in his work tracing the president's agenda, is interested mainly in the high-priority domestic items therein.[16] Therefore the president's agenda, as Light defines it, is somewhat different from the president's program taken as a whole, as discussed here. Both emphasize issues receiving presidential attention and thus elevated from the mass of bills associated with the executive branch as a whole. But the program, as discussed in Chapter Three, is the president's comprehensive accounting of problem and proposal across the full range of government action. Thus programmatic items may move on or off the immediate "agenda." The State of the Union address may, over the course of an administration, account for the latter; but it is too small a vessel to contain the entire program, and so does not provide the systematic basis for analysis needed here.

Congressional Quarterly Boxscores

Some researchers looking for broader data have utilized the legislative "Boxscore" listings compiled by Congressional Quarterly from 1947 through 1975 and published in that organization's annual *Almanac*. Each year, CQ scoured presidents' public statements to extract "legislative proposals which were clear-cut enough to be pinned down."[17] These included requests for congressional action from the State of the Union address, the Budget Message, the Economic Report, special substantive messages, letters, press conferences, and speeches. Not counted are measures advocated by executive branch officials other than the president; nominations submitted to the Senate; measures endorsed but not specifically submitted by the president; exhortations to Congress that do not require legislation; or routine appropriations requests.

As such these data are quite comprehensive, but problematic nonetheless.[18] For my purposes, two difficulties with the Boxscore information as published are most crucial.

First and most obvious, the time period covered by the Boxscores falls far short of the scope of this project, which extends for more than two decades past 1975. Indeed, because of a shift in methodology after the 1953 scores were calculated, the Boxscores are internally consistent only from 1954 to 1975. This first limit is partly a result of a broader flaw: since these data were not considered reliable for their stated purpose of measuring presidential success in Congress, CQ stopped calculating them.

Second, the treatment of Boxscored proposals is not entirely consistent over time. CQ's methods of subdividing presidential proposals shifted from year to year. Some items do not seem to appear in public sources, and thus are hard to verify; some are overly vague; some do request "negative" action despite the journal's stated ground rules. And by excluding all appropriations requests the Boxscores bypass an increasingly important component of policy.

Nonetheless, scholars owe CQ a great debt. The set of Boxscore items — though not the CQ definition of "success" — is a close cousin to the dataset developed for this project.[19]

The Public Papers of the Presidents

As noted earlier, not all items that the executive branch as a whole sends to Congress for consideration can be considered part of the president's program. At a minimum, it seems plausible that items included in the program must have received at least some personal attention from the president, though they need not be on his "must list" or, in fact, be objectively important. In addition, the programs must be broadly comparable over time in order to analyze accurately any trends of centralization therein.

To meet these criteria, this project uses the compilations of the *Public Papers of the President (PPP)* covering 1949 through 1996. These volumes are published annually by the National Archive and Record Administration's Office of the Federal Register and encompass, as their title implies, all public communications of the president during a given year. This draws on most of the same material as the Congressional Quarterly Boxscore data in one replicable and readily available source.

As in CQ, items included in the count are presidential communications to Congress, in the form of messages, speeches, or letters that make specific legislative proposals. Each item is therefore sponsored by the president, in writing, and associated with him personally; he is to this extent committed to its substance and passage.

A request for legislation might include anything from an energy bill to a suggested joint resolution to an omnibus special message on a single topic (for example, agriculture, highway construction, or mutual security). The common denominator is that the president is making a specific legislative request that contemplates action by both chambers of Congress. As a result, vague policy wish lists are excluded: something like Harry Truman's 1949 pronouncement that "the national tax policy should be flexible and should be promptly adjusted to the changing needs of business and consumers in the course of evolving economic events" — or George W. Bush's 2001 call for "fair and balanced" election reform — is too amorphous for inclusion.[20] Endorsements of extant legislation filed by others (such as Carter's 1978 endorsement in his State of the Union address of Humphrey-Hawkins full employment legislation) are also left out.

Items were counted only once per Congress. Once a piece of legislation is on the table, so to speak, further presidential mentions to the same body of legislators are considered endorsements. Thus if a president mentioned an item in eight consecutive years (by definition, to little avail), it would be included in the first, third, fifth, and seventh years' counts. Further, if a proposal from the State of Union, Economic Report, or Budget Message was repeated in another substantive communication to the same Congress (most often in a special message on a specific subject), it was only counted once unless the specifics of the request had changed in between. Such an item would be catalogued as part of whichever message provided more specific details on its provisions.

Diverging from CQ, I also included messages embodying supplemental budget requests, were also included, although only in cases where the president sent a separate communication asking for a specific dollar amount in the current fiscal year. That is, where presidents pulled items out of the budget and made separate requests regarding their outcome (whether to add spending or, in the case of rescission requests, to cut it), they were counted separately from the budget message as a whole.

Requests that Congress not act (for example, "do not raise taxes this year") were not included, with the exception of items that were drafted and sent by the president but that could become law automatically without congressional action. The most prominent example of this is reorganization plans submitted to Congress under Reorganization Act authority; such acts became law unless Congress passed a resolution of disapproval within a time certain. Like other legislation, such plans are formulated in the executive branch and transmitted to Congress for action — it is just that in this case, as in few others, presidents prefer inaction.

Note that the "two chamber" rule means that treaties are excluded from the data. While this reduces the number of foreign policy proposals included in the study, the impact is actually quite limited. The reason is that the *PPP* included only "important" treaties until editorial policy shifted in the 1970s. Though JFK, for example, submitted nearly seventy treaties, protocols, and conventions to the Senate for ratification,[21] only three appear in the three years of Kennedy's public papers. By the time of the Carter administration, however, even routine instruments asking for the Senate's "advice and consent" are included.

Note that this inconsistency is an aberration within the *PPP*. It is certainly true that over the period in question the papers expand, from one annual volume in most years prior to 1965 to three in recent election years. But the inclusion of additional material over time does not reflect a change in what was deemed proper to include: thus it does not undercut the goal of constructing an unbiased dataset. In part, the "thickening" reflects the workload placed on the executive branch by the legislative: the papers are filled with reports to the Congress pursuant to statute, even after the proximate need for those reports (for example, the conflict in Cyprus) has faded from the headlines. Mostly, though, the papers simply reflect presidents' increased prolixity stemming from their needs and opportunities to "go public."[22] Jimmy Carter's town meetings are harbingers of Ronald Reagan's weekly radio addresses and Bill Clinton's talk show appearances, all faithfully recorded.

Using the coding rules above, I used the *PPP* to make two counts. First, the *messages* sent to Congress by each president were tabulated. A message was defined as a communication from the president to Congress on a single topic on a single day. For the most part these are discrete one- or multipart requests (for example, "Special Message on Health Care"; "Letter to the Speaker of the House and President of the Senate Transmitting the Elementary and Secondary Education Act of 1965"). Keep in mind that this definition can sometimes mean that one communication may constitute more than one message: some omnibus communications from the president contain more than one subject and thus were counted as more than one message. This was often true of the State of the Union, the Economic Report, and the Budget Message, and sometimes of broad special messages as well, such as Eisenhower's May

1960 "Message on the Legislative Program" and its analogues across other administrations. It could also occur if the president made clear in his communication to Congress that more than one bill was being transmitted.[23] Less commonly, proposals eventually folded into one bill ended up in parts of two messages.[24]

The basic rule, then, is that messages in the *PPP* were counted as such unless the president made it clear that the items therein were separable or that multiple pieces of legislation were attached: any piece of legislation that the president sent as one piece and wanted to see adopted as sent was considered one message, no matter how realistic the prospects of that outcome. After all, the message is at the heart of presidential legislative formulation: it is "not just a proposal for action; it is itself a form of action that involves setting objectives and defining strategies of bargaining."[25]

Using this definition tended to create bigger units than are common in the Boxscore version. In general, though, it seemed appropriate to utilize the vehicle by which a president chooses to present his policy proposal, however discrete or enormous, to the Congress. This allows for greater consistency of items in the sample across time. And it makes sense to adhere, in the data, to the object of interest: the policy proposal or package actually prepared in the executive branch. Should the National Performance Review package filed as one bill in October of 1993 be studied as one presidential message, or as the thirty-plus segments reviewed by congressional committees? Given the aims of this project, the former makes more sense. As John Kennedy noted in his 1963 tax message, "the changes listed below" — forty-six of them, all told — "are an integral part of a single tax package." Similarly, Gerald Ford stressed in unveiling his 1975 omnibus energy bill that "[this] is a very comprehensive program and we are having put in one bill all of the legislative proposals. . . . We are doing this because we want it to be, as it is, a comprehensive approach to the problem of energy."[26]

Similar quotes could be presented for every administration. The point is that the message's size is a question of presidential choice that is itself of interest, and represents information that should not be discarded.

That said, some messages are more complex than others, and to gain another vantage on the size and scope of a given presidential program, a second count of the number of specific *proposals* contained in each message was also tabulated.[27] I adjusted these data to be consistent with the coding rules for messages: namely, proposals repeated within a single Congress were counted only the first time; treaties were not included; and reorganization plans were. The number of proposals does not serve as a perfect proxy for complexity, but is useful descriptive information nonetheless.

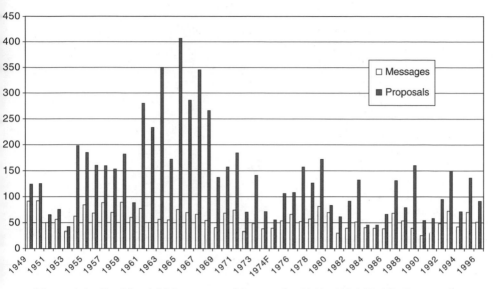

Figure 4.1 Presidential Messages and Proposals, 1949–1996 (*Public Papers of the Presidents*). There are two entries for 1974, representing both Presidents Nixon and Ford.

The Data

Using these criteria, I identified a total of 2,796 messages comprising 6,926 proposals across the ten-presidency, forty-eight-year period.[28] These data are summarized here in two ways, by year and by president. Figure 4.1 shows the yearly trend in presentation; the numbers behind the graph may be found in the Appendix, table A.1. A breakdown by administration is presented in table 4.1, listing the average number of messages and proposals (along with the number of proposals per message) sent each year by each president over his entire tenure.

The relatively high number of messages and low number of proposals per message in the Truman and Eisenhower years partially reflects that the Budget Message (as a text, outside of dollar amounts) and Economic Report were once much more common vehicles for discrete, specific presidential policy suggestions than they are now. Although both these presidents sent special messages to Congress, it was left to Kennedy and Johnson to craft the huge omnibus messages that marked the 1960s. Keep in mind, as already noted, that while the number of proposals (and proposals per message) is a useful comparative figure, it is not an exact measure of the size of a given item. This is because even quite large program items can appear in the *PPP* as one or a few pro-

TABLE 4.1
Legislative Messages and Proposals, by President

President	Average Messages per Year	Average Proposals per Year	Average Proposals per Msg.
Truman (1949–1952)	72.3	97.3	1.35
Eisenhower (1953–1960)	69.1	145.9	2.11
Kennedy (1961–1963)	61.0	287.7	4.72
Johnson (1963–1968)	63.8	295.2	4.63
Nixon (1969–1974)	53.9	136.2	2.53
Ford (1974–1976)	65.3	111.2	1.70
Carter (1977–1980)	64.8	134.5	2.08
Reagan (1981–1988)	44.6	81.3	1.82
Bush (1989–1992)	35.5	91.8	2.58
Clinton (1993–1996)	58.8	111.8	1.90
Total	58.3	144.3	2.48

Source: Public Papers of the Presidents, 1949–1996.

Note: Averages for Ford and Nixon, who both served in 1974, are pro-rated. Note that LBJ did not submit additional recommendations in 1963; thus his average is based on five full years in office and Kennedy's on three.

posals, a matter discussed further when message "complexity" is operationalized in Chapter Five.

The messages can also be broken down by policy type, albeit rather crudely. Of the 2,796 total messages, 68 percent are largely domestic in nature; 20 percent largely foreign; 7 percent are budgetary items affecting both foreign and domestic policy; and 5 percent are reorganizational proposals that also straddle both arenas. Note that if those treaties appearing in the *PPP* were included in the mix, foreign affairs would become about a third of the whole; if all treaties sent to Congress were considered, the number of foreign policy items would close on 50 percent.[29] Because many domestic policies have some element of international relations contained therein (with the rise of "intermestic" policy, the reverse is even more true), and because nearly all proposals have some sort of budgetary impact, a more nuanced coding of policy type was developed for the smaller sample (this is detailed in Chapter Five).

The Sample

It is impossible to come to any conclusion about the formulation processes governing 3,000 policy initiatives. Thus a random sample of 384 legislative proposals was drawn. Since the source of messages overall — not the overall number of messages or proposals — is the quantity of

TABLE 4.2
Characteristics, Universe, and Sample of Presidential Legislative Proposals

	Universe	Sample
Mean proposals/message	2.5	3.1
Median no. of proposals/message	1	1
Mode no. of proposals/message	1	1
% Domestic	68	67
% Foreign	20	23
% Budget	7	5
% Reorganization	5	5

interest, the sample was stratified by administration in order to ensure a steady number of initiatives over time and to avoid oversampling from more active presidents.[30]

The sample size was chosen in order to allow for reliable generalizations between administrations. The full sample provides sixteen items for each of the twenty-four Congresses in the time series — hence, $n = 32$ for a normal four-year term, with presidents serving less than a full term prorated for time served.[31] This second stratification by Congress is appropriate because each two-year Congress is the temporal unit within which an administration's policy formulation process must work. Indeed, Section 8-e of OMB Circular A-19 notes that clearance "advice on the relationship of legislation to the President's program generally applies to all sessions of each Congress but does not carry over from one Congress to the next."[32]

As table 4.2 indicates, quick comparison with the overall universe of proposals shows that the sample is in fact representative. A list of sampled items is presented in the appendix as table A.2.

Note that summary statistics examining the sample will be weighted, to correct for the fact that some proposals were more likely to have been included in the sample than others. That is, since an equal number of observations were taken from each Congress, program items sent by presidents with a large agenda were less likely to be sampled than program items sent by less active presidents. In order to draw accurate generalizations from the sample about the entire population of program items, it is necessary to give more weight to the former items.[33] This procedure is quite common in survey research, where a small subpopulation must be oversampled to ensure that it can be accurately analyzed.[34]

CODING CENTRALIZATION: DELVING INTO PREHISTORY

In the context of case study or judicial review we are used to thinking about legislative history. This project, however, demands the mirror image. That is, a legislative "prehistory" of the presidential initiative's ancestry within the executive branch was established so that its preponderant source within the executive branch could be determined.

Tracing the origins and development of even a modest piece of legislation could fill the pages of a book; many books are filled just that way.[35] Any translation of the real-world policymaking process into a blunt numerical assessment must inevitably misapprehend that process to some degree. Nonetheless it is a necessary simplification, if generalizations about presidential management of the programmatic process are to be sketched and tested. Importantly, what is presented here is an ordinal, not an absolute, measure of centralization. It is not the exact locus but the relative centralization of the process of policy formulation that is in question.

For this study, the source of a piece of legislative policy was placed in one of five categories, from least to most centralized:

1. the product of the Cabinet departments and/or executive agencies;
2. of mixed White House/departmental origin, with the departments taking the lead role;
3. of mixed origin, with the White House in the lead;
4. the product of centralized staff outside the White House Office, such as in the Budget Bureau/OMB or CEA; or
5. the product of staffers within the White House Office itself.

This framework is congruent with the limited extant work in this area. For example, Harold Wolman and Astrid Merget develop a six-part typology of presidential policy development processes, ranging from what they term the "legislative clearance model" at the decentralized end of the process to the "White House Staff model" at the other extreme. In between are various mixtures of White House and departmental staff involvement. Likewise, Daniel Ponder's categories of the White House–departmental relationship within his notion of "staff shift" are similarly centralized, decentralized, or mixed.[36]

Wolman and Merget separate out an "outside task force model," but this is not necessary here since task forces, too, can be categorized along an axis of centralization. In general, task forces and commissions of various sorts tend to be formed precisely when the president is dissatisfied with the proposals arising from the line departments; as such, they are frequently brought under the aegis of the White House staff.[37] The strategic use of commissions by presidents is well documented. Eisenhower chief of staff Sherman Adams relates with some relish that when ideas for the 1954 foreign economic policy message were brought to Ike by staff economist Gabriel Hauge and others, the president liked them — but "[he] needed first a study by a commission or citizens' committee which would bring in recommendations for a new foreign trade program and support it when [he] sent it to Congress." One was appointed, and the desired recommendations were obtained.[38]

Some commissions, however, while nominally controlled by the president, either are made up mainly of departmental secretaries or are politically independent, perhaps even appointed by earlier presidents. The Outdoor Recreation Resources Review Commission (ORRRC) cochaired by Senator Clinton Anderson and Laurance Rockefeller is a good example. While the ORRRC's report of early 1962 became the basis for several Kennedy proposals in the area of land conservation, the body itself had been appointed in 1958 by President Eisenhower and could hardly be said to be under the (Kennedy) White House's control. In cases like this the resultant proposals were considered to be decentralized in origin.[39]

A similar standard applies to program ideas that have been floating in Congress, which is quite common; certainly few major ideas spring fullgrown from the executive branch alone.[40] The Kennedy program in 1961 was sent up quickly in part because "it had the great virtue of familiarity. Eisenhower's vetoes had left the Democrats a ready-made list of bills."[41] Still, the president must invest staff resources in transforming congressional ideas into presidential ones, at least in presentation. Since the proposal is something of a known quantity, this tactic usually lowers presidents' informational costs, which in turn, as argued in Chapter Two, makes a decentralized strategy more likely. But this doesn't have to be the case. In the Kennedy instance, speed was deemed of the essence, and so even before the new administration took office the Bureau of the Budget (using a carefully compiled "Kennedy-pedia" of campaign commitments) and a number of task forces had been at work scouring the political landscape for ideas and initiatives. Those that emerged are best seen as products of a centralized process.[42]

I noted above that a policy's level of centralization is based on its "preponderant" source within the executive branch. The term is borrowed from Lawrence Chamberlain, who used it in his 1946 study of policy initiation to evaluate whether a bill was mainly a legislative or an executive product.[43] The tribute is appropriate, since I have simply shifted the terms of the question: instead of asking about the legislative and executive branches, my targets are the executive and—with a nod to Nelson Polsby—the presidential.[44] In any case the term is a useful way to acknowledge that most proposals have many sires but that responsibility for the overall form and content of the presidential proposal can generally be assigned. Most proposals spring not from a moment's flash of inspiration but from a sometimes tortured process.[45] But the guiding question is not whether a department (or the White House) ever saw or even was assigned the drafting of a proposal; anything reaching the level of presidential utterance will generally receive a wide range of input. On the one hand, the legislative reference process and the practicalities of sending a presidential message to Congress ensure at least some EOP involvement in any item in the president's program. On the other, the technical aspects of drafting are often carried out in the departments even when the ideas come from outside them.[46] Mixed processes are common, as will be seen, and important; but not every proposal should be coded "mixed."

The key dimensions, then, are who took the *initiative* in proposing or presenting the policy; who had the *influence* to prevail in arguments over thrust and design; and who had the *capacity* to flesh out the package with programmatic and legislative substance. These were assessed, wherever possible, using archival sources, mainly the Bureau of the Budget/Office of Management and Budget records held by the National Archives, and the subject and staff files in seven presidential libraries.[47] A wide variety of other sources were also used: the *PPP* themselves; oral histories and interviews; various issues of the Congressional Quarterly *Weekly Report* and *Almanac*; the *National Journal*; memoirs; secondary texts of political science and history; national newspapers; and testimony from the bills' committee hearings.

Only specific references to a given staffer, staff group, department, agency, commission, or task force as the author of policy proposals were utilized. Archival sources were checked against the secondary literature, and vice versa. Where insufficient facts were available regarding a given item, no code was assigned.[48] Still, it should be kept in mind that not all coding decisions were made on the basis of equivalent information.

As a result it may be useful to give some examples of how specific codes were assigned — that is, what does a centralized, or mixed, process actually look like? Again, the key factors were where an idea originated; who had successful input into the specifics of the policy; and who had the capacity for the substantive knowledge needed to prepare the message or draft (though as noted, providing a technical drafting service is not considered to be substantive input into a policy's formulation if the specifics were dictated elsewhere.) The examples here are drawn from different administrations and cover different subjects. They supplement the illustrations from the Eisenhower and Clinton administrations presented in the first chapter.

Decentralized

On November 10, 1989, President Bush unveiled his Homeownership and Opportunity for People Everywhere package — HOPE, for short. Its central element was a program of $2.15 billion in matching grants to states and nonprofit institutions trying to build up affordable housing stock, mainly by rehabilitating public housing, government-held vacant housing, and foreclosed housing in the FHA portfolio. Another $728 million would go into a three-year effort to find social services and health care for the homeless. The low-income housing tax credit would be extended, and fifty "enterprise zones" created in distressed urban and rural areas, within which capital gains taxes would be eliminated. An additional fifty "housing opportunity zones" would provide tax and regulatory incentives for building affordable housing. First-time home buyers would be able to use money in Individual Retirement Accounts (IRAs) toward a down payment, without penalty.

This set of proposals was developed, drafted, and presented to the president by Housing and Urban Development Secretary Jack Kemp and the HUD staff.[49] It received little or no help along the way from the White House, OMB opposed it vigorously on the basis of its cost and its overall philosophy. The Treasury Department also raised objections to the extension of the low-income housing credit.

In part, the radical departure from Reagan-era attacks on housing, and on HUD, appealed to the "kinder, gentler" Bush; nonetheless, a Senate staffer noted that "it was not easy for Kemp to get his bill," given White House and OMB sniping.[50] Administration officials, indeed, gave Kemp credit for "a major victory" in the policy formulation process.[51]

Mixed: Department Lead

On April 6, 1977, President Jimmy Carter sent Congress the Youth Employment and Demonstration Projects Act, part of the administration's larger effort to stimulate a sluggish national economy. Here the overall process was departmental at the outset, then mediated by the White House and OMB when agency disagreement threatened the administration's momentum on the issue.

In his fiscal stimulus message of January 31, 1977, President Carter requested $1.5 billion for youth employment. "These proposals reflected the concerns of the secretary of labor [Ray Marshall], who was committed to jobs programs that focused on the most disadvantaged sectors of the labor force."[52] No details, though, emerged until March, when it became clear that Congress was not, by itself, going to come up with a bill satisfactory to the administration — "the threat of runaway legislation [is] clear," warned White House aide Stuart Eizenstat in a memo to Carter. In response, the Labor Department constructed a measure and draft message that took bits and pieces of various pending bills — including, at the urging of the Domestic Policy Staff, a new federal Young Adult Conservation Corps.[53] A message was to be appended to this by the DPS. "This," Eizenstat noted, would ". . . spell out the new proposal outlined above. We believe such a message is critical to regaining the Administration's initiative in this area. OMB and all affected agencies agree."[54] Carter concurred.

After the message was drafted Labor continued to take the lead; around March 29 it submitted a draft bill to OMB, which circulated it for comments. The number (and occasional vehemence) of responses received prompted OMB to convene an interagency meeting on April 5 to hammer out the details. Even then not all departments were happy. However, as OMB staffer Naomi Sweeney reported, they were "willing to go with it as amended," and that was enough. On April 6 the bill went to Congress.[55]

Mixed: White House Lead

On March 8, 1971, President Richard Nixon sent Congress a Special Message on Special Revenue Sharing for Manpower, incorporating the Manpower Revenue Sharing Act of 1971. This was partly motivated by the failure of a broader revenue sharing act developed by the Treasury Department and sent to Congress in August 1969.[56] By 1971, although Labor and to a lesser extent Treasury had a good deal of input in shaping the bill, the process was clearly driven (and the final specifics dictated) by the staff of the White House Domestic Council working closely with Office of Management and Budget personnel.

After Domestic Council director John Ehrlichman presented a new revenue-sharing package to the Cabinet in January 1971, Labor Secretary James Hodgson suggested that a manpower act be folded into a new version of the larger plan. The White House staff briefly resisted this but soon, instead, took over the details. By early February, Secretary Hodgson had been in touch with OMB head George Shultz, who assigned deputy director Dick Nathan to the issue. After a flurry of White House meetings, Nathan reported to Edwin Harper of the Domestic Council that "we agreed upon a procedure to get a specific proposal developed. . . . The Department will prepare this week a paper spelling out the various alternatives along with their recommendations for handling the difficult issues raised in Secretary Hodgson's memorandum to George Shultz. I will meet again with [Labor] early next week to identify those points which require a presidential decision."[57]

Labor's draft proved to be less than satisfactory, prompting a flurry of White House memos. On March 1, Ehrlichman wrote to Hodgson noting that he had reviewed with the president "the several policy issues which my staff and OMB have discussed with the Department on Manpower Special Revenue Sharing." In each instance, the president decided against Labor's position.[58] On March 24, Hodgson and two of his assistant secretaries met with their EOP counterparts, but got no satisfaction: "Ehrlichman, Shultz, and Nathan were all in there to go pure revenue sharing, and they prevailed." Of the $2 billion requested in the bill, only $300 million was to remain in Labor's control, with the rest going directly to the states.[59]

Centralized in the Executive Office of the President

President Harry Truman's budget message for fiscal year 1950, presented to Congress on January 10, 1949, contained a proposal to abolish the Department of Agriculture's Regional Agricultural Credit Corporation (RACC). This initiative came directly from the Bureau of the Budget, arising originally in a 1947 internal review of agricultural credit operations.

In December 1947, a Budget Bureau staff document drawing on the findings of the internal review noted that "the purpose of this memorandum is to present the reasons why the Regional Agricultural Credit Corporation of Washington, D.C., should be abolished and its functions transferred to the Secretary of Agriculture. The main reason is that the RACC has now substantially completed the program for which it was originally established." The BoB's position was transmitted to the Agriculture Department, and in late February 1948, Acting Secretary of Agriculture N. E. Dodd replied to budget director Webb on this issue and other related bureau recommendations. Agriculture disliked most of the BoB ideas, though Dodd admitted regarding the RACC that "we see no basic objection to this recommendation, although we are not convinced that any advantages would accrue from the proposed change." Despite — or perhaps because of — this faint praise, a reorganization plan was developed in BoB to phase out RACC. However, since "representatives of the Department . . . showed considerably more enthusiasm for its objectives than Undersecretary Dodd's letter originally indicated," by the end of March 1948 the bureau suggested that the department submit legislation that would effect the same reorganization. Budget then successfully pushed for its inclusion as a message within the president's fiscal 1950 budget.[60]

Centralized in the White House Office

Presidents made protracted efforts into the 1970s on behalf of home rule for the District of Columbia — whose government, as Lyndon Johnson complained, "had been operating in the same archaic way since

Reconstruction days," run by a board of appointed commissioners whose lawmaking was subject to presidential and congressional veto.[61] On February 2, 1965, Johnson proposed that Congress allow the District to elect its own mayor and city council.

In this he followed partly in the steps of the Kennedy administration, and indeed, had retained JFK staffer Charles Horsky in the White House as his Advisor for National Capitol Affairs. Horsky served as a one-man rallying point for District residents and conduit into the White House for D.C. government officials. In late 1964 he worked with the District's general counsel and general administration director to draft new home-rule legislation, with occasional technical help from the Budget Bureau and Justice Department. He also worked the political side of the fence, checking in regularly with prominent District residents and with citizen groups like the Washington Home Rule Committee. A wide array of questions had to be resolved: what residency requirement and voting age should be put in place for elections? Should there be a referendum within the District to accept the new form of government? How to transfer power to the new government, and which agencies should be abolished? How many councillors? District or at-large? Paid how much?[62]

On December 18, 1964, Horsky summarized the results of his labors in a memo to Johnson. By the end of January, the bill and its message were "finally and thoroughly cleared and . . . ready to go as soon as you approve this message."[63]

A Snapshot of Centralization: Comparative Statics

With these considerations in mind, what does the coding show?

There are any number of ways to break down the account of centralization provided thus far. Looking at the data as a whole, as in table 4.3, reveals that presidents have been quite flexible in their policy formulation strategies. We can estimate that about a quarter of program items have been produced by the departments, a quarter by each of the mixed strategies (totaling half of all items), and a quarter led by some part of the EOP. Still, while these results might imply that this variety of strategies has been used consistently over time, table 4.3 does not get at this question directly. After all, the decentralized items might come at the beginning of the time series, the centralized items at the end, and the mixed items in the middle.

Examining the mean level of centralization Congress by Congress, however, indicates that centralization does not trend upward over time (see figure 4.2). As might be expected, these data show a good deal of

TABLE 4.3
Policy Formulation Strategies, 1949–1996

	Level of Centralization	Weighted % of total	Frequency in sample (n = 366)
0	Decentralized	22.9	83 (22.7%)
1	Mixed (dept. led)	24.9	93 (25.4%)
2	Mixed (WH led)	28.0	104 (28.4%)
3	EOP	11.1	39 (10.7%)
4	WHO	13.2	47 (12.8%)

variation, but within a relatively narrow band and without any evident pattern. Table 4.4 puts the centralization figures in a more intuitive way, presenting the (weighted) mean level of centralization associated with each president. Again we see a fair amount of variation, in ways we might expect: Eisenhower is at the low end of the centralization spectrum, Nixon and Reagan (though also Ford) at the high end. Once more, though, there is no upward trend over time; the terminus nearly matches the origin.

Since the linear centralization hypothesis is tied to time and environment and explicitly not to presidents,[64] it is most useful to disaggregate

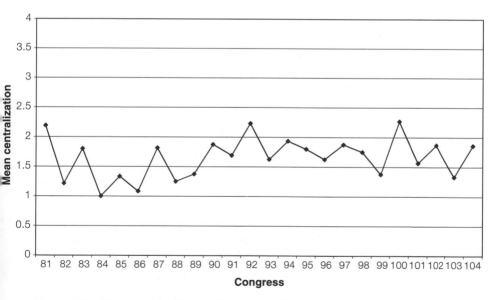

Figure 4.2 Mean Level of Centralization, by Congress

TABLE 4.4
Level of Centralization, by President, 1949–1996 (weighted means)

	Mean	S.E.
Truman (1949–1952)	1.60	.241
Eisenhower	1.36	.171
Kennedy	1.58	.240
Johnson	1.61	.215
Nixon	1.86	.212
Ford	1.85	.318
Carter	1.72	.239
Reagan	1.77	.169
Bush	1.69	.244
Clinton (1993–1996)	1.58	.238
Total ($n = 366$)	1.67	.072

the weighted data down into equal blocks not equivalent to actual administrations. Table 4.5 arranges the cross-tabulated data into eight six-year periods.[65] It shows that there are shifts across time, but not in the direction predicted by positing a relentless process of centralization. Instead, extra-departmental sources of presidential proposals have long been prominent; White House and EOP involvement is already quite pronounced in the earliest period. By the period ending in 1996, a rough equilibrium seems to have settled in, with the departments and the White House each preponderantly responsible for roughly half of the proposals.

Presented graphically this finding is even more striking. Graphed by six-year period, whether broken down by individual code (figure 4.3) or

TABLE 4.5
Source of Legislative Proposals, by Period (weighted)

Period	Decentralized	Dept.-led	EOP-led	Centralized
1949–1954	26.6%	19.9%	27.2%	26.3%
1955–1960	33.3	32.1	27.7	7.0
1961–1966	27.3	24.1	30.1	18.6
1967–1972	15.6	26.7	26.3	31.4
1973–1978	19.5	26.4	25.6	28.5
1979–1984	16.2	26.0	29.7	28.1
1985–1990	26.2	23.3	24.4	26.1
1991–1996	22.4	22.4	34.1	21.1

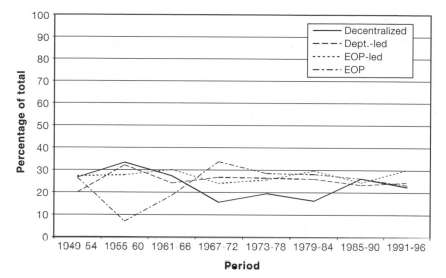

Figure 4.3 Processes of Program Formulation, 1949–1996

collapsed into simple "department-led" and "EOP-led" categories (figure 4.4),[66] the centralization "trend" most nearly resembles a flat line. The results bounce around somewhat—the level of centralization is, as the conventional wisdom might predict, much the lowest during the six-year period dominated by the (second) Eisenhower administration. But again no trend can be discerned. Eisenhower's lack of reliance on purely centralized strategies (coded 4), further, disguises the involvement of White House personnel in program formulation: figure 4.5 shows that "mixed" formulation strategies (coded 1 or 2) rose during that same six-year period. Figure 4.5 as a whole serves as an instructive indicator of the frequency of such mixed strategies in the president's program: they make up approximately half of all formulation strategies, not just overall, but in each time period. This point will be revisited later.

Overall, these comparative statics are inconsistent with the linear centralization hypothesis. Centralization has been utilized by presidents across the postwar era, and there is no sign that its use has greatly increased over time. The clear evidence, instead, is that presidents use a wide range of formulation strategies over time—a finding potentially encouraging for contingent centralization. But it doesn't get to the heart of the question, since the hypotheses of contingency require an explication of the conditions under which presidents make management decisions. That task comes next.

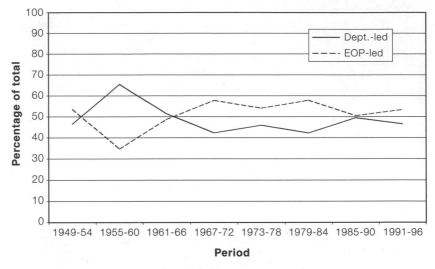

Figure 4.4   Department- and EOP-led Program Formulation

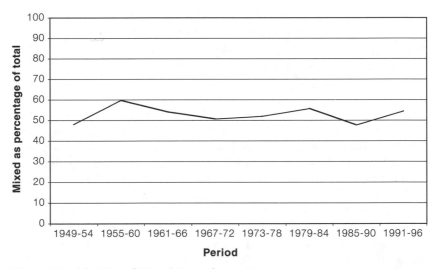

Figure 4.5   The Use of Mixed Formulation Strategies

Conclusion

Systematic analysis of the president's program is well overdue. In part this is because that program has long been like a bird in the upper reaches of a rain forest: known to exist, heard from, but rarely more than glimpsed.

This chapter meets the objections raised regarding the current state of the literature in Chapter Two by replacing anecdote with analysis: it provides a rationale for, and presents, a comprehensive new dataset covering nearly five full decades of presidential legislation. In the next three chapters, that data will be used to analyze presidential information needs and sequential bargaining strategies — first within the administration itself, and then with Congress.

CHAPTER FIVE

Putting Centralization
to the Test

THE theory of contingent centralization developed in Chapter Two predicts that presidents' strategies for utilizing centralized or decentralized staff organizations are centered on the informational transactions they conduct to formulate individual policy items. Chapter Three's qualitative review and Chapter Four's presentation of comparative quantitative data suggested that presidents do in fact cast a wide net in putting together legislative proposals, and that this has been true across the postwar era. That is, the answers to whether and when presidents centralize are "yes," and "not always . . . it depends."

The present chapter's goal is to elaborate systematically the factors on which the question of centralization depends. The first section will review and operationalize the hypotheses presented in Chapter Two. The second, and most extensive, presents the results of statistical analysis, using more than 350 observations of presidential legislative policy proposals from 1949 through 1996 to assess the relative strength of theories of linear and contingent centralization. The concluding section sums up the lessons of this exercise.

The questions in this chapter turn on a president's bargains with the executive branch. In some ways this is merely the first stage of a sequential bargaining process. Having worked to formulate an item for the presidential program, the president must then bargain with Congress to see that policy enacted. This implication of centralization—how the strategy matters for presidential relations with, and success in, Congress—is reserved for Chapters Six and Seven.[1]

CENTRAL HYPOTHESES

Contingent centralization hypothesizes, consistent with work in transaction cost economics, that presidents will seek the cheapest reliable information regarding policy formulation. As elaborated in Chapter Two, a number of observable implications follow from this tenet, indicating when it is managerially more cost effective to obtain centralized versus decentralized expertise on policy formulation. We should expect more centralization when:

- the program item deals with cross-cutting jurisdictions;
- the program item has reorganizational or personnel management implications;
- the proposal is produced quickly, in reaction to a crisis or a focusing event;
- the approach or issue is new to the president's program; or
- the president's centralized capacity for program development is enlarged by the need to produce a large overall program.

We would in turn expect to see less centralization when:

- the issue at hand is particularly complex or technical;
- the preferences of the bureau with substantive jurisdiction over the proposal in question are close to those of the president; or
- congressional preferences, likewise, are closer to those of the president.

The flip side of each hypothesis also obtains — for example, we would expect to see more centralization as presidential preferences diverge from Congress, and less for simpler proposals within one department's jurisdiction.

Each of these issues is addressed in turn below, along with the data used to test them in the quantitative analysis that follows. In each instance the reader is referred back to Chapter Two for more detailed discussion of the hypotheses outlined here.

Conditions Favoring Centralization

Some policy contexts make it relatively more expensive for presidents to obtain reliable information from the wider executive branch about the expected value of proposing a given program item to Congress. All else equal, this should lead to more centralization.

CROSS-CUTTING JURISDICTIONS

The narrow vantage of departments makes it difficult for them to give presidents useful advice on issues that cut across the purview of multiple departments. Centralized staff are better able to take a broad view. I measure this by calculating the number of departments or agencies with jurisdiction over the substance of a given program item. The more there are, the more centralized the formulation process is likely to be. This count is reconstructed from archival sources, especially Budget Bureau/Office of Management and Budget clearance records that track the departments given the opportunity to comment on the item before it is transmitted to Congress,[2] or from secondary sources where archival data were not available, taking into account all departments reported to be interested or which testified on the legislation at congressional committee hearings. In instances where a Cabinet or sub-Cabinet-level committee or task force was formed, the "cross-cutting" figure was determined by counting its members. Organizations in the Executive Office of the President were not included in this count.[3]

For example, in 1950 Harry Truman proposed the consolidation of education programs serving children living on federal property. Five agencies were involved: the Federal Security Agency, the General Services Administration, and the departments of Defense, Agriculture, and Interior.[4] In 1981 Ronald Reagan created a Technical Working Group to flesh out his "new federalism" proposals. Besides White House and OMB officials, the departments of Agriculture, Education, Health and Human Services, Housing and Urban Development, Labor, and Treasury were represented.[5] In the first case, the cross-cut variable would be coded 5; in the second, 6.[6]

PROGRAMMATIC CAPACITY

As hypothesized in Chapter Two, the repeated transaction of related bargains leads to something of an economy of scale, making the institutionalization of a more widely policy-proficient White House staff more efficient for the president. This makes any given item more likely be centralized: once a structure is in place to "make" legislative policy, the more likely it is to be used.

Two measures help to track this capacity. One is the size of the president's program: the total number of messages sent by the president to Congress in the year of the sampled message. The larger the overall legislative agenda, the more related tasks are repeated and the more overall coordination is required—thus the more likely that centralized staff resources will be institutionalized.

A more direct measure of capacity is the size of the president's centralized staff, defined here as the EOP as a whole.[7] In this case the staff is seen as the *result* of bargaining strategies and needs, turning around the usual direction of the causal arrow. This variable does not target program formulation quite so neatly, since a large number of staff is less important than their day-to-day function. However, it provides a useful proxy for the upper limit of presidential centralizing capacity.[8]

REORGANIZATIONAL AND MANAGERIAL IMPACT

Since departments are turf conscious, their input on issues of governmental management—proposals that affect their own structure or personnel—is unlikely to be seen by presidents as reliable. Therefore each sampled item was coded on a three-point scale (0, 1, 2) indicating its impact on departmental organization or personnel. A proposal entailing no reorganization is assigned a code of 0 (this accounts for about 70 percent of the sample). A proposal that reshapes an extant institution or creates a new organization to implement a task laid out elsewhere in the measure receives a 1; an example here is President George H. W. Bush's 1989 savings and loans rescue and restructuring package. Finally, reorganization plans, personnel pay or civil service restructuring proposals, or other items with reorganization as their main objective (for example, the 1953 statute creating the Department of Health, Education, and Welfare, or the 1971 bill proposing a new Federal Executive Service) are assigned a 2.[9]

TEMPORAL PRESSURES

Temporal pressures may help shape the formulation of a given legislative proposal. One obvious instance is when the request is in response to a happening external to the White House, a "crisis" or (in John Kingdon's terminology) a "focusing" event: an episode that focuses public (and thus political) attention on a given issue. In such cases the president and other elected officials are under pressure to "do something" about the problem at hand. If presidents see bureau operations as inherently dilatory, we might expect presidents to turn to in-house advice when time is short.

This measure is operationalized as a dichotomous variable, coding proposals created in specific response to external shocks as 1. Focusing events are usually natural disasters at home or triggering events abroad. In these data, examples include the 1957 launch of the Sputnik satellite, the massive 1976 oil spill off the New England coast, the 1983 Soviet destruction of a Korean Airlines passenger aircraft, and the 1992 hurricanes in Hawaii and Florida. Every solution needs a problem, of course; most proposals are designed in response to some societal condition. The state of the economy, for example, is the rationale for a variety of remedial legislation. The crisis category as conceived here, however, is limited to shorter-term focusing events.

ISSUE NOVELTY

How new is a proposal to the president's program? Chapter Two laid out presidential plaints surrounding the supposed inability of bureaus to develop fresh, innovative ideas, and hypothesized that presidents will pursue a more centralized formulation strategy for proposals that represent a new approach to policy problems.

Paul Light has categorized items on the presidential agenda as "old" and "new." Indeed, his recent work in this area emphasizes the "derivative presidency" — that is, the tendency of recent presidents to offer not bold, novel ideas, but refinements or adjustments in existing ones. The original Medicaid law is given as an example of a new program, an increase in the minimum wage as an old one.[10]

I build on this to create a dichotomous variable coded 1 for new policy items, 0 for old ones. A proposal is considered old if (a) the current president has offered it before,[11] or (b) the proposal is offered subject to a procedure laid down in current law without seeking to change the terms of that statute.

An example of category (a) would be Jimmy Carter's Hospital Cost Containment Act, offered in 1977 and 1979: the 1979 version would be considered "old." (Light also tracks repeated items; recall, though, from Chapter Four that for my purposes items repeated within the same Congress are counted only the first time.)

Category (b) includes simple extensions of current law (such as Bill Clinton's 1995 proposal to re-authorize for five years the Ryan White CARE Act regulating AIDS funding) and cases in which a simple change in benefit level is substituted within an existing statute. For example, as with Light, this would include increases in the minimum wage or in the number of weeks unemployment benefits are available — but not changes in the categories governing who is eligible. Another, less intuitive example, would be the addition of wilderness areas to the current national stocks, as George Bush proposed in 1992. (Had Bush instead suggested amending the law governing the eligibility of potential wilderness areas, it would count as "new.")

Kingdon has observed that the prophet's lament "nothing is new under the sun" is often an accurate description of the national policy agenda. One Carter administration official objected to the White House's complaint that HEW had "worked up the same old hash" in the health care area by observing "well, there isn't anything around *except* the same old hash."[12] To take just that one example, some variant of the issue of national health insurance reform appears in my sample not only in the Carter presidency but also under Truman, Nixon, Clinton, and the elder Bush. A definition that sees "new" items largely as items "new to the current president," as here, may therefore overestimate the number of such items.[13] At the same time, it more accurately reflects the decision-making process presidents face. Presidential backgrounds and interests vary widely; even existing law may be new to some. The very longevity on the national stage of topics such as health care bears witness to a complexity whose dimensions and ramifications presidents will want to master before associating themselves with a particular policy approach.

Conditions Favoring Decentralization

Less centralization is expected when the relative cost to the president of reliable information shifts in favor of the departments or other extra–White House sources, usually Congress.

As already noted, the size of the overall program seems likely to spur centralization as staff organizations and procedures are institutionalized to meet a recurring bargaining need. But as the complexity of any given measure increases, the more likely it is that departmental expertise will be required to craft legislative language matching presidential desires. A negative coefficient is therefore expected for this variable.

However, this prediction is not unalloyed. Given that programmatic devils lurk in the drafting details, even as presidents realize their need for substantive expertise they will seek assurances that bureau preferences are not replacing their own. I hypothesize a mixed process, with departmental and centralized resources combined in some manner.

The idea of complexity as conceived here is comparable to Light's other major policy dimension in *The President's Agenda*, one dividing agenda proposals along "large/small" lines.[14] In the analysis below, complexity was initially measured by including as a separate variable the number of individual proposals in the presidential message.[15] This indicator, however, was undercut by the form in which even complicated bills are frequently transmitted to Congress, in messages that read, more or less, "pass my proposed legislation." For example, Truman's 1950 "Point Four" message on foreign aid contains just two proposals. Gerald Ford's 1975 hugely complex Aviation Act deregulating the airlines contains just one. Overall, a simple count of the raw number of proposals may hide a multitude of sins.

I have therefore adopted instead Light's "large/small" dichotomy, expanding the scale from two increments to three to provide more variation within the data. Nontechnical messages, extensions of existing law, or dollar requests that do not change existing law receive a code of 1. An example here is Bill Clinton's 1995 request to create a commission on campaign finance, flowing from his famous New Hampshire handshake with House Speaker Newt Gingrich. Other legislative proposals require some specialized substantive knowledge to be conceived and drafted effectively. Those requiring this sort of technical expertise, but in a clearly delimited area, receive a code of 2. Examples include Eisenhower's 1960 proposal to adjust the interest rate ceiling on Treasury-issued bonds or Reagan's 1987 plan to phase out direct student loan programs. As messages grow larger in scope, bringing to bear expertise in a multitude of policy areas, the appropriate code is 3. The Point Four and airline deregulation examples would fall into this category. Note that this is not the same thing as the "cross-cutting" dimension, which takes into account the number of bureaus with an interest in a piece of legislation rather than the substantive challenges of formulating it.[16]

BUREAU PROXIMITY TO PRESIDENT

Presidential management problems with relation to the executive branch are exacerbated by the fact that bureaus have multiple principals to which they must respond — including accountability to their own statutory authority. Presidents have therefore tried to control executive branch personnel, seeding the bureaus with staff loyal to presidential desires. As a Clinton White House aide commented in 1993, "people make policy, and unless you look for the people who have policy visions that track with the President, you are not going to have policies emerging from the departments that track with the President."[17] This strategy is often associated in the literature with the Reagan and Nixon administrations, but it is hardly limited to them. Gabriel Hauge of the Eisenhower staff, for example, recounted to chief of staff Sherman Adams that "if we had men at the Under Secretary, Assistant Secretary and Special Assistant level in every Department and principal Executive Office Agency who burned with zeal for the President . . . I think it would make a real difference all through the Departments and in the record they make."[18]

As suggested in Chapter Two, presidents who succeed in finding such men and women of zeal might adjust for this by reducing centralization. After all, a department controlled by appointees fully committed to a president's interests could be more safely entrusted with program formulation. Richard Nathan, who worked for Richard Nixon, described enhanced control over appointments as part of a president's "administrative strategy." Terry Moe calls this overall strategy "politicization," and suggests that presidents search for "responsive competence" rather than for the public administrator's ideal of "neutral" competence.[19]

Is politicization sufficient to curb presidents' fears of intermarriage with "the natives"? Or, in an era of seemingly perpetual divided government, are the views and loyalties even of rabidly partisan appointees mitigated through the centrifugal forces of the executive agencies and their various constituents? The informational vantage suggests the former should hold true, or at least more true. If so, centralization should decline with the number of political appointees serving across the departments and agencies.

Over time, the Civil Service Commission and its successor agency, the Office of Personnel Management, have collected data on the proportion of executive branch civilian jobs covered by merit protections. This percentage can be used as a proxy for politicization of the executive branch over time.[20]

Other measures are also utilized. For example, departments headed by a secretary who is a longtime associate or former staffer of the president should be deemed more reliable. Thus a dichotomous variable distinguishes items associated with departments where such a secretary was in place. Thirty-five secretaries with close presidential ties were identified over the 1949–1996 period; they are listed in the Appendix.[21] However, as discussed in Chapter Two, careful choice of a secretary is presumably insufficient to enforce responsiveness throughout a large department. After all, more than 1.8 million people worked for the executive branch in 2000; just 536 of them were presidential appointees requiring Senate approval.[22]

Another cut might follow Chapter Two's suggestion that all departments are not created equal. Some are better situated to give presidents useful counsel: recall Cronin's notion, later refined by Cohen, of inner and outer Cabinet departments. The inner departments — State, Defense, Justice, and Treasury — have broad mandates and the ability to stress advice over advocacy. Other departments, created to satisfy the desires of a given constituency (such as farmers or teachers) for organizational representation in government have a narrower focus and, from the president's perspective, more incentive to provide biased information.[23] A separate variable was therefore included to test whether the inner Cabinet departments are indeed given more responsibility for policy formulation. This variable is coded as an outer/inner Cabinet dummy (inner = 1), which is predicted to have a negative coefficient: inner Cabinet positions should be associated with less centralization.

If, as predicted here, the result of politicization is decentralization, it implies that administrative strategies are not a complement to but a substitute for centralization. Given that both have costs, presidents might choose to pursue one but rarely both at once. Nixon's administrative strategy, as described by Nathan, came in sequence *after* the effort to create a White House "counterbureaucracy" had proved ineffective. Likewise, Weko reports that the incoming Clinton administration took from the Carter administration a desire to decentralize, but cites an aide who claimed that a small White House (itself, of course, not achieved) would be made possible by careful control over appointments. "Carter's [decentralization] is totally different," he said, "from the way we wanted to do it. We wanted this president to have the benefit of having *his* people in place to push *his* program and *his* plans."[24]

CONGRESSIONAL PROXIMITY TO THE PRESIDENT

The multiple principals problem noted above implies that presidents should be more trusting of bureaus' advice when the preferences of those principals align. Politicizing tries to shift bureaus' own preferences; but congressional ties to the president are also crucial. Not only can presidents obtain information from legislative sources more easily when legislators share presidential preferences, but bureaus' links to Congress should trouble the president less as legislative and executive desires converge.

One proxy for preference is, of course, political party. The majority status of the president's party in each chamber therefore matters. Even a one-vote majority gives a party power to organize the chamber, control the flow of bills to the floor, and appoint a disproportionate number of committee staff versed in the pursuit of party goals. Centralization seems more likely when divided government holds sway, and less likely under conditions of unified government.

A variety of divided government measures were constructed, including a simple dichotomous variable (with a code of one indicating one or more chambers under the control of the opposition party), and a measure averaging the number of presidential co-partisans in House and Senate. While a majority of one is the first hurdle, the more members sharing presidential preferences the more resources should be available, and the more likely consistent signals will be sent to the bureaus.[25] In practice problems of multicollinearity prevent using measures for House and Senate separately (the size of the presidential cohort in the two chambers correlate at $r = .89$). The mean of the two, though, correlates with each chamber's measure at $r > .97$, and was therefore used.

Party and preference cannot be assumed to be equivalent. Keith Krehbiel, in fact, has argued that "preferenceship" is analytically prior to partisanship, at least in recent Congresses.[26] A good deal of effort in the congressional studies literature has therefore gone into estimating directly the ideology of legislators. Here I will utilize the " 'real' ADA scores" developed by Tim Groseclose, Steven Levitt, and James Snyder.[27] This measure takes the vote-based scores issued annually by the interest group Americans for Democratic Action (ADA), long utilized as a means of placing legislators on a liberal-conservative axis, and scales them to allow for comparability across chambers and year — thus transforming "nominal" to "real" values in the way that those studying fiscal time-series data must.[28] This conversion provides a way to track the ideology of the median and mean voters in House and Senate over time, and a parallel ideological score for individual presidents. The mean and median scores for each chamber of each Congress were then subtracted from the president's score, with the absolute value of that difference serving as a measure of the president's ideological distance from Congress. Congressional and presidential scores on this measure are provided in the Appendix, table A.5.

Different specifications were tested, but I will generally report the results of the Senate median score (that is, the distance between the president and the median senator). Because means may remain relatively constant even as polarization between the legislative parties increases — and because the median voter is a staple of decision analysis — using the median score makes more theoretic sense. Using the Senate rather than the House makes little difference (the two correlate at $r = .89$). Another measure tested uses the median of the House Rules Committee as the point of comparison with the president, because of its direct relevance to legislative agenda setting and its usual congruence with floor and majority party preferences. Thus common space coordinates were applied to committee members in combination with the comprehensive listing of House and Senate committee assignments compiled by Garrison Nelson and updated past 1992 by Charles Stewart and Jonathan Woon. Again, the absolute value of the difference between the presidential score and the committee median was calculated: the larger the ideological distance, the more centralized a process is hypothesized.[29]

An interesting extension of this ideological test would disaggregate legislative ideology to the level of the individual subject-matter committee level. As discussed later, congressional committees are assembled in large part to reflect the larger organization of the executive branch, and are linked closely to the agencies over whose substance they have jurisdiction. Presidents might fine-tune their centralizing strategies to reflect their ideological congruence not just with the Congress as a whole but with the committee most closely tied to the legislation in question. A number of problems must be worked out, though, for this to be an accurate measure.[30] At the moment, theory outstrips data; this is a lack that future research would do well to remedy.

Linear Centralization

To test the thesis of linear centralization, a simple variable representing the year is included in the analysis. If the cause of centralization is tied to trends in the macro-environment over time, the year variable should be strongly positive. Chapter Four, of course, suggested it will not prove so.

Although time is used to represent the linear process of centralization, keep in mind that it is more properly considered as a proxy for the overall workload on the president required by the size of government and its responsibilities (recall figure 3.1). Indeed, the simple "year" variable utilized here correlates at $r = .99$ with the size of the governmental outlay budget, in real dollars, and at $r = .89$ with the number of pages in the *Federal Register*, making the inclusion of these commonly used variables superfluous.

Additional Hypotheses and Controls

Presidency scholarship suggests several additional hypotheses that are not firmly associated with either contingent or linear centralization but that might provide their own explanation for centralization. These should be included in any model, since their omission might lead to bias.

First, *policy type* should be examined. Policy is usually divided into at least three arenas: domestic, foreign, and economic. It is not clear what impact on centralization the first two classifications should have. Although some presidents have sought explicitly to be their own secretary of state, much of the activity associated with the National Security Council staff who serve as the focus of "foreign policy in the White House" accounts is nonlegislative.[31] And as noted in Chapter Three, Congress has vested legislative responsibility for some policy items (for example, fishery agreements) directly in the departments. This suggests that foreign policy items with a legislative component might actually be less centralized than their domestic counterparts. But this may not be true over time. Presidents early in the cold war waged great battles over mutual security programs, for example, which were often developed within the EOP-based Mutual Security Administration. So no prediction is made as to the direction of the foreign/domestic divide's impact on centralizing strategy overall.

The salience of intermestic policy in the last half of the twentieth century cautions against the use of a simple dummy variable. Thus whether a policy is foreign or domestic was coded on a five-point scale, from -2 (indicating a policy proposal that is entirely domestic) to 2 (entirely foreign). An example of the former is the 1989 amendments to the Head Start education program; the latter includes a 1955 funding request for highway construction through Central and South America. In between are issues like immigration, tariffs, and military spending.[32]

Since both foreign and domestic policy items can have budgetary and economic ramifications, a proposal's budgetary impact is coded separately. Estimating exact spending is a thankless task: exact amounts are rarely set forth in presidential messages. Further, should one account for short-term costs or long? Should one record actual or projected, nominal or real, spending? Following Light, I divide items simply into "nonspending" and "spending" categories.[33] A code of 0 indicates trivial budgetary effects, while an item receives a code of 1 if the policy has direct effects on spending or revenue. If OMB exerts control over the process, we should expect a positive coefficient.

The general salience of fiscal affairs is another important control. As discussed in Chapter Three, when budgetary constraints are high—

when deficits are larger—we should expect presidents to bring policy formulation under closer control. To measure the nation's financial health, I use a "budget situation" measure developed by David Mayhew, which divides the federal budget deficit or surplus for a given fiscal year by the total federal outlays for that year.[34]

An additional policy context potentially encouraging centralization is the *priority or salience of an item within the program*. Shouldn't presidents want to bring their cherished, controversial items "in house," under close guard? The Clintons' 1993 health care proposal leaps to mind as a confirming example.

It is not self-evident that presidential interest predetermines the placement of policy formulation. Other, equally high-priority items have been centered in the departments (for example, voting rights in 1965 or tax reform in 1986). Nor does surveillance equate to involvement: a watchful eye doesn't always come attached to a red pen. As Clinton's first labor secretary, Robert Reich, points out, "even policies in which the President and White House staff are particularly interested often originate in a department with particular expertise or incentive to move the ball."[35]

Further, keep in mind that all of the items in these data are already part of the president's program, which as defined here means they already breach a crucial threshold of consequence. That is, each is a "priority" to the extent it has ascended into the rarified air of personal presidential attention and written commitment. I have argued that the central issue governing presidential management choices in this area is the cost of reliable information. If so, priority issues may inspire more monitoring, but there is no a priori reason to suppose that (controlling for complexity and so on) the White House will be the source of, as well as the sight-line to, the policy.

Still, this is an important control, and two measures seem plausible. One is a dichotomous variable marking items included in presidents' State of the Union addresses; as I argued in Chapter Four, this speech provides a better list of presidential priorities than it does a comprehensive accounting of the program as a whole. It is clearly the case that presidents do rank items within their program, though this has received sparse empirical analysis.[36]

A second measure gets at a close variant of this question. That is, have more salient or contentious issues moved into the White House over time? Even if the balance within the entire program remains fairly constant, it could be that "hard cases" are centralized. Again, this is addressed partially by the objections above and partially by controlling for the proposal's size and complexity. Consistent measures of ex ante policy controversy (that is, before it is formulated and presented to

Congress) do not exist. However, an additional dichotomous control variable representing items highly salient to the national policy debate, as measured by inclusion ten or more times in unsigned *New York Times* editorials during a given Congress, was included in the analysis below.[37] Items on this list are highly visible and, often, highly controversial: which causes which is arguable, but salient items usually become important to the president even if they didn't start out that way.

Finally, a counter (from 1 up to a potential maximum of 96) controls for the month of the presidency in which the request was presented. Presidents have often been urged to "move it or lose it,"[38] and the White House staff—or task force reports put together by centralized staff during the transition—are closest at hand for this purpose. We might therefore expect a negative coefficient for this variable. That is, as the term progresses, presidents' knowledge of (and trust in) the wider executive branch increases, and they have more time to wait for departmental production. If presidents come into office promising Cabinet governance, however, one might expect the opposite to hold true—early attempts to allow departmental autonomy, followed by a centralized crackdown, à la Nixon and Carter.

A word should be added about the potential impact of individual presidents on the process. Few would deny the relevance of a president's personal skills and inclinations to the conduct of his administration; Erwin Hargrove, among others, has strongly argued that scholars must seek to understand the "relation of [personal] style to policy making."[39] Clearly presidents enter office with varying talents for, and proclivities toward, management. The conventional wisdom, for example, draws strong contrasts between the hands-off Reagan and the detail-driven Carter, the collegial Kennedy and the reclusive Nixon.

But scholars have found this an elusive concept in which to ground research drawing general conclusions about multiple presidents. I do not claim that all behavior is institutionally driven. But I do claim that presidents with widely diverging personal traits will react to similar management situations in similar ways. This emphasis on what Hugh Heclo calls the "deep structure" of the presidency, as already discussed, has driven an important part of the field's research agenda in recent years.[40]

As a statistical control on differences across administrations, I ran the models below including dummy variables for each individual president. Controlling for the other aspects of the management environment, I did not expect them to be significant in themselves: they were not. Each coefficient for the presidency dummy control variables proved to be both individually and jointly insignificant. This suggests that—again, when controlling for the management contexts elaborated here—presidential style is not an important predictor of presidential choice with regard to the formulation of legislative proposals. Rather, institutional variables account for much of the variation often attributed to individual presidents.

Because the contingent centralization model does not make theoretical claims about presidential style (except, indeed, to deny its empirical power when controlling for the management environment), the analysis below does not include them. This proves to make little difference in the substantive findings, with one exception. (For details, see the Appendix, table A.6.) Without the administration dummies, the variable measuring the ideological distance between the president and the Senate floor median becomes a much stronger predictor of centralization. This makes sense, given that ideology is a personal attribute—removing nine dummy variables, each of which is effectively controlling for ideology, serves to free up the latter measure.

Summary

The variables discussed above and the predicted direction of their coefficients are summed up in table 5.1. The dependent variable, again, is an index of centralization. Centralization was measured in four categories from 0 to 3. Zero represents a decentralized process and three a completely centralized one, with mixed processes in between. This combines the two most centralized categories discussed in Chapter Four, the wider EOP and the White House staff proper, since they do not prove to be analytically (or statistically) distinct.[41]

STATISTICS AND SUBSTANCE

The analysis below is conducted using ordered probit estimation.[42] Ordered probit models are designed to analyze situations in which the main variable of interest has discrete outcomes that can be ranked ordinally. Their use is appropriate here because the dependent variable—the ordinal account of a given request's level of centralization—is categorical, but not necessarily evenly spaced. That is, a level of centralization coded 0 might not always be the same distance from a level coded 1 as a 2 is from a 3. Ordinary least-squares (OLS) regression is not appropriate for categorical variables unless the "spacing of the outcome choices can be assumed to be uniform,"[43] and in these data this assumption is not extended. However, it should be noted that running the same specifications in an OLS model gives similar results.[44]

Unlike their linear counterparts, the coefficients estimated by maximum likelihood models such as probit are difficult to interpret at a

TABLE 5.1
Summary of Independent Variables: Centralization

Variable	Measured as	Predicted Impact on Centralization
Contingent Centralization		
Cross-cutting jurisdictions	Number of agencies	Positive
Programmatic capacity		
Program size	Annual number of messages	Positive
Staff size	EOP staff size	Positive
Reorganization impact	Index (0–2)	Positive
Crisis/focusing event	Dichotomous (crisis = 1)	Positive
Issue novelty	Dichotomous (new = 1)	Positive
Politicization	% of civilian executive branch employees under merit/civil service protection	Positive (more merit employees → more centralization)
Politicization	Dichotomous ("trusted secretary" = 1)	Negative
Politicization	Dichotomous (inner Cabinet = 1)	Negative
Congressional proximity (party)	Average % of House and Senate members of the president's party	Negative (more co-partisans → less centralization)
Congressional proximity (ideology)	Ideological distance between president and floor median ("real ADA" scores)	Positive (larger distance → more centralization)
Congressional proximity (ideology)	Ideological distance between president and House Rules Committee (Poole-Rosenthal common space coordinates)	Positive (larger distance → more centralization)
Complexity	Index (1–3)	Negative (mixed strategy expected)
Linear Centralization		
Time	Year	Positive
Other		
Presidential priority	Dichotomous (included in State of the Union = 1)	Positive

TABLE 5.1 (*cont.*)

Variable	Measured as	Predicted Impact on Centralization
Salient/controversial issue	Dichotomous (salient = 1)	Positive
Policy type (dom./for.)	Index (domestic = −2, to foreign = 2)	Negative?
Policy type (budget implications)	Dichotomous (spending impact = 1)	Positive
Fiscal climate	Ratio of deficit or surplus to total outlays	Negative? (surplus → less centralization)
Month of administration	Measured from start of presidency	Negative?
Individual president	Dichotomous variables representing each president	Control (see pp. 98–99)

glance. Although coefficients' direction and statistical significance can quickly be determined, the substantive impact on the dependent variable they impute to each explanatory variable can only be interpreted jointly, transformed into probabilities. (That is, a unit change in x does not lead to a unit change in y, all else equal; rather, a change in x results in a shift, with probability z, in y's placement among the four categories, holding other independent variables constant.) The tables of coefficients will therefore be followed by more intuitive presentations of variables' substantive significance.

The question of weighting discussed in Chapter Four should be briefly revisited. Recall that the data here represent a random sample of presidential program items, stratified by Congress so that less programmatically active presidents are not undercounted in the analysis. The result is that different items in the population have different probabilities of selection for the sample. Thus earlier descriptions of the sample (that is, its summary statistics) needed to be weighted so that they accurately described the population of program items as a whole.

In using the sample in the predictive models that follow, correction for stratification itself is still appropriate. But corrective reweighting is less necessary when using the sample in predictive models, because the model design makes the implicit claim that the parameters of its explanatory variables are constant across groups. That is, if the weighted model varies much from the unweighted, it implies that the model itself is wrong. In fact there is little discrepancy and so the unweighted results are presented below.[45]

The Causes of Centralization

Tables 5.2 and 5.3 present the results of the main tests of centralization. Table 5.2 presents the broad model of contingent centralization described above. Two models are presented; as indicated, a variety of alternate specifications were also tested, and where these produced intriguing results they are described in the discussion that follows.

Again, probit coefficients make little intuitive sense in isolation. Thus a more substantive understanding of the impact of each variable may be obtained by transforming the coefficients into probabilities. This transformation indicates the percentage point change in the probability of obtaining a result in one of the categories of centralization, given a specified shift in one independent variable and holding all other independent variables at their means. These impact figures, which give intriguing nuance to the raw coefficients, are presented in table 5.3.[46] In some cases a shift in range is most intuitive, in others a smaller change more common. However, to make comparisons more meaningful across variables, table 5.3 standardizes the shift by presenting the impact of a change in an independent variable from its 10th to 90th percentile value.[47] (The exception is for dummy variables, whose impact is measured as a shift from 0 to 1.) This helps exclude influential outliers at either end of the centralization spectrum, while giving a realistic sense of the potential impact of each variable.

Selected results from Table 5.3 are presented in Figures 5.1 and 5.2.[48] These represent the impact of the same 10th to 90th percentile shift in each independent variable (again, holding the other variables constant at their means) on the probability of a program item's falling into the bookend categories of centralization: that is, of being wholly centralized or decentralized.

Note that the quantitative tables present an array of information about each independent variable, including its coefficient, the standard error of that coefficient, the associated t-statistic obtained from dividing the first by the second, and the probability that the coefficient in question was obtained by chance even though the true coefficient equals 0, using a two-tailed test. Most quantitative analysis considers a coefficient significant if this probability is less than 5 percent (that is, $p < .05$), and I will generally use this standard. It is worth noting, though, that there is no magic associated with this number — "surely God loves .06 nearly as much as .05" — or indeed in the process of null hypothesis testing generally.[49] The key is knowing how uncertain we are

TABLE 5.2
The Context of Centralization (ordered probit)

	Coeff. (S.E.)	t-stat. (Prob.)	Coeff. (S.E.)	t-stat. (Prob.)
Cross-cutting jurisdiction	.161	5.98	.161	5.70
	(.027)	(.000)	(.028)	(.000)
Program size	.005	1.20	.007	1.91
	(.004)	(.233)	(.004)	(.057)
Staff size	.0004	2.83	.0004	2.62
	(.0002)	(.005)	(.0002)	(.009)
Reorg. impact	.357	3.68	.373	3.87
	(.097)	(.000)	(.096)	(.000)
Crisis	−.100	−0.58	−.073	−0.41
	(.171)	(.560)	(.178)	(.681)
New item	.845	6.10	.838	6.08
	(.138)	(.000)	(.138)	(.000)
Complexity	−.349	−3.94	−.345	−3.92
	(.089)	(.000)	(.088)	(.000)
Politicization				
Merit %	−.044	−1.18		
	(.037)	(.240)		
Inner Cabinet	−.221	−1.76		
	(.126)	(.080)		
"Trusted secretary"			−.215	−1.23
			(.175)	(.221)
Congressional proximity				
Divided gov't	.074	0.51		
	(.145)	(.610)		
Avg. % Cong. seats			−.004	−0.51
			(.008)	(.610)
Senate median	.010	2.15	.009	1.98
	(.005)	(.032)	(.005)	(.049)
Year	−.012	−1.15	−.002	−0.33
	(.010)	(.251)	(.006)	(.742)
Priority item (State of Union)	.259	1.78	.233	1.58
	(.146)	(.077)	(.148)	(.115)
Policy salience	.094	0.50	.077	0.41
	(.191)	(.621)	(.189)	(.683)
Policy type (dom./for.)			−.092	−2.24
			(.041)	(.026)
Policy type (budget impact)	.181	1.32	.169	1.23
	(.137)	(.188)	(.137)	(.219)
Budget situation (deficit as % of outlays)	−2.203	−2.56	−2.294	−2.64
	(.860)	(.011)	(.870)	(.009)

TABLE 5.2 (*cont.*)

	Coeff. (S.E.)	t-stat. (Prob.)	Coeff. (S.E.)	t-stat. (Prob.)
Month of term	−.003	−0.83	−.003	−0.79
	(.003)	(.406)	(.003)	(.431)
N	366		366	
LL	−440.0		−438.7	
Prob. > χ²	.000		.000	
% correctly predicted	42.4		41.5	
PRE	19.5		18.3	

Note: The dependent variable here is an ordinal index of centralization (0–3). Coefficients are calculated using ordered probit analysis, correcting for the stratified nature of the sample; *t*-statistics are presented for each coefficient; and the probability of having obtained a given coefficient purely by chance is presented in parentheses below each *t*-statistic, using a two-tailed test. Cut point coefficients are not reported. LL stands for the "log likelihood" value of the equation, which indicates through a chi-squared test whether the model leads to a significant improvement in explaining the variance of the dependent variable compared with simply tracking the overall distribution. PRE stands for the proportionate reduction in error in predicting specific categorical outcomes compared with the overall distribution.

about a particular finding; a figure of .10 or more might plausibly be considered significant. Since any measure of uncertainty is potentially useful to the reader, I have included the $p < \alpha$ figure for each variable in each model.

Discussion

Overall, the model fits the data quite well. Despite the wide array of specifications tested, the results of the probit analysis consistently indicate strong support for contingent centralization, and almost none for linear centralization.

LINEAR CENTRALIZATION

Although the coefficient for the "year" variable tracking centralization as a function of time is positive in at least some specifications, it is consistently tiny and statistically insignificant. Controlling for the contexts of the management environment, time is not an important predictor of centralizing strategies. This is true when variables that trend somewhat over the time period being studied — such as the budget situation variable and overall politicization — are removed from the model. It

TABLE 5.3
Impact of Independent Variables on the Likelihood of Centralization

	Level of Centralization			
Variable	0 Department	1 Mixed (Dept.)	2 Mixed (EOP)	3 (WHO/EOP)
Cross-cut	**−19.8**	**−11.0**	**8.8**	**22.0**
Program size	*−5.5*	*−3.0*	*2.7*	*5.8*
Staff size	**−13.1**	**−8.4**	**5.4**	**16.0**
Reorg. impact	**−14.9**	**−11.8**	**4.5**	**22.3**
Crisis	3.2	1.1	−1.8	−2.5
New item	**−25.3**	**−7.0**	**13.7**	**18.6**
Complexity	**17.2**	**9.9**	**−7.6**	**−19.5**
Proximity to bureau				
Merit %	7.7	4.0	−3.8	−8.0
Inner Cabinet	*4.9*	*2.3*	*−2.4*	*−2.0*
"Trusted secretary"	4.6	1.7	−2.5	−1.7
Proximity to Congress				
Divided gov't	−1.9	−0.9	0.9	1.9
% Cong. seats	2.1	1.1	−1.1	−2.1
Distance from Senate	**−10.9**	**−5.9**	**5.2**	**11.6**
Distance from Rules	*−9.4*	*−5.3*	*4.4*	*10.4*
Year	**12.2**	**6.2**	**−5.7**	**−12.7**
Priority item	*−6.5*	*−4.0*	*3.0*	*7.5*
Policy salience	−1.8	−1.6	0.6	2.8
Policy (dom./for.)	*10.1*	*4.4*	*−5.4*	*−9.1*
Budget impact	*−5.1*	*−2.4*	*−2.6*	*4.8*
Budget situation	**14.3**	**7.9**	**−6.6**	**−15.5**
Month of term	*4.2*	*2.1*	*−2.1*	*−4.2*

Note: Figures indicate the percentage change in the probability of obtaining a result in one of the categories of centralization, from least to most centralized, given a shift in the independent variable from its 10th percentile value to its 90th percentile value, holding all other variables at their mean. (The shift for dummy variables is from 0 to 1.) For example, a figure of 8.8 in the fourth column would indicate that such a shift in the relevant independent variable resulted in a 8.8 percentage point increase in the likelihood of seeing the president follow an EOP-led mixed strategy. Rows are set boldface if original coefficient statistically significant at $p < .05$ level; italic if $p < .10$ (two-tailed tests). The standard errors underlying the coefficient will determine the width of the confidence intervals associated with each.

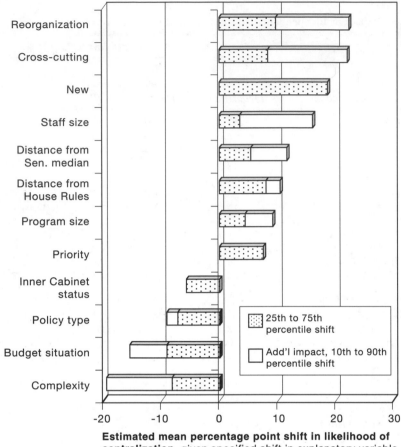

Figure 5.1   Determinants of Centralization

is true when the equation controls for individual presidents (who, of course, provide their own sequence in time), and when it does not.

As noted in Chapter Three, scholars have suggested that the institutionalization of the presidency has gone through a sequence of phases, reaching a stable plateau in the mid-1970s. Ragsdale and Theis, for example, argue that institutional space is more or less filled; as a result, we are now in a period in which "the institution makes presidents as much if not more than presidents make the institution."[50] The data here provide an additional opportunity to test this theory, by dividing them into "pre-institutionalized" and "institutionalized" periods (1949–1974

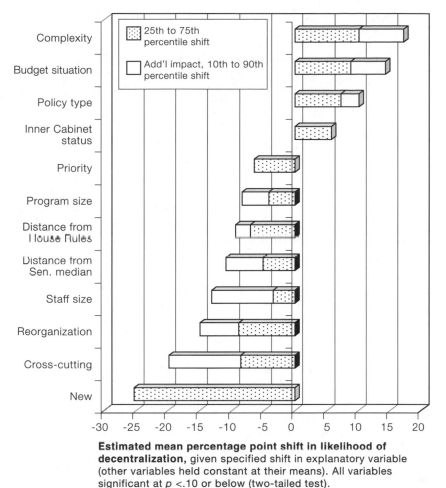

Estimated mean percentage point shift in likelihood of
decentralization, given specified shift in explanatory variable
(other variables held constant at their means). All variables
significant at *p* <.10 or below (two-tailed test).

Figure 5.2 Determinants of Decentralization

and 1975–1996, respectively).[51] If the eras are separable on the dimension of the president's program, we might expect to see linear centralization in the earlier period but not the later.

In fact we see it in neither (results not presented here). While the indicators of contingent centralization remain the best predictors of presidential behavior in this area, tracking by time does not prove positive and significant even in the earlier era. This makes sense, according to the "phase shift" hypothesized in Chapter Two: centralization, in that view, becomes a viable strategy for presidents with the institutionalization of the legislative program in the late 1940s. Since then, the managerial incentives imposed upon presidents in this area seem to have been relatively stable.

The coefficients with the strongest explanatory power are those associated with variables linked to contingent centralization. They are largely in the predicted direction and meet a high level of statistical significance. This is particularly striking in the areas where centralization increases because of the added efficiencies in "making" rather than "buying" policy formulation expertise. Policies that cut across numerous agency jurisdictions, those with a strong impact on bureau organization or personnel, and those that are new to the president are all dramatically more likely to be centralized than those lower on these measures (all at $p \leq .001$, two-tailed test, across all models). They remain robust regardless of the specification tested.

Transforming the coefficients to obtain their simulated impact on the centralization decision gives a sense of their substantive import. For example, ceteris paribus, a proposal cutting across six departments (the variable's 90th percentile) has a 22 percentage point higher probability of being centralized, and a 20 percentage point lower probability of being decentralized, than does a proposal within a single department. A "new" item has a 19 percentage point higher probability of being highly centralized—and a 25 percentage point lower probability of being decentralized—than an "old" one. Moving from the 10th to the 90th percentile in terms of an item's reorganizational impact, all else equal, results in a 22 percentage point increase in the likelihood of centralization. A one-category shift—from an item with no reorganizational impact to one with limited impact (that is, from the 25th to the 75th percentile), makes centralization about 10 percentage points more likely. Each of these estimated impacts should be read with their underlying standard error kept in mind: the breadth of a 95% confidence interval for a cross-cutting item is much narrower than for, say, the year variable, because we can be more certain that the coefficient of the former is closer to its "true" value. For example, in ninety-five out of one hundred trials, the impact of the shift in cross-cutting jurisdictions on the likelihood of a wholly centralized formulation process should be no less than 14 percentage points and no more than 30 points (as above, the mean value is 22 points). Compare this with the year variable. Its impact, as noted in table 5.3, seems impressive (if wrongly signed for linear centralization), suggesting a shift of about 12 percentage points toward the likelihood of decentralization. But this masks a huge standard deviation: our multiple trials this time would yield values ranging from positive 8 points to more than negative 33. Thus not only the impact but the direction of that impact is up in the air. By contrast, the low standard errors of the main variables of interest on this dimension indicate that we can be fairly confident of their effect.

The capacity variables also have some impact. Items sent as part of larger agendas seem somewhat more likely to be centralized, though this depends on the combination of variables modeled: it is much stronger in the absence of the measure of merit percentage, although the two do not correlate highly. (Since merit percentage itself, as noted below, is not a strong measure, some confidence in the program size variable seems warranted.) Staff size proves a stronger indicator. As the size of the centralized executive office staff moves from its 10th to its 90th percentile, the likelihood of a fully decentralized strategy drops by more than a dozen percentage points, all else equal, while that of a fully centralized strategy rises more than 15. Note, though, that this percentile shift represents a doubling of staff size, from 1,200 to 2,400 or so people. A shift from the 25th to the 75th percentile (an increase of 300 staffers) reveals a rise in the likelihood of a centralized strategy rising by just 3 percentage points.

Only the crisis variable completely fails to predict centralization, despite the original expectation. In fact, crises seem to lead, if anywhere, to decentralization. It is hard to be confident about this result; still, it is possible that items pushed to prominence by external shocks might prod presidents to expand their range of consultation, rather than contract it.

CONTINGENT CENTRALIZATION: DECENTRALIZING STRATEGIES

The findings support three of the hypotheses predicting decentralization. As expected, complexity strongly moves the formulation process toward decentralization ($p < .001$). As proposals cross the range of technical complexity, all else equal a decentralized strategy's likelihood is increased 17 percentage points, and that of a wholly centralized formulation decreased nearly 20 percentage points. The additional hypothesis that mixed strategies are prompted by complex proposals is also supported: this is explored at the end of the discussion.

Although the coefficients of their relevant variables are signed as predicted, neither the fact nor the size of a congressional majority of the president's party seems to matter much to presidential strategy.[52] Nor, in fact, does centralization overall appear to be strongly linked to divided or unified government: while centralization does decrease under unified government, the difference of means is not statistically significant.[53] Interestingly, an additional variable controlling for the party of the president also proved to be insignificant, controlling for the broad managerial context.[54]

However, the coefficient representing the ideological distance between the president and the Senate median voter is positive and significant. This shows strong support for the notion that the cost of expertise outside of the White House — as available both from Congress directly and through departments receiving consistent signals from their executive and legislative principals — increases as the president's preferences diverge from those of Congress. The result is increased centralization: indeed, ceteris paribus, moving from the 10th to the 90th percentile estimates of that divergence implies an 11 percentage point decrease in the chances of following a decentralized strategy, and a 12 percentage point increase in the likelihood of a fully centralized process. Parallel results are obtained when using the president's distance from the House Rules Committee, though the distance from the floor median is a more robust measure. Again, examination of presidential congruence with individual subject-matter committees would be an interesting extension of this finding.

Variables associated with politicization and bureau proximity yield mixed results. The strongest finding is that items falling under the jurisdiction of inner Cabinet departments are less likely to be centralized ($p < .08$, though this is a two-tailed test). We cannot be quite as confident in this finding as others, since it falls away when the equation also contains the measure of the proposal's placement on the foreign/domestic policy axis variable (hence, the two are presented in separate models in table 5.2). The reason, as the policy variable's own negative coefficient indicates, is that foreign policy items are linked to decentralization. Because the entire roster of the inner Cabinet — State, Defense, Treasury, and Justice — deals with issues that have foreign policy ramifications, the distinct impact of the policy and inner Cabinet measures is hard to disentangle, especially given the bluntness of the Cabinet measure.[55]

The coefficient of the variable denoting "trusted secretaries," those who were former EOP staffers or longtime associates of the president, is also negative, as predicted, but not close to statistically significant. Nor is the coefficient of the merit percentage variable.[56]

ALTERNATE HYPOTHESES/CONTROLS

Alternate hypotheses drawn from the literature on the institutional presidency had mixed utility in predicting centralization. The strongest finding here is that the fiscal context does affect policy formulation. As the deficit grows as a proportion of federal outlays, centralization increases; or, conversely, as the budget situation "improves," moving toward balance or surplus, decentralization becomes more likely. When moving from the 10th to the 90th percentage values (from, approximately, the budget situation in the early to mid-1980s to that in the early 1960s), the likelihood of centralization declines by about 14 percentage points.

Examining the different aspects of policy type suggests that as items move from the domestic to foreign policy side of the index, presidents decentralize their formulation ($p < .05$). This suggests that, at least as far as legislation is concerned — an important caveat — the influence of White House–based foreign policy staffs may be more limited than sometimes presumed. Spending items were more likely to be centralized, but not significantly so. Likewise, an item's salience had little impact on a program item's formulation. Top presidential priorities included in the State of the Union address, marking presidential items of top priority, are about 7 percentage points more likely to be centralized, all else equal ($p < .08$). As suggested, this effect is likely moderated by the elite status all items included in the president's program share. Still, this finding suggests that tracking the enhanced gradations of presidential attention within the program — defining the president's "must list" consistently over time — would help delineate how that attention interacts with a president's search for information, expanding the explanatory leverage of contingent centralization.

MIXED STRATEGIES

We should keep in mind an important fact: the president's range of choices goes beyond a mere dichotomy between centralization and decentralization. As we saw in Chapter Four, only about a quarter of presidential program items are formulated preponderantly in departments, and another quarter in the EOP proper. Rather, formulation strategies frequently blend departmental and EOP personnel in creative ways. It was suggested earlier that technically complex items might serve as prime candidates for these sorts of mixed strategies. This phrase, while not meant in its precise game theoretic sense, does retain a link to the concept of expected utility: when will blending White House and departmental expertise maximize the president's? Presidents need the expertise departments can offer, but worry that expert advice may mask other agendas. More bluntly, they fear being taken advantage of by people who know more than they do about the fine print. One way to avoid this is to place agency people in harness with White House or EOP personnel.

To examine this question, the dependent variable was recoded so that "mixed" items (whether departmentally or EOP led) were broken away from all others. Then a probit analysis was conducted; item complexity was hypothesized as a strong positive predictor of whether a given program proposal is formulated using a mixed strategy. This model as a whole (not reported here) performed quite poorly in predicting the overall use of such strategies. However, as predicted, complex items demonstrate strong substantive significance for presidential choice in this regard. Ceteris paribus, an increase in the complexity of an item increases its chances of being formulated through a mixed strategy by about 13 percentage points ($p < .002$).

SUMMARY

This chapter has tested a number of models derived from the hypotheses laid out in Chapter Two, where insights from transaction cost economics were applied to presidential decisions about formulating the legislative program. Here, those hypotheses were linked to the dataset laid out in Chapter Four and specific measures discussed and defined.

The quantitative tests presented here provide solid support for notions of contingent centralization. Even controlling for a wide array of contexts, presidents seemed to respond consistently to the management environment that faced them.

Most of the hypotheses predicting increased centralization — encompassing managerial contexts such as new items, cross-cutting issues, or matters of reorganization and personnel management — were robustly supported. They mattered across time and partisan context. So did measures assessing the cost of non–White House expertise. As presidential proximity to legislative floor medians grew, so did the likelihood of decentralization; likewise, inner Cabinet departments were more likely to be entrusted with policy formulation. Technical complexity was also a strong predictor of decentralized — most often, mixed — strategies.

The statistical analysis presented here is the first step, not the last. It should be read in a probabilistic sense — these results presume that "all else is equal," but in the world of presidential politics tradeoffs must frequently be made across divergent dimensions. Further, better measures of politicization will be especially useful to further research.

Nevertheless, the results to date provide a solid base for that research agenda, and provide a strong indication that presidents centralize in response to the management environment rather than by reflex. As a result they mark a solid step forward in our knowledge of presidential management of the executive branch.

With a better sense of the roots of centralization in hand, we are now in a position to address another question posed at the start of this book: whether a centralizing strategy "works" for the president in terms of congressional success. What impact does presidential management of the formulation process have on a given proposal's ultimate disposition?

The next two chapters explore the connection between the design process and congressional reaction to a given proposal. As we shall see, presidents are caught between competing imperatives: creating a legislative program that matches their preferences and maximizing their success in Congress. Centralization does not succeed in squaring the circle.

CHAPTER SIX

Congress Is a Whiskey Drinker:
Centralization and Legislative Success

IN 1965 Lyndon Johnson's congressional liaison, Larry O'Brien, was asked, "How do you twist an arm?" His reply: "If you're talking about persuasion: we initiate by proposing."[1]

Indeed, the bargaining process with Congress surrounding a proposed piece of legislation begins with its presentation—with what it contains and how it is assembled, with when it arrives and even with its title.[2] As Nixon aide Bryce Harlow warned the new administration, "Your cooperation in consulting with Congressional experts before an announcement is made or a decision irretrievably fixed could save us all a great deal of grief later on. Sometimes a changed word or two will result in acceptance and support of a program."[3] Or as Johnson himself put it: "Congress is like a whiskey drinker." That is, "You can put an awful lot of whiskey into a man if you just let him sip it. But if you try to force the whole bottle down his throat at one time, he'll throw it up."[4]

The broad point is that the size, substance, and timing of legislative proposals matter for their reception by the Congress. Jon Bond and Richard Fleisher, having tested a wide series of hypotheses on sources of president-centered power over legislative outcomes, concluded that "a president's greatest influence over policy comes from the agenda he pursues and the way it is packaged."[5] As Paul Quirk writes, "a president's legislative success often will depend on the ability to design winning proposals that serve his objectives and yet provide the basis for winning coalitions in Congress."[6] Managing a bill's substance is therefore a key task for presidents seeking success in Congress.

But scholars have given this connection less attention than it deserves. The literature on presidential success in Congress is extensive; however, it tends to examine roll-call votes in something of a vacuum, independent of the process that went into formulating the policy in the first place.[7] In a review of presidential-congressional relations, Bond and Fleisher, writing with Glen Krutz, concluded that "our knowledge remains limited," in part because "we don't have systematic measures of the nature of the policy proposals on the presidents' agendas."[8]

This chapter and the next explore the connection between one aspect of the nature of a policy proposal—its provenance and design process—

and the congressional reaction to it. The key question of interest here is whether centralized policy proposals fare better in Congress than do their decentralized counterparts. More formally, does use of a centralizing strategy in formulating a given policy proposal increase the probability of its passage through Congress, controlling for the nature of the policy proposal and other contextual factors known to be important to presidential success? Centralization does seem a plausible tool for this task. The stakes for presidential success in Congress are high — recall Roy Ash's exhortation to President Nixon that "legislating is governing" — and centralization is theorized as a means of matching presidential capacity to lofty expectations.

But this asks too much. The focus of this book suggests that centralization will actually detract from presidents' legislative success. There is an institutional disconnect between the White House staff and legislators: the White House's informational connections to the lawmakers who first consider administration proposals — especially committee and subcommittee members — are far more tenuous than those of departmental staffs. Reinforcing this, the different institutional vantages and different political incentives of the White House and Congress make it hard for the two branches to cooperate fully. These handicaps are partially mitigated when Congress deals more directly with the bureaucracy.

The theory of contingent centralization suggests that the negative impact of centralization may even be overdetermined. Recall that in Chapter Five the managerial hypotheses modeling contingent centralization were generally supported: namely, innovative proposals which cross-cut a variety of departmental jurisdictions, which implemented reorganizations of the executive branch, which were part of a large presidential workload, or which were formulated in times when reliable extra–White House expertise was particularly expensive were more likely to be centralized. These are precisely the conditions under which congressional support for presidential proposals is likely to be lower. Indeed, many of the very organizational and management factors that lead presidents to centralize the formulation side of a given legislative proposal tend to make it harder for Congress to act decisively on such an item. Contingent centralization suggests that in general, centralizing hurts presidents' legislative efforts.

This is ironic. Centralization is a useful, even a necessary, instrument for presidents seeking to extract effective coordination from a sprawling executive branch. But the means bolstering management of the executive branch may undercut the ends of legislative success.

This chapter will first lay out the disjunction between Congress and the president's inner circle, then discuss two sets of control variables: those suggested by the expectations of contingent centralization, and others from the wider literature on presidential-congressional relations. Including these in the analysis will allow a more accurate estimate of the impact of centralization itself. Chapter Seven will present the methods and additional data used to test this question and assess the results — along with the broader implications for presidential policy formulation. While this will be discussed in more detail below, it is worth mentioning at the outset that "success" here differs somewhat from much of the literature, which uses the term with respect to the percentage of recorded votes on which the president took a public position and prevailed. It differs, too, from congressional "support," which refers to the average percentage of the roll-call vote received by the president's position on important votes. I will use "success" to denote the partial or full enactment into law of a presidential proposal.[9] The analysis tries to tease out systematically a number of the presidential strategies (with regard, for example, to timing, scope, size, and even consultation with Congress) crucial to that success.

CENTRALIZATION AND CONGRESSIONAL SUCCESS

The process by which a legislative proposal is formulated affects its substance. Therefore, if the substance of a proposal matters for its reception by Congress, so does the process behind it. Here that process has been characterized as centralized, decentralized, or some mix of the two, depending on the deployment of the White House and departmental staffs.

As noted earlier, centralization is itself associated with a number of executive branch organizational issues that themselves might be thought to have a negative impact on a proposal's chances of congressional adoption. However, even controlling for these factors, and for others found to be important by the wider presidency-Congress literature, centralization itself should still detract from success.

Why? In part because presidential success in Congress hinges on the informational and agenda-setting nature of the formulation process. Michael Malbin argues:

> Public issues involve. . . . as many sides, or opinions about the best possible public policy, as there are actors. So if the president hopes to persuade others to accept his proposals, he must work with committee and party leaders in Congress to structure a situation in which his proposals are accepted as the best of the alternatives that are practically available. Since structuring a vote means limiting the choices open to members, it presupposes maintaining good working relations with committee and party leaders, the people who hold the levers needed for structuring, and also with followers, whose choices will be limited.[10]

So why should centralization hurt presidents in Congress, all else equal? The crux, I hypothesize, is that it makes "good working relations" difficult, for reasons once again informational and institutional. First, centralization disrupts established informational networks and limits interbranch consultation; second, presidents and members of Congress want different things, vantages which breed a culture of suspicion between the branches that is exacerbated when policy formulation is kept within the White House.

Centralization and Legislators' Information

Consider the world from the point of view of a member of Congress. Like the president, she needs information about the likely impact on real-world outcomes stemming from the various proposals in front of her. Committees are created, at least in part, to serve as conduits of such information to the legislature as a whole. Committees are granted jurisdictional monopolies, which encourage them to specialize substantively, and gate-keeping power over the progression of legislation.[11]

Committees, in turn, are closely connected to an executive branch counterpart.[12] It is enough here to note that committees tend to develop close connections to the departments or agencies handling the same substantive matters as the committee. Although presidents' connections to congressional leadership are often centralized, at the committee level those connections are largely through the departments, not the White House staff or even the Office of Management and Budget.[13] For the committees, as one staffer put it, oftentimes OMB "is essentially this very mysterious organization. . . . The communication channels just don't cross there."[14] As discussed earlier, the efficacy of information flow even between department and committee depends in part on whether the branches are united or divided by party and, within that, by their ideological congruence; the latter might even vary committee by committee.

On the whole, though, information flows more freely through the established networks between committee and department than between White House and committee: in fact, given the separation of speech-writing and even of the congressional liaison from program development in recent years, the White House itself may find it hard to speak with one voice. Nicholas Calio, George W. Bush's liaison to Congress, boasted in 2001 that "there is an absolute integration of legislative affairs and policy" in the White House. This was notable because, as he added, "believe it or not, that's unusual."[15]

Consultation with relevant members of Congress on the formulation of a proposal is thus more common when the formulation process is at least partly decentralized. In the White House, consultation may not be ex ante but, instead, after the fact: as an aide to Ronald Reagan put it, "A decision has been made, now we need to set up the consultation."[16] More generally, with the legislative leadership, consultation tends to be "more on the landing, not the takeoff. By the time the leadership is involved, the context is pretty well set."[17]

Those responsible for shepherding presidential legislation through Congress recognize that prior consultation helps the process succeed. Carter legislative liaison Frank Moore pleaded in 1978 with the White House for a "process of developing legislative proposals" that would include "consultation planned in advance. . . . [W]henever possible key committee members and staff members should have an opportunity to have some input in the drafting of the President's legislative pro- posal. . . . [P]rior to submission, briefings on the contents of the legisla tion should be held for committee chairmen, subcommittee chairmen, Congressional leadership and appropriate constituency groups."[18]

Lyndon Johnson is rightly presented as a stellar legislative bargainer, but it is too little noted that much of this skill was utilized before the presentation of a bill. "The trick," Johnson noted, "was to crack the wall of separation enough to give the Congress a feeling of participation in creating my bills without exposing my plans at the same time to advance congressional opposition before they even saw the light of day. It meant taking risks, but the risks were worth it. . . . I insisted on con- gressional consultation at every single stage."[19] Even FDR's "Hundred Days" were marked by similar solicitude to legislators.[20]

The idea is to garner the lay of the political landscape, to gather intelligence and feedback. This does not imply that the president's as- sessment of a proposal's chances will be perfect; far from it. Nor does it suggest that all congressional suggestions will be incorporated into the president's proposal — this is a matter of presidential choice.[21] Specifics seem more likely to be changed when processes are decentralized, but recall that such processes are decentralized in part because presidential and congressional preferences coincide in the first place. And even when changes are made, this may be a preferable strategy to bargaining over a bill on the floor. The latter is more costly, because more public, and because the stakes of defeat rise for the president as the salience of a vote increases. The trade-offs that President Clinton was forced to make to collect votes for his 1993 deficit reduction package serve as a case in point.[22]

There are, certainly, reasons not to give members of Congress ad- vance information on the president's policies. As an aide to Gerald Ford put it, "There is an underlying suspicion of Congress. You tell one of them and all the others will find out. The first thing they do is go out and tell the press. . . . [Y]ou don't want them making the announcement."[23] This is hardly a recent problem for presidents: the Eisenhower administration's attempts to amend the Taft-Hartley labor law nearly ran aground when the discussions between the Commerce and Labor departments and key members of Congress were leaked to the *Wall Street Journal* in the summer of 1953. White House counsel Bernard Shanley quickly termed the leaked details part of "a working draft," and no proposals were sent until 1954.[24]

Lack of consultation may also be strategic. Presidents may not feel there is much point to consulting on the provisions of a campaign proposal, for example, to whose details they are already committed. Presidents seeking to appear as strong leaders may not want to give the impression that they are bending to Congress's will. Indeed, presidents may not actually place a premium on passing legislation: they may calculate instead that the issue is more valuable than the bill, that political success accrues from legislative failure, or, at the least, that it is important to have a comprehensive record of proposals (passed or not) on which to run. Disagreement may be a strategic good.[25]

This is especially true in times of divided government. The special session of the "Do-Nothing" 80th Congress called by President Truman in 1948 provides a concentrated example; President Bush's programmatic agenda grew wildly as reelection approached in 1992 (see figure 4.1); and later in the 1990s President Clinton vied with the Republican-led 104th and 105th Congresses in similar ways. Still, if the goal is legislative success — and few would claim that failure is a viable electoral strategy in the long run — without consultation presidents run the risk of having few supporters when support is needed.[26]

Congress versus the White House

The notion of "strategic disagreement" usefully resurfaces in a parallel institutional context, for the branches have different interests and different cultures, a divergence exacerbated by centralization. Presidents, it is frequently argued, have the general interest at heart, while Congress's success lies in its members' obeisance to local, territorial concerns.[27] Morris Fiorina puts it this way: "Individual district interests are special interests, whose sum is *not* the national interest."[28]

Frequent friction between members of Congress and White House staff is one result. The latter see the former as parochial, unable to see the national interest over their district boundaries. Recall the "underlying suspicion" of Congress voiced by the Ford staffer above.

Members of Congress, for their part, find the White House too quick to equate the president's interest to the national interest, as well as arrogantly out of touch with the realities of holding elected office. Speaker Sam Rayburn, watching John Kennedy's Ivy League–educated national security advisers debate Vietnam, reportedly whispered to the vice president that he wished at least one of those staffers had ever been elected to something, somewhere.[29] Kennedy himself chided longtime aide Ken O'Donnell, "You have never been elected to anything by anybody. . . . Elected officers have a code . . . no matter whether they like each other or hate each other—those who have not achieved that approbation of the people have got troubles."[30] Thirty years later, during the debate over Bill Clinton's health care package, Representative Jim McDermott berated White House staffer Ira Magaziner, an Oxford graduate: "I didn't go to Rhodes [Scholar] University, I don't even know where it is. But I got elected to Congress, and you never ran, and you don't know s— about nothing."[31]

Johnson staffer O'Brien noted that one of "the basic facts of political life   is that we cannot suggest to members of Congress, individually or collectively, that they commit political hari-kari."[32] But legislators feel that presidents' staffs too often ask just that—and a centralized formulation process makes it less likely that those staffs will engage in the information gathering needed to forestall it. From a legislator's point of view, a centralized proposal thus often comes from the White House with the burden of proof on the president's shoulders. The member of Congress has more doubt about it (in that she knows less about it than about an equivalent proposal formulated in the departments)—and is likely to be less willing to grant the benefit of that doubt to its formulators. Barbara Sinclair's discussion of the Clinton presidency suggests that this disconnect is present, even unavoidable, in unified as well as in divided government.[33]

Again, this is not to say that presidents may not have reasons to centralize. It is only to suggest that we should not expect centralization to help presidents succeed legislatively.

Energy Legislation, 1977 and 1979

To round out the theoretical expectations traced so far, it is worth examining a pair of brief contrasting case studies. These focus on the formulation of President Carter's two major energy proposals, which were sent to Congress in 1977 and 1979. Selecting these cases controls for the presidential personality, for the broader political context, and even for the subject matter of the resultant proposal—but allows exploration of the divergent formulation strategies involved and their effect on congressional reaction and eventual legislative success.

In 1977 Carter wanted a comprehensive package, one that sought to solve the interlocking problems associated with the energy crisis in the most coherent, rational way. The president suffered that most peculiar of curses: he got what he asked for. But Congress passed nothing until the very last day of the 1978 session, and then its final product was barely a shadow of Carter's original proposals.

In 1979, by contrast, the president's proposal—while still comprehensive—was constructed piece by piece in a painstakingly consultative manner. That passage was arduous too, but most of the package did indeed pass. By the 1980 campaign, Carter was claiming that he deserved an "A" on energy matters—"that's one of the great achievements of our Administration."[34]

ENERGY IN THE 95TH CONGRESS: "CHEWING ON A ROCK"

January 1977 dawned cold and got colder. There was snow in Miami, and ice eight inches thick on the Mississippi River. The bitter winter, with help from a flawed natural gas distribution system, caused energy supplies to run critically low across the country.

In February President Carter announced that he would send a national energy plan to Congress within ninety days. On April 18, he made a televised speech from the White House library, clad in a cardigan, to declare that the energy crisis was the "moral equivalent of war." Two days later he presented his battle plan: an enormous omnibus measure, by some counts containing 113 proposals, "one of the most complex legislative packages ever devised."[35]

For all its intricacy, the package had been formulated as part of a "virtually covert operation" by a tiny task force of independent economists, lawyers, and energy experts led by White House energy adviser James Schlesinger.[36] There was almost no consultation with Cabinet departments, many of which had a stake in the legislation, and even less contact with members of Congress.[37] Secrecy was no accident: Carter "insisted" that it be "utter and complete."[38] Indeed, the editor of Schlesinger's drafts was none other than Carter himself. Even the new Domestic Policy Staff led by Stu Eizenstat was out of the loop.[39] Though the plan rested heavily on tax proposals, Treasury Department taxation specialists were largely ignored; Secretary Michael Blumenthal's objections to the package, when he finally saw it, were quickly overridden.[40] Other relevant departments—Transportation, Commerce, and HUD, for example—were also shut out.

The idea of a closely centralized process was to prevent special interests from picking off discrete portions of what Carter felt had to be a comprehensive measure. The appeal of legislative consultation was further diminished by the fact that Congress had stalemated over energy policy since the Nixon administration. To do things quickly, and to make sure the proposal was internally consistent, centralization seemed optimal. And the trains ran on time: the ninety-day deadline was met.

But as Carter soon learned, the process itself damaged the chances for policy change. Members of Congress knew little about the package and felt not only slighted but confused; as a result, as one summary of the process gently put it, "they were miffed."[41] Further, the bill's provisions were politically naive: items were included that had been decisively rejected in the past, and whose resubmission damaged the chances of other, novel proposals.[42] Since not many people in the administration knew how the bill was structured, few could sell it — or even adequately describe it — to lawmakers. Soon it transpired that the draft legislation also had "serious technical problems," which further undercut legislators' confidence.[43]

Recognizing that seventeen committees and subcommittees had some jurisdiction over President Carter's energy package, House Speaker Thomas P. ("Tip") O'Neill (D-Mass.) created a temporary "super" energy committee. This thirty-seven-member body was to hold hearings, parcel the bill out to other committees, receive recommendations back within a set time, and then compile (and/or amend) those committees' work for a final recommendation to the floor. In the end, a conglomeration of five bills was voted on as one.[44] Although the Carter gasoline tax was scrapped, the House passed the bulk of the National Energy Plan on August 5.

That marked the end of the happy part of the story. In the Senate the bill, in the words of *Congressional Quarterly*, "was butchered."[45] Senate Finance chair Russell Long (D-La.) represented the heart of the oil and gas industries, and was in no mood to compromise. Eventually the Senate passed not one bill but five, each so different from the administration version that a conference committee met for nearly a year before reporting its proposals. It was not until late 1978 that a bill finally passed, surviving by only one vote in the House. It bore scant resemblance Carter's original proposals. The new taxes were replaced by tax credits, or dropped entirely; only the original conservation proposals came close, and even there mandatory standards for utilities and new buildings were deleted.[46]

What happened? As suggested above, "much of the criticism leveled at the program had to do with how it was formulated and presented to Congress."[47] By using such a heavily centralized process, Carter failed to preempt the wide array of political problems associated with the energy issue or to give advance notice of the administration's approach to legislators — who would, after all, ultimately have to judge it. If lawmakers couldn't get information from the administration, where else were they to turn but to the very interest groups Carter hoped to avoid?

Energy issues were tough political issues: Tip O'Neill thought that "this perhaps has been the most parochial issue that could ever hit the floor."[48] But the chosen drafters were apolitical by nature and by direction; political advice even from other White House staffers was unsought and, when provided, ignored. Further, failing to draw on departmental technical expertise cost the drafters additional credibility. It was not just a question of information, but also that the White House misjudged congressional incentives on the issue. The end result, as Carter said, made getting an energy package through Congress like "chewing on a rock."[49]

ENERGY AND THE 96TH CONGRESS: "BOTH HANDS WASH THE FACE"

To his credit, Carter learned from this ordeal. "The important insight to be derived from [the 1977–78] story for understanding the evolution of the policy development process in the Carter White House," Erwin Hargrove later concluded, "is that most of the principal actors decided that a less tightly-held, more open consultative process might have increased Congressional acceptance and reduced the time required for passage."[50] As Eizenstat put it, the experience was "symbolic of what happens when you try to put things together too quickly and without the type of consultation that's necessary."[51]

The energy issue certainly didn't go away—indeed, in January 1979 the Iranian revolution interrupted world oil supplies, and in late March nuclear power advocates were given pause by the accident at Pennsylvania's Three Mile Island plant. During the winter, Carter directed Eizenstat to work with Schlesinger to convene an interagency group to develop new energy proposals.

It is instructive to note that Carter did not ask Eizenstat to create the new energy package within the White House, but rather to coordinate an effort in which the bulk of the work would be farmed out to the substantive agencies involved. Indeed, the Energy Department did most of the drafting. The group involved representatives from eight departments as well as House and Senate leaders, congressional chairmen and rank-and-file members with a particular interest in energy issues, even consumer and business groups.[52] "Contrast that process with the first energy process," Eizenstat later said:

> Here we had every single agency around a table twice as big as this room, attended on the average by fifteen to twenty people every single bloody afternoon for weeks and weeks and weeks and weeks. EPA, Treasury, OMB, CEA, Department of Transportation . . . everybody and his brother. It was a very open, very involved process, very consultative process, we did a lot of work on the Hill, talked to Jim Wright, talked to Scoop, talked to the people who were moving the synthetic [fuels] bill in the House, . . . had

the agencies involved. . . . Interest group discussions, extensive discussions with the business community . . .

And by God when we got through with that process we had a really first rate decision memorandum for the President and we had a policy passed, every single item passed except the energy mobilization board.[53]

The resulting plan was again large, complex, and comprehensive. In an April 1979 "status report" to the President, Eizenstat commented that "this is very technical legislation" and estimated that seventeen titles would be needed to fill out the omnibus package.[54]

This time, though, the White House made a concerted effort to produce draft bills that were both technically accurate and politically palatable. "A group of DPS, CL, DOE, OMB and Treasury has been working on a full-time basis to develop the windfall profits tax and the Energy Security Fund legislation," Eizenstat told Carter. Digging below the acronyms, this meant the group included Treasury and Energy Department staffers, along with OMB and the Domestic Policy Staff—and also Congressional Liaison. Indeed, Eizenstat stressed, "as part of our efforts, I along with this group have met with the staffs of [a long list of members of Congress]."[55]

Adopting a congressional perspective and providing reliable information to members made a big difference. As noted by Eizenstat, in contrast to the 1977 bill, the majority of Carter's 1979 proposals were in fact adopted. This wasn't particularly easy, even after all the effort that had gone into formulation; energy remained a daunting political struggle, given legislators' natural reluctance to raise costs on their constituencies.[56] But the complaint was no longer one about information: members of Congress knew the options and the alternatives. Now the question was, in Malbin's terms, whether Carter's plan was the best practicable choice. That Congress decided in the affirmative was in no small part due to the changes in the formulation process, which were along dimensions instructive for thinking about the role of centralization: toward inclusion and consultation and toward respect for the congressional perspective. As Majority Whip John Brademas (D-Ind.) had earlier observed, "[the president] is learning that the left hand washes the right, and they both wash the face."[57]

CONTINGENT CENTRALIZATION
AND CONGRESSIONAL DECENTRALIZATION

Two brief histories, however apt, don't clinch a case. But in the Carter examples are the seeds of why centralization may not prove a useful strategy for succeeding in Congress.

Before proceeding further, some key control variables must be developed, because certain factors associated with centralization might also be expected to have an independent negative impact on legislative success. Recall that presidents centralize as the number of departments involved in a policy matter increase; centralization rises as the reorganizational impact of a proposal rises; new program items are more likely to be centralized than old ones; centralization becomes less likely when the preferences of departments' sometimes competing principals are more closely aligned; and finally, more technically complex items are generally less centralized, though some White House participation is likely in their formulation.

There is theoretical reason to believe that each of these affects not only centralization but congressional reaction to legislation generally. Thus they must be controlled for in any broader analysis.

Cross-Cutting Jurisdictions

To the extent that presidents address issues that straddle the jurisdictions of more than one executive department, they assure themselves of running afoul of Congress. The reason is simple: while not a one-to-one fit, the congressional committee system parallels the organization of the executive branch, matching up committee jurisdictions with those of agency counterparts.[58]

Making matters more problematic for presidents is the sheer number of committees with a claim to jurisdiction over broad proposals. For example, subcommittees of larger bodies such as Appropriations and Ways and Means also have responsibility for working with departmental programs (for example, the Human Resources subcommittee of Ways and Means deals with human services issues), and committees such as Governmental Affairs in the Senate and Government Reform in the House exercise oversight over a wide range of substantive topics. This accounting does not even get to the Budget committees, or committees dealing with rules, the organization of each chamber, or ethics. In 1998 the House had 112 committees and subcommittees, and the Senate 88.[59] As Woodrow Wilson noted a century ago, Congress is a "disintegrate ministry"; today that description is, if anything, even more apt. It has not been undone by sporadic attempts at Congress's own version of centralized coordination.[60]

Indeed, over time, the situation has become more difficult for presidents as party ties — never very binding in the American system — have grown looser and the sanctioning power of congressional leadership weaker. Samuel Kernell describes this shift as an evolution from group-oriented "institutionalized pluralism" to a free-wheeling "individualized pluralism."[61] His focus is on the difficulty this poses for presidential bargaining over legislative issues; but there is an organizational analogue as well. Subcommittees, expanding in number in the 1970s, had their own Bill of Rights ensconced in the legislative rules. And committees at all levels constantly vie for an ever larger piece of the legislative pie. "This is a guaranteed prescription for fragmentation. How many committees in Congress now work on environmental issues? Dozens, each from their own perspective, and each with its own glacial strategy for encroaching on the few jurisdictionally ambiguous issues that remain."[62] When issues cannot fit neatly into one box, Congress's reaction has been not to expand the box but to make a copy of it for everyone. As the number of players increases, so does the number of veto points and the likelihood of stalemate.

It is true that the textbook view of "how a bill becomes a law" has been partly superseded by unorthodox and even ad hoc procedures for handling important legislation.[63] Yet these procedures themselves have arisen in perverse tribute to the fact that Congress is just as it has always been: decentralized, fragmented, even atomized.[64] As Ford counselor Jack Marsh told a Cabinet meeting, "the Congress' inability to discuss major issues is now an issue in and of itself. There are many jurisdictional disputes; there is fragmentation, factionalism."[65]

From a president's point of view this often means the undoing of what he has so carefully overseen in the formulation process. A bill put together as an omnibus presentation may be quickly dismembered upon referral to committee. In January 1963, for example, President Kennedy made a conscious decision to send to Congress "the widest range of programs he could assemble" within a message on education. An omnibus bill comprising more than forty proposals was duly transmitted to Congress. These were soon separated into at least nine bills in the House and Senate.[66] More recently, Bill Clinton's National Performance Review (NPR) package was filed as one bill in October of 1993. But it contained proposals dealing with each of the fourteen Cabinet departments and other executive agencies besides, and by the 1994 session the bill had been divided into more than thirty segments for congressional review across seventeen committees in the House alone.[67]

Kennedy was driven to complain about this treatment to House Rules chairman Howard "Judge" Smith, arguing, tongue firmly in cheek, that in "requiring . . . a division of a single program into more than one bill" the "organization of Congress may be deficient."[68] But the joke is, after all, on presidents. A bill sent to more than one committee during the 98th Congress, for example, was less than half as likely to be approved on the House floor than singly referred measures.[69] Indeed, evidence suggests that even as the Republican majority scaled back (slightly) on the number of full committees after 1994, it increased the incidence of multiple referrals.[70]

Congressional leaders have, at times, attempted to restructure the legislative decision process so as to aid presidential efforts—the 1977 energy package is a textbook case. The fact that *any* bill passed is generally credited to Speaker O'Neill's organizational wrangling.[71] In 1995, new Speaker Newt Gingrich (R-Ga.) began to employ a series of his own task forces outside of the normal committee process. But while this again illustrates the relative inefficiency of that process, it is not an example that should inspire presidents—especially not those of the opposition party.

The Clinton health care plan provides a gloomy counterexample. While in the spring of 1993 the Clintons, and legislative allies such as Senator Jay Rockefeller (D-W. Vir.), had urged creation of another supercommittee drawn mainly from the three major committees with principal jurisdiction on health care matters, House Speaker Tom Foley (D-Wash.) and Majority Leader Dick Gephardt (D-Mi.) shot down the idea. Participation was to be maximized, not streamlined, they argued. "It doesn't work that way," Gephardt said. "The least you can do is go through the committee process."[72] Efforts to craft the health care bill so that it would be sent only to the Senate's sympathetic Labor and Human Resources Committee were similarly futile, in part because the Congressional Budget Office ruled that the plan's employer mandate was a tax and thus within Senate Finance's jurisdiction as well.[73]

Reorganization

Because presidents find it difficult to trust departmental assessments of reorganizational proposals, they tend to centralize the formulation of such items. But much of the narrative on committee jurisdiction applies to reorganization too. Because committees are often tied to executive organization, moving a bureau from one department to another will often shift oversight responsibility (and control of budgetary authorizing language) from one committee to another. James Q. Wilson has noted that "in debating such laws, Congress is exceptionally sensitive to the implications of any reorganization for its own internal allocation of power. . . . A willingness to surrender turf is as rare among members of Congress as it is among cabinet secretaries."[74]

Congressional interest in administrative reform—in the sense of improving executive management—has, over time, been episodic at best.[75] One cause is a certain proprietary sense over the departments and agencies as they stand, since they were created by Congress in the first place.

The Constitution is tacit on the subject, so the bureaucracy was created as departments seemed desirable. Often, this was as new constituencies arose with claims on and ties to government. When presidents seek to reorganize, the question quickly becomes one of legitimacy, of the "right" to interfere with established patterns.

Put in those terms the debate sounds grander than perhaps it is. The heart of the matter is a second point: that structure matters for power, and that a "responsive" bureau means something different to a member of Congress than it does to the president. For each, not surprisingly, responsiveness is defined in terms of his own needs. The president wants to establish a line of executive command; members of Congress want to gain access to the decision-making process and to influence it in discrete instances. The president's electoral incentives are for effective adminis-tration, those of Congress for "fixing" bureaucratic problems. Taken to an extreme, this divergence implies that Congress prizes inefficiency (at least as defined by management consultants) in the executive branch.[76] Short of that, restructuring an agency reorients its relationship with the interest groups that are linked to it and may even have helped to create it. This is fundamentally threatening to those interests and, by exten-sion, to their allies in Congress.[77] Presidents are hardly immune from interest-group pressure. Still, the territorial imperative (both geographic and jurisdictional) is far stronger in Congress than in the presidency.[78] Similarly, it is safe to say that presidents' interest in creating organiza-tions that do not overlap, that are aligned along functional lines — that simply "make sense" — far outstrips that of most individual members of Congress.[79]

Issue Novelty

New program items, Chapter Five demonstrated, are likely to be more centralized than their venerable counterparts. But it is a basic tenet of American government that the status quo is favored over change, and incremental change over comprehensive reform. In part this flows from the organizational imperatives traced above: any policy running the leg-islative gauntlet requires support both wide and deep to survive multi-ple veto points and dilatory tactics.[80]

As a result, successful coalition leaders often follow the unwritten rule of universalism — legislation is easier to pass if it provides payoffs for a broad array of districts. But this tends to simultaneously expand expectations for the proposal and to make its outcomes less effective. Johnson and Carter official Charles Schultze got at both points when he noted that during the Great Society "there was a lot of boodle being handed out in large numbers of small boodle."[81]

Another result is that building support for a given proposal takes time — in part simply to convince legislators that at stake is a problem requiring solution, not simply a condition of life.[82] Ideas float around in what John Kingdon has called the "policy primeval soup," combining and recombining until form and opportunity coincide.[83] New ideas, like new wine, don't go down smoothly.

It is worth stressing that just because an item is new to the president's program, as defined in Chapter Five, does not make it new to Congress. The four or eight years of a presidency are eclipsed by even a two-term senator; committee chairs, indeed, have usually risen to their position through seniority. We might expect that the negative impact of items deemed new in this data, then, is relatively muted.

Available Expertise

A strong theoretical prediction of contingent centralization was that the partisan and especially the ideological makeup of Congress had an impact on presidential centralizing strategies. The informational vantage predicts that this compatibility lowers the cost of outside expertise. Since, as already discussed, congressional committees are closely linked to departmental personnel, presidents feel it safer to delegate the task of policy formulation to the department/committee tandem. Indeed, the closer the policy preferences of the president and the Congress, the less likely were presidents to centralize.

This connection needs to be reiterated with regard to the president's congressional success. Reorganizational ramifications and cross-jurisdictional issues weigh down proposals in Congress not simply because legislators are hostile to presidential policy goals (though they may be). Rather, those proposals face institutional barriers grounded in the historical nature and development of Congress. With regard to partisan and ideological congruence, though, presidents can "buy" policy formulation from departments and their congressional overseers because reliable expertise is available, which is in turn because the two parties to the bargain want the same thing. Where that compatibility is lacking, we should expect less presidential success in Congress overall.

The empirical evidence for this point is overwhelming, and as it is itself one of the "usual suspects" of the presidential-congressional relations literature it will be discussed further in the next section. Here I will merely reiterate that party and ideology are not necessarily the same thing. Both should matter for presidential success in Congress: we might expect to see ideology matter quite a bit for the availability of resources, given presidents' traditionally weak ties to party structures, but committee staff expertise is much less accessible to a president of the minority party in Congress, if only because the minority commands far fewer staffers.[84]

Complexity

Because complex proposals require subject-matter expertise not often available in the White House, such program items tend not to be wholly centralized. However, for many of the reasons associated above with "new" and cross-cutting issues, these types of proposals are harder to get through Congress as well.[85] Thus the complexity measure is expected to be a countervailing control, making this class of *de*-centralized program items harder to pass. Recall that a mixed process was forecast for complex items; how the division of labor is patterned may prove to be crucial for legislative success here.

Workload

Finally, the size of the president's program will also matter for his congressional success. This is not simply a matter of members' hostility toward any one of the president's proposals. Rather, it is a matter of time: there is only so much of it. A two-year session contains 520 weekdays, minus holidays, minus recesses, and, frequently, minus Mondays and Fridays so as to allow travel to the district. In the 106th Congress of 1999–2000, the House was in formal session for 272 days, the Senate for 303, or about 2,200 hours apiece. In that time 10,840 bills and other measures were introduced.[86]

Given these statistics, it is clear that mere delay can serve as a powerful weapon of denial. Items that are part of the presidential program do tend to be privileged in the sense that they receive at least some attention from Congress.[87] Even so, the agenda can be easily overloaded. Clinton press secretary Mike McCurry was on the mark when, in reply to a question about why the administration was holding back a certain proposal, he observed, "Because we are frying a lot of fish right now, and the kettle is only so big."[88] Jimmy Carter admitted in 1977 he had "overestimated the Congress in its ability to deal with complicated subjects expeditiously," adding, "I think you've noticed that the burden of work we've put on the Congress has just been more than they could handle in the time allotted."[89] Earlier that year, Speaker O'Neill had urged Carter to cut back on his program, hoping the president would name four or five major bills he wanted to get done. But even after some very broad hints, the president's list contained not seven but seventy items.[90]

Lyndon Johnson, while possessed of an enormous legislative agenda of his own, knew his "whiskey drinkers" well and made certain that his proposals did not clog the work of any one committee.[91] But the true anti-Carter, in this sense, is Ronald Reagan. Political scientists have praised him for keeping his agenda short and his priorities clear, especially in his first year.[92] Clearly this does give those proposals some advantage.

Even so, this "lesson" of the Reagan experience may not be a model for all presidents: George H. W. Bush, for example, did not receive plaudits for his small agenda but instead was judged deficient on "the vision thing." The more pressing difficulty for presidents generally may be in reconciling the advice to set a small agenda with the fact of large problems. Early in his first term, Bill Clinton liked to argue that the nation's problems were so interconnected that they all had to be addressed, and so he tried: tax, health care, and welfare reform proposals had to be carefully sequenced (and passed) if the whole program was to work properly. As a result, when one item bogged down, they all did. The upshot, Clinton told an interviewer, was "that, if I can use a business analogy, my product jumped ahead of my process."[93] Or perhaps, more specifically, of congressional limitations on processing.

EMPIRICAL FACTORS IN PRESIDENTIAL SUCCESS IN CONGRESS

As noted at the start of this chapter, the empirical literature analyzing presidential success in Congress has done little to peer behind the White House curtain. However, an extensive body of work details the factors known to contribute to that success overall.

Although there is some work on presidents' roles in committee deliberations[94] — an important venue for influence, given the structure of the American legislative process — the bulk of the literature in this area has focused on the presidential impact on roll-call votes on the floor of Congress. There are a variety of dependent variables utilized, the two most prominent of which are the presidential support scores of individual members of Congress and presidential success in winning roll-call votes on which the president has taken a position.[95] Discussion over the propriety of these measures has become heated at times, and as elaborated in Chapter Seven, I will use a different measure tracking the proportion of a presidential proposal that becomes law. There is much more consensus, however, on the independent variables' side of the equation.

Empirical studies have identified three main categories of explanation for presidential support on the floor of Congress: political parties and ideology (which themselves can be distinguished), policy type, and the president's popularity with the general public. Others have already been covered above. I will discuss each of the three, briefly, in reverse order, then discuss several additional controls.

A fourth category which will not be discussed here, but which has an ongoing presence in the literature, is that of presidential leadership skills. There are two reasons for the omission. First, this area is closely tied to the personalities of individual presidents, and thus inconsistent with this project's aim of seeking to specify the institutional impact of the *presidency* on policy outcomes. Second, systematic attempts to test the "skills" hypothesis have tended to conclude that this is a factor that works only "at the margins."[96] Relying on such explanations cannot distinguish, for example, why very different presidents have similar rates of success in Congress — or why the same president's success varies so much year to year, even issue to issue. One recent review of the field notes, "Not one study of presidential-congressional relationships that has systematically examined several presidencies and numerous legislative events over an extended period of time has found presidential legislative skills to be a potent explanation for variations in congressional responses to the president."[97] Most observers would agree with the blanket statement that a skilled president is more likely to succeed than an unskilled one. Defining any of the terms in that sentence, though, elicits controversy. What constitutes skill? What makes one a "better" leader? Are these definitions themselves conditional on environmental attributes separable from the president himself?

This is not the same as saying that presidents themselves never matter, or that leadership skills, used appropriately at the right time (the judgment of which is surely another attribute of such skill), are never effective tools. But the analysis here addresses systematically a number of those presidential strategies (with regard, for example, to timing, scope, size, even consultation with Congress) that are themselves often considered, historically, to be "leadership skills."

Presidential Popularity

There is "virtual unanimity" among presidents and their aides in asserting "the importance of the president's public standing to an administration's legislative success."[98] Nonetheless, the evidence of a direct translation of publicity to success is mixed, and a fierce debate rages in the literature over whether public approval of the president has a meaningful impact on congressional approval of his policies. A variety of specifications have been suggested and tested, attempting to get both at issues of timing and at subsets of the data more closely attuned to, and tuned into by, individual members of Congress.[99] To the extent that a relationship is found here, we would expect it to be positive; still, as with leadership skills, the overall judgment is that popularity has only a marginal effect. At times this might be substantively quite important: policy is often made, after all, at the margins.

Policy Type

The great divide here is between foreign and domestic policy. A broad literature on the "two presidencies" argues (or sometimes aims to debunk) the notion that presidents are far more successful on foreign policy initiatives than in domestic affairs. The original thesis, as put forth by Aaron Wildavsky more than thirty years ago, is somewhat dated. Still, the latest empirical findings, complicated by the rise of so-called intermestic issues, do continue to show some evidence that politics stops at the water's edge — that presidents do receive more support in foreign affairs than in domestic. The divergence tends to be sharper for members not in the president's party, and mainly in the Senate.[100]

Related to this is the question of external focusing events, as developed in Chapter Five. The nation and the Congress tend to "rally 'round the flag" when foreign crises emerge. The dramatic increase in George W. Bush's popular approval rating after the terrorist attacks of September 2001 is an obvious example. In 1995, even with public opinion running two to one against President Clinton's decision to deploy peacekeeping troops to Bosnia, Republican majority leader Bob Dole worked to push Clinton's resolution requesting support of deployment through the Senate.[101] An analogue on the domestic side is disaster relief after hurricanes, earthquakes, and the like. Further, focusing events that shine the spotlight on a given policy need can often serve as a catalyst for action.[102] For example, the wreck of the tanker *Argo* off the Massachusetts coast in December 1976 prompted the incoming Carter administration to develop a legislative proposal reworking the statutes governing cargo ship safety standards and oil spill liability.[103] A version of that proposal became law in 1978.

Political Parties and Ideology

This is where most studies of presidential success in Congress hang their hats: party (and, with more data recently available, ideology) is consistently the biggest predictor of support for the president. Majority party presidents, quite simply, do better on the floor of Congress than do minority party presidents; and the larger the majority, the better the president does. Kenneth O'Donnell, who worked for both Kennedy and Johnson, noted that the latter's greatest legislative victories came in the

89th Congress, which had immense Democratic majorities. After the disastrous 1966 midterms, "he couldn't get Mother's Day through."[104]

The rise of candidate-centered campaigning loosened the already wobbly electoral link between party and member of Congress; at the same time, the 1980s and 1990s witnessed a resurgence in party voting, as the ideological span within each party shrank and that between the two parties grew. Party and ideology, then, are closely linked; but both have independent importance in congressional voting decisions.[105] Most observers agree, with Paul Light, that "party seats remain the gold standard for presidential agenda setting. Short-term gains in presidential approval can make the influence of those seats more liquid perhaps, but cannot convert a Republican seat into a Democratic seat unless that approval creates coattails in the next election."[106] And even this last link is hard to judge. In general, while the size of the president's "mandate" is conceded as a subjective factor, this is a fuzzy question — mandates are constructed, and may have little to do with the true bases of voter choice.[107]

NEXT STEPS

This chapter has argued that a centralized formulation process should be expected to have a negative effect on a given proposal's success in Congress, even controlling for those causes of centralization that also affect success. In addition, it has laid out other theories of presidential success in Congress that must also be included in testing centralization's effect on the president's programmatic prospects. The theoretical stage is set: Chapter Seven places methods and data upon it.

CHAPTER SEVEN

The Odds Are with the House: The Limits of Centralization

A JOKE going around the White House in advance of Jimmy Carter's 1978 trip to Atlantic City sums up a real truth about presidential power. "I may not be much of a gambler," Carter's punchline proclaimed, "but I have learned one important gambling principle since being in office: the odds are always with the House."[1]

They are, indeed: Congress was and is the first branch of American government. The previous chapter suggested one consequence: to the extent centralization is a management strategy designed to overcome the informational pathologies of presidential relations with the executive bureaucracy, Congress will be affronted by its creations — perhaps as a matter of ideological preference, but certainly as a matter of organizational interest.

This chapter places that argument into the context of a model testing presidential success in Congress. As predicted, centralization proves to be a dubious management strategy for presidents seeking to maximize the chances of passing their programs into statute. This is so even when controlling for factors potentially confounded with centralization and for those the presidential-congressional relations literature argues drive the legislative process overall.

CENTRALIZATION AND LEGISLATIVE SUCCESS

Defining Centralization and Success

In Chapter Four an index of centralization was developed and utilized as the dependent variable in a series of ordered probit analyses. Here that index will flip to the other side of the equation as an independent variable. As before, a proposal may be considered decentralized, mixed but departmentally led, mixed with the EOP or White House in the lead role, or centralized.[2]

The dependent variable is a president's success in Congress. As noted earlier, most of the literature defines "success" in reference to the roll-call votes on which the president took a public position and prevailed, or uses instead a measure of congressional "support," that is, the mean percentage of the vote received by the president's position on important matters. As conceived in this chapter, "success" is not tied to individual roll-call votes. Instead success is assessed according to (a) whether legislation makes its way to the president's desk in a form sufficiently agreeable to him that he is willing to sign it into law, and (b) how closely that legislation resembles the president's original proposal. This approach parallels that taken by Mark A. Peterson in his important study of presidential-congressional relations, *Legislating Together*.[3]

This formulation helps to isolate the legislative response to presidential initiatives, rather than measuring presidential position taking on the congressional agenda, only some items of which are presidentially inspired. It also allows consideration of two dimensions not always recognized in the literature, but important nonetheless.

First, success is not an all-or-nothing proposition; while victory can often be symbolized by an up-or-down roll-call vote, it is the substance that reaches (or fails to reach) the enrollment stage that normally shapes perceptions of a president's legislative leadership, and his legacy. Indeed, sometimes the very fact that any substance at all has made it that far is what matters most. Presumably, the president prefers enactment of his proposals as submitted. But in many or even most cases, he will accept less. Some questions lend themselves more easily to split-the-difference outcomes—funding issues generally have clearer lines than do moral ones. But even with the latter, success often depends on compromise. As a result, presidents think hard about vetoing even measures that have moved quite some distance from their original proposal. The *Public Papers* are rife with presidential signing statements to the effect that "this is a good start, but only a start." Bill Clinton commented in 1996, signing a contested welfare reform act, that "the bill I'm about to sign, as I have said many times, is far from perfect, but it has come a very long way."[4] Since nothing is so often the output of the American system, the argument that a bill is "better than nothing" has stronger merits than true believers of all ideological stripes like to concede.

So it is important to allow for the possibility of compromise as an outcome separate from defeat. To do this, "success" is operationalized for this analysis as an ordinal index, running from 0 to 3, which can be examined using ordered probit. This follows Peterson's model; however, where Peterson puts his analysis in terms of the level of conflict engendered by a given proposal (the specific parts of a given message), I calculate the proportion of the substance of the original message that reaches the president's desk.[5] This ranges from defeat of a presidential initiative (by vote or inaction), to a president's getting some, most, or all of what he wants. Whenever feasible, I have quantified this as a percentage of the number of specific provisions that were approved, of those offered. That is, a president could get none (0), less than half (1), more than half (2), or substantially all (3) of what he proposed.[6]

The second important dimension of "success" is time. As long as a proposal passed before the end of the president's time in office, it was counted as successful along the dimensions just described. Thus congressional action does not have to come in the calendar year in which the measure was originally proposed, as required by the CQ Boxscores discussed in Chapter Four.

This temporal extension better reflects reality, and prevents us from underestimating success.[7] President Eisenhower proposed Hawaiian statehood for seven years before it was accepted by Congress. President Reagan presented proposals for port modernization in early 1983 that became law in late 1986. These are rightly counted as policy successes. That presidents feel it is never too late to try for congressional enactment is exemplified by their tendency even in their last two weeks in office to resubmit favored proposals to the new Congress.

Four sources were used to determine the progress of presidential proposals: Congressional Quarterly *Almanacs* (1975–1996), the Congressional Quarterly Boxscores published for 1949–1975 (as extended to account for proposals' passage in subsequent years), the Congressional Universe database available through Reed Elsevier, Inc.'s on-line Lexis-Nexis service, and the internal status reports cited earlier on cleared administration-sponsored legislation prepared by the Division of Legislative Reference in the Office of Management and Budget.[8]

Summary statistics for the sampled items are presented in table 7.1, weighted to provide a more accurate estimate of the entire population of presidential proposals (though these results vary from the unweighted results by no more than two-tenths of 1 percent in any category). Overall, presidential initiatives fare quite well. Table 7.1 indicates that between 1949 and 1996, presidents won approval of slightly less than 30 percent of the messages they sent to Congress, lost on about 40 percent, and compromised on the remainder. This is quite congruent with Peterson's findings covering 1953–1984. He found that presidents won on about 35 percent of their proposals, lost 45 percent, and gained a compromise on 19 percent. Similarly, a more recent study by George Edwards and Andrew Barrett, using somewhat different criteria, found that presidential program items succeeded about 40 percent of the time between 1953 and 1996.[9]

Keep in mind that this study measures presidential success only with regard to the president's program. This is likely not a representative sample of all presidential-congressional interaction. Since all the sampled items here are on the presidential agenda, the results obtained do

TABLE 7.1
Presidential Success in Congress (on presidential initiatives)

Success	Frequency	Percentage
0 Defeat or inaction	147	39.4
1 Partial (<50%)	46	12.1
2 Partial (>50%)	72	19.5
3 All	113	28.9
Total	378	100.0

Note: Weighted mean: 1.38 (S.E. = 0.07).

not provide leverage on whether such items succeed at a higher rate than others.

Certainly presidential items do not succeed by virtue of that status alone; Peterson's analysis of the Eisenhower through Reagan administrations shows that a full quarter of presidential proposals were simply ignored. This was less true for larger or more innovative items, however. Further, some recent scholarship indicates that items on the presidential agenda do have a better chance of surviving their congressional ordeal, given the president's ability to get his priorities heard by both chambers and the low likelihood that vetoes will derail the legislative process in such cases.[10] Further, presidents might game the process in order to shorten the odds of their program's succeeding, starting with the choice of whether to send legislation at all. As one staffer commented in the late 1950s, "It is my feeling that there will be very little opportunity for new legislation during the next two years. For that reason I think we should hold to a very minimum any recommendations that we send to the Congress in order to keep our batting average from being too low."[11] Presidents could even pre-empt anticipated congressional reaction by taking stands only on popular issues and avoiding divisive ones, though at least one major analysis did not find this to be true.[12]

An additional caveat regarding legislative success should be raised. As discussed earlier, turning a proposal into law is not the only standard of success from the president's point of view, though it is usually the most important one. Where presidents seek an issue, not a bill, the analysis below will be less useful in explaining legislative outcomes.

Table 7.2 breaks success down by administration, presenting both weighted and unweighted mean success rates (a mean of 3 would mean that the president succeeded in attaining everything he asked for). As we might expect, Gerald Ford was least successful. In the weighted data,

TABLE 7.2
Mean Success, by President, 1949–1996

President	Weighted Mean	S.E.	Unweighted Mean	S.D. (N)
Truman (1949–1952)	1.28	.203	1.45	1.26 (31)
Eisenhower	1.73	.152	1.65	1.30 (63)
Kennedy	1.38	.262	1.30	1.35 (27)
Johnson	1.67	.199	1.74	1.25 (38)
Nixon	1.06	.196	1.07	1.23 (43)
Ford	0.85	.275	0.85	1.23 (20)
Carter	1.63	.234	1.59	1.29 (31)
Reagan	1.31	.160	1.29	1.22 (62)
Bush	1.18	.223	1.16	1.24 (31)
Clinton (1993–1996)	1.54	.209	1.53	1.22 (32)

the "winner" is Dwight Eisenhower, followed closely by Jimmy Carter and Lyndon Johnson. These results are tightly bunched enough to put LBJ highest if the data are unweighted, with Eisenhower second and Carter third. Although the high standing of Eisenhower may be surprising — his ranking on roll-call success is not as impressive, as Bond and Fleisher document — it is consistent with Peterson's findings.[13] The only shift in relative rank between the two datasets (keeping in mind that his analysis ends in 1984) is that the current study finds Carter to have been more successful. This is likely a function of the use of messages rather than their component proposals as the chief unit of analysis. Interestingly, Carter's support scores over time were quite high.[14]

It is important to note that aggregate results can hide wide variation. For example, Bill Clinton (using data only from his first term) ranks fourth, but this masks a dramatic drop-off in success from the 103rd to the 104th Congresses.[15] Year-by-year success rates are presented in the Appendix, table A.7, though the low *n* available for any given year means they should be interpreted with care.

Independent Variables

Centralization, of course, is the key independent variable. Additional measures associated with more or less centralization, as detailed in Chapter Six, have their own theoretical basis for inclusion; their second job is to serve as guards against finding a spurious relationship between centralization and success. To the extent that they help to predict (de)centralization, placing them on the same side of the equation as centralization will inflate the standard errors of each, making the analysis a stronger test of each measure. Variables include:

• *Cross-cutting jurisdictions.* A negative coefficient is predicted: the higher the number of jurisdictions involved, the less likely is success. This variable is defined in the same way as in Chapter Five; see the discussion there for more detail.

• The *reorganizational impact* of a policy, defined as it was earlier; a negative coefficient is predicted. However, note that formal reorganization plans submitted under authority of the Reorganization Act of 1949 (and subsequent extensions through the Carter administration) became law unless a resolution of disapproval was passed in Congress. This reversed the normal burden of action (or perhaps, rather, the burden of inertia) and gave such plans a significant boost. A dummy variable is therefore included to represent and control for reorganization plans, with a strong and positive coefficient expected for that measure.

• *Workload.* This variable is the total number of bills and joint resolutions filed in a given Congress.[16] A negative coefficient is expected, since an overloaded congressional agenda should result in the passage of fewer presidential measures. Utilizing the number of presidential proposals gave similar results.

• As before, *new items* are measured dichotomously (new = 1), with a negative coefficient expected. However, as noted in Chapter Six, what is new to the president may be old news to Congress. If so, this variable will likely prove insignificant.

• The *percentage of seats in Congress held by the president's co-partisans.* This, of course, is expected to be positive and quite telling in presidential success: the more Democrats in Congress during the term of a Democratic president, for example, the more proposals the latter is likely to see approved. As noted in Chapter Five, problems of multicollinearity prevent the use of both chambers in a single equation. Thus a single measure averaging the percentage of seats held in each chamber was utilized. Different permutations of each variable were estimated in separate models — using, for example, just the Senate's percentage of presidential co-partisans, and dummy variables for divided government — with little divergence. This makes sense: while simple majority status in and of itself is important, to attain success even majority presidents will almost always need to build cross-partisan coalitions. Thus the actual size of their partisan cohort is the appropriate measure.

• The *president's ideological distance from Congress.* The "real ADA" scores described in Chapter Five were used here to estimate the president's ideological proximity to the median voter in each chamber, calculated by taking the absolute value of the difference between the legislative median and the president. The Senate median and the estimates of the president's distance from the House Rules Committee (even more relevant to success, since this committee must consider most legislation moving through the lower chamber) were also used again here. As before, the latter are based on Poole-Rosenthal common space coordinates.

• *Policy complexity.* The three-point index developed earlier was utilized. Since complicated bills are, a priori, harder to pass than simple ones, a negative coefficient is predicted.

• The *priority* variable, measured by an item's inclusion in the State of the Union address, was mildly associated with increased centralization in Chapter Five and is included to address a complicating question of potential endogeneity. If presidents centralize controversial items that are harder in themselves to pass, the real determinant of failure in Congress is not centralization but the proposal's ex ante level of divisiveness. As discussed earlier, this relationship is hard to untangle, in part because of the difficulty in assessing policy controversy prior to a proposal's being formulated. The salience measure defined in Chapter Five was not utilized here, since it was not associated with centralization and its theoretic impact on success is ambiguous.[17]

• *Presidential approval.* As discussed in Chapter Six, there is little agreement on the proper specification of this variable or on whether it affects congressional voting behavior. Scholars have utilized annualized figures, state-specific polls, and measures of "shifts in range," generally but not inevitably to little result.[18] The simplest option is most appropriate here: it measures the percentage approving of the president in the most recent Gallup poll before a given program item's transmission to Congress.[19]

• If the *"two presidencies"* thesis holds true, presidents should get more of what they want in foreign policy. Thus the earlier measure of whether a policy is foreign or domestic in nature is included. Keep in mind that because the data used here exclude treaties, controversial foreign policy items may be undercounted here. On the other side of the scale, more or less routine foreign agreements requiring congressional approval *are* represented.[20] A positive coefficient is therefore expected, but should not be read as a conclusive test of the "two presidencies" thesis.

• *Focusing events* have a strong pull on the congressional agenda, enhancing members' desire to act in a manner for which they can take credit.[21] Thus the crisis variable from Chapter Five is used here as well, designating items sent to Congress by the president in response to an external event. A positive coefficient is again expected.

• *Time* is designated as the month of the president's term. The co-efficient of this variable should be negative, if only because the later something is proposed, the less time it has to get physically through the legislative process. But scholars have also argued that presidential effectiveness follows a cycle that peaks at the start of a term—the honeymoon period—and troughs in the fourth year, when the president is either running for reelection or serving as a "lame duck."[22] Either way, as the president's term progresses, prospects for legislative success should decline.[23]

• Since *staff size* proved to be associated with centralization, it should be included in this model as well as a control. No a priori prediction is made here as to its coefficient's likely direction; presumably an enlarged congressional relations staff would improve a president's odds for success, but a large EOP might also tend to isolate itself more from congressional consultation. The latter effect, though, should be picked up by the centralization variable itself.

• A last control variable takes into account the broad *fiscal climate* legislators face. When budgetary resources are scarce, proposals might well meet with less success (though, since proposals might *cut* spending, this should not invariably be true). The budgetary situation variable was therefore included. A positive coefficient would indicate that as surpluses grow, presidents have increasing success in Congress. Since centralization decreases under those circumstances, as shown in Chapter Five, inclusion of this control also prevents omitted variable bias.

As discussed throughout, the models used here do not try to measure directly the role and skill of the president himself—from aspects of his personality to his level of engagement in his legislative agenda to his use of his staff lobbyists in the Office of Legislative Affairs.[24] Still, as an additional check, differences across administrations were tested by utilizing dummy variables for each president. As discussed below, these prove to be insignificant, a finding that emphasizes the role of systemic factors. Table 7.3 sums up the discussion so far.

FINDINGS

Table 7.4 presents two ordered probit models assessing the basic "success" model with alternate measures of ideological proximity. The first column includes a floor measure of the ideological distance between Congress and president; the second uses instead a measure of the distance between the president and the congressional committee, calculated using common space coordinates. Other variants tested are dis-

TABLE 7.3
Summary of Independent Variables: Success in Congress

Variable	Measured as	Predicted Impact on Success in Congress
Centralization		
Centralization	Index (0–3)	Negative
Associated with (De)centralization and with success		
Cross-cutting	Number of agencies	Negative
Reorganization	Index (0–2)	Negative
Reorganization Plan	Dichotomous (reorg. plan = 1)	Positive
Workload	Number of proposals to a given Congress	Negative
Issue novelty	Dichotomous (new = 1)	Negative
Complexity	Index (1–3)	Negative
Congressional proximity (party)	Average % of House and Senate members of the president's party	Positive (more co-partisans → more success)
Congressional proximity (ideology)	Ideological distance between president and Sen. floor median ("Real ADA" scores)	Negative (larger distance → less success)
Congressional proximity (ideology)	Ideological distance between president and the House Rules Committee (Poole-Rosenthal common space coordinates)	Negative (larger distance → less success)
Associated with Success		
Policy type (foreign/domestic)	Index (−2 [domestic] to 2 [foreign])	Positive ("two presidencies")
Presidential approval	Gallup poll most closely preceding item	Positive
Month of term	Counted from start of administration, reset after re-election	Negative
Crisis (focusing event)	Dichotomous (crisis = 1)	Positive
Controls		
Priority/controversy	Dichotomous (included in State of the Union = 1)	Negative?
Staff size	EOP staff size	Control (positive?)

TABLE 7.3 (cont.)

Variable	Measured as	Predicted Impact on Success in Congress
Budget situation	Fiscal year deficit or surplus divided by total federal outlays	Control (positive?) (bigger surplus → more success)
Presidential style	Administration dummy variables	Control

Note: The dependent variable is an index (0–3) indicating an item's level of success in Congress.

cussed below, where appropriate. However, there was little statistical or substantive change in most variables across the specifications tested.

The alternate analysis that includes the nine dichotomous variables representing individual presidents, is not presented here in full. As in the earlier analysis of centralization, these variables prove insignificant. Since this offers little reason to think that personal skills have a *systematic* impact on congressional success, and since the model presented here offers no theoretical justification for keeping the dummies in the model, table 7.4 has the dual advantages of parsimony and substantive punch. As in Chapter Five, the biggest statistical change when the dummies are removed is the enhanced impact of the ideological distance between president and Congress. Again, this makes sense: given the difficulty of measuring ideology in the first place, and especially of distinguishing it from the person of the president, the capture of stray variation implemented by the inclusion of individual controls quite plausibly confounds its impact.[25] It should perhaps be stressed that using the presidency dummies makes no difference in the measure or magnitude of the main variable of interest for this analysis, centralization. That remains a consistent predictor of presidential frustration in Congress, no matter what specification is used.

Discussion

As expected, the "usual suspects" are strong predictors of legislative success. However, even controlling for these, centralization proves to be a considerable drain on presidential prospects in Congress.

Figure 7.1 puts this finding graphically. Utilizing the procedure for transforming ordered probit coefficients described in Chapter Five, I estimated the impact of moving centralization across its range — from least to most centralized. As figure 7.1 shows, this shift increases

TABLE 7.4
Determinants of Presidential Success in Congress (ordered probit)

	Floor Median		Rules Committee Median	
	Coeff. (S.E.)	t-statistic (Prob.)	Coeff. (S.E.)	t-statistic (Prob.)
Centralization	−.147 (.069)	−2.14 (.033)	−.147 (.071)	−2.22 (.027)
Cross-cutting jurisdiction	.027 (.028)	0.98 (.328)	.027 (.028)	0.96 (.336)
Reorg. impact	−.111 (.103)	−1.07 (.284)	−.111 (.098)	−1.13 (.257)
Reorganization plan	2.079 (.619)	3.36 (.001)	2.061 (.579)	3.56 (.000)
Workload	−.000 (.000)	−0.41 (.684)	−.000 (.000)	−0.53 (.594)
New issue	.117 (.151)	0.78 (.437)	.105 (.151)	0.69 (.488)
Complexity	−.177 (.092)	−1.92 (.056)	−.181 (.091)	−2.00 (.046)
Avg. % Cong. seats	.017 (.008)	2.07 (.039)	.014 (.008)	1.81 (.070)
Senate median	−1.012 (.794)	−1.27 (.203)		
House Rules			−.846 (.489)	−1.73 (.083)
Policy type (dom./for.)	.252 (.043)	5.87 (.000)	.254 (.043)	5.89 (.000)
Pres. approval	.009 (.005)	1.71 (.089)	.009 (.005)	1.69 (.091)
Month of term	−.012 (.006)	−2.18 (.030)	−.012 (.005)	−2.26 (.024)
Crisis	.564 (.193)	2.92 (.004)	.559 (.191)	2.93 (.003)
Priority	−.046 (.136)	−0.34 (.734)	−.058 (.141)	−0.41 (.682)
Budget situation	−.926 (.853)	−1.09 (.278)	−.736 (.799)	−0.92 (.357)
Staff size	−.000 (.001)	−0.17 (.862)	−.000 (.001)	−0.22 (.826)
n	363		363	
LL	−417.9		−417.3	
Prob. $> \chi^2$	.000		.000	

TABLE 7.4 (cont.)

	Floor Median		Rules Committee Median	
	Coeff. (S.E.)	t-statistic (Prob.)	Coeff. (S.E.)	t-statistic (Prob.)
% correctly predicted	53.4		53.4	
PRE	24.9		24.9	

Note: The dependent variable here is an ordinal index of presidential success in Congress (0–3), as defined above. Coefficients are estimated using ordered probit analysis, correcting for the stratified nature of the sample. In the first column of each model are presented each variable's coefficient and its standard error; the second column gives the t-statistic for the coefficient and the probability of having obtained that value simply by chance, using a two-tailed test. Cut point coefficients are not reported. LL stands for the "log likelihood" value of the equation, which indicates through a chi-squared test whether the model leads to a significant improvement in explaining the variance of the dependent variable compared with simply tracking the overall distribution. PRE stands for the proportionate reduction in error in predicting specific categorical outcomes compared with the overall distribution.

the chances that a program item will fail outright by 16 percentage points, ceteris paribus, and decreases the likelihood that a president will achieve even limited compromise by close to 15 percentage points.

To aid in the interpretation of the model as a whole, a number of similar transformations were calculated and are presented in figures 7.2 and 7.3.[26] As before, these indicate the percentage change in the probability of obtaining a result in one of the categories of centralization, given a shift in one independent variable and holding all other independent variables at their means. In order to make value changes comparable across what may be very different ranges, the shift is once again put in percentile terms, showing a change from the 10th to 90th percentile value of each measure (except for dichotomous variables, which are shifted from 0 to 1). The shift between the 25th and the 75th percentile is again shown as a subset of the larger change.

Figure 7.2 reflects the independent variables' impact on presidential success — the impact of the percentile shift on the likelihood of the president's getting essentially all of what he asked for (that is, "success" = 3). Figure 7.3 reverses the question to examine presidential failure. The two are related, of course, but they are not mirror images. Once again, the variables' underlying confidence intervals should be taken into account when assessing their impact.

As noted, the standard measures of presidential success remain strong predictors in these data. The coefficient for the percentage of seats held

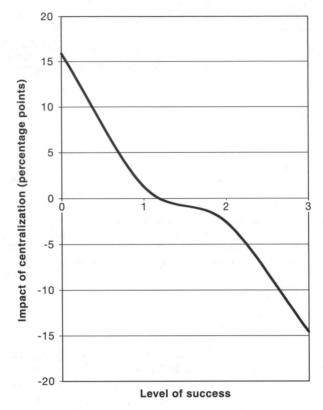

Figure 7.1   Impact of Centralization on Success in Congress (estimated mean impact given shift in range, other variables constant; simulated from ordered probit equation).

by the president's party in Congress is strongly significant and positive; this holds true for a simple divided government dummy variable as well. Moving from the 10th to the 90th percentile level of seats (a shift from 42 to 64 percent of seats), all else equal, results in a 12 percentage point increase in the likelihood of the president's getting a proposal passed in its entirety, and a near-symmetric 13 percentage point decrease in the likelihood that he will get nothing at all. That shift, obviously, is of landslide proportions; for comparison's sake, a shift from the mean value (51 percent) up one standard deviation (to 59.8 percent) results in shifts of $+5.0$ and -5.3 percentage points in the likelihood of success and failure, respectively.

The impact of the ideological distance between the president and Congress is largely tied up in the party measure, at the aggregate level; each strengthens notably in alternate specifications when the other is

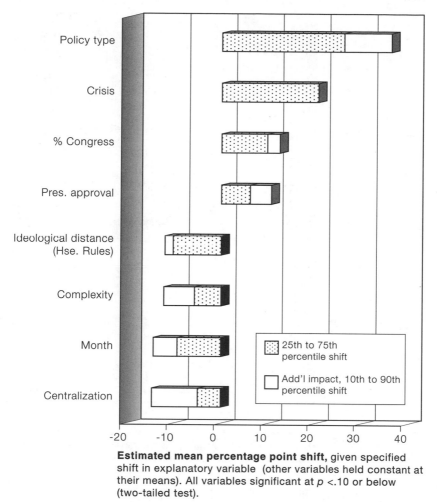

Estimated mean percentage point shift, given specified shift in explanatory variable (other variables held constant at their means). All variables significant at $p < .10$ or below (two-tailed test).

Figure 7.2   Determinants of Success in Congress

excluded.[27] But when measured at the committee level, the coefficient representing the president's ideological distance from House Rules is independently significant (at $p < .05$ in specifications without party controls, and at $p < .10$ with them, as in the second column of table 7.4). The larger the gap from the president to the median voter on the House Rules Committee, for example, the less likely is his program item to win approval: for any single proposal, moving from the 10th percentile distance to the 90th percentile decreases the chance of success by 13 percentage points, all else equal.

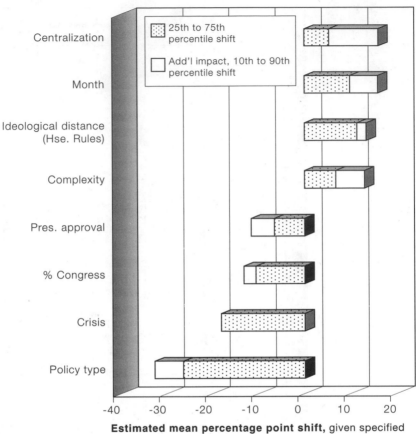

Estimated mean percentage point shift, given specified
shift in explanatory variable (other variables held constant at
their means). All variables significant at $p < .10$ or below
(two-tailed test).

Figure 7.3   Determinants of Failure in Congress

The more complex a given message, the more likely the president is to
have to compromise. Further, the earlier in his term the president pro-
poses an item to Congress, the more likely he is to get what he wants
(indeed, shifting from the 10th to the 90th percentile here shows the
chance of outright failure increasing about 16 percentage points as time
ticks on, ceteris paribus).

Foreign policy proposals and those prompted by critical external
events are also far more likely to gain congressional approval, all else
equal. The trigger of a focusing event increases the chances of presidential success by 18 percentage points. And in these data, purely foreign
items are some 30 percentage points less likely than purely domestic

items to fail to pass in any form. Again, because of the nature of the data it is unclear how pure a test of the "two presidencies" this proves to be. Still, it is a strong finding, and perhaps not surprising: recent examinations of the thesis have utilized presidents' success or support on roll-call votes, and it makes sense for presidents to fare better on their own foreign policy initiatives than when taking positions on a range of measures that includes congressional proposals.[28] All of these variables have coefficients that are statistically significant at $p < .05$ or below. The coefficient for presidential popularity is in the expected direction — indicating that more popular presidents are more successful ($p < .10$) — but this is not a powerful finding substantively. A 20-point shift upward in approval (from 46 to 66 percent approval) implies just a 6 percentage point jump in the likelihood of unalloyed presidential success, all else equal.

Most of the other variables are in the expected direction but are not statistically significant. Workload has a negative coefficient — the larger the legislative agenda, the less likely any one part of it is to pass, but this effect is not robust across specifications (though in some models, not reported here, $p < .10$); likewise, items with a reorganizational impact are less successful, with the strong exception of formal reorganization plans.[29]

It is worth concluding by considering in more detail the impact of centralization on success. In all specifications, its coefficient is negative and strongly significant. This finding bolsters the theoretical expectations of Chapter Six: centralizing program formulation has its managerial uses, but it is not an effective strategy for success in Congress.

As already seen in figure 7.1, a shift from a department-centered formulation process to one kept within the White House can affect presidential success rates quite dramatically. The flip side is also true: a decrease in centralization across its range (that is, from 3 to 0) increases the president's chances of getting what he wants by 14 percentage points and decreases the chance of outright failure by 16 percentage points, all else equal. Even controlling for a variety of other conditions, centralizing matters for success — less than party or crisis, but usually more than complexity or ideology.

The result is a burden presidents don't need — and that they take upon themselves when they follow a centralizing strategy. Still, the results suggest a useful strategy for presidents. As figures 7.2 and 7.3 indicate, the impact of centralization on success is strongest in its tail values as opposed to its mid-range: much of the shift in success comes as centralization moves from its 10th to its 90th percentile as opposed to its 25th to its 75th percentile values. Thus, while shifting from a preponderantly department-led process to one that is EOP-led weighs

down success by 15-plus percentage points, shifting from a mixed process led by the departments to a mixed process led by EOP staff decreases the president's chances of complete legislative success by slightly
more than 5 percentage points. This effect is hardly negligible, and it
is quite consistent: each shift across a single category decreases the
chances of success, and increases those of failure, by between 5 and 6
percentage points. But it does suggest that, all else equal, presidents
comfortable with managing both EOP and departmental staff will lose
relatively little by putting the former in charge of a mixed process.
Using the White House staff as a substitute for the departments may be
fatal to legislative success; using it to coordinate them instead seems to
keep the damage within limits.[30] The bruise to the legislative process
may well be worth the risk to presidents seeking to simultaneously maximize their executive initiative and legislative clout.

Concluding Questions

This chapter has demonstrated that centralized formulation processes
hurt the chances that an item on the presidential program will receive
congressional support. Information and bargaining again play a key
role, this time from the legislative perspective. Members of Congress
know less about an item being crafted in the White House than they do
about a departmental production, and have less reason to believe that
the information they do receive from EOP sources is reliable. When
congressional expertise was available to presidents, decentralization was
a more likely choice. This implies a level of prior consultation with
Congress (and possibly with departmental constituencies) more extensive than that usually obtained with centralized processes, helping to
bridge the institutional and attitudinal disconnect between presidential
staffers and members of Congress.

Why would a president centralize, knowing his chances of failing in
Congress increase? One answer is that he may *not* know, at least not
until the experience of his term has brought the lesson home.

Even then, though, presidents might rationally turn to centralization.
For one thing, this result should be seen in probabilistic, not determinis-
tic, terms. One should not conclude automatically that a corresponding
counterfactual (program X would have passed, had a decentralized process been followed) holds true in any given case.[31] For another, presidents are caught in a cross fire. On the one hand, they need to manage
the executive branch in such a way as to ensure the compilation of a
program consistent with their preferences. On the other, they need that
program passed through an entirely separate institution. Presidents
might be better off decentralizing policy more generally, but the burdens

of management are often sufficient incentive to shift the process the other way: formulation comes first in temporal sequence, and short-term needs often trump long-term strategy in political life. Skillful governance of a mixed process may be one cost-effective, if hardly cost-free, answer to the dilemma. As I have argued throughout, presidents will make this decision on a case-by-case basis, influenced by the informational options available to them in each instance.

The expectation that presidents can lead — even control — Congress is unrealistic in any case. As Kenneth Collier argues, "Americans continue to expect a level of legislative leadership from their president unsupported by the system of separation of powers created by the founders and made even more unlikely by the independent-minded lawmakers that voters send to Washington."[32] But if the expectations are fanciful, the realities of executive branch management put them even further out of reach. It is not surprising that, as discussed in the next chapter, presidents have sometimes sought to expand their policy reach outside the legislative arena.

Indeed, simultaneously riding herd on the modern presidency and the modern Congress is a task worthy of a rodeo cowboy. It's enough to make presidents reach for the whiskey bottle themselves.

CHAPTER EIGHT

Hard Choices

"EVERY president wants to make policy," note Laurence Lynn and David Whitman, and every president since Harry Truman has put the heart of his policy agenda into a legislative program.[1] The president's program represents his comprehensive evaluation of the nation's problems and his specific proposals for addressing them. As such it is the product of any number of hard choices.

This book opened by sketching the process by which President John F. Kennedy translated principle into policy proposal in the field of civil rights. From the outset of the modern presidency to George W. Bush and beyond, presidents facing the demand for annual programmatic proposals face parallel sets of choices, similar institutional and management needs. In making critical decisions at the intersection of substance and strategy, presidents need information about where each road leads. Each program item represents a presidential choice among many potential streams of advice about policy and politics. Where should presidents invest their resources for policy formulation?[2]

We can now fill in some of the ongoing contexts that guide those choices. I have argued that though choice is constant, the basis for choice is contingent. Presidents seek to obtain reliable information about the political and substantive ramifications of their legislative program at minimal cost, and utilize their staff and extra-staff resources accordingly. They pay heed to the specifics of each proposal and to the political environment in which it must flourish. They seek to minimize their transaction costs as they bargain for information and expertise, effectively manipulating a complex institutional palate. In short, the chief executive is indeed an executive.

This concluding chapter does three things. It reviews the findings presented earlier and places them in the broader context of a research agenda exploring the institutional and administrative presidencies. It discusses the limitations of this approach, and makes suggestions for future research. Finally, it suggests the utility of a model of informational bargaining in examining presidential behavior and assessing presidential leadership.

OLD QUESTIONS, NEW FINDINGS

This study was motivated by two related facts. First, the institution of the president's legislative program, now a half century old, shifted the burden of legislative agenda setting. Presidents found their very ability to lead assessed by their proficiency with, and success in, their congressional endeavors. Yet we knew little about the way in which the president's program was formulated, or even what it contained, year to year. The empirical record has been grounded mainly in focused case studies or in limited subsets of presidential proposals.

Second, while study of the "institutional presidency" has become a cornerstone of the field—rooted in the development of large and specialized White House staffs—there has been little progress made in cumulative theorizing about how presidents use those staffs and others as part of a broader management effort. When will presidents rely on White House staff, when on the Cabinet, to perform needed tasks? How has this relationship developed? Has it changed over time?

The theory of centralization has dominated the study of this question.[3] This approach, building on the rational choice branch of the new institutionalism, posits that presidents react to an increasingly balky institutional environment by shifting policy formulation resources away from the wider executive branch bureaucracy and toward organizations and staffers closer to hand and more responsive to their needs. That is, presidents centralize; and given the near-linear rise in the size and complexity of the government they seek to control, the result will be a similarly increasing proportion of program formulation in the White House rather than via the older, but now unworkable, model of "Cabinet government."

The inherent plausibility of linear centralization has enshrined it as the academic conventional wisdom. Still, while the data problems noted earlier make its claims hard to assess, even on its own terms it falls short. This is not because its basic logic is flawed: presidents do react to their institutional environment, trying to maximize their impact on governmental outputs. But the implication of that very insight is that the dimension of the environment most relevant to the choices at hand must be scrutinized. And if we look to the institutional environment surrounding presidential choices with regard to legislative program development, we see not a sharp line but the blur of motion. The analytic key is the transaction—each item in the president's program—not the aggregate level of output. And each comes in its own setting, with dimensions defined in part by the nature of the item itself. Although the macro-environment will matter for creating presidential capacity to choose different formulation strategies—presidents with no program did not need to create tools for centralized policy formulation — the institutional dimensions associated with individual program items should be the primary influences on presidential choices regarding program management. Centralization, then, is not linear, but contingent.

If so, what conditions underlie presidential decision making? The choice of formulation strategies will hinge on the relative costs of each programmatic transaction, as measured in the currency of information. As they formulate their program items, presidents need to know what potential solutions exist, the effect each option will have, and the prospect each has for attracting political support. Presidents want to offer an item closest to their preferences and most likely to "solve" the problem at hand, without losing sight of political realities. To calculate this, they must choose how to manage the policy formulation process. That is, they must choose whether to centralize and to what degree. This choice will be guided by a calculation of which source of information provides the optimal combination of reliability and cost — the cheaper, in a managerial sense, the better. The cost of information cannot be calculated to the cent. But we can define what the transaction costs paradigm calls "shift parameters" — conditions under which some options are more costly than others — and thus make predictions about the effects, in direction and intensity, of different management environments on presidents' choices regarding centralization and policy formulation.

Chapter Two presented a number of such parameters. Centralized information will be relatively cheaper, I argued, when the president wants quick action or when an issue is new to a president; when a proposal cuts across a number of departmental jurisdictions, or when it seeks to reorganize or reorient agency management; or when a large total agenda makes it more efficient for presidents to institutionalize a staff to perform the repeated tasks associated with that agenda, with the size of that staff serving as a post hoc indicator.

The cost of decentralized policy formulation will fall, in relative terms, when a given proposal is technically complex. Decentralization will also be cheaper when presidents have ready access to reliable legislative and bureaucratic resources and advice, and reside in close ideological proximity to their preferences. That is, presidents will decentralize when the preferences of the bureaus are more congruent with the president — either because the president has successfully "politicized" a given agency or because the leanings of its congressional co-principals are also in line with presidential desires.

These hypotheses were tested using a comprehensive new database of legislative program items, whose provenance was tracked through archival and secondary research. Little evidence was found of increased centralization over time; instead, it became clear that presidents have been flexible centralizers (and decentralizers) from the genesis of the legislative program to the present day. Ordered probit analysis showed further that, even controlling for a wide range of alternative hypotheses, the informational conditions underlying contingent centralization held up as strong predictors of presidential formulation strategies. Temporal variables showed no substantive or statistical significance. But each of the five shift parameters noted above had a role in centralization or decentralization. Chapter Five provides a detailed discussion of those findings. In brief, innovative proposals that cross-cut a variety of departmental jurisdictions, that implemented reorganizations of or personnel reforms in the executive branch, that were new to the president, that occurred when centralized capacity was high, or that were formulated in times when reliable extra–White House expertise was particularly expensive were significantly more likely to be centralized. Decentralized (most often, as expected, mixed) strategies were most common when proposals were technically complex. Centralization rose with a president's ideological distance from legislative median voters and declined as that distance diminished.

Centralization also declined when an inner Cabinet department was involved in policy formulation. This suggests that politicization is a substitute strategy for centralization rather than a complement to it, though a more definite conclusion awaits future research.

A negative finding is worth noting: the coefficients for the dichotomous variables controlling for each individual president under study proved to be both individually and jointly insignificant. This suggests that when controlling for the management contexts elaborated here, presidential style is not an important predictor of presidential choice with regard to the formulation of legislative proposals. Rather, institutional variables account for much of the variation often attributed to individual presidents. This does not mean that presidential skill has no role in presidential managerial success. But presidents do seem to respond consistently to the management environment that faces them. Under some conditions centralization appears to be a necessary strategy if the president is to extract from the executive branch a policy proposal that suits his preferences. Its benefits are in its managerial capacity to bend a sprawling executive branch to presidential judgment.

But how well does centralization work in terms of a key presidential objective for the program, namely, its success in Congress? The idea, after all, is that centralization cuts the Gordian knot tying presidents to the inflated expectations of their leadership ability. But the findings here are that centralization's blade is too dull for that task.

In fact, the very contexts that make centralization attractive make legislative success less likely, given the institutional structure and imperatives of the legislative branch. Congress is fragmented; the legislative gauntlet is time consuming and marked with a plethora of veto points. An item crossing or reorganizing departmental (and therefore congressional committee) jurisdictions will already face an uphill battle.

Yet even then, controlling for all this, items resulting from a centralized formulation process should do less well in Congress than comparable items formulated elsewhere. The reason stems from Congress's own informational dynamics. Consultative connections are poorly developed between the White House and the committees that shape congressional consideration, in sharp contrast to the networks that link legislature and bureaucracy. Further, centralized staffers (with the president's political needs firmly in mind) often give short shrift to the competing incentives facing legislators. The result is an institutional disconnect. All else equal, centralization should be a drag on legislative success.

So it is. As detailed in Chapter Seven, the "usual suspects" of the presidential-congressional relations literature are strong predictors of program success: party, ideology, policy type, and focusing events all play a major role. But even so, centralization proves a consistent predictor of presidential frustration. Moving from a wholly decentralized to a wholly centralized process increases the chances of a president's failing to achieve even limited compromise on a given program item by more than 15 percentage points. More limited shifts decrease the likelihood of success by 5 or 6 percentage points each time a process grows more centralized, all else equal.

Why do presidents centralize, if they know it hurts their prospects of success?

The first reason is that they may not know it, at least not until well into their term. The lack of institutional memory in the modern White House means that presidents and their staffs learn much the hard way, and the impact of centralization is likely no exception. Ignorance combines with arrogance — the notion that what prior presidents have failed to do, our newly victorious band of brothers and sisters will achieve with ease — to dangerous effect.[4]

However, two other factors make centralization attractive even to informed and humble presidents. One is that sequence matters. The immediate task is to manage policy formulation; achieving a legislative proposal that meets the president's needs and matches his preferences is a hard task in its own right. Presidents might be forgiven for letting the short-term need outweigh the long-run goal. The long run, after all, political actors tend to think, can always be fixed when and if it gets here.

So it is important, finally, to remember that the damage done by centralization is probabilistic. It is one factor among many that presidents must juggle, and all else is rarely equal. Whether the managerial benefits outweigh the legislative baggage a centralized process may carry with it down Pennsylvania Avenue is for each president to decide. The answer, I suspect, will often be yes. But as with so much else in American politics, tactical choices about program management may accrue unanticipated strategic consequences. Centralization is supposed to provide an advantage to presidents, but proves instead a mixed blessing. At the least, these results highlight an ongoing dilemma of presidential power in a separated system — and should make presidents think twice.

In the end, then, this study answers three central questions. First, what does the president's program actually look like, in terms of its scope and substance? Second, under what conditions do presidents follow a centralizing strategy, and are these consistent with the predictions derived from a model of contingent centralization grounded in informational transaction costs? Third, do centralizing strategies enhance presidents' chances of legislative success in Congress? Taken together, the second and third questions — most broadly answered "yes" and "no," respectively — provide an assessment of the contexts under which centralization "works" for presidents.

LIMITS AND EXTENSIONS

The research presented here is compatible with an array of other scholarship on the institutional presidency, exploring how the organizational role presidents play makes sense of the behavior of very different individuals. Although different scholars have meant different things by "institutionalization" as it reflects the presidency, an institutional perspective generally seeks to examine the office as an ongoing collection of regularized processes and roles. It argues that the "cumulative heritage of precedent and multitude of expected actions which have come to be associated with the office over time" set up incentives and constraints for presidential action.[5] And so it moves away from using presidents themselves as dependent variables and toward examining presidential *choices* in a specific strategic context. Since the 1940s, the formulation of a legislative program has been a task each president must address — the set of choices presidents make to meet that expectation are best examined as institutional choices, not quirks of personality. The findings of this book will, I hope, go some way toward convincing readers of the utility of this approach.

Note though that an institutional vantage need not ignore real-life complexity. Chapter Three, for example, showed that the conventional account of presidential program formulation, a picture broadly in line with the predictions of linear centralization, was too tightly cropped. A step back revealed a more complicated mosaic of presidential management, showing that the capacity for centralized strategies was in place as early as the Truman administration (that is, in a supposedly decentralized era), and that for every account of centralization or decentralization in the conventional wisdom there is an equal and opposite account to be put forth. Searching for regularities in presidential behavior stemming from the president's institutional vantage actually required the consideration of more qualitative detail, not less.

The appropriate response here was to pursue large-n statistical analysis. This will not always be the case; it depends on the question being asked.[6] But the experience of researching this book does suggest that both qualitative research and quantitative research need to be determinedly and reciprocally cumulative. After all, a continuing caution for the field as political methodology grows ever more complex is that coding can only be as reliable as the research that underlies it. In the areas of interest to presidency scholars, good measures are hard to find, and measurement error is rife among those that can be calculated. Data may be truncated, interrupted, inconsistent, or even inaccurate — a problem encountered even in statistical series collected by government agencies[7] — or they may simply not be good proxies for the underlying dynamic of interest. In part this is because the complexities of the office are inherently difficult to quantify; in part, though, it is because consolidating such data has not been a priority of scholars interested in the subfield.[8] Both conditions demand attention. We need to sharpen our questions and also to gather the rich detail of presidential politics into coherent vantages on those questions. Systematic quantitative analysis must be built on careful archival work: these approaches need to be viewed as symbiotic, not exclusive, tools for researching the presidency.

THE LEGISLATIVE PROGRAM AND UNILATERAL ACTION

If extant data impose one limit on what we understand about the presidential program, the very nature of that program imposes a limit on the understanding it imparts about presidential policymaking in general. Not all policy formulation, after all, is legislatively grounded, and a number of observers have descried a rise in presidential administrative strategies that take advantage of opportunities for unilateral action.[9] If dealing with Congress brings grief, presidents might be forgiven for asking: why bother with Congress at all? The wave of regulations promulgated by the outgoing Clinton administration after the 2000 election make this question particularly salient.

Rulemaking was not a new strategy, though, even to President Clinton. In 1995 he had mused to an interviewer, "I had overemphasized in my first two years . . . the importance of legislative battles as opposed to the other things that the president ought to be doing. And I think now we have a better balance of both using the Presidency as a bully pulpit and the President's power of the Presidency to *do* things, actually accomplish things, and . . . not permitting the Presidency to be defined only by relations with the Congress."[10] As Clinton's presidency progressed, the *Public Papers* revealed a wide range of efforts to "do things" via executive order, executive agreement, or directive memoranda to the departments and agencies. The regulations rushed into print in advance of George W. Bush's inauguration—ranging from ergonomic protections for American workers to limits on road building in the national parks—served in this sense as merely the icing on the cake.[11] The general strategy finds a ready echo in other administrations. For example, an aide to the elder George Bush, Dan McGroarty, argues that President Bush did in fact care about domestic issues, "but everything we did was DOA [dead on arrival] in Congress. How long do you think that an operation will continue doing that over and over and over and over again when everything is declared DOA? As opposed to going to the constitutional side of the equation—the latitude the president has in foreign policy, the interest and expertise George Bush has in foreign policy, the events of the world in 1989? Given all of those factors, where do you spend your time?"[12]

As this comment suggests, presidents have a number of ways to avoid grappling with Capitol Hill. Foreign policy, where (as discussed in Chapter Five) legislation is often less necessary and presidential unilateral capacity more developed, is an appealing vehicle. Another is to reshape the policy landscape with "one stroke of the pen" via executive order, as presidents often promise, and sometimes deliver.

The question, then, is not whether unilateral action is important to presidents: it is, and probably more so than generally credited.[13] At the same time, as Fleisher and Bond note, "there is little of significance that does not eventually come to the floor of the House or Senate."[14] Legislative and executive strategies exist together in the presidential toolbox: each supplements the other. George W. Bush, for example, used both instruments in responding to the terrorist attacks of September 2001. On September 24 he issued an executive order freezing the financial assets of twenty-seven persons and organizations linked to global terrorism; two weeks later he swore in Pennsylvania governor Tom Ridge as director of a new EOP agency created by executive order, the Office of Homeland Security. At the same time, Bush asked for a wide array of legislation ranging from congressional authorization for the use of "all necessary and appropriate" military force (see P.L. 107-40), to $20 billion in emergency supplemental spending, to a bailout package for the airline industry, to tax relief aimed at stimulating the economy, to law enforcement measures designed to ease the detection and detention of suspected terrorists. The strategies were linked both temporally and substantively. Some of the executive actions would ultimately prompt the formulation of new legislation; some of the legislation would in turn strengthen the ability of the president to act unilaterally. This symbiosis is not new: a 1961 memo from the Budget Bureau pointed out to the Kennedy White House that "executive orders . . . can occasionally cause more of a stir than legislation, and they can have a lot to do with the President's legislative relations."[15]

The interesting question is how to explicate that link. Each means of policymaking has costs and benefits to presidents and to the political process as a whole. Still, presidents are adept at figuring out the relative payoffs they accrue from different managerial choices, given the context in which they are made. Each managerial context within the wider macro-environment lends its own push to the direction of that wider arena. Recall the discussion of "phase shifts" in Chapter Two. The phase shift activating presidents' unilateral strategies and that making possible centralized legislative policy formulation come at different times — but once in place each shapes the other, making each strategy more or less attractive. That is, the choice of whether to follow an executive-centered or legislative strategy can be thought of as another part of the bargaining sequence, one analytically prior to that discussed in this book: before formulating legislation, the president must decide that a legislative strategy offers the most cost-effective solution to his policymaking problem. In creating the Office of Homeland Security by executive order, for example, the second President Bush rebuffed those in Congress who wanted to create a new Cabinet department for the same purpose. In this decision, as in others, the president had to gauge a set of managerial contexts, some of them quite familiar. What sort of policy is it: is the executive action within the president's formal powers? Where does it fit along the White House–departmental divide? How close is Congress to the president — that is, how likely are legislators to approve the president's statutory request or to overturn a presidential executive order? What impact will evading, or engaging, Congress, have on future interbranch relations? Rarely is the decision a simple question of substitution. A hostile Congress is neither a necessary nor a sufficient condition for unilateral action.[16]

All else equal, presidents should prefer legislation to executive action, for several reasons. One is that it broadens the scope of presidential authority. Although presidents have often pushed the boundaries, they are constrained by law in what they can achieve by unilateral action in the absence of statutory delegation.[17] And such action may well fail outright. The relative permanence of legislation is its trump card: executive orders can be superseded by acts of Congress, by court order, or by subsequent executive orders. Something of a ping-pong effect can ensue: President Clinton, taking office in 1993, reversed President Reagan's executive order limiting aid to organizations providing abortion counseling abroad, which was then reinstated by President Bush in January 2001.[18] Congress, while handicapped by its own collective action problems, can act swiftly when it chooses. And in many cases deterrence is enough: in 1993, a Clinton promise to eliminate discrimination against gays in the armed services was hastily recast when widespread opposition arose in the military and in Congress.[19] Congress later enhanced its ability to overturn regulations, using this review power in 2001 to annul Department of Labor standards regarding repetitive stress injuries and workplace ergonomics.[20]

Even if Congress fails to reverse a presidential decision, broad unilateral change can have a grave impact on presidential-legislative relations. A 1967 case illuminates the point: that year's Civil Rights Act focused on eliminating discrimination in housing, but President Johnson rejected demands by some in the black community that he issue an executive order to that effect.[21] Johnson "thought that any act like this which was done purely by the White House without the support of Congress would be greeted as a virtual usurpation of authority and power."[22] Given that the president *must* deal with Congress on a wide range of issues, a real risk is that even successful unilateral action can poison the well.

In short, abiding policy change requires widespread political support. As a Nixon staffer commented on his boss's use of executive orders, "we could have accomplished much more through legislative channels. If you want some lasting impact, it has to come through statutes."[23] And presidents with an eye on their place in history want just that. This requires in turn that presidents build consensus — in short, it requires the hard work of educating and persuading. Presidents seeking to unite, not divide, will find greater payoffs on the legislative side of the ledger.

With all this in mind, presidents may decide that some impact is better than none. The costs of legislative failure are high, after all, especially for activist presidents. Clinton aide Rahm Emanuel commented, "sometimes we use [an executive order] in reaction to legislative delay or setbacks. Sometimes we do it to lead by example and force the legislative hand. Obviously, you'd rather pass legislation that can do X, but you're willing to make whatever progress you can on an agenda item."[24]

Further, while executive action seen as illegitimate can undermine a president's reputation, skillfully used it may also serve as a valuable bargaining tool. For while, as already noted, most important matters will at some point arrive in Congress, it matters how and under what circumstances they get there. For example, an executive order might reshape the burden of action, shifting the status quo: legislators will find it easier to block proposed change than to act affirmatively to overturn the facts on the ground.[25] By changing the sequence of decisions, and the costs and benefits associated with them, the president can structure congressional choice. When presidents consider legislative policy formulation, they must take into account the institutional terrain their prior choices have created. This calculation might itself shape the centralization decision. At the least, it should make us cognizant that bargaining presidents are at the heart even of the institutional presidency.

THE STRUCTURE OF LEADERSHIP: INFORMATION AND PRESIDENTIAL MANAGEMENT

This brings us full circle. How does the president become a leader, rather than a clerk; how does he channel the demands and expectations of other actors to his own advantage? One way is through the structuring of others' choices, and his own. Each president must submit a legislative program, but the shaping and formulation of that program — its substance, its relation to other presidential objectives, and its perception by the public and by other political actors — is largely discretionary. "Legislative drafting," Lyndon Johnson once noted, "is a political art."[26] These are hard choices, and in them lie the seeds of presidential success or failure.

Much important contemporary work on the presidency and Congress has returned to an old notion, the separation of powers that underlies the American system of government.[27] This serves to emphasize the importance of interbranch bargaining to outcomes of policy and politics, a lesson reinforced by the findings here. The presidential vantage is not atop government, as we often persist in thinking, but as part of an interlocking system of competing powers and "tandem institutions."[28] Despite presidents' natural craving for "control," there is a tactical connection between politics and policy that requires inclusion rather than command. In the American system, policy is made *by* politics, not above them.

But this is not the story's only moral. Another is that at least part of the outcome of a given interbranch bargaining process hinges on the intrabranch bargaining that precedes it. Presidents who succeed in structuring to their own advantage the sequential bargains the program requires, with their own staffs and with Congress, will be those most effective in the exercise of presidential power. Presidential leadership rests on presidential management. And Dwight Eisenhower was right: "Leadership is as vital in conference as it is in battle."[29]

How might presidents do a better job of this? One answer lies in linking Eisenhower's insight to one rather older: Napoleon Bonaparte's observation that "a leader has the right to be beaten — but never the right to be surprised."[30] This book has focused on the kinds of informational transactions presidents conduct and the consequences for legislative policy formulation of different advising processes in the executive branch. Different organizational choices mean the president gets different information. The underlying challenge for presidents seeking to limit surprises is to structure their flow of advice to attain the information they want and need. The underlying challenge for scholars is to help them do it.

One key to future research is the broader exploration of presidential staff structures in informational terms. What impact do different advisory structures have on the nature and amount of information the president receives?[31] In a real sense, the near infinite supply of potential information facing the president is like the chaos public choice theorists see in mass unstructured preferences: decisions cycle endlessly unless some sort of equilibrium is imposed.[32] Decisions about staff institutions serve as an agenda, ordering — but also limiting — the information made available to the president. Like any sort of decision tree, the shape of the executive office hierarchy will affect the options and "narrow the choice set" available for presidential consideration.[33] That is, since "policymaking involves making comparisons (of pieces of information, of policy options, or of proposals for implementation), . . . an organization's structure affects who compares what with what, so that different structures can produce different policy outcomes."[34] Systematic study of those structures can help us give presidents good advice about how to get good advice. Given the bounds within which presidents operate, the ability to lead might well depend on the president's skill in protecting his prerogatives of choice. Limitations, as the Framers realized long ago, are not without their advantages; "without omniscience, omnipotence might be dangerous."[35] But must presidents fall so far short of omniscience?

Once again centralization serves as a good jumping-off point. It is often argued that the policy outcomes produced by centralization are worse than their decentralized counterparts; even many of those who accept centralization as inexorable castigate presidents' quest for responsiveness. Walter Williams, for example, decries "the destructive nature of responsive competence for presidential policymaking when loyalists have limited policy skills."[36] Yet it seems clear, given the scope and complexity of contemporary public policy, that from an informational vantage presidents need a responsive staff. The president does need help, perhaps more so today than ever. As John Hart notes, "politicization of the institutional presidency has been a cause of concern to post-Watergate reformers because it runs counter to so many of the . . . textbook virtues of neutral competence. To a succession of presidents, however, these virtues are found only in textbooks."[37]

That said, there seems to be a ceiling as well as a floor on the use of centralized staff for policy advice and development.[38] There is not enough space, physically or institutionally, in the White House; and White House staff simply don't know enough to help presidents fill out their entire programmatic agenda. As a result presidents must learn the best means of working with the wider bureaucracy, of making bureaus' preferences more congruent with their own—and of learning from what the bureaus have to offer. Cabinet councils and interdepartmental committees offer one means of doing this; the many observations of mixed strategies, where presidents seek to provide leadership and direction without losing the benefits of consultation, suggest that this is an area of ongoing experimentation. Presidents must seek to organize their offices in such a way as to assure themselves a flow of information that takes advantage of the differential talents of their various staff resources.

The point returns to the presidential perspective. From a president's viewpoint, a problem is not domestic or foreign—it is a problem, period, and must be dealt with of a piece with a dismaying number of other problems. This requires tying together the pieces of information and advice garnered from different sources. Clearly, a president has to do this by himself. But the manner in which he organizes his staff, and structures the flow of information within his administration, makes it easier or harder. That way leadership lies.

Leadership requires thought. And when centralization is a reaction to managerial needs—the result of judgments about the options, costs, and benefits presented by the institutional environment—it is a valuable instrument of presidential power. When centralizing is reflexive, however, the result of no thought at all, bad bargains result for presidents and polity. Presidents have the capacity to make the executive branch work for them. We might rightfully hope they add to it an equal portion of discernment, so that it also works for us.

Additional Data and Alternate Specifications

TABLE A.1
Messages and Proposals, by Year, 1949–1996

President	Year	Messages	Proposals
Truman	1949	91	124
	1950	92	125
	1951	50	65
	1952	56	75
Eisenhower	1953	33	42
	1954	62	198
	1955	84	185
	1956	68	160
	1957	88	159
	1958	69	153
	1959	89	182
	1960	60	88
Kennedy	1961	77	280
	1962	50	233
	1963	56	350
Johnson	1964	55	172
	1965	75	407
	1966	69	286
	1967	66	345
	1968	54	266
Nixon	1969	40	137
	1970	68	157
	1971	74	184
	1972	33	70
	1973	48	141
	1974	38	71
Ford	1974	39	55
	1975	53	106
	1976	66	108
Carter	1977	52	157
	1978	57	126
	1979	81	172
	1980	69	83

TABLE A.1 (*cont.*)

President	Year	Messages	Proposals
Reagan	1981	29	61
	1982	39	91
	1983	51	132
	1984	40	45
	1985	39	45
	1986	38	66
	1987	68	131
	1988	53	79
Bush	1989	39	160
	1990	25	54
	1991	30	58
	1992	48	95
Clinton	1993	72	149
	1994	42	71
	1995	70	136
	1996	51	91
Total		2,796	6,926

TABLE A.2
Sampled Items, by Congress

The abbreviation "Msg" refers to "message," "SpM" to "Special Message." Date given is appearance in *Public Papers of the President* of item's transmission to Congress; where this differs from the date of the original message, the message date is also referenced below.

81st Congress

1949	5-Jan	Extend export control authority [State of the Union]
1949	10-Jan	Abolish Regional Agricultural Credit Corp [Budget Msg]
1949	21-Feb	SpM on the Extension of the Institute of Inter-American Affairs
1949	22-Apr	SpM on Health Care
1949	28-Apr	Authorize U.S. membership in International Trade Organization
1949	20-Jun	Reorganization Plan 6 of 1949 (U.S. Maritime Commission)
1949	20-Jun	Reorganization Plan 5 of 1949 (Civil Service Commission)
1949	24-Jun	SpM recommending Point 4 legislation
1950	9-Jan	Merge education programs for children on federal property [Budget Msg]
1950	23-Jan	Revenue Act of 1950
1950	3-Mar	SpM on the Coal Strike

TABLE A.2 (*cont.*)

1950	13-Mar	Reorganization Plan 9 of 1950 (Federal Power Commission)
1950	6-Apr	SpM on Unemployment Insurance
1950	5-May	SpM on Small Business
1950	9-May	Reorganization Plan 25 of 1950 (National Security Resources Board)
1950	19-Jul	SpM on Korea (Defense Production Act Extension)

82d Congress

1951	8-Jan	Taft-Hartley Amendments [State of the Union]
1951	9-Jan	Provide states with congressional redistricting guidelines
1951	12-Jan	Public financing for rental housing [Economic Report]
1951	15-Jan	Reduce loan authority of Rural Electrification Administration [Budget Msg]
1951	15-Jan	Payroll tax to fund national health insurance [Budget Msg]
1951	27-Feb	SpM on Increasing Postal Rates
1951	13-Jul	SpM on Employment of Agricultural Workers from Mexico
1951	27-Jul	Finance UN Palestinian refugee program
1951	20-Aug	Funding for Midwest flood relief
1951	27-Sep	SpM on Conflict of Interest Legislation
1952	9-Jan	Aid states' public assistance programs [State of the Union]
1952	21-Jan	Allow federal workers to receive training at private institutions
1952	22-Jan	Coal mine safety legislation
1952	6-Mar	SpM on Mutual Security
1952	10-Apr	Reorganization Plan 4 of 1952 (Dept. of Justice)
1952	23-May	Recommendations regarding federal personnel

83d Congress

1953	2-Feb	Aid schools operating in defense areas [State of the Union]
1953	20-Feb	Resolution on subjugated peoples
1953	12-Mar	Reorganization Plan 1 of 1953 (Dept. of HEW)
1953	12-Mar	Defray expenses of advisory committee on education
1953	14-Apr	SpM on the disposal of government-owned synthetic rubber facilities
1953	2-May	Establish a Commission on Foreign Economic Policy
1953	20-May	SpM recommending tax legislation
1953	1-Jun	Reorganization Plan 9 of 1953 (Council of Economic Advisers)
1953	1-Jun	Reorganization Plan 8 of 1953 (U.S. Information Agency)
1954	7-Jan	Forfeit citizenship of those convicted of conspiring to use force against the United States [State of the Union]
1954	11-Jan	SpM on Agriculture
1954	14-Jan	SpM on Old Age and Survivors Insurance and Federal Grants-in-Aid for Public Assistance Programs

TABLE A.2 (*cont.*)

1954	21-Jan	Increase of aid to D.C. for public works [Budget Msg]
1954	24-Feb	Recommendations regarding federal personnel policies
1954	30-Mar	SpM on Foreign Economic Policy
1954	23-Jun	SpM on Mutual Security Program

84th Congress

1955	6-Jan	Amend Taft-Hartley law to protect rights of economic strikers in representation elections [State of the Union]
1955	6-Jan	Advisory commission on the arts within HEW [State of the Union]
1955	10-Jan	Expand presidential tariff authority in foreign economic policy
1955	17-Jan	Increase the $275m debt limit [Budget Msg]
1955	17-Jan	Extend Mexican farm labor (*"bracero"*) program [Budget Msg]
1955	22-Feb	SpM on National Highway Program
1955	4-Mar	Requesting extension of the 1951 Renegotiation Act
1955	1-Apr	Requesting $75m to complete the Inter-American Highway
1955	27-May	Amendments to the 1953 Refugee Relief Act
1955	11-Jun	Authorize Atomic Energy Commission to provide research reactors, fuel, training to friendly nations; subsidize half the cost
1956	5-Jan	Improve education for adult American Indians [State of the Union]
1956	5-Jan	Authorize Upper Colorado Basin, Fryingpan power projects [State of the Union]
1956	16-Jan	Provide aid to states to combat juvenile delinquency [Budget Msg]
1956	17-Jan	Water resources policy package
1956	24-Jan	Grant better terms on federally insured mortgages for those displaced by urban renewal [Economic Report]
1956	19-Mar	SpM on Mutual Security Program

85th Congress

1957	5-Jan	SpM requesting authority in Middle East to deal with "aggression"
1957	10-Jan	Approve U.S. membership in the Organization for Trade Cooperation [State of the Union]
1957	16-Jan	Increase patent fees [Budget Msg]
1957	16-Jan	Extend Small Business Act; SBA amendments [Budget Msg]
1957	16-Jan	Authorize increased interest rates on home loans made by or guaranteed by the Veterans Administration [Budget Msg]
1957	31-Jan	SpM on Immigration

TABLE A.2 *(cont.)*

1957	5-Mar	SpM on Drought and Other Natural Disasters
1957	22-Mar	Authorizing U.S. membership in the Int'l Atomic Energy Agency
1958	13-Jan	Adjust and improve veterans' compensation [Budget Msg]
1958	20-Jan	Revise distribution formula under Title I of Farm Tenant Act [Economic Report]
1958	20-Jan	Revise interest rate ceilings on Federal Housing Administration-insured mortgages [Economic Report]
1958	20-Jan	Authorize the secretary of labor to promulgate safety standards for longshoremen [Economic Report]
1958	30-Jan	SpM requesting 5-year extension of Reciprocal Trade Agreements Act
1958	26-Feb	Constitutional amendment regarding vice president when president is temporarily disabled
1958	2-Apr	SpM on Space Science and Exploration
1958	23-Jun	SpM on United States-Euratom agreement

86th Congress

1959	19-Jan	Amend Postal Policy Act of 1958 [Budget Msg]
1959	19-Jan	Fix tax loopholes/inequities [Budget Msg]
1959	19-Jan	Extend current excise and corporate tax rates for one year [Budget Msg]
1959	19-Jan	Alaska Omnibus Act [Budget Msg]
1959	19-Jan	Authorize sale of revenue bonds by the Tennessee Valley Authority [Budget Msg]
1959	20-Jan	Revise federal contracting laws ("8-hour laws") [Economic Report]
1959	29-Jan	SpM on Agriculture
1959	13-Mar	SpM on the Mutual Security Program
1960	12-Jan	Adjust upward or eliminate the interest rate ceiling on Treasury bonds
1960	18-Jan	Revise Federal Savings and Loan Insurance Corporation reserves and financing [Budget Msg]
1960	18-Jan	Cap water waste treatment facility construction at $20m [Budget Msg]
1960	18-Feb	U.S. participation in the International Development Association
1960	17-Mar	SpM on Immigration
1960	3-May	Public lands/wildlife range program [SpM on Legislative Program]
1960	16-May	SpM on the Freedom Monument
1960	23-Aug	SpM on Dominican Republic's sugar quota

TABLE A.2 *(cont.)*

87th Congress

1961	6-Feb	Provide aid to children of unemployed parents (see 2/2 msg)
1961	9-Feb	Increase the number of federal judgeships
1961	20-Feb	Distressed Area Redevelopment Act (see 2/2 msg)
1961	13-Apr	SpM on the Regulatory Agencies
1961	17-Apr	Add an assistant secretary of HEW for international affairs
1961	17-Apr	Farm Bill (see 3/16 msg)
1961	25-May	Increase USIA budget for SE Asia, Latin America [SpM on Urgent National Needs]
1961	26-May	Foreign Assistance Act (see 3/22 msg)
1961	29-May	"Manpower" worker retraining program (see 5/25 msg)
1961	7-Jun	Youth Opportunities Act
1961	29-Jun	Proposing U.S. Disarmament Agency (see 5/25 msg)
1962	20-Jan	Extend corporate income tax and excise tax rates through FY63 [Economic Report]
1962	30-Jan	SpM requesting $100m to purchase UN bonds
1962	19-Feb	Public Works Acceleration Act
1962	20-Mar	Stimulating the construction of coal slurry pipelines (see 3/1 msg)
1962	4-Apr	Creating a land conservation fund (see 3/1 msg)

88th Congress (Kennedy)

1963	17-Jan	Update the schedule of patent fees [Budget Msg]
1963	17-Jan	Enact new dairy legislation [Budget Msg; and see 1/31 msg]
1963	21-Jan	Facilitate civilian use of gov't-financed research [Economic Report]
1963	29-Jan	SpM on Education
1963	5-Feb	Mental Retardation Facilities and Community Mental Health Centers Construction Assistance
1963	11-Feb	Establish a national foreign affairs academy
1963	18-Feb	Urban Mass Transportation Act (see 4/5/62 msg)
1963	4-Apr	District of Columbia Charter Act
1963	27-May	Reorganization Plan 1 of 1963 (FDR Library)
1963	12-Jun	Civil Rights Act [SpM on Civil Rights and Jobs]
1963	22-Jul	SpM on Railroad Rules Dispute

88th Congress (Johnson)

1964	21-Jan	Increased disposal of stockpiles [Budget Msg]
1964	27-Jan	Creating Department of Housing and Community Development
1964	9-Mar	Create National Commission on Automation and Technological Progress
1964	16-Mar	SpM on War on Poverty (Economic Opportunity Act)

TABLE A.2 (*cont.*)

1964	28-Apr	Providing economic development for Appalachia
1964	27-May	Earthquake disaster relief and rebuilding aid for Alaska

89th Congress

1965	13-Jan	SpM on Immigration
1965	28-Jan	Increase Social Security benefits by 7% [Economic Report]
1965	28-Jan	Eliminate requirement of Federal Reserve banks to maintain a gold certificate reserve [Economic Report]
1965	2-Feb	SpM on Home Rule for the District of Columbia
1965	2-Mar	SpM on Cities (Omnibus Housing Act)
1965	17-Mar	Voting Rights Act (see 3/15 msg)
1965	13-Apr	Proposing a new power plant at the Grand Coulee Dam ($364m)
1965	4-May	Requesting $700m for Vietnam
1965	17-May	Excise Tax Reduction Act
1965	26-May	Regulate outdoor advertising
1966	20-Jan	Constitutional amendments changing electoral college, House terms
1966	24-Jan	Increase temporary debt limit [Budget Msg]
1966	28-Feb	Establish a national visitor's center in District of Columbia
1966	7-Mar	Federal Salary and Fringe Benefits Act
1966	18-Aug	Exempt officers' combat pay from taxation
1966	8-Sep	SpM on Fiscal Policy

90th Congress

1967	24-Jan	Supplemental spending of $12.3b for Vietnam
1967	26-Jan	User fees for highways, aviation, inland waterways [Economic Report]
1967	9-Feb	SpM on Foreign Aid
1967	15-Feb	SpM on Equal Justice (Civil Rights Act of 1967)
1967	28-Feb	SpM on Education and Health (Education Professions Development Act)
1967	17-Mar	SpM on the quality of American government (Intergovernmental Manpower Act)
1967	6-Jun	Power Reliability Act
1967	26-Sep	SpM proposing a U.S. contribution to the special funds of the Asian Development Bank
1968	29-Jan	Increase diesel fuel, truck taxes [Budget Msg]
1968	29-Jan	Continuing funding for SST prototype plane [Budget Msg]
1968	1-Feb	Strengthen the mortgage credit market [Economic Report]
1968	26-Feb	Reorganization Plan 2 of 1968 (urban mass transit)
1968	27-Feb	SpM on Agriculture
1968	30-Apr	SpM amending IMF agreement (Special Drawing Right reserve)

TABLE A.2 *(cont.)*

1968	6-Jun	Gun control proposals
1968	26-Jun	Gas pipeline safety legislation (see 2/6 msg)

91st Congress

1969	25-Feb	SpM on Reform of the Postal Service
1969	21-Apr	SpM on Reform of the Federal Tax System (revised surtax extension)
1969	30-Apr	Grant Consolidation Act
1969	2-May	SpM on Obscene and Pornographic Materials
1969	28-May	SpM on Foreign Aid
1969	11-Aug	SpM on Welfare Reform (Family Assistance Plan)
1969	7-Nov	Add, 1000 air traffic control positions for current FY
1970	26-Feb	Eliminate the select reserve within the Coast Guard ready reserve [Federal Economy Act]
1970	27-Feb	Emergency Public Interest Protection Act (re labor disputes)
1970	3-Mar	SpM on Education Reform
1970	3-Mar	Avert pending rail strike
1970	20-Mar	SpM on Small Business
1970	25-Mar	Strengthen explosives/bombings law
1970	23-Apr	SpM on Draft Reform
1970	21-May	Emergency School Aid Act
1970	9-Jul	Reorganization Plan 3 of 1970 (Environmental Protection Agency)

92d Congress

1971	26-Jan	Extend and amend Defense Production Act [Resubmission Msg]
1971	26-Jan	Clarify president's authority to designate the chair of the Federal Power Commission [Resubmission Msg]
1971	2-Feb	SpM proposing a Federal Executive Service
1971	18-Feb	SpM on a National Health Strategy
1971	24-Feb	SpM on Consumer Protection
1971	8-Mar	SpM on Special Revenue Sharing for Manpower
1971	9-Apr	Provide an additional 100,000 neighborhood youth corps summer jobs
1971	21-Apr	International Development and Humanitarian Assistance Act
1971	28-Apr	Proposing fourteen new national wilderness areas
1972	20-Jan	Boost funding for sea-based deterrent forces (to $900m) [written State of the Union msg]
1972	20-Jan	Raise military retirement and survivor benefits [written State of the Union msg; see 3/23 msg]
1972	21-Jan	Legislation arbitrating West Coast dock strike
1972	4-Feb	Funding for bicentennial plans in District of Columbia

TABLE A.2 *(cont.)*

1972	13-Jun	Requesting expression of support (from both houses) for interim SALT agreement
1972	17-Jul	(Tropical Storm) Agnes Disaster Recovery Act
1972	4-Aug	SpM on Historic Monuments (National Land Use Policy Act)

93d Congress (Nixon)

1973	11-Jan	Extend Economic Stabilization Authority (Phase III)
1973	30-Mar	Authorize the president to reduce or suspend tariffs (see 4/10 msg)
1973	16-Apr	SpM on Strategic Stockpile Disposal
1973	18-Apr	SpM on Energy Policy
1973	10-Sep	Raise the minimum wage [Legislative Goals Msg]
1973	19-Oct	Requesting additional foreign aid for Israel and Cambodia
1974	7-Feb	Extending authorizing legislation for the ACDA
1974	19-Feb	SpM on Economic Adjustment Assistance
1974	20-Feb	SpM on Health
1974	4-Mar	Revise veterans' disability compensation program
1974	27-Mar	Campaign finance reform legislation (see 3/8 msg)
1974	2-Aug	Establish permanent Cost of Living Task Force in EOP

93d Congress (Ford)

1974	12-Sep	Restore financial integrity to Railroad Retirement System [Legislative Priorities Msg]
1974	8-Oct	Remove acreage limitations remaining on rice, peanuts, cotton [Economic Msg]
1974	18-Nov	Authorize military construction funds [2d Legislative Priorities Msg]
1974	18-Nov	Create Commission on Regulatory Reform [2d Legislative Priorities Msg]

94th Congress

1975	15-Jan	Cuts in corporate taxes [State of the Union]
1975	9-Jun	Create an Office of Science and Technology Policy
1975	26-Jun	Nuclear Fuel Assurance Act
1975	1-Jul	Provide Commonwealth Status to N. Mariana Islands
1975	16-Jul	Compromise legislation on oil decontrol
1975	8-Oct	Aviation Act (airline regulatory changes)
1975	10-Oct	Establish an Energy Independence Authority
1975	20-Oct	National Food Stamp Reform Act
1976	9-Feb	Medicare amendments
1976	13-Feb	Approve revisions in naval budget respecting Aegis-armed ships
1976	23-Mar	Child nutrition reform legislation (block grant consolidation)

TABLE A.2 (*cont.*)

1976	30-Apr	Drug abuse legislation (see 4/27 msg)
1976	26-May	Amend security assistance bill to eliminate cap on P.L. 480 (Food for Peace) aid to South Korea
1976	26-May	Amend Senate language delaying authorization of B-1 bomber
1976	19-Jul	Substitute language for Watergate Reorganization and Reform Act
1976	22-Jul	Higher education student loan proposals [Legislation msg]

95th Congress

1977	31-Jan	Tax rebate [Economic Recovery Program msg]
1977	31-Jan	Public works/CETA expansion [Economic Recovery Program msg]
1977	21-Feb	U.S.-South Korea fishery agreement
1977	17-Mar	Comprehensive Oil Pollution and Liability Act
1977	6-Apr	Youth Employment and Demonstration Projects Act (see 3/9 msg)
1977	6-Apr	Msg on Consumer Protection (Agency for Consumer Advocacy)
1977	25-Apr	Child Health Assessment Program
1977	21-Oct	Transferring certain U.S. defense assets to the Republic of Korea
1978	28-Feb	Elementary and Secondary Education Act Amendments
1978	27-Mar	Msg on National Urban Policy
1978	1-May	U.S.-Canada Reciprocal Fisheries Agreement for 1978
1978	23-May	Reorganization Plan 2 of 1978 (Civil Service Commission)
1978	24-May	Create national commission on the International Year of the Child
1978	5-Jun	Cut military assistance budget by $48m [rescission msg]
1978	8-Jun	Long-term loans for New York City
1978	28-Sep	Requesting extension of multilateral trade negotiation authority

96th Congress

1979	25-Jan	Real Wage Insurance tax plan [State of the Union]
1979	25-Jan	Law Enforcement Assistance Administration reform [State of the Union]
1979	25-Jan	Expand D.C. home rule [State of the Union]
1979	26-Jan	Revising statutes governing ties to Taiwan after PRC recognition
1979	1-Mar	Stand-by gasoline rationing plan
1979	6-Mar	Hospital Cost Containment Act
1979	10-Apr	Requesting $100m in economic aid for Turkey

TABLE A.2 (*cont.*)

1979	26-Apr	Proposing Windfall Profits Tax and Energy Security Trust Fund
1979	21-Jun	Deregulation of trucking industry
1979	12-Sep	Proposing Low Income Energy Assistance Program
1980	21-Jan	Increase veterans' job training and disability benefits [State of the Union]
1980	21-Jan	Pass implementing legislation for International Sugar Agreement
1980	28-Jan	Governing leasing program in Alaska national petroleum reserve
1980	4-Jun	U.S.-Morocco agreement on the peaceful uses of nuclear energy
1980	19-Jun	Allow export of nuclear fuel to India
1980	28-Aug	Extend unemployment benefits [Economic Renewal Program msg]

97th Congress

1981	18-Feb	Program for Economic Recovery [Omnibus Budget Reconciliation Act]
1981	19-Mar	Cut $2.8b in thirty-three budget areas [budget rescission msg]
1981	21-May	Social Security Trust Fund proposals
1981	30-May	Extend veterans' educational assistance program (VEAP)
1981	2-Jun	Extend most-favored-nation trade status of Romania, Hungary, PRC
1981	24-Sep	Increase transportation user fees [fall budget package msg]
1981	24-Sep	Reduce FY82 nondefense spending 12% [fall budget package msg]
1982	26-Jan	New Federalism proposals [State of the Union]
1982	6-Feb	Convert CETA program into a block grant [Budget Msg]
1982	6-Feb	Boost spending for military personnel and operations [Budget Msg]
1982	23-Mar	Enterprise Zone Tax Act
1982	24-May	Federal Energy Reorganization Act
1982	22-Jun	Education Opportunity and Equity Act
1982	13-Sep	Criminal Justice Reform Act
1982	22-Sep	National Debt Retirement Act (sale of surplus federal property)
1982	30-Nov	Highway repair program (see 11/27 msg)

98th Congress

1983	25-Jan	Port modernization program [State of the Union]
1983	31-Jan	One-year freeze on federal civilian and military pay and pensions [Budget Msg]

TABLE A.2 *(cont.)*

1983	31-Jan	Tax high-cost employee health insurance options [Budget Msg]
1983	31-Jan	Reduce minimum wage for youth summer jobs [Budget Msg]
1983	2-Mar	Amend IMF agreement to increase U.S. contribution
1983	8-Mar	Constitutional amendment allowing prayer in schools
1983	16-Mar	Comprehensive Crime Control Act
1983	17-Mar	Equal Education Opportunity Act (Chap 1 vouchers)
1983	19-Apr	Recommendations regarding defense modernization (MX, etc.)
1983	27-Apr	Request reprogramming of Central American aid
1983	2-May	U.S.-GDR fishery agreement
1983	5-Sep	Requesting a resolution condemning the Soviet attack on Korean passenger jet (KAL 007)
1983	12-Sep	National Productivity and Innovation Act (patent, copyright reform)
1984	1-Feb	Deregulation of financial institutions [Budget Msg]
1984	12-Sep	Develop limited binary chemical weapon deterrent
1984	27-Sep	Requesting $110m to improve security at U.S. diplomatic missions

99th Congress

1985	3-Jan	Proposing $1b hunger relief program for Africa
1985	6-Feb	increase Nicaraguan *contra* humanitarian aid (see 4/4 msg)
1985	22-Feb	Superfund reauthorization legislation
1985	23-Feb	Agricultural Adjustment Act of 1985
1985	4-Mar	Build twenty-one additional MX missiles
1985	26-Apr	Proposing four additions to wilderness system
1985	29-Apr	U.S.-Israel Free Trade Area implementation act
1985	29-May	Tax reform
1985	31-Jul	Federal management improvement/productivity package
1985	23-Sep	Create $300m export subsidy fund
1985	8-Nov	Unitary Tax Repeal Act
1986	6-Feb	Antiterrorism program ["America's Agenda" msg]
1986	24-Apr	Defense management/organization legislation (Packard Commission)
1986	6-May	$354m arms sale to Saudi Arabia
1986	3-Jun	Msg on Strategic Modernization Program
1986	15-Sep	Drug-Free America Act (see 8/4 msg)

100th Congress

1987	5-Jan	Terminate federal direct student loan program [Budget Msg]
1987	5-Jan	Privatize Alaska Power Administration [Budget Msg]

TABLE A.2 (*cont.*)

1987	27-Jan	Amend Foreign Corrupt Practices Act [written State of the Union msg]
1987	27-Jan	Recapitalize FSLIC [written State of the Union msg]
1987	29-Jan	Amend statutes governing air pollution regulations to recognize new antipollution technologies
1987	24-Feb	Add catastrophic care health insurance to Medicare
1987	12-Mar	Federal Credit Reform Act (loan sales)
1987	6-May	Msg on Energy Security
1987	9-Nov	U.S.-Japan agreement on the peaceful uses of nuclear energy
1988	25-Jan	Restrict use of Legal Services Corporation funds [written State of the Union msg]
1988	25-Jan	Job training/welfare reforms [written State of the Union msg]
1988	25-Jan	Privatize gov't employee housing [written State of the Union msg]
1988	18-Feb	Privatize Rural Telephone Bank in REA [Budget Msg]
1988	24-Feb	Truth in Federal Spending Act
1988	17-Mar	Requesting transfers within FY88 continuing resolution (for Coast Guard, Justice, NASA, SBA)
1988	8-Jun	President's Pro-Life Act of 1988

101st Congress

1989	9-Feb	Urban enterprise zones [State of Union-type address]
1989	9-Feb	Capital gains tax cut [State of Union-type address]
1989	22-Feb	Financial Institutions Reform, Recovery, and Enhancement Act
1989	15-Mar	Head Start amendments
1989	21-Mar	Minimum wage revisions
1989	9-May	D.C. funding restrictions/proposals
1989	12-Jun	Clean Air Act amendments
1989	14-Jun	U.S.-Denmark fishery agreement
1989	7-Jul	(Congressional) Honoraria Reform Act of 1989
1989	6-Sep	Support for East European Democracies aid to Poland and Hungary (see 7/10 msg)
1989	26-Oct	Food safety and pesticide proposals
1989	10-Nov	"HOPE" (Homeownership and Opportunity for People Everywhere) Act
1990	31-Jan	Elevate EPA to Cabinet rank [State of the Union]
1990	22-Mar	National Tree Trust Act
1990	14-Sep	Enterprise for the Americas Initiative (see 6/27 msg)
1990	20-Oct	Amendments to pending Civil Rights Act of 1990

102d Congress

1991	22-May	"America 2000" education legislation
1991	24-Jul	Cut $5m from Dept. of Defense budget [budget rescission msg]

TABLE A.2 (*cont.*)

1991	9-Oct	Implementing act for U.S.-USSR trade agreement
1992	28-Jan	Provide health insurance tax credit to low-income families [State of the Union]
1992	28-Jan	Allow penalty-free use of IRA savings for medical and educational expenses [State of the Union address]
1992	3-Apr	FREEDOM Support Act (aid to former USSR)
1992	28-Apr	Job Training 2000 legislation (see 1/17 msg)
1992	12-May	Urban Aid initiative ("weed and seed" programs for Los Angeles, etc.)
1992	12-May	Extend emergency unemployment compensation benefits
1992	13-May	National Youth Apprenticeship Act
1992	23-Jun	U.S.-Estonia fishery agreement
1992	27-Jul	Proposing wilderness areas (Wyoming)
1992	13-Aug	Community Opportunity Pilot Project Act (see 7/31 msg.)
1992	8-Sep	Hurricane relief for Florida and Hawaii
1992	15-Sep	Reallocation requests for Dept. of Defense, Asian Development Bank
1992	16-Sep	Family Leave Tax Credit Act

103d Congress

1993	17-Feb	$30b economic stimulus package [Administration Goals msg]
1993	17-Feb	Raise income taxes on wealthy [Administration Goals msg]
1993	1-Apr	Comprehensive Child Immunization Act
1993	1-Apr	Foreign Operations Assistance Act (aid to Russia)
1993	21-Apr	"Goals 2000: Educate America Act"
1993	5-May	Student Loan Reform Act
1993	15-Jun	Reauthorize (but restructure) Radio Free Europe and Radio Liberty
1993	2-Jul	Defense conversion legislation
1993	5-Jul	Safe Schools Act
1993	22-Sep	Address on Health Care (see also 10/27 msg)
1994	19-Jan	$8.6b for California earthquake disaster assistance
1994	11-Feb	Immigration proposals
1994	15-Mar	Re-Employment Act of 1994 (see 3/9 msg)
1994	18-Jul	U.S.-Lithuania fishery agreement
1994	27-Sep	Uruguay Round Implementation Act (GATT)
1994	15-Dec	Create single voucher for job training programs [Middle-Class Bill of Rights msg]

104th Congress

1995	5-Jan	Campaign finance reforms
1995	9-Feb	Major League Baseball Restoration Act
1995	29-Mar	Establish District of Columbia Financial Authority

TABLE A.2 *(cont.)*

1995	3-May	Immigration Enforcement Improvements Act
1995	10-May	Gun-Free School Zones amendments
1995	13-Jun	Reconciliation plan leading to balanced budget in ten years
1995	16-Jun	Create bipartisan campaign finance commission
1995	5-Jul	Reauthorize Ryan White CARE Act (AIDS services) for five years
1995	26-Aug	National Parks financial amendments
1995	13-Nov	"Clean" increase in debt limit
1995	27-Nov	Implementing peace agreement in Bosnia-Herzegovina
1995	7-Dec	ERISA Enforcement Improvement Act
1996	9-Feb	Reverse requirement that armed forces discharge personnel with HIV
1996	26-Feb	Amend pending Cuban sanctions bill to provide compensation for families of pilots shot down by Cuba
1996	24-Jun	Amend Constitution to safeguard various rights for crime victims
1996	5-Aug	International Crime Control Act

TABLE A.3
(Weighted) Source of Legislative Proposals, by Period

Period	Decentralized	Dept.-led	EOP-led	EOP	WHO
1949–1954	26.6%	19.9%	27.2%	11.1%	15.2%
1955–1960	33.3	32.1	27.7	2.3	4.7
1961–1966	27.3	24.1	30.1	7.3	11.3
1967–1972	15.6	26.7	24.0	13.4	20.3
1973–1978	19.5	26.4	25.6	13.0	15.5
1979–1984	16.2	26.0	29.7	19.8	8.4
1985–1990	26.2	23.3	24.4	12.0	14.1
1991–1996	22.4	24.4	30.1	4.8	18.4

TABLE A.4
"Trusted Secretaries," 1949–1996 (dates refer to service as departmental secretary; prior service to the president is in parentheses)

Truman (1949–1953 only)
 John Snyder, Treasury, 1/20/49–1/20/53 (EOP staff; longtime associate)
Eisenhower
 Herbert Brownell, Jr., Justice, 1/20/53–1/27/58 (campaign manager)
 Arthur Flemming, HEW, 8/1/58–1/20/61 (EOP staff)

TABLE A.4 (*cont.*)

Fred Seaton, Interior, 6/8/56–1/20/61 (EOP staff)
Kennedy
  Robert F. Kennedy, Justice, 1/20/61–11/22/63 (campaign manager; brother)
Johnson
  Clark Clifford, Defense, 3/1/68–1/20/69 (longtime associate)
  Lawrence O'Brien, Postmaster General, 11/3/65–4/26/68 (EOP staff)
  Marvin Watson, Postmaster General, 4/26/68–1/20/69 (EOP staff)
  Lee White, Federal Power Commission, 1966–1969 (EOP staff)
Nixon
  Robert Finch, HEW, 1/20/69–6/23/70 (longtime associate)
  Henry Kissinger, State, 9/22/73–8/9/74 (EOP staff)
  John Mitchell, Justice, 1/20/69–6/12/72 (campaign manager)
  Peter Peterson, Commerce, 2/21/72–2/2/73 (EOP staff)
  William Rogers, State, 1/20/69–9/3/73 (longtime associate)
  George Shultz, Treasury, 6/12/72–5/8/74 (EOP staff)
  Caspar Weinberger, HEW, 2/12/73–8/9/74 (EOP staff)
Ford
  Henry Kissinger, State, 8/9/74–1/20/77 (EOP staff)
  Donald Rumsfeld, Defense, 11/20/75–1/20/77 (EOP staff)
  Bill Usery, Labor, 2/10/76–1/20/77 (EOP staff)
  Frank Zarb, Federal Energy Administration, 1974–1977 (EOP staff)
Carter
  James Schlesinger, Energy, 10/1/77–8/24/79 (EOP staff)
Reagan
  James Baker III, Treasury, 2/25/85–8/18/88 (EOP staff)
  Bill Brock, Labor, 4/29/85–12/17/87 (EOP staff)
  Frank C. Carlucci, Defense, 11/23/87–1/20/89 (EOP staff)
  William Clark, Interior, 11/21/83–2/7/85 (EOP staff)
  Elizabeth Dole, Transportation, 2/7/83–12/3/87 (EOP staff)
  John Herrington, Energy, 2/7/85–1/20/89 (EOP staff)
  Edwin Meese III, Justice, 2/25/85–8/12/88 (EOP staff)
  William French Smith, Justice, 1/22/81–2/25/85 (longtime associate)
  Caspar Weinberger, Defense, 1/20/81–11/23/87 (gubernatorial staff)
Bush
  James A. Baker III, State, 1/20/89–8/23/92 (longtime associate)
  Andrew H. Card, Jr., Transportation, 2/24/92–1/20/93 (EOP staff)
Clinton (1993–1996 only)
  Robert Reich, Labor, 1/20/93–1/10/97 (longtime associate)
  Mickey Kantor, Commerce, 4/12/96–1/21/97 (EOP staff)
  Robert Rubin, Treasury, 1/10/95–7/2/99 (EOP staff)

TABLE A.5
"Real ADA" Ideology Scores

Year	Senate Median	President
1949	18.36	72.43
1950	18.01	80.81
1951	17.15	78.55
1952	18.08	75.57
1953	18.56	34.43
1954	14.14	22.90
1955	17.09	54.21
1956	26.56	41.26
1957	28.52	47.29
1958	23.96	37.11
1959	35.99	17.41
1960	41.17	23.70
1961	40.78	68.35
1962*	40.78	68.35
1963	40.36	81.44
1964	40.34	81.33
1965	48.31	82.41
1966	43.58	67.65
1967	36.84	55.34
1968	37.90	89.34
1969	40.30	33.99
1970	37.05	15.91
1971	35.06	10.59
1972	36.27	25.71
1973	49.99	10.89
1974	46.37	18.93
1975	51.05	17.48
1976	46.58	3.14
1977	49.54	81.34
1978	48.75	91.35
1979	47.87	79.13
1980	47.03	74.30
1981	32.91	1.36
1982	36.71	6.75
1983	33.46	0.79
1984	39.79	1.63
1985	33.45	− 0.14
1986	34.86	3.98
1987	48.71	− 5.67
1988	47.85	− 4.64
1989	40.49	0.11
1990	44.12	− 2.94

TABLE A.5 (cont.)

Year	Senate Median	President
1991	47.88	−0.38
1992	52.28	−3.39
1993	51.26	66.29
1994	49.98	85.24
1995	38.40	89.15
1996	34.11	93.44

Source: Tim Groseclose, Steven D. Levitt, and James M. Snyder, Jr., "Comparing Interest Group Scores across Time and Chambers: Adjusted ADA Scores for the U.S. Congress," American Political Science Review 93 (1999): 33–50. President-equivalent scores calculated by George Krause (1949–1994) and Dan Ponder (1995–96).
*No scores were issued for 1962, so the values for 1961 are repeated.

TABLE A.6
The Context of Centralization (ordered probit analysis, including presidency dummy variables)

Variable	Coeff. (S.E.)	t-stat. (Prob.)
Cross-cutting	.163	5.94
	(.027)	(.000)
Program size	.006	1.39
	(.005)	(.166)
Staff size	.0005	1.99
	(.0002)	(.047)
Reorg. impact	.359	3.69
	(.097)	(.000)
Crisis	−.053	−0.30
	(.181)	(.768)
Old/new	.850	5.91
	(.144)	(.000)
Bureau Proximity		
Merit %	−.049	−1.19
	(.041)	(.236)
Inner Cabinet	−.206	−1.63
	(.126)	(.104)
Congressional proximity		
Avg.% Cong. seats	−.001	−0.05
	(.023)	(.958)
Distance from Senate median	.012	1.65
	(.007)	(.099)
Item complexity	−.352	−3.94
	(.090)	(.000)

TABLE A.6 (*cont.*)

Variable	Coeff. (S.E.)	t-stat. (Prob.)
Year	.233	0.84
	(.277)	(.402)
Budget situation	−1.940	−1.61
	(1.202)	(.108)
Policy type: spending impact	.161	1.17
	(.138)	(.243)
Policy salience	.100	0.50
	(.199)	(.616)
Priority	.244	1.63
	(.150)	(.103)
Month	−.024	−1.02
	(.024)	(.307)
Individual presidents		
Eisenhower	−.858	−0.69
	(1.24)	(.489)
Kennedy	−2.641	−0.79
	(3.358)	(.432)
Johnson	−3.555	−0.85
	(4.199)	(.398)
Nixon	−4.605	−0.83
	(5.568)	(.409)
Ford	−6.109	−0.86
	(7.136)	(.393)
Carter	−6.699	−0.86
	(7.754)	(.388)
Reagan	−7.460	−0.84
	(8.914)	(.403)
Bush	−9.588	−0.86
	(11.135)	(.390)
Clinton	−10.668	−0.87
	(12.209)	(.383)
N	366	
LLF	−438.5	
prob. $> \chi^2$	.000	
% correctly predicted	42.1	

Note: This model parallels the first column of Table 5.2. The independent variable is an ordinal index of centralization (0–3), as defined in Chapter Five. Coefficients are calculated using ordered probit analysis, correcting for the stratified nature of the sample. *T*-statistics are presented for each coefficient; and the probability of having obtained a given coefficient purely by chance is presented in parentheses below each *t*-statistic, using a two-tailed test. The dichotomous variable representing the Truman administration is omitted, as are cutpoint estimates.

TABLE A.7
Presidential Success Rates in Congress, Annual

President	Year	Mean Success	S.D.	N
Truman	1949	2.25	1.16	8
	1950	1.88	1.13	8
	1951	0.89	1.17	9
	1952	0.67	1.03	6
Eisenhower	1953	2.38	1.19	8
	1954	2.29	0.76	7
	1955	1.80	1.32	10
	1956	1.33	1.37	6
	1957	1.50	1.31	8
	1958	1.88	1.36	8
	1959	1.50	1.41	8
	1960	0.50	1.07	8
Kennedy	1961	1.91	1.30	11
	1962	1.20	1.64	5
	1963	0.73	1.10	11
Johnson	1964	2.33	0.81	6
	1965	2.00	1.15	10
	1966	2.17	1.33	6
	1967	0.88	1.13	8
	1968	1.50	1.41	8
Nixon	1969	1.00	0.89	6
	1970	1.00	1.22	9
	1971	0.13	0.35	8
	1972	2.00	1.41	8
	1973	1.67	1.51	6
	1974	0.83	1.33	6
Ford	1974	0.75	1.50	4
	1975	1.00	1.31	8
	1976	0.75	1.16	8
Carter	1977	1.50	1.31	8
	1978	2.13	1.36	8
	1979	1.40	1.26	10
	1980	1.33	1.37	6
Reagan	1981	1.57	1.51	7
	1982	0.78	1.20	9
	1983	1.23	1.24	13
	1984	1.67	1.53	3
	1985	1.80	1.23	10
	1986	1.60	0.55	5
	1987	1.25	1.39	8
	1988	0.86	1.21	7

TABLE A.7 (*cont.*)

President	Year	Mean Success	S.D.	N
Bush	1989	1.33	1.23	12
	1990	1.50	1.29	4
	1991	1.00	1.73	3
	1992	0.92	1.24	12
Clinton	1993	1.80	1.14	10
	1994	2.00	1.26	6
	1995	1.25	1.29	12
	1996	1.00	1.15	4

NOTES

~~~~~~

The presidential filing systems differ slightly in their assignment of subject codes to areas within the central files, with new codes added over time. The most common subject used here is "LE," or general legislation, though LE can also be used with specific subjects—for example, LE/ED indicates legislation regarding education.

Cites to archival holdings normally give the file or record group, the title, date, and correspondents on a given document, the box number, folder title (in brackets), and the archive in question.

PREFACE

1. Moynihan quoted in Richard L. Berke, "Bush is Providing Corporate Model for White House," *New York Times* (March 11, 2001): A1; Glenn Kes-

sler and Dana Milbank, " 'Review Board' Rules the Funding Process," *Washington Post* (March 1, 2001): A1.

CHAPTER ONE. MANAGING THE PRESIDENT'S PROGRAM

1. Taylor Branch, *Parting the Waters: America in the King Years, 1954–63* (New York: Touchstone, 1988), 699, 808f; Richard Reeves, *President Kennedy: Profile of Power* (New York: Touchstone, 1993), 521–22; Arthur M. Schlesinger, Jr., *Robert Kennedy and His Times*, paperback ed. (New York: Ballantine, 1979), 372f.

2. Ted Sorensen, notes dated 6/14/63, no title. WHCF: President's Office Files: Legislative Files, Box 53, [6/63], JFKL. Everett Dirksen (R-Ill.) was the Senate minority leader, Mike Mansfield (D-Mont.) the majority leader. Arthur Vandenberg was a Republican senator from Michigan who in the 1940s was key to passage of President Harry Truman's Marshall Plan for postwar European reconstruction. Along with the Sorensen memo and the other sources cited above, see Theodore C. Sorensen, *Kennedy* (New York: Harper & Row, 1965), 494–98, for a discussion of some of the options Kennedy considered. A memo from powerful Senate staffer Bobby Baker to Majority Leader Mansfield makes clear the magnitude of the problem; he felt it "virtually impossible to secure 51 Senators who will vote for the President's bill." See Robert Baker to Sen. Mansfield, "Civil Rights Possibilities," memo of 6/27/63. WHCF: President's Office Files: Legislative Files, Box 53, [6/63], JFKL.

3. Isaiah Berlin, "Two Concepts of Liberty," in his *Four Essays on Liberty* (New York: Oxford University Press, 1969), 170.

4. Fred I. Greenstein, "Change and Continuity in the Modern Presidency," in Anthony King, ed., *The New American Political System* (Washington, D.C.: American Enterprise Institute, 1978), 45–46.

5. Quoted in Sorensen, *Kennedy*, 353.

6. Press conference of 16 December 1997, *Public Papers of the President: 1997, vol. 2* (Washington, D.C.: Government Printing Office, 1998), 1774.

7. John W. Kingdon, *Agendas, Alternatives, and Public Policies*, 2d ed. (New York: HarperCollins, 1995), 23. See also Frank R. Baumgartner and Bryan D. Jones, *Agendas and Instability in American Politics* (Chicago: University of Chicago Press, 1993), 241.

8. For a good review of empirical work in this area, and an important extension of it, see George C. Edwards III and Andrew Barrett, "Presidential Agenda Setting in Congress," in Jon R. Bond and Richard Fleisher, eds., *Polarized Politics: Congress and the President in a Partisan Era* (Washington, D.C.: CQ Press, 2000).

9. Edwards and Barrett found that 97.6 percent of presidential initiatives obtained agenda status between 1935 and 1996 (ibid., 120).

10. Ash to Nixon, "Strengthening the Presidency," memo dated 8/24/73. WHCF: Staff Member and Office Files: Roy Ash, Box 7, [Ash Memos to the President, Feb. 1973 to Dec. 1973], NPMP, 3; interview with Stuart Eizenstat, head of Carter's Domestic Policy Staff (Miller Center Interviews, Carter Presidency Project, vol. 13, January 1982, JCL), 105. Even as George W. Bush pre-

pared to take office after the disputed 2000 election, pundits opined that he "dearly needs some legislative successes early next year to show that he can be the 'uniter' he promised to be." See Alison Mitchell, "Winning: Now He Must Persuade the Voters," *New York Times* (December 17, 2000): IV-1, and, similarly, Francine Kiefer and Abraham McLaughlin, "Bush Starts on Clear, Simple Plan," *Christian Science Monitor* (January 22, 2001): 1.

11. Jon R. Bond, Richard Fleisher, and Glen S. Krutz, "An Overview of the Empirical Findings on Presidential-Congressional Relations," in James Thurber, ed., *Rivals for Power: Presidential-Congressional Relations* (Washington, D.C.: CQ Press, 1996), 104.

12. Paul Quirk, "What Do We Know?" in William Crotty, ed., *Political Science: Looking toward the Future*, vol. 4 (Evanston, Ill.: Northwestern University Press, 1991), 47. See also Jon R. Bond and Richard Fleisher, *The President in the Legislative Arena* (Chicago: University of Chicago Press, 1990), 230.

13. See, for example, the essays in George C. Edwards III, John H. Kessel, and Bert A. Rockman, eds., *Researching the Presidency: Vital Questions, New Approaches* (Pittsburgh: University of Pittsburgh Press, 1993), and Edwards and Stephen J. Wayne, eds., *Studying the Presidency* (Knoxville: University of Tennessee Press, 1983).

14. See the sources in Chapters Six and Seven.

15. Stephen J. Wayne, *The Legislative Presidency* (New York: Harper and Row, 1978); Paul C. Light, *The President's Agenda: Domestic Policy Choice from Kennedy to Clinton*, 3d ed. (Baltimore: Johns Hopkins University Press, 1999). The first edition of Light's work was published in 1982.

16. See especially Terry M. Moe, "The Politicized Presidency," in John Chubb and Paul E. Peterson, eds., *New Directions in American Politics* (Washington, D.C.: Brookings Institution, 1985); Moe and Scott A. Wilson, "Presidents and the Politics of Structure," *Law and Contemporary Problems* 57 (1994): 1–44; Thomas J. Weko, *The Politicizing Presidency: The White House Personnel Office, 1948–1994* (Lawrence: University Press of Kansas, 1995). For a broader discussion of new institutionalism, see Peter Hall and Rosemary C. R. Taylor, "Political Science and the Three New Institutionalisms," *Political Studies* 44 (1996): 936–57, or Moe, "The New Economics of Organization," *American Journal of Political Science* 28 (1984): 739–77. The latter's title is a reminder that new institutionalism's concepts flow partly from an economics-oriented take on organization theory.

17. Moe, "The Politicized Presidency," 246.

18. Daniel E. Ponder, in *Good Advice: Information and Policy Making in the White House* (College Station: Texas A&M Press, 2000), 10–13 and 197–200, provides a useful discussion and review of the literature on this point.

19. Charles M. Cameron, *Veto Bargaining: Presidents and the Politics of Negative Power* (New York: Cambridge University Press, 2000), 246.

20. Quoted in Francis Heller, ed., *The Truman White House: The Administration of the Presidency, 1945–1953* (Lawrence: Regents Press of Kansas, 1980), 99. Emphasis in original.

21. For a good review, see Karen M. Hult, "Advising the President," in George C. Edwards III, John H. Kessel, and Bert A. Rockman, eds., *Researching*

the Presidency: Vital Questions, New Approaches (Pittsburgh: University of Pittsburgh Press, 1993). Chapters Two and Three below detail the program it-self—as substance, not symbol—as presidential choice, not something foisted upon the president by the executive branch or the public. See also Jeffrey E. Cohen, *Presidential Responsiveness and Public Policy-Making* (Ann Arbor: University of Michigan Press, 1997).

22. On the institutional presidency see, inter alia, John P. Burke, *The Institutional Presidency* (Baltimore: Johns Hopkins University Press, 1992); Matthew J. Dickinson, *Bitter Harvest: FDR, Presidential Power, and the Growth of the Presidential Branch* (New York: Cambridge University Press, 1997); John Hart, *The Presidential Branch*, 2d ed. (Chatham, N.J.: Chatham House, 1995); Terry M. Moe, "Presidents, Institutions, and Theory," in George C. Edwards III, John H. Kessel, and Bert A. Rockman, eds., *Researching the Presidency: Vital Questions, New Approaches* (Pittsburgh: University of Pittsburgh Press, 1993); Ponder, *Good Advice*; Charles E. Walcott and Karen M. Hult, *Governing the White House: From Hoover through LBJ* (Lawrence: University Press of Kansas, 1995); Shirley Anne Warshaw, *The Domestic Presidency: Policy Making in the White House* (Boston: Allyn and Bacon, 1997). On the administrative presidency see, inter alia, Colin Campbell, *Managing the Presidency: Carter, Reagan, and the Search for Executive Harmony* (Pittsburgh: University of Pittsburgh Press, 1986); Robert Durant, *The Administrative Presidency Revisited* (Albany: State University of New York Press, 1992); Judith Michaels, *The President's Call: Executive Leadership from FDR to George Bush* (Pittsburgh: University of Pittsburgh Press, 1997); Richard Nathan, *The Administrative Presidency* (New York: Wiley, 1983); Richard W. Waterman, *Presidential Influence and the Administrative State* (Knoxville: University of Tennessee Press, 1989).

23. See Moe, "The Politicized Presidency."

24. James P. Pfiffner, "Presidential Constraints and Transitions," in Steven A. Shull, ed., *Presidential Policymaking: An End-of-Century Assessment* (Armonk, N.Y.: M. E. Sharpe, 1999), 23–24. See also Michael L. Mezey, *Congress, the President, and Public Policy* (Boulder, Colo.: Westview Press, 1989), 91; and Michaels, *The President's Call*, chap. 2.

25. In "The Politicized Presidency," Moe adds a second key result, politicization, which is described as the seeding of the wider bureaucracy with presidential loyalists and/or ideologues. This strategy is related to, and I would argue subsidiary to, choices about centralizing: if one can trust one's appointees in the departments, the cost of a decentralized policy process diminishes. Moe seems to consider centralization and politicization as complementary strategies; I will argue that they are better seen as substitutes.

26. Paul C. Light, *Thickening Government* (Washington, D.C.: Brookings Institution, 1995).

27. They became part of P.L. 83–761. The Eisenhower speech is in *PPP*, January 14, 1954, 62ff. For details, see Nelson Rockefeller to the President, letter of 10/20/53, WHCF: Official Files 99-G-1, [State of the Union Message (1953)], DDEL; Robert J. Donovan, *Eisenhower: The Inside Story* (New York: Harper, 1956), 172–73; Edward D. Berkowitz, *Mr. Social Security: The Life of Wilbur J. Cohen* (Lawrence: University Press of Kansas, 1995), 91f.; Bureau of

the Budget, "Legislative Recommendations of the President, 83rd Congress, 2d session, report of 9/15/54," 4, in RG 51, Legislative Reference Division Subject Files 1939–70 (series 39.39), Box 5, [Status Reports — 83rd Congress, 2d Session], NA-II.

28. *PPP*, September 22, 1993, 1558ff., and October 27, 1993, 1835f. The bill itself (HR3600, 103d Congress) ran 1,342 pages, according to Peter G. Gosselin, "Clinton Makes Pitch, Delivers Health Plan," *Boston Globe* (October 28, 1993): A1. The voluminous secondary literature on the topic includes Haynes Johnson and David S. Broder, *The System*, paperback ed. (Boston: Little, Brown, 1997); Theda Skocpol, *Boomerang: Clinton's Health Security Effort and the Turn against Government in U.S. Politics* (New York: W. W. Norton & Company, 1996); and Paul Starr, *The Logic of Health Care Reform*, rev. ed. (New York: Whittle Books/Penguin Books, 1994).

29. Lawrence R. Jacobs and Robert Y. Shapiro, *Politicians Don't Pander: Political Manipulation and the Loss of Democratic Responsiveness* (Chicago: University of Chicago Press, 2000), 89, and chap. 3 generally.

30. Known as the "Intensive Care Unit." George Stephanopoulos, *All Too Human: A Political Education* (Boston: Little, Brown, 1999), 198. See also Elizabeth Drew, *On the Edge: The Clinton Presidency*, paperback ed. (New York: Simon & Schuster/Touchstone, 1994), 191–95, and Johnson and Broder, *The System*, 112–17. The departments qua departments did get some begrudged input into the draft of the Health Security Act that followed the president's September address. At that point, "the drafters came over from the departments and the bill grew by about four hundred pages," as Magaziner later complained. See *The System*, 169. Skocpol, *Boomerang*, 50–60, is particularly valuable on the formulation process as her analysis is based on White House memos not yet widely public.

31. *PPP*, April 2, 1958, 269–73. Ike left room here for presidential discretion: NASA was to have control of all space activities "except for those projects primarily associated with military requirements" (p. 270) as determined by the president.

32. Stephen Ambrose, *Eisenhower, vol. 2: The President* (New York: Simon and Schuster, 1984), 457–58; *PPP*, April 2, 1958, 270.

33. James Everett Katz, *Presidential Politics and Science Policy* (New York: Praeger, 1978), 35–37, 105–6, 119–20; Enid Schoettle, "The Establishment of NASA," in Sanford A. Lakoff, ed., *Knowledge and Power* (New York: Free Press, 1966). In March 1958 Eisenhower wrote to the secretary of defense and the National Advisory Committee for Aeronautics informing them of (not asking them about) the upcoming special message. He tells them they are to talk to the Budget Bureau or to Killian if they have objections. Memo of 4/2/58, no title, WHCF: Confidential files, Box 44, [NASA (1)], DDEL. See also the memos of Killian aide Robert Piland to Killian in this folder and in [NASA (2)], for example, "Notes on NASA," memo of 4/10/58. In later years, when Gerald Ford was considering reinstituting a science advisory structure in the White House, Vice President Nelson Rockefeller asked Eisenhower science staffers what they had accomplished; the creation of NASA was prominent among their responses. See Henry Simmons to Jim Cannon, "Presidential Science Advice,"

memo of 3/18/75, and James Killian, letter to Rockefeller, 3/20/75, both in Domestic Council: James Cannon Files, Box 32, [Science and Technology Policy, Office of, March 12–31, 1975], GRFL.

34. Quoted by R. Gordon Hoxie at a conference on the Eisenhower presidency. See Shirley Anne Warshaw, ed., *The Eisenhower Legacy: Discussions of Presidential Leadership* (Silver Spring, Md.: Bartleby Press, 1992), 150.

35. *PPP*, December 7, 1995, 1858.

36. See the *Congressional Record* of December 20, 1995, Senate Statements on Introduced Bills and Joint Resolutions, comments of Senator Simon on the Pension Audit Improvement Act of 1995; *PPP*, 1858f.; Robert Reich to author, e-mail communication, October 28, 1999; Rachel Markun, "Prospects for Pension Legislation in 1997," *Defined Contribution Plan Investing* (December 24, 1996): 2.

37. For a more formal treatment of this topic, see Andrew Rudalevige, "The Institutional Perspective and the Presidency: The Organization of Information and the Structure of Leadership," paper presented at the annual meeting of the American Political Science Association, Washington, D.C., August 1997.

38. Richard E. Neustadt, *Presidential Power and the Modern Presidents* (New York: Free Press, 1990), 128–29.

39. These concepts, derived from institutional economics, are discussed in more detail in Chapter Two. Important work in the field includes Moe, "The New Economics of Organization," and David Epstein and Sharyn O'Halloran, *Delegating Powers: A Transaction Cost Politics Approach to Policy Making under Separate Powers* (New York: Cambridge University Press, 1999).

40. Dickinson, *Bitter Harvest*; Ponder, *Good Advice*.

41. See Cohen, *Presidential Responsiveness and Public Policy-Making*; Light, *The President's Agenda*; Peterson, *Legislating Together*; Wayne Steger, "Presidential Policy Initiation and the Politics of Agenda Control," *Congress and the Presidency* 24 (1997): 17–36.

42. Jim Keogh to George Shultz, Bob Finch, and John Ehrlichman, no title, memo of 12/23/70. WHCF: Subject Files: EX LE, Box 3, [16 of 39, December 3–28, 1970], NPMP; Ted Sorensen to the President, "Legislative Priorities," 6/11/62. WHSF: Theodore Sorensen papers, Box 58, [Memos Re: Legislation 1962], JFKL.

43. Light, *The President's Agenda*; Wayne, *The Legislative Presidency*. See also John Kessel, *The Domestic Presidency* (Scituate, Mass.: Duxbury Press, 1975); Richard E. Neustadt, "Presidency and Legislation: Planning the President's Program," *American Political Science Review* 49 (1955): 980–1021; Ponder, *Good Advice*.

44. For example, Richard E. Cohen, *Washington at Work: Back Rooms and Clean Air* (New York: Macmillan, 1992); Steven Waldman, *The Bill*, rev. ed. (New York: Penguin, 1996).

45. For example, Peter M. Benda and Charles Levine, "Reagan and the Bureaucracy," in Charles O. Jones, ed., *The Reagan Legacy: Promise and Performance* (Chatham, N.J.: Chatham House, 1988).

46. For example, Shirley Anne Warshaw, *Powersharing: White House–Cabinet*

Relations in the Modern Presidency (Albany: State University of New York Press, 1996); Warshaw, *The Domestic Presidency*).

47. This draws on Michael Malbin, "Presidential Proposals to Congress and Related Roll Call Votes, 1789–1993," in Elaine K. Swift et. al., *Database of Congressional Historical Studies, 1789–1988* [computer file] (Ann Arbor, Mich.: Inter-University Consortium for Political and Social Research, 2001). I worked with the Malbin research team in error checking the 1949–1992 proposals against my own reading of the *Public Papers of the Presidents*, and in adding 1993–1996 to the ICPSR dataset. Divergences between my data and Malbin's are explained in Chapter Four.

48. Lawrence Chamberlain, *The President, Congress, and Legislation* (New York: Columbia University Press, 1946), chap. 12.

49. Nathan, *The Administrative Presidency*; Durant, *The Administrative Presidency Revisited*; Terry M. Moe and William G. Howell, "The Presidential Power of Unilateral Action," *Journal of Law, Economics, and Organization* 15 (1999): 132–79.

50. Metternich, quoted in Henry A. Kissinger, *A World Restored* (Boston: Houghton Mifflin, 1957), 135.

CHAPTER TWO. BARGAINING, TRANSACTION COSTS, AND
CONTINGENT CENTRALIZATION

1. See, for instance, Shirley Anne Warshaw, *Powersharing: White House–Cabinet Relations in the Modern Presidency* (Albany: State University of New York Press, 1996); James P. Pfiffner, ed., *The Managerial Presidency*, 2d ed. (College Station: Texas A&M University Press, 1999).

2. Walter Williams, "George Bush and Executive Branch Domestic Policymaking Competence," *Policy Studies Journal* 21 (Winter 1993): 703. See also John P. Burke, *The Institutional Presidency* (Baltimore: Johns Hopkins University Press, 1992), 181ff., and especially Terry Moe, "The Politicized Presidency," in John Chubb and Paul E. Peterson, eds., *New Directions in American Politics* (Washington, D.C.: Brookings Institution, 1985).

3. Bradley H. Patterson, Jr., *The White House Staff: Inside the West Wing and Beyond* (Washington, D.C.: Brookings Institution, 2000), 5.

4. Schultze oral history of March 28, 1969 (AC 83–17), LBJL, 48. Ford chief of staff (and later Cabinet member) Donald Rumsfeld, who ran the OEO under Nixon, agreed: "an operating agency . . . doesn't belong there [in the EOP]." See Samuel Kernell and Samuel L. Popkin, eds., *Chief of Staff* (Berkeley: University of California Press, 1986), 107. On the USTR, see I. M. Destler, *American Trade Politics*, 2d ed. (Washington, D.C.: Institute for International Economics, 1992).

5. Nixon quoted in Jack Anderson, "Kissinger: One Man State Department," *Washington Post* (October 18, 1974): D19. In what follows, the words "bureaucracy," "departments," "agencies," and "bureaus" will be used more or less interchangeably to refer to all Cabinet departments and operating agencies within the executive branch.

6. David Lowery, "The Presidency, the Bureaucracy, and Reinvention: A Gentle Plea for Chaos," *Presidential Studies Quarterly* 30 (2000): 79–108; Paul C. Light, *The Tides of Reform* (New Haven: Yale University Press, 1997).

7. On Clinton's transition report, see Jack Nelson and Robert J. Donovan, "The Education of a President," *Los Angeles Times Magazine* (August 1, 1993). On Cabinet government generally, see Anthony J. Bennett, *The American President's Cabinet* (New York: St. Martin's, 1996); Jeffrey E. Cohen, *The Politics of the U.S. Cabinet* (Pittsburgh: University of Pittsburgh Press, 1988); Warshaw, *Powersharing.*

8. See Graham Allison, *Essence of Decision* (Boston: Little, Brown, 1971), 176.

9. Leslie Gelb, "Muskie and Brzezinski: The Struggle over Foreign Policy," *New York Times Magazine* (July 20, 1980).

10. James Q. Wilson, *Bureaucracy* (New York: Basic Books, 1989), 173. Both the White House and the department staffs are bureaucracies, in Wilson's usage.

11. James MacGregor Burns, *Presidential Government: The Crucible of Leadership* (Boston: Houghton Mifflin, 1965), 129. See also John Hart, *The Presidential Branch*, 2d ed. (Chatham, N.J.: Chatham House, 1995), chap. 4.

12. George Stephanopolous, *All Too Human: A Political Education* (Boston: Little, Brown, 1999), 210.

13. Or, as only Henry Kissinger would put it, "propinquity counts for much." See Kissinger, *White House Years* (Boston: Little, Brown, 1979), 47; this is a truth to which the quadrennial battle over West Wing office space testifies. See also Hedrick Smith, *The Power Game*, paperback ed. (New York: Ballantine Books, 1988), 300f., and for the wider point, Jeffrey Pfeffer, *Managing with Power: Politics and Influence in Organizations* (Boston: Harvard Business School Press, 1992), 118–25.

14. See, for example, John H. Kessel, "The Structures of the Carter White House," *American Journal of Political Science* 27 (1983): 431–63; Kessel, "The Structures of the Reagan White House," *American Journal of Political Science* 28 (1984): 231–58; Joseph Pika, "White House Boundary Roles: Marginal Men amidst the Palace Guard," *Presidential Studies Quarterly* 16 (Fall 1986): 700–15.

15. See William T. Bianco, *Trust: Representatives and Constituents* (Ann Arbor: University of Michigan Press, 1994); Oliver Williamson, "Calculativeness, Trust, and Economic Organization," in Williamson, *The Mechanisms of Governance* (New York: Oxford University Press, 1996), chap. 10.

16. On principal-agent relations, see B. Dan Wood and Richard W. Waterman, *Bureaucratic Dynamics: The Role of Bureaucracy in a Democracy* (Boulder, Colo.: Westview Press, 1994), chap. 2. With respect to the White House, Kennedy counsel Ted Sorensen argued that presidents must watch "who is able to invoke the president's name, who is using the president's telephone, and who is using the president's stationery. That's serious. If you have hundreds of people doing that, there is no way you can keep them out of mischief." Quoted in Kernell and Popkin, *Chief of Staff*, 106.

17. See Joel Aberbach and Bert Rockman, "The Political Views of U.S. Senior Federal Executives, 1970–92," *Journal of Politics* 57 (1995): 838–52, and Ab-

erbach and Rockman, *Inside the Web of Politics* (Washington, D.C.: Brookings Institution, 2000).

18. Harold Seidman and Robert Gilmour, *Politics, Position, and Power*, 4th ed. (New York: Oxford University Press, 1986), 82. Ronald Reagan's system of Cabinet Councils was designed to combat this by keeping Cabinet secretaries at the White House for large portions of their workweek; Bill Clinton tried a "touchy-feely" Cabinet retreat at Camp David in early 1993. See Chester Newland, "Executive Office Policy Apparatus: Enforcing the Reagan Agenda," in Lester Salamon and Michael S. Lund, eds., *The Reagan Presidency and the Governing of America* (Washington, D.C.: Urban Institute Press, 1984), and Stephanopoulos, *All Too Human*, 129ff. But as Bradley Patterson points out, "ask a federal employee 'for whom do you work?' and the answer will always be 'for the Bureau of Land Management'—or the FBI, or the IRS, or the Navy—never 'I work for the president.'" *White House Staff*, p. 18.

19. Richard F. Fenno, Jr., *The President's Cabinet* (Cambridge: Harvard University Press, 1959), 6.

20. True D. Morse, oral history of October 9, 1967 (no. 40), DDEL, 21.

21. John Brehm and Scott Gates, *Working, Shirking, and Sabotage: Bureaucratic Response to a Democratic Public* (Ann Arbor: University of Michigan Press, 1997), chap. 1; Wood and Waterman, *Bureaucratic Dynamics*. For an early formal review of the divergence, along these lines, between presidential and bureaucratic preferences, see Jonathan Bendor, Serge Taylor, and Roland Van Gaalen, "Stacking the Deck: Bureaucratic Missions and Policy Design," *American Political Science Review* 81 (1987): 873–96.

22. Kathryn Dunn Tenpas and Matthew J. Dickinson, "Governing, Campaigning, and Organizing the Presidency: An Electoral Connection?" *Political Science Quarterly* 112 (Spring 1997): 51–66.

23. R. Douglas Arnold, *Congress and the Bureaucracy: A Theory of Influence* (New Haven: Yale University Press, 1979); D. Roderick Kiewiet and Mathew D. McCubbins, *The Logic of Delegation* (Chicago: University of Chicago Press, 1991). For a good review, and strong extension, of this literature, see David Epstein and Sharyn O'Halloran, *Delegating Powers: A Transaction Cost Politics Approach to Policy Making under Separate Powers* (New York: Cambridge University Press, 1999), chap. 2.

24. Herbert Kaufman, *The Administrative Behavior of Federal Bureau Chiefs* (Washington, D.C.: Brookings Institution, 1981), 164. See also Morris Fiorina, *Congress: Keystone of the Washington Establishment*, 2d ed. (New Haven: Yale University Press, 1989); Wilson, *Bureaucracy*, chap. 13.

25. For a discussion of these models, see Jeffrey M. Berry, *The Interest Group Society*, 3d ed. (New York: Longman, 1997), 194ff.

26. Kaufman, *Administrative Behavior*, 66.

27. Quoted in Erwin Hargrove and Samuel A. Morley, eds., *The President and the Council of Economic Advisers: Interviews with CEA Chairmen* (Boulder, Colo.: Westview Press, 1984), 235.

28. Mark Alger to Walter Minnick, "Location of Counsellors in the Executive Office of the President," memo of 11/22/72. WHSpF: Staff/Office Files of John Dean, Box 63, [3 of 5], NPMP.

29. In other subfields of political science, information is a crucial element in the study of institutions. Perhaps most prominent in the current American politics literature is the debate over the role of congressional committees as informational institutions for the full chamber; see, for example, Keith Krehbiel, *Information and Legislative Organization* (Ann Arbor: University of Michigan Press, 1991).

30. Two early and influential works on this point are Theodore J. Lowi, *The Personal Presidency* (Ithaca, N.Y.: Cornell University Press, 1985); Bert A. Rockman, *The Leadership Question* (New York: Praeger, 1984).

31. Quoted in Patrick Anderson, *The Presidents' Men*, paperback ed. (Garden City, N.Y.: Anchor Books, 1969), 394.

32. Terry Moe, "The Politicized Presidency," 239. The term "responsive competence" is Moe's. More generally, see Colin Campbell, *Managing the Presidency: Carter, Reagan, and the Search for Executive Harmony* (Pittsburgh: University of Pittsburgh Press, 1986); Hugh Heclo, "The Office of Management and Budget and the Presidency: The Problem of Neutral Competence," *Public Interest* 38 (1975): 80–98.

33. For a cogent review, see Peter Hall and Rosemary C. R. Taylor, "Political Science and the Three New Institutionalisms," *Political Studies* 44 (1996): 936–57. Other useful sources are Robert E. Goodin, "Institutions and Their Design," in Goodin, ed., *The Theory of Institutional Design* (New York: Cambridge University Press, 1996); Thomas Hammond, "Structure, Strategy, and the Agenda of the Firm," in Richard P. Rumelt, Dan E. Schendel, and David J. Teece, eds., *Fundamental Issues in Strategy: A Research Agenda* (Boston: Harvard Business School Press, 1994); Gary J. Miller, *Managerial Dilemmas* (New York: Cambridge University Press, 1992); and Moe, "The New Economics of Organization," *American Journal of Political Science* 28 (November 1984): 739–77.

34. Terry M. Moe and Scott A. Wilson, "Presidents and the Politics of Structure," *Law and Contemporary Problems* 57 (Summer 1994): 43.

35. Moe, "The Politicized Presidency," 246. See also pp. 237–38, 241.

36. For a vigorous debate on this subject, see the essays — particularly those by Erwin Hargrove, Gary King, and Terry Moe — in George C. Edwards III, John H. Kessel, and Bert A. Rockman, eds., *Researching the Presidency: Vital Questions, New Approaches* (Pittsburgh: University of Pittsburgh Press, 1993).

37. See Moe, "The Politicized Presidency," 251–62.

38. Oliver Williamson, *The Mechanisms of Governance* (New York: Oxford University Press, 1996), 6, 89. Williamson credits John R. Commons's 1930s work as the source of transaction-oriented approaches (see p. 26).

39. This is Richard E. Neustadt's definition of presidential power.

40. I share new institutionalists' general assumptions about presidential preferences: that is, the president prefers a "better" outcome to a "worse" one. He may rank his options as he chooses, but would rather win than lose and will prefer a course of action that is "cheaper" (managerially) to more expensive options, all else equal.

41. Parallel to this transaction-level argument, Mazmanian and Sabatier point out more generally that public policy inputs vary, issue by issue: thus while any particular Buick is as easy to make as any other Buick, a government

regulator faces easier or harder cases with which to turn "raw material" into implemented policy. See Daniel A. Mazmanian and Paul A. Sabatier, *Implementation and Public Policy* (Glenview, Ill.: Scott, Foresman, 1983).

42. Stephen Skowronek, *The Politics Presidents Make* (Cambridge: Harvard University Press, 1994), 49–56.

43. Of which Moe has been a prominent advocate: see his "New Economics of Organization."

44. Richard E. Neustadt, *Presidential Power and the Modern Presidents* (New York: Free Press, 1990), 128–29.

45. Barry D. Karl, *Executive Reorganization and Reform in the New Deal* (Cambridge: Harvard University Press, 1963), 246.

46. Hall and Taylor, "Political Science and the Three New Institutionalisms," 951.

47. See, for example, Peter W. Sperlich, "Bargaining and Overload: An Essay on *Presidential Power*," in Aaron Wildavsky, ed., *The Presidency* (Boston: Little, Brown, 1969); Samuel Kernell, *Going Public*, 3d ed. (Washington, D.C.: CQ Press, 1997).

48. The State of the Union address is an arguable exception. As argued in Chapter Four, though, the State of the Union is far from a complete compilation of the president's program in most years. Further, the proposals it presents are often vague exhortations, fleshed out more fully in subsequent subject-specific messages.

49. See Epstein and O'Halloran, *Delegating Powers*, 38ff.; Williamson, *Mechanisms of Governance*; and the cites below.

50. Krehbiel, *Information and Legislative Organization*. John Mark Hansen, similarly, discusses legislators' informational needs vis-à-vis interest groups; see his *Gaining Access: Congress and the Farm Lobby, 1919–1981* (Chicago: University of Chicago Press, 1991). More broadly, game theorists have found that outcomes are extremely sensitive to informational conditions.

51. Norman C. Thomas, "Presidential Advice and Information: Policy and Program Formulation," *Law and Contemporary Problems* 35 (1970): 540–72. Long before this, even, Leonard White's standard public administration textbook listed as the first requirement of the (then novel) EOP to "ensure that the chief executive is adequately and currently informed." White, *Introduction to the Study of Public Administration*, 3d ed. (New York: Macmillan, 1948), 52.

52. But see Matthew J. Dickinson, *Bitter Harvest: FDR, Presidential Power, and the Growth of the Presidential Branch* (New York: Cambridge University Press, 1997), esp. 9–14; Daniel E. Ponder, *Good Advice: Information and Policy Making in the White House* (College Station: Texas A&M Press, 2000).

53. Ronald Coase, "The Nature of the Firm," *Economica* 4 (1937): 386–405.

54. Oliver Williamson is probably the most prominent scholar in this area; see Williamson, *Markets and Hierarchies* (New York: Free Press, 1975); *The Economic Institutions of Capitalism* (New York: Free Press, 1985); and the collected essays in *The Mechanisms of Governance*, especially chapter 3. But see also Kenneth Arrow, *Information and Economic Behavior* (Technical Report 14SNR, Harvard Project on Efficiency in Decision Making, 1973); Harold Dem-

setz, "The Theory of the Firm Revisited," *Journal of Law, Economics, and Organization* 4 (1988): 141–61; Oliver Hart, "An Economist's Perspective on the Theory of the Firm," in Oliver Williamson, ed., *Organization Theory: From Chester Barnard to the Present and Beyond*, expanded ed. (New York: Oxford University Press, 1995); Paul Milgrom and John Roberts, "Bargaining Costs, Influence Costs, and the Organization of Economic Activity," in James E. Alt and Kenneth A. Shepsle, eds., *Perspectives on Positive Political Economy* (New York: Cambridge University Press, 1990).

55. See most notably Epstein and O'Halloran, *Delegating Powers*; this approach is broadened somewhat in John D. Huber, Charles R. Shipan, and Madelaine Pfahler, "Legislatures and Statutory Control of Bureaucracy," *American Journal of Political Science* 45 (April 2001): 330–45.

56. See Dickinson, *Bitter Harvest*, 224, for a parallel discussion of presidential choices to institutionalize bargaining resources.

57. Ash oral history, August 4, 1988, NPMP, 15.

58. See on this point Randall Calvert, "The Value of Biased Information," *Journal of Politics* 47 (1985): 530–55. One could argue (compare Bianco, *Trust*; Williamson, *Mechanisms of Governance*, chap. 10) that the question of expertise is a subset of that of preferences (since the president prefers correct information to incorrect).

59. Seidman and Gilmour, *Politics, Position, and Power*, 80. See also Judith Michaels, *The President's Call: Executive Leadership from FDR to George Bush* (Pittsburgh: University of Pittsburg Press, 1997), 53.

60. A. James Reichley, *Conservatives in an Age of Change* (Washington, D.C.: Brookings Institution, 1981), 126.

61. Quoted in Patterson, *White House Staff*, 31.

62. See, for example, Daniel Patrick Moynihan, *Coping* (New York: Random House, 1973), 322.

63. Lyndon B. Johnson, *The Vantage Point: Perspectives on the Presidency, 1963–69*, paperback ed. (New York: Popular Library, 1971), 326. More broadly, Thomas and Wolman note presidents' concern regarding "a dearth in imagination in agency-oriented proposals which tend to be remedial and incremental rather than broadly innovative." See Norman C. Thomas and Harold L. Wolman, "Policy Formulation in the Institutionalized Presidency: The Johnson Task Forces," in Thomas E. Cronin and Sanford D. Greenberg, eds., *The Presidential Advisory System* (New York: Harper and Row, 1969), 126.

64. Jimmy Carter oral history in Kenneth W. Thompson, ed., *Portraits of American Presidents, vol. 8: The Carter Presidency* (Lanham, Md.: University Press of America, 1990), 6. Carter is quick to add that he "never acted unilaterally on a recommendation by Brzezinski that involved international policy" (p. 7). On the broader point of time horizons and their results, see John Kingdon, *Agendas, Alternatives, and Public Policies*, 2d ed. (New York: Harper-Collins, 1995), 33.

65. Robert B. Reich, *Locked in the Cabinet* (New York: Knopf, 1997), 150.

66. Joseph A. Califano, Jr., oral history of June 16, 1973 (AC 74–69), LBJL, 35.

67. Eugene Bardach, *Getting Agencies to Work Together* (Washington, D.C.: Brookings Institution, 1998), 232. See also Wilson, *Bureaucracy*, 269ff.

68. Quoted in Kernell and Popkin, *Chief of Staff*, 112. See also Laurence E. Lynn, Jr., and David DeF. Whitman, *The President as Policymaker: Jimmy Carter and Welfare Reform* (Philadelphia: Temple University Press, 1981), 4.

69. At the same time, the increased technical complexity of any one policy item, especially within a single department's jurisdiction, may spark increased departmental involvement. This is discussed further below.

70. Or at least to make their own work, pulling problems into the White House the president might rather avoid. Ted Sorensen's comment noted above gets at this point. So does Ronald Reagan's wistful comment about the Iran-*contra* affair: "Every day I go to bed, I realize there are hundreds if not thousands of people out there who say they're speaking on my behalf whom I've never met. . . . That's kind of scary." Quoted in Bob Woodward, *Shadow: Five Presidents and the Legacy of Watergate*, paperback ed. (New York: Simon & Schuster/Touchstone, 2000), 136.

71. James Gaither oral history of January 17, 1969 (AC 72–21), LBJL, 7.

72. See, for example, Light, *The Tides of Reform*; Peri Arnold, *Making the Managerial Presidency*, 2d rev. ed. (Lawrence: University Press of Kansas, 1998) discusses both the general trend and the Nixon plan in some detail.

73. William Carey (Executive Assistant Director, BoB) to Larry O'Brien, "Congressional Liaison, Bureau of the Budget," memo of 3/10/61. RG 51, LRD Subject Files, 1939–70 (series 39.39), Box 10, [White House Correspondence — 1961], NA-II.

74. The Reorganization Act of 1949 gave presidents the power to submit reorganization plans to Congress, which would be adopted unless disapproved by either chamber. This authority, after intermittent extensions (see, for example, P.L. 95–17), expired in April 1981. Note though that many reorganizations (such as the creation of new Cabinet departments) could not be accomplished under Reorganization Act authority.

75. *Congressional Quarterly Almanac, 1982*, 303ff.; Robert D. Hershey Jr., "Reagan Said to Consider Saving Energy Dept.," *New York Times* (December 16, 1981): A22; Howell Raines, "Reagan Adopts Plan to End Energy Department and Shift Its Duties," *New York Times* (December 17, 1981): A1; Paul Taylor, "Reagan, as Promised, Will Ask Congress to Dismantle Energy Department," *Washington Post* (December 18, 1981): A16.

76. Arnold, *Making the Managerial Presidency*, 348.

77. Quoted in Paul Starobin, "The Broker," *National Journal* (April 16, 1994), 882.

78. Lynn and Whitman, *President as Policymaker*, 265. See below, however, for their full assessment of this strategy.

79. Whitaker oral history of 12/30/87, NPMP, 33. Or as Carter transportation secretary Brock Adams, after being fired, complained of the White House staff, "There's a difference between campaigning and governing. Governing takes a different kind of person. You can't govern [by] being against government." Quoted in Phillip G. Henderson, *Managing the Presidency: The Eisen-*

hower Legacy, from Kennedy to Reagan (Boulder, Colo.: Westview Press, 1988), 62. More generally, see Charles O. Jones, *Passages to the Presidency: From Campaigning to Governing* (Washington, D.C.: Brookings Institution, 1998).

80. Quoted in Dick Morris, *Behind the Oval Office* (New York: Random House, 1997), 98.

81. Longtime Washingtonian Clark Clifford, for one, suggests getting a third opinion from people outside government, so that the president is not trapped between departmental advocacy and White House sycophancy. See *Counsel to the President* (New York: Random House, 1991), 423–24. Nicholas Katzenbach, attorney general and undersecretary of state under Lyndon Johnson, disagreed — but, notably, also on informational grounds. He argues that "the danger of outside advice to a president is that it comes from extremely able people with good judgement who are just badly informed. . . . It really is hard to master [a complex issue] on a weekend and to come up with very sound advice." Oral History of November 23, 1968 (AC 78–24), LBJL, 9.

82. Quoted in Lynn and Whitman, *President as Policymaker*, 266.

83. John Snow to Task Force, "Aviation Bill," memo of 9/3/75. WHSF: DC: Judith Hope files, Box 12, [Aviation Act of 1975 Sept.–Dec. 1975], GRFL.

84. Arthur Okun oral history, in Hargrove and Morley, *The President and the Council of Economic Advisers*, 278.

85. See, for example, Terry Moe, "The Politics of Bureaucratic Structure," in John Chubb and Paul E. Peterson eds., *Can the Government Govern?* (Washington, D.C.: Brookings Institution, 1989). Further, as discussed in Chapter Three, another connection of centralization to Congress is that Congress itself sometimes dictates the president's formulation strategy by statutorily empowering given departments to act in certain areas or by realigning the incentives for presidential action (as with, for example, the granting of broad reorganization authority, which tends to prompt reorganization proposals).

86. Committee staff expertise is less available to a president of the (congressional) minority party, if only because there are fewer staffers. This is especially true on the House side, where two-thirds of committee staff are hired by the majority members. In the Senate, the balance more closely reflects the partisan balance. Tim Groseclose and David C. King, "Little Theatre: Committees in Congress," in Herbert F. Weisberg and Samuel C. Patterson, eds., *Great Theatre: The American Congress in the 1990s* (New York: Cambridge University Press, 1998), 138.

87. Keith Krehbiel, *Pivotal Politics: A Theory of U.S. Lawmaking* (Chicago: University of Chicago Press, 1998).

88. Moe, "The Politicized Presidency." See additionally Robert Durant, *The Administrative Presidency Revisited* (Albany: State University of New York Press, 1992); Michaels, *The President's Call*; Richard Nathan, *The Plot That Failed: Nixon and the Administrative Presidency* (New York: Wiley, 1975); Nathan, *The Administrative Presidency* (New York: Wiley, 1983); Richard W. Waterman, *Presidential Influence and the Administrative State* (Knoxville: University of Tennessee Press, 1989).

89. Notes from meeting of 11/17/72, 10 a.m., WHSF: Haldeman: Notes

Files, [Oct. 1, 1972–Nov. 17, 1972, Part I], NPMP. "Harlow" is Nixon (and formerly Eisenhower) adviser Bryce.

90. "Minutes of Cabinet Meeting of 1/29/75," 5. James E. Connor Files, Box 4, GRFL. This concern is pervasive. For example, a memo to high-ranking White House staff early in the Eisenhower administration urges them to "get some tough guy in the personnel department of the Agriculture Department. The place is saturated below high levels with people who do not want department to succeed. . . . these people can sabotage any Secretary without the Secretary even knowing about it." See Victor Johnston to Wilton Persons, Gerald Morgan, and Jack Martin, "Suggestions for Department of Agriculture," memo of 10/23/53, WHSF: Gerald Morgan Files (no. A67-19), Box 1, [Agriculture Legislation no. 2], DDEL.

91. See Waterman, *Presidential Influence and the Administrative State*. Haldeman's discussion above about using dismantled EOP offices as a vehicle for politicization supports this notion.

92. Thomas E. Cronin, *The State of the Presidency* (Boston: Little, Brown, 1975), 191–96; the quoted passage is from p. 191.

CHAPTER THREE. THE PRESIDENT'S PROGRAM:
HISTORY AND CONVENTIONAL WISDOM

1. Minority report, House Commerce Committee, 1910 (H. Rept. 923, 61st Congress, 2d session), quoted in Lawrence Chamberlain, *The President, Congress, and Legislation* (New York: Columbia University Press, 1946), 422–23.

2. Letter, Senate Majority Leader Mike Mansfield to President Lyndon Johnson, 3/19/65. RG 51, LRD Subject Files, 1939–70 (series 39.39), Box 7, [Legislative Program Material — 89th, 1st — 1965], NA-II.

3. Mary Parker Follett, *The Speaker of the House of Representatives* (New York: Longmans, Green, 1896), 325; see also Sidney Milkis and Michael Nelson, *The American Presidency: Origins and Development, 1776–1998* (Washington, D.C.: CQ Press, 1999), 171. For excellent overarching accounts of presidential involvement in the legislative process, see Wilfred E. Binkley, *President and Congress*, 3d rev. ed. (New York: Vintage, 1962), and James L. Sundquist, *The Decline and Resurgence of Congress* (Washington, D.C.: Brookings Institution, 1981), chap. 6.

4. Theodore Roosevelt, *An Autobiography* (1913; reprint, New York: Da Capo Press, 1985), 292.

5. Louis W. Koenig, *The Chief Executive*, rev. ed. (New York: Harcourt, Brace and World, 1968), 136. See also Edward S. Corwin, *The President: Office and Powers*, 5th rev. ed. updated by Randall W. Bland, Theodore T. Hindson, and Jack W. Peltason (New York: New York University Press, 1984), 307–8.

6. Sundquist, *Decline and Resurgence*, 130–31.

7. See Koenig, *The Chief Executive*; Sundquist, *Decline and Resurgence*. Note that the president himself has no standing to introduce bills in Congress; this is done by a friendly legislator in either or each chamber. It is relatively rare

but not unknown that a president is unable to find a congressional sponsor for his proposal, even one who will simply introduce the measure "by request."

8. See especially Frank Freidel, *Franklin D. Roosevelt: A Rendezvous with Destiny* (Boston: Little, Brown, 1990), 94–99; James MacGregor Burns, *Roosevelt: The Lion and the Fox* (New York: Harcourt, Brace and World, 1956), 166–68; Binkley, *President and Congress*, 295–303. Bernard Fay writes that far from acting like a dictator, Roosevelt bargained hard in consultations before bills' introduction, and "behaved in fact very much more like a French Premier who never can make a move without having previously obtained the assent of his majority." Fay, *Roosevelt and His America* (Boston: Little, Brown, 1933), 332.

9. Chamberlain, *The President, Congress, and Legislation*. This work, which covered 1870 to 1940, was updated in the wake of similar claims during the Great Society, with similar conclusions: see Ronald C. Moe and Steven C. Teel, "Congress as Policy-Maker: A Necessary Reappraisal," *Political Science Quarterly* 85 (1970): 443–70.

10. See P.L. 79–304, codified at 15 U.S.C. 1021 et seq.

11. This section and the next draw on Richard E. Neustadt, "Presidency and Legislation: Planning the President's Program," *American Political Science Review* 49 (December 1955): 980–1021, esp. 996–1013.

12. Quoted in Francis H. Heller, ed., *The Truman White House: The Administration of the Presidency, 1945–1953* (Lawrence: Regents Press of Kansas, 1980), 90. See also Neustadt, "Planning the President's Program," 999–1000.

13. In 1964, for example, BoB staffer P. S. ("Sam") Hughes hammered this home to White House counsel Lee White: "There is nothing new and significant to talk about. . . . The consensus here is that the Conservation message, like several of the other messages under consideration, is not only unnecessary but undesirable in the present circumstances and we accordingly recommend that there be no Conservation message." (There wasn't, at least not in 1964.) See Hughes to White, "Comments on Interior Draft of Conservation Message," memo of 1/22/64. RG 51, Legislative Reference Division Subject Files 1939–70 (series 39.39), Box 11, [White House Correspondence—1964], NA-II.

14. Neustadt, "Planning the President's Program," 980.

15. No author, "Legislative Coordination, Clearance and Scheduling for the 1st session of the 81st Congress," 11/9/48. RG 51, Legislative Reference Division Subject Files 1939–70 (series 39.39), Box 3, [Legislative Program—81st Cong., 1st Session], NA-II. See also a November 1958 memo to the file from P. S. Hughes of the BoB's Office of Legislative Reference entitled "Action on November 5 'Preliminary List of Potential Legislative Recommendations of the President.'" Hughes marked items with notations such as "WH staff classify as departmental" or "status doubtful. Probably not more than departmental." RG 51, Legislative Reference Division Subject Files 1939–70 (series 39.39), Box 5, [Presidential Legislative Recommendations—86th Cong.], NA-II.

16. Maurice Stans to Arthur Flemming, letter of 12/17/59. RG 51, Subject Files of Director 1952–61 (series 52.1), Box 8, [Coordination and Clearance (E5–3)], NA-II.

17. Neustadt, "Planning the President's Program," 1000.

18. Ibid., 1015.

19. Al Stern to Stu Eizenstat, "96th Congress," memo of 11/27/78. WHCF: Subject Files: LE, Box LE-2, [11/1/78–12/31/78], JCL. The context is "the beating we took in the 95th Congress."

20. Stephen J. Wayne, *The Legislative Presidency* (New York: Harper and Row, 1978).

21. Richard E. Neustadt, "Statement before the Subcommittee on National Security Staffing and Operations of the Senate Committee on Government Operations, March 25, 1963," in Henry M. Jackson, ed., *The National Security Council: Jackson Subcommittee Papers on Policy-Making at the Presidential Level* (New York: Praeger, 1965), 252.

22. Budget Circular 49 to this effect was issued in December 1921. See Richard E. Neustadt, "Presidency and Legislation: The Growth of Central Clearance," *American Political Science Review* 48 (September 1954): 644.

23. Through Budget Circulars 336 (1935) and 344 (1937), respectively. The National Emergency Council was an interdepartmental committee with a functioning staff secretariat.

24. Shelley Lynne Tomkin, *Inside OMB: Politics and Process in the President's Budget Office* (Armonk, N.Y.: M. E. Sharpe, 1998), 18–20. Note that the Legislative Reference Division itself was not brand new; it was a reworking of the continuation of the Division of Coordination, a 1940 creation whose name, budget director Harold Smith feared, was not bland enough to avoid congressional attention. (Interview with Richard E. Neustadt, April 10, 2000.)

25. The LRD at this point did not prevent departments from transmitting legislation to Congress, though later it would. Rather, it noted whether the proposed law was "in accord" with, "consistent with," or "not in accord" with the president's own priorities; a fourth category registered "no objection to" the proposal from the president's perspective. The president's letter in 1947 asked simply for "a report showing the character of legislation of concern to the Department . . . which you anticipate may be considered by the Congress." (Letter from President Truman to Cabinet secretaries and agency heads, 9/26/47. RG 51, Legislative Reference Division Subject Files 1939–70 (series 39.39), Box 3, [80th Congress, 2nd session] NA-II.) For a useful summary of the clearance process, see Lester M. Salamon, "The Presidency and Domestic Policy Formulation," in Hugh Heclo and Salamon, eds., *The Illusion of Presidential Government* (Boulder, Colo.: Westview Press, 1981), 180–81.

26. Bureaus were to prepare their preliminary legislative program by September 15. "Our purpose," the budget director wrote, "is to provide more time than has heretofore been feasible for study and analysis and proper integration of legislative proposals with the President's Budget recommendations." Frank Pace, Jr., to Heads of Executive Departments and Establishments, "The Preliminary Legislative Program Requested in the 1951 Call for Estimates," Bulletin 50–5, 8/31/49. RG 51, Office Files of Director Frank Pace 1947–50 (series 47.3a), Box 1, [(Meetings — Truman-Pace), May–Aug. 1949], NA-II. See also Neustadt, "Planning the President's Program," 1008.

27. The text of Circular A-19, as last revised September 20, 1979, is available through the OMB website at *http://www.whitehouse.gov/omb/circulars/a019/a019.html*.

28. P. S. Hughes [OLR] to David Bell [incoming budget director] and Theodore Sorensen [incoming counsel to the president], "Legislative Coordination and Clearance Procedure," memo of 12/19/60, p. 1. RG 51, Subject Files of the Director 1952–1961 (series 52.1), Box 8, [Coordination and Clearance (E5–3)], NA-II.

29. Budget outlays adapted from Office of Management and Budget, *Budget of the United States, Fiscal Year 2002* (Washington, D.C.: Government Printing Office, 2001), Historical Table 1.3; *Federal Register* data provided by Matt Dickinson and updated by the author from information provided by the Office of the Federal Register.

30. See Paul C. Light, *Thickening Government: Federal Hierarchy and the Diffusion of Accountability* (Washington, D.C.: Brookings Institution, 1995), table A-1.

31. See the cites below or in Chapter One. There are some notable efforts at more systematic analysis, including John H. Kessel, *The Domestic Presidency* (Scituate, Mass.: Duxbury Press, 1975); Paul C. Light, *The President's Agenda: Domestic Policy Choice from Kennedy to Clinton*, 3d ed. (Baltimore: Johns Hopkins University Press, 1999 [first published in 1982]); Neustadt, "Planning the President's Program"; and Wayne, *The Legislative Presidency*. However, Light's admirable book focuses on a subset of the overall program (see Chapter Four on this point), and Kessel's is focused on the Nixon Domestic Council. Neustadt's covers only the Roosevelt, Truman, and early Eisenhower years. Wayne's indispensable work ends with the Carter administration.

32. For discussions of the distinction, see Larry Berman, *The Office of Management and Budget and the Presidency, 1921–1979* (Princeton: Princeton University Press, 1979); Matthew J. Dickinson, *Bitter Harvest: FDR, Presidential Power, and the Growth of the Presidential Branch* (New York: Cambridge University Press, 1997), 106–8, 212–13.

33. Heller, *The Truman White House*; Salamon, "The Presidency and Domestic Policy Formulation;" Arthur Maass, "In Accord with the Program of the President? An Essay on Staffing the Presidency," *Public Policy* 9 (1953): 77–93; Alfred Dick Sander, *A Staff for the President: The Executive Office, 1921–1952* (New York: Greenwood, 1989); Wayne, *The Legislative Presidency*.

34. Salamon, "The Presidency and Domestic Policy Formulation," 181; see also Phillip G. Henderson, *Managing the Presidency: The Eisenhower Legacy, from Kennedy to Reagan* (Boulder, Colo.: Westview Press, 1988), 50–57; Stephen Hess, *Organizing the Presidency*, 2d ed. (Washington, D.C.: Brookings Institution, 1988); Alfred Dick Sander, *Eisenhower's Executive Office* (Westport, Conn.: Greenwood, 1999); Wayne, *The Legislative Presidency*.

35. Arthur Schlesinger, *A Thousand Days: John F. Kennedy in the White House*, paperback ed. (New York: Fawcett, 1965), 631 (and see, relatedly, 195ff., 390–2). See also Hugh Davis Graham, "Short Circuiting the Bureaucracy in the Great Society: Policy Origins in Education," *Presidential Studies Quarterly* 12 (1982): 407–20; Henderson, *Managing the Presidency*, 127ff.; Bradley H. Patterson, Jr., *Ring of Power: The White House Staff and Its Expanding Role in Government* (New York: Basic Books, 1988), 272.

36. Patrick Anderson, *The Presidents' Men*, paperback ed. (Garden City,

N.Y.: Anchor Books, 1969); Graham, "Short Circuiting the Bureaucracy in the Great Society"; Norman C. Thomas and Harold L. Wolman, "Policy Formulation in the Institutionalized Presidency: The Johnson Task Forces," in Thomas E. Cronin and Sanford D. Greenberg, eds., *The Presidential Advisory System* (New York: Harper and Row, 1969).

37. Quoted in Charles Roberts, ed., *Has the President Too Much Power?* (New York: Harper's Magazine Press, 1974), 152–53.

38. The shift to OMB, and the creation of the Domestic Council, was achieved by Reorganization Plan 2 of 1970, sent to Congress on March 12, 1970; OMB was then formally created by Executive Order 11541 in July 1970. Joel Havemann, "White House Report: OMB's Legislative Role Is Growing More Powerful and More Political," *National Journal* (October 27, 1973): 1589–98; Ronald C. Moe, "The Domestic Council in Perspective," *The Bureaucrat* 5 (1976): 251–72; Raymond J. Waldmann, "The Domestic Council: Innovation in Presidential Government," *Public Administration Review* 36 (1976): 260–68.

39. Richard Nathan, *The Plot That Failed: Nixon and the Administrative Presidency* (New York: Wiley, 1975).

40. I. M. Destler, "National Security II: The Rise of the Assistant 1961–1981," in Hugh Heclo and Lester M. Salamon, eds., *The Illusion of Presidential Government* (Boulder, Colo.: Westview, 1981); John Prados, *Keepers of the Keys: A History of the National Security Council from Truman to Bush* (New York: Morrow, 1991); Christopher C. Shoemaker, *The NSC Staff: Counseling the Council* (Boulder, Colo.: Westview, 1991).

41. See the cites above, as well as Roy Ash's oral histories at the NPMP; John Ehrlichman, *Witness to Power: The Nixon Years* (New York: Simon and Schuster, 1982), 92–94; John Hart, *The Presidential Branch*, 2d ed. (Chatham, N.J.: Chatham House, 1995), 137–38; Tomkin, *Inside OMB*, 48–50.

42. Terry Moe, "The Politicized Presidency," 259. See on this score R. Gordon Hoxie, "Staffing the Ford and Carter Presidencies," in Bradley D. Nash et al., eds., *Organizing and Staffing the Presidency* (New York: Center for the Study of the Presidency, 1980).

43. Shirley Anne Warshaw, *Powersharing: White House–Cabinet Relations in the Modern Presidency* (Albany: State University of New York Press, 1996), 94 and chap. 4 generally.

44. *PPP*, January 23, 1977; Joseph A. Califano, Jr., *Governing America* (New York: Simon and Schuster, 1981), 26; Warshaw, *Powersharing*, 106–7.

45. Chester Newland, "Executive Office Policy Apparatus: Enforcing the Reagan Agenda," in Lester Salamon and Michael S. Lund, eds., *The Reagan Presidency and the Governing of America* (Washington, D.C.: Urban Institute Press, 1984), 140.

46. Ford, it should be noted, also rethought his "spokes" organization. He started, though, with a "staff coordinator" as one of those spokes and in quiet and rather de facto fashion allowed that position (occupied by Dick Cheney) to expand to a formal chief of staff by 1976. See Hess, *Organizing the Presidency*, chap. 8.

47. See Hart, *Presidential Branch*, 140; Hess, *Organizing the Presidency*, chap. 9; Warshaw, *Powersharing*, chap. 5.

48. James Baker, Ed Meese, and Mike Deaver.

49. The Reagan years inspired a slew of commentary and, in fact, the thesis of Moe's "Politicized Presidency." More broadly see Anthony J. Bennett, *The American President's Cabinet* (New York: St. Martin's Press, 1996), chap. 9; Kenneth E. Collier, "Behind the Bully Pulpit: The Reagan Administration and Congress," *Presidential Studies Quarterly* 26 (1996): 805–15; Dick Kirschten, "Decision Making in the White House: How Well Does It Serve the President?" *National Journal* (April 3, 1982): 584–89; Richard Nathan, *The Administrative Presidency* (New York: Wiley, 1983); Newland, "Executive Office Policy Apparatus: Enforcing the Reagan Agenda"; Frederic A. Waldstein, "Cabinet Government: The Reagan Management Model," in Joseph Hogan, ed., *The Reagan Years: The Record in Presidential Leadership* (New York: Manchester University Press, 1990); Shirley Anne Warshaw, "White House Control of Domestic Policymaking: The Reagan Years," *Public Administration Review* 55 (1995): 247–53; Thomas Weko, *The Politicizing Presidency: The White House Personnel Office, 1948–1994* (Lawrence: University Press of Kansas, 1995).

50. Colin Campbell, "The White House and Presidency under the 'Let's Deal' President," in Colin Campbell and Bert A. Rockman, eds., *The Bush Presidency: First Appraisals* (Chatham, N.J.: Chatham House, 1991); John Podhoretz, *Hell of a Ride: Backstage at the White House Follies, 1989–1993* (New York: Simon and Schuster, 1993); Burt Solomon, "Send in the Clones," *National Journal* 24 (March 21, 1992): 678–83.

51. Note that Clinton also created an Office of Environmental Policy within the Office of Policy Development (see Hart, *Presidential Branch*, 91). John P. Burke, "The Institutional Presidency," in Michael Nelson, ed., *The Presidency and the Political System*, 6th ed. (Washington, D.C.: CQ Press, 2000), esp. 424; I. M. Destler, *The National Economic Council: A Work in Progress*, Policy Analyses in International Economics, vol. 46 (Washington, D.C.: Institute for International Economics, 1996); Elizabeth Drew, *On the Edge: The Clinton Presidency*, paperback ed. (New York: Touchstone, 1994).

52. Sidney Milkis and Michael Nelson, *The American Presidency: Origins and Development, 1776–1998*, 3d ed. (Washington, D.C.: CQ Press, 1999), 376.

53. Michael L. Mezey, *Congress, the President, and Public Policy* (Boulder, Colo.: Westview Press, 1989), 91. See also Burke, "The Institutional Presidency," 423–25.

54. See Lyn Ragsdale and John Theis, "The Institutionalization of the American Presidency," *American Journal of Political Science* 41 (1997): 1280–1318; George A. Krause and Jeffrey E. Cohen, "Opportunity, Constraints, and the Development of the Institutional Presidency: The Issuance of Executive Orders, 1939–1996," *Journal of Politics* 62 (February 2000): 88–114.

55. Reliable and consistent White House staff size figures are hard to obtain. The best figures readily available are those presented by John Hart in *The Presidential Branch*. See table 4.2, column C, on p. 116, updated by table 4.3, on p. 119. The 1949–1976 figures in Hart rely on the work of Stephen Wayne in *The Legislative Presidency*, 220–21. I have added detailees (computed as full-time equivalents) to the salaried staff count in Table 4.3 in order to make this figure

comparable with Wayne's, and filled in 1994–1996 from the same source Hart uses (reports filed pursuant to the White House Personnel Authorization Employment Act of 1978, P.L. 95–570). Thanks to Matt Dickinson for providing those figures and data on 1977 and 1978. Note that a chart of overall EOP staff would show similar ups and downs: the two staff figures correlate at over .70.

56. Shirley Anne Warshaw, *The Domestic Presidency: Policy Making in the White House* (Boston: Allyn and Bacon, 1997), 12.

57. Quoted in Kenneth W. Thompson, ed., *Portraits of American Presidents*, vol. 5: *The Johnson Presidency* (Lanham, Md.: University Press of America, 1986), 29. Theda Skocpol, similarly, comments in *Boomerang: Clinton's Health Security Effort and the Turn against Government in U.S. Politics* (New York: W. W. Norton, 1996), that the "planning process that fleshed out the Clinton Health Security plan was not all that different from the process run by the Committee on Economic Security in 1934–1935 to draft Franklin Roosevelt's Social Security legislation" (14).

58. See on this point Peri Arnold, *Making the Managerial Presidency: Comprehensive Reorganization Planning*, 2d rev. ed. (Lawrence: University Press of Kansas, 1998), chap. 5 and 354; see also Ronald C. Moe, *The Hoover Commissions Revisited* (Boulder, Colo.: Westview Press, 1982); William E. Pemberton, *Bureaucratic Politics* (Columbia: University of Missouri Press, 1979).

59. Clark Clifford, with Richard Holbrooke, *Counsel to the President* (New York: Random House, 1991); Sander, *A Staff for the President*, 79–86, 154ff. See too the oral histories in Kenneth W. Thompson, ed., *Portraits of American Presidents, vol. 2: The Truman Presidency* (Lanham, Md.: University Press of America, 1984).

60. Quoted in Heller, *The Truman White House*, 73.

61. No author, "Legislative Coordination, Clearance and Scheduling for the 1st session of the 81st Congress," 11/9/48, 3–4. RG 51, Legislative Reference Division Subject Files 1939–70 (series 39.39), Box 3, [Legislative Program—81st Cong., 1st Session], NA-II.

62. Two memos from Richard Neustadt, then at the BoB, to OLR head Roger Jones are instructive. In the fall of 1949, Neustadt urged that OLR take an active role in rating the preliminary agency proposals received through responses to Circular A-11. "MacPhail's idea in taking on all the work we have set forth for Legislative Reference is that it is the only way to do a good job on this thing and keep our own hand in properly and insure that White House staff is kept in touch at every step. That latter applies particularly to the idea that *we will prepare* the highlight supplement on legislation for the President's highlight memorandum." Neustadt to Jones, "Bureau Procedure for Utilizing Agency Legislative Programs Submitted under Sec. 86, 'Call for Estimates,'" memo of 9/6/49 (emphasis added). RG 51, Legislative Reference Division Subject Files, 1939–70 (series 39.39), Box 4, [Legislative Program—81st Congress, 2nd session], NA-II. In May 1950 Neustadt suggested that OLR pick up another function, that of monitoring congressional action on items in the presidential program. Neustadt to Jones, "Weekly Reports on Anticipated Congressional Schedules," memo of 5/15/50. RG 51, Legislative Reference Division Subject Files, 1939–70 (series 39.39), Box 4, [Legislative Program—82nd Congress, 1st

session], NA-II. Neustadt added in his 1954 *APSR* article that while Webb did not abdicate all responsibility in the legislative area, "as a practical matter, Legislative Reference's White House ties became both real and generally respected" ("Growth of Central Clearance," 660).

63. See Berman, *Office of Management and Budget*, 40; Edward S. Flash, Jr., *Economic Advice and Presidential Leadership* (New York: Columbia University Press, 1965), 44–45; Robert E. Merriam, "The Bureau of the Budget as Part of the President's Staff," *Annals of the American Academy of Political and Social Science* 307 (1956): 15–23. The Truman Library files and oral histories of staffers such as George Elsey, Roger Jones, Charles Murphy, Richard Neustadt, Frank Pace, Harold Seidman, Elmer Staats, and James Webb provide the best primary sources; they are summarized in Matthew J. Dickinson and Andrew Rudalevige, "Revisiting the Golden Age: Responsiveness and Competence at the Bureau of the Budget, 1945–1952" (paper presented at the annual meeting of the American Political Science Association, San Francisco, August 2001).

64. L. C. Gibson to Mr. Garber, "Comments on Tentative List of Legislative items for 81st Congress," memo of 9/16/48, 2. RG 51, Legislative Reference Division Subject Files, 1939–70 (series 39.39), Box 3, [Legislative Program— 81st Cong., 1st Session], NA-II.

65. Interview with Richard E. Neustadt, April 10, 2000.

66. Patterson, *Ring of Power*, 272.

67. Sherman Adams, *Firsthand Report: The Story of the Eisenhower Administration* (New York: Harper and Brothers, 1961); Milton Eisenhower, *The President Is Calling* (Garden City, N.Y.: Doubleday, 1974); Bradley H. Patterson, Jr., "Team and Staff: Dwight Eisenhower's Innovations in the Structure and Operations of the Modern White House," *Presidential Studies Quarterly* 24 (1994): 277–98; Sander, *Eisenhower's Executive Office*; Thomas R. Wolanin, *Presidential Advisory Commissions: Truman to Nixon* (Madison: University of Wisconsin Press, 1975).

68. Quoted in Shirley Anne Warshaw, ed., *The Eisenhower Legacy: Discussions of Presidential Leadership* (Silver Spring, Md.: Bartleby Press, 1992), 99. See also Hart, *The Presidential Branch*, 212.

69. See Berman, *Office of Management and Budget*, 52–57; Aaron Wildavsky, *The New Politics of the Budgetary Process*, 2d ed. (New York: HarperCollins, 1992), 97–99.

70. Dodge to Adams and Shanley, "The Handling of Legislation Related to the President's Program by the Dept of Agriculture," memo of 3/1/54. RG 51, Subject Files of the Director 1952–1961 (series 52.1), Box 8, [Coordination and Clearance (E5–3)], NA-II.

71. Sherman Adams to Secretary of Agriculture Ezra Taft Benson, letter of 3/3/54. RG 51, Subject Files of the Director 1952–1961 (series 52.1), Box 8, [Coordination and Clearance (E5–3)], NA-II.

72. (Acting) Secretary of Agriculture [True D. Morse] to Sherman Adams, letter of 4/2/54. RG 51, Subject Files of the Director 1952–1961 (series 52.1), Box 8, [Coordination and Clearance (E5–3)], NA-II. The attached note is dated April 14, 1954. Of course, given the outcome, it might be Dodge who didn't get it—Agriculture knew full well what it was doing. An additional example comes

from 1958. "It should be called to your attention," OLR head Roger Jones informed BoB director Percival Brundage, "that the Bureau of the Budget did not participate in any way in the development of the President's message on extension of the Reciprocal Trade Act, or in the coordination and clearance of the bill that was sent to the Congress by the Secretary of Commerce on January 30. . . . [S]uch handling is clearly contrary to the President's instructions." Jones to Director, untitled, memo of 2/7/58, RG 51, Legislative Reference Division Subject Files, 1939–70 (series 39.39), box 5, [Legislative Program 85th [Congress]], NA-II. A broader treatment of this subject (that also deals well with the Truman years) can be found in Frederick C. Mosher, *A Tale of Two Agencies* (Baton Rouge: Louisiana State University Press, 1984).

73. For a comprehensive treatment of the functions and scope of the present-day executive office staff, see Bradley H. Patterson, Jr., *The White House Staff: Inside the West Wing and Beyond* (Washington, D.C.: Brookings Institution, 2000).

74. See Wayne, *The Legislative Presidency*, 79. Again, though, keep in mind that the Budget Bureau was clearly working for the White House.

75. Newland, "Executive Office Policy Apparatus," 138. See also Berman, *Office of Management and Budget*, 80, 102; Wayne, *The Legislative Presidency*, 79–82.

76. For good overviews, see Emmette S. Redford and Richard T. McCulley, *White House Operations: The Johnson Presidency* (Austin: University of Texas Press, 1986); Nancy Kegan Smith, "Presidential Task Force Operation during the Johnson Administration," *Presidential Studies Quarterly* 15(1985): 320–29; Thomas and Wolman, "Policy Formulation in the Institutionalized Presidency." The oral histories of Joseph Califano, James Gaither, and Larry Levinson at the LBJL are also very useful; a number of these interviews were conducted by Stephen Wayne during his research for *The Legislative Presidency*, and are summarized there (pp. 110–11).

77. Charles L. Schultze, oral history of March 28, 1969 (AC 83–17), LBJL, 34.

78. HEW (including the Office of Education), Labor, NSF, and OEO. Of the remaining members, one was Doug Cater of the White House staff, two were from BoB, and two from the White House's Office of Science and Technology. See the report of the task force in WHSpF: Legislative Background: Education Professions Development Act of 1967, Box 1, [Report of the Interagency Task Force on Education, 10/31/66, Folder 1], LBJL; see also James C. Gaither to the files, "Education Professions Development Act of 1967," memo of 11/15/68. WHSpF: Legislative Background: Education Professions Development Act of 1967, Box 1, [Background Summary], LBJL.

79. Joseph A Califano, Jr., oral history of June 16, 1973 (AC 74–69), LBJL, 2.

80. Ibid., 5.

81. Oral history of Califano assistant James Gaither, January 15, 1969, LBJL, 2. He adds that after 1967, "for the first time members of the White House staff could really get very deeply into the substance of these programs and actually make a substantive contribution rather than just serving as the vehicle for pulling together all the ideas for consideration by the President."

82. Bill Hunter (aide to John Ehrlichman), quoted in Kessel, *The Domestic Presidency*, 95.

83. Joan Hoff, *Nixon Reconsidered* (New York: Basic Books, 1994), 53.

84. Dom Bonafede and John K. Iglehart, "White House Report: End of Counselor System Enlarges Policy-Forming Role of Cabinet," *National Journal* (May 19, 1973): 726–29; Weko, *The Politicizing Presidency*, 109–21.

85. Robert S. Gilmour, "Central Legislative Clearance: A Revised Perspective," *Public Administration Review* 31 (1971): 152.

86. Richard M. Pious, "Sources of Domestic Policy Initiatives," in Harvey C. Mansfield, Sr., ed., *Congress against the President* (New York: Praeger, 1975), 102.

87. Pious's comment may go too far: see, for example, Gilmour, "Central Legislative Clearance," 156; Kessel, *The Domestic Presidency*. Still, a surprising amount of testimony from Nixon insiders supports the Pious argument in rather similar terms. CEA chair Herb Stein, for example, claimed that "[T]hey were basically not policymaking people on the Domestic Council. . . . it was a paper handling staff and an adjunct to the Congressional Liaison Office, but they were primarily involved in making sure that the various departments submitted the necessary papers." See Stein's oral history in Erwin C. Hargrove and Samuel A. Morley, eds., *The President and the Council of Economic Advisers: Interviews with CEA Chairmen* (Boulder, Colo.: Westview Press, 1984), 373. Likewise, OMB director Roy Ash argued, "The Domestic Council never was created with real policy-makers. Never. . . . [I]t didn't have a staff that was intellectually oriented toward the analysis and thinking through of broad policy issues. They were too much oriented to the operational, the case work, the political." See Ash's oral history of January 13, 1988, NPMP, 45. Longtime Nixon assistant and Cabinet secretary George Shultz piled on: "The presence of the new Domestic Council staff, rather than contributing to White House policy analysis, all too often simply extended the advocacy process to the White House itself by providing departmental advocates with an Executive Office beachhead." See George P. Shultz and Kenneth Dam, *Economic Policy beyond the Headlines* (New York: W. W. Norton, 1977), 161. Even Domestic Council staffers admitted that a lot of their time was spent "fire-fighting" (Kessel, *Domestic Presidency*, 95–97). John Whitaker notes that the council staff worked closely with the OMB. OMB, he recalls, "could give you all kinds of facts. . . . So, we would jointly write memos to the President. . . . OMB had more of the substantive parts and I had more of the politics." See Whitaker's NPMP oral history of December 30, 1987, 32.

88. See Nathan, *The Plot That Failed*, 52. Nathan argues, in fact, that the two strategies are inconsistent, not complementary.

89. John Osborne, *White House Watch: The Ford Years* (Washington, D.C.: New Republic Books, 1977), 49.

90. Ibid., 85; Wayne, *Legislative Presidency*, 122ff.

91. As Treasury Secretary William Simon chided council director Jim Cannon, "the draft memo dated December 8 is improved, but still doesn't provide the information the President would need to make informed decisions. . . . I realize that your staff are not experienced in this very complex policy area, and

that the time pressure is intense. But the financial issues here are second to none in magnitude, and the harm done by an unwise decision is especially difficult to undo. I urge you to allow enough time to permit my staff to work directly with yours so that a more accurate, readable, and compact decision instrument can be produced." Simon to Cannon, "Decision Memo for the President on Social Security," memo of 12/10/75. WHSF: Domestic Council: Arthur Quern files, Box 9, [Social Security 12/10/75–1/31/76], GRFL.

92. For a detailed examination of the EPB, see Roger B. Porter, *Presidential Decision Making: The Economic Policy Board* (New York: Cambridge University Press, 1980); this roster is on p. 43.

93. Hart, *Presidential Branch*, 89, 140, and Warshaw, *Powersharing*, chap. 5, argue the "pro" side; beyond the cites above, at least two leading students of the presidency conclude differently: see Norman C. Thomas and Joseph A. Pika, *The Politics of the Presidency*, rev. 4th ed. (Washington, D.C.: CQ Press, 1997), 349.

94. Weko, *The Politicizing Presidency*, 121–23.

95. Stephen Wayne, "Comments: Politics instead of Policy," in Lester Salamon and Michael S. Lund, eds., *The Reagan Presidency and the Governing of America* (Washington, D.C.: Urban Institute Press, 1984), 176.

96. Here Hart, and Thomas and Pika, agree. See Hart, *Presidential Branch*, 90–91; Thomas and Pika, *Politics of the Presidency*, 349–50.

97. Quoted in William A. Niskanen, *Reaganomics* (New York: Oxford University Press, 1988), 306. Niskanen himself disagrees, arguing that the councils served the worthwhile purpose of slowing program development and thus reducing the frequency of policy errors.

98. Niskanen notes that James Baker, when he became Treasury secretary, rarely brought Treasury items before the relevant Cabinet Council (*Reaganomics*, 307). Edwin Meese, while attorney general, continued to chair the Domestic Policy Council and had Justice staff in charge of its working groups. See Robert Pear, "Meese Playing Central Role in Domestic Policy Now," *New York Times* (September 17, 1986): B8.

99. Truman's submission of his State of the Union and budget messages as a single combined document in 1946 was designed to drive home this point; the phrase quoted is from the introductory passage of that message (January 21, 1946).

100. Kenneth A. Shepsle, "The Changing Textbook Congress," in John Chubb and Paul E. Peterson, eds., *Can the Government Govern?* (Washington, D.C.: Brookings Institution, 1989), 259.

101. Wildavsky, *New Politics of the Budgetary Process*, 216; see also Donald F. Kettl, *Deficit Politics* (New York: Macmillan, 1992).

102. See the Congressional Budget and Impoundment Control Act of 1974 (P.L. 93–344). This created a process by which presidents must request congressional permission to rescind previously appropriated spending (hence, "rescission" messages). The Line Item Veto Act of 1996 (P.L. 104–130), struck down by the Supreme Court in June 1998, briefly gave President Clinton the power of "enhanced rescission"—that is, his recommendations on spending cancellations were deemed approved unless Congress passed a resolution reinstating the funds in question.

103. Calculated from the *Public Papers of the Presidents*. Note that Ford and Carter each sent an additional rescission message as lame ducks (in 1977 and 1981, respectively); these are not included here.

104. From 42 USC 2153 (a)(9). The 1978 language also requires consultation with the Arms Control and Disarmament Agency, which was later folded into the State Department. Like reorganization plans, nuclear export agreements normally go into effect unless disapproved by Congress—a key exception is if the president chooses to waive the requirements of the law relating to the certification of nonproliferation, in which case Congress must affirmatively approve the agreement.

105. See 16 USC 1822–1823.

106. After all, in November 1990, Bush chief of staff John Sununu said in a speech that "there's not a single piece of legislation that needs to be passed in the next two years for this president." Quoted in Milkis and Nelson, *The American Presidency: Origins and Development*, 363. Still, given that the size of the presidential program is itself a presidential choice, even this issue has implications for management.

107. Joel Aberbach, "The President and the Executive Branch," in Colin Campbell and Bert A. Rockman, eds., *The Bush Presidency: First Appraisals* (Chatham, N.J.: Chatham House, 1991), 238; and see Martin Laffin, "The President and the Subcontractors: The Role of Top Level Policy Entrepreneurs in the Bush Administration," *Presidential Studies Quarterly* 26 (1996): 550–66.

108. See Warshaw, *Powersharing*, 169–70.

109. Ibid., 186–88, 194–96; see also Hart, *Presidential Branch*, 90–91.

110. For such a portrait see the essays in Colin Campbell and Bert A. Rockman, eds., *The Clinton Presidency: First Appraisals* (Chatham, N.J.: Chatham House, 1996). See also Burt Solomon, "Drawn and Redrawn, the Lines in the West Wing Get Blurrier," *National Journal* (January 15, 1994): 134.

111. Indeed, as noted in Chapter Two, the new president's transition report on personnel evidently failed to discuss the White House staff. Jack Nelson and Robert J. Donovan, "The Education of a President," *Los Angeles Times Magazine* (August 1, 1993). See also Drew, *On the Edge*; Dick Morris, *Behind the Oval Office* (New York: Random House, 1997), 97–98.

112. Warshaw, *Powersharing*, 215–19.

113. Weko, *The Politicizing Presidency*, 125–26.

114. Interview with John Donahue, former assistant secretary of labor, February 25, 2000.

115. See Gary King, "The Methodology of Presidential Research," in George C. Edwards III, John H. Kessel, and Bert A. Rockman, eds., *Researching the Presidency: Vital Questions, New Approaches* (Pittsburgh: University of Pittsburgh Press, 1993).

CHAPTER FOUR. THE PRESIDENT'S PROGRAM: AN EMPIRICAL OVERVIEW

1. The memo argues that Eisenhower proposed 23 "major recommendations" in 1953 and 42 in 1954, of which 12 and 17 passed, respectively. Kennedy's figures are 33 of 53 for 1961 and 40 of 55 for 1962—a rather more

optimistic survey than most contemporary observers conceded. No author (presumably the Office of Congressional Relations), n.d., "Review of Major Legislation of Kennedy/Eisenhower Administration," President's Office Files: Legislative Files, Box 52, [Review of Major Legislation of Kennedy/Eisenhower Administration], JFKL.

2. John [Markus, OMB] to Frank Moore, memo of 6/1/77. WHCF: Subject Files, Box LE-1, [LE 5/1/77–6/30/77], JCL.

3. For Johnson: Lawrence F. O'Brien and Joseph A. Califano, "Final Report to President Lyndon B. Johnson on the 89th Congress," 10/24/66. WHSF: Joseph Califano Office Files, Box 49, [Legislation], LBJL. For Clinton: No author credited, "President Clinton's Record of Accomplishment on the Two-Year Anniversary of His Inauguration," Office of the Press Secretary, the White House, January 19, 1995.

4. Jim Keogh to George Shultz, Bob Finch, and John Ehrlichman, no title, 12/23/70. WHCF: Subject Files: EX LE, Box 3, [16 of 39, December 3–28, 1970], NPMP; Ted Sorensen to President Kennedy, "Legislative Priorities," 6/11/62. WHSF: Theodore Sorensen papers, Box 58, [Memos Re: Legislation 1962], JFKL.

5. See Paul C. Light, *The President's Agenda: Domestic Policy Choice from Kennedy to Clinton*, 3d ed. (Baltimore: Johns Hopkins University Press, 1999), 4; Shelley Lynne Tomkin, *Inside OMB: Politics and Process in the President's Budget Office* (Armonk, N.Y.: M. E. Sharpe, 1998), 162–63. As Light found in his original 1982 study, the full list includes a wide range of items that should not be classified as presidential, even when considering only items receiving OMB approbation as "in accord with the program of the President." Light therefore utilized items that were listed by OMB as in accord with the president's program but that also appeared in one or more State of the Union addresses (see p. 41).

6. Records covering 1949–1979, with occasional gaps, are in the archives. For two examples of such documents see "Legislative Recommendations of the President, 83rd Congress, 2nd Session: Final Report, September 15, 1954," RG 51, Office of Legislative Reference Subject Files, 1939–70 (series 39.39), Box 5, [Status Reports — 83rd Congress, 2nd Session], NA-II; or "Major Presidential Legislative Proposals: 90th Congress, 1st Session," 12/8/67, WHSF: Joseph Califano Office Files, Box 50, [Legislation 1968 — 2], LBJL. OMB provided 1989–1996 clearance records to me directly, along with somewhat differently formatted (and far less comprehensive) documents covering 1987 and 1988. Since Light had access to similar material, his updates of *The President's Agenda* have faced similar problems. In updating his work to include the Reagan presidency, he was unable to duplicate his first dataset (1961–1980) for the 1981–1988 period (see *The President's Agenda*, 241). Light's 1981–1988 data include instead all items mentioned by President Reagan in an inaugural or State of the Union address and later submitted as a legislative proposal included in Congressional Quarterly's annual *Almanac* for that year. Presumably the Bush and Clinton agendas were calculated the same way (see ibid., chap. 12, 277ff.).

7. See, for example, Light, *The President's Agenda*; Jeffrey E. Cohen, *Presidential Responsiveness and Public Policy-Making* (Ann Arbor: University of

Michigan Press, 1997). Raw data are found in Lyn Ragsdale, *Vital Statistics on the Presidency: Washington to Clinton*, rev. ed. (Washington, D.C.: CQ Press, 1998), table 8-3.

8. See, for example, Mark A. Peterson, *Legislating Together* (Cambridge: Harvard University Press, 1990); Steven A. Shull, *Domestic Policy Formation: Presidential-Congressional Partnership?* (Westport, Conn.: Greenwood Press, 1983); Robert A. Spitzer, *The Presidency and Public Policy: The Four Arenas of Presidential Power* (University: University of Alabama Press, 1983); Wayne P. Steger, "Presidential Policy Initiation and the Politics of Agenda Control," *Congress and the Presidency* 24 (Spring 1997): 17–36.

9. Quoted in Kenneth W. Thompson, ed., *Portraits of American Presidents, vol. II: The Bush Presidency, pt. 2* (Lanham, Md.: University Press of America, 1998), 97. This problem is not new. As a Budget Bureau staffer complained to the Johnson White House, "Everybody wants his own pet project mentioned, and the State of the Union message tends to evolve into a laundry list. . . . [T]he situation has become almost ridiculous, particularly since the same tendencies are evident in both the Budget Message and the Economic Report." Philip S. Hughes to Bill Moyers, "Legislation to be mentioned in the State of the Union Message," memo of 12/29/64. RG 51, Legislative Reference Division Subject Files (series 39.39), Box 7, [1965 (89th C.) Legislative Program Materials], NA-II.

10. For Truman, see Acting Director F. J. Lawton to Sen. Alexander Wiley, letter of 3/16/49. RG 51, Subject Files of the Director, 1947–52 (series 47.3), Box 2, [E4–5 (Legislative Programs)], NA-II. For Eisenhower, see the *PPP*, January 16, 1957; likewise, in his State of the Union address for 1958, Eisenhower noted specifically that "there are many items in the Administration's program . . . with which I am not dealing today. . . . I am reserving them for treatment in separate communications." In 1970, Nixon noted in his State of the Union address that "at this point I do not intend to go through a detailed listing of what I have proposed or will propose." In 1986, Reagan said, "This week I will send you our detailed proposals; tonight, let us speak of our responsibility to redefine government's role."

11. See, for example, the relevant *PPP* for 1973, 1974, 1980, 1987, and 1988.

12. BoB International Division (Barie) to Director, "1962 Supplemental for USIA for Radio and TV Activities in Latin America and Southeast Asia," memo of 5/19/61. WHCF: Subject files, Box 184, [FG 296: USIA 1/20/61–7/31/61], JFKL. Ford's messages were sent to Congress on September 12 and November 18, 1974.

13. In 1989, for example, the State of the Union address had been given by outgoing President Reagan. Instead, new president George H. W. Bush gave an address "to Congress and the Nation" on February 9, 1989. For a list of State of the Union dates and substitutes covering 1953–1989, see Cohen, *Presidential Responsiveness*, 254. To this list one could add Bill Clinton's February 17, 1993, address on "Administration Goals" and George W. Bush's "Address to the Joint Session of Congress" of February 27, 2001.

14. Richard E. Neustadt, *Presidential Power and the Modern Presidents* (New York: Free Press, 1990), 5.

15. Cohen, *Presidential Responsiveness*, 36–37.

16. Light, *The President's Agenda*, 5. As he notes there, "our definition will remain rather restrictive."

17. *Congressional Quarterly Almanac, 1954*, 42.

18. Various scholars have critiqued the Boxscore methodology quite comprehensively; for a cogent review, see Peterson, *Legislating Together*, 305–15.

19. A dataset in production around the same time as mine—partly in conjunction with it—will provide a corrected collection of Boxscore data dating from the beginning of the Republic to the mid-1990s. See Michael J. Malbin, "Presidential Proposals to Congress and Related Roll Call Votes, 1789–1993," in Elaine K. Swift et al., *Database of Congressional Historical Statistics, 1789–1988* [computer file] (Ann Arbor: Inter-University Consortium for Political and Social Research, 2001). The current project's relationship to the work of Malbin and his colleagues is noted more fully below.

20. *PPP*, January 7, 1949; "Text of Bush's Address to Congress," *Washington Post* (February 28, 2001): A11.

21. Ragsdale, *Vital Statistics*.

22. Samuel Kernell, *Going Public*, 3d ed. (Washington, D.C.: CQ Press, 1997); Jeffrey K. Tulis, *The Rhetorical Presidency* (Princeton: Princeton University Press, 1987).

23. For example, on April 21, 1971, President Nixon sent Congress a message on foreign aid that made explicit reference to two bills: the International Security Assistance Act and the International Development and Humanitarian Assistance Act. For my purposes this would constitute two messages, one on each topic.

24. This includes items like President Clinton's health care program from September and October 1993. Clinton's original address included a number of specific proposals but was followed up with a letter transmitting the actual legislation, which contained a number of additional proposals.

25. Edward V. Schneier and Bertram Gross, *Legislative Strategy: Shaping Public Policy* (New York: St. Martin's, 1993), 118.

26. *PPP*, January 24, 1963; *PPP*, January 29, 1975.

27. This was done in conjunction with the dataset mentioned above (Malbin, "Presidential Proposals to Congress and Related Roll Call Votes, 1789–1993"). I worked with the Malbin research team in error checking the 1949–1992 proposals against my own reading of the *PPP*, and in adding 1993–1996 to the ICPSR dataset. Many thanks to Professor Malbin for his permission to use this dataset before its official publication with the ICPSR.

28. These figures, and those in table 4.1, do not include messages and proposals presented by presidents in the "lame duck" period before they are to leave office but after a new Congress has been seated (for example, January 3–19, 1981).

29. Ragsdale notes in *Vital Statistics on the Presidency*, table 7-2, that 1,052 treaties were signed by presidents between 1949 and 1984, after which clear

tabulation is difficult. There are 462 messages transmitting 483 treaties in the *PPP* between 1949 and 1996.

30. As discussed below, the sample data were then weighted where appropriate to ensure that the opposite problem — too much stress on less active presidents — did not occur. In the analyses below, of course, *n* will vary since it may be impossible to assign some of the codes associated with a given observation.

Note that this analysis makes an implicit assumption: that sampling from the presidential items sent to Congress represents a random sample of all items for which a presidential decision to centralize or not is actually made (that the number of things for which a centralization decision is made but not observed, because they were never entered in the *PPP*, is negligible). However, even if this proved untrue, the results of the analysis would still be unbiased as long as the errors in observation were not correlated with the errors in the models predicting centralization presented in Chapter Five. There is no reason to believe they are so correlated.

31. A pilot study of 125 observations was first coded in order to develop the estimated standard deviation of the universe of items. The sample size of 384 was then chosen to minimize sampling error while allowing for comparisons between the strata. See William G. Cochran, *Sampling Techniques*, 3d ed. (New York: Wiley, 1977); Gary T. Henry, *Practical Sampling* (Newbury Park, Calif.: Sage Publications, 1990).

32. See *http://www.whitehouse.gov/omb/circulars/a019/a019.html*.

33. The probability of a given item being sampled was 16/(messages sent to a given Congress). Weighted analyses were conducted using the "svy" and "pweight" commands in Stata 6 statistical software. Although standard errors were also calculated using a finite population correction mechanism (adjusting for the difference between sampling with and without replacement), results were virtually identical and so standard errors reported here do not include this adjustment.

34. See Christopher Winship and Larry Radbill, "Sampling Weights and Regression Analysis," *Sociological Methods and Research* 23 (November 1994): 230–57. For a good application in political science, see Sidney Verba, Kay Schlozman, and Henry Brady, *Voice and Equality* (Cambridge, Mass.: Harvard University Press, 1995).

35. Even within the confines of the items sampled here, see, for example, Jeffrey H. Birnbaum and Alan Murray, *Showdown at Gucci Gulch* (New York: Random House, 1987); Richard Cohen, *Washington at Work: Back Rooms and Clean Air* (New York: Macmillan, 1992); or Daniel P. Moynihan, *The Politics of a Guaranteed Income: The Nixon Administration and the Family Assistance Plan* (New York: Random House, 1972).

36. See Harold L. Wolman and Astrid E. Merget, "The Presidency and Policy Formulation: President Carter and the Urban Policy," *Presidential Studies Quarterly* 10 (1980): 402–15; Daniel E. Ponder, *Good Advice: Information and Policy Making in the White House* (College Station: Texas A&M University Press, 2000). Note that Wolman and Merget also include an option for a purely congressional initiative.

37. See Wolman and Merget, "The Presidency and Policy Formulation," 403.

See also Norman C. Thomas and Wolman, "Policy Formulation in the Institutionalized Presidency: The Johnson Task Forces," in Thomas E. Cronin and Sanford D. Greenberg, eds., *The Presidential Advisory System* (New York: Harper and Row, 1969); and BoB Director to Office and Division Directors, "Instructions for Bureau Analysis of Task Force Recommendations," memo of 11/9/67. WHSF: Matthew Nimetz, Box 15, [Legislative Program Development Procedures], LBJL.

38. Sherman Adams, *Firsthand Report: The Story of the Eisenhower Administration* (New York: Harper and Brothers, 1961), 377. On the Democratic side, note Charles Schultze's comment that commissions are often used "where you know darn well what you want to do, and a task force simply becomes a means of dragooning people into accepting it." Schultze, oral history of March 28, 1969 (AC 83–17), LBJL, 36.

39. Johnson's attorney general, Ramsey Clark, argued that this is actually quite common. "These commissions don't work in a vacuum; the major part of their staff support is the Department of Justice and other federal agencies," he noted. "And I don't believe there has been one where there hasn't been . . . a very substantial input from the federal agencies and their guiding and helping shape [the final outcome]." Oral History of April 16, 1969 (AC 79–33), LBJL, 10.

40. Light, *The President's Agenda*, 89–90; interview with Nick Littlefield, former staff director and chief counsel to Senate Committee on Labor and Human Resources, October 23, 1999. For the larger point, see Charles O. Jones, *The Presidency in a Separated System* (Washington, D.C.: Brookings Institution, 1994); John W. Kingdon, *Agendas, Alternatives, and Public Policies*, 2d ed. (New York: HarperCollins, 1995); and Andrew J. Taylor, "Domestic Agenda Setting, 1947–1994," *Legislative Studies Quarterly* 23 (1998): 373–97.

41. Harry McPherson, *A Political Education: A Washington Memoir* (1972; reprint, Boston: Houghton Mifflin, 1988), 189.

42. Interview with Theodore C. Sorensen, former counsel to President Kennedy, March 7, 1999; Hugh Davis Graham, "Short Circuiting the Bureaucracy in the Great Society: Policy Origins in Education," *Presidential Studies Quarterly* 12 (1982): 408; Sorensen, *Kennedy* (New York: Harper and Row, 1965), 234–40; and, generally, the series of task force reports in the transition files of the JFKL Pre-Presidential Files.

43. Lawrence Chamberlain, *The President, Congress, and Legislation* (New York: Columbia University Press, 1946).

44. John Hart popularized this apt phrase in his *The Presidential Branch*, 2d ed. (Chatham, N.J.: Chatham House, 1995), but he gives credit for the term to Polsby (see p. viii).

45. Though the former certainly exist as well — Clinton assistant secretary of labor John Donahue told me the educational tax incentives first proposed by the president in late 1994 sprang from the "kind of idea you have in the shower." Interview, February 25, 2000.

46. More broadly still, in the Johnson administration at least, the Office of Legal Counsel in the Justice Department played a role in drafting nearly every bill. Domestic aide Joe Califano commented that "I got [Justice] to agree to take

on the job of making sure that every bill mentioned in a presidential program conformed with what the President said and wanted the bill to do. . . . They took it after the Budget Bureau, did a final check on it. They had a very good impact on the bill. Many technicians on the hill told me the legislation was much better drafted." Oral history of June 16, 1973 (AC 74–69), LBJL, 22.

47. The Harry S. Truman Library, Dwight D. Eisenhower Library, John F. Kennedy Library, Lyndon B. Johnson Library, Gerald R. Ford Library, Jimmy Carter Library, and the Richard M. Nixon Presidential Materials Project.

48. Hence, the n of observations coded on this variable equals 366 (of a possible 384).

49. Martin Laffin, "The President and the Subcontractors: The Role of Top Level Policy Entrepreneurs in the Bush Administration," *Presidential Studies Quarterly* 26 (Spring 1996): 550–66; Gwen Ifill, "Bush Housing Proposals Reflect Kemp Philosophy," *Washington Post* (November 12, 1989): A9; *Congressional Quarterly Almanac, 1989*, 654f., and *Congressional Quarterly Almanac, 1991*, 334. HUD staff of note here include the assistant secretary for community planning and development, Anna Kondratas, and Kemp aide Thomas Humbert, who worked with tenant activists on ownership issues.

50. Leslie Maitland, "Plan For Homeless Is Called Modest," *New York Times* (November 26, 1989): I-35.

51. David Hoffman, "Bush Outlines Housing Initiative but Leaves Funding Unclear," *Washington Post* (November 11, 1989): A14.

52. Melvyn Dubofsky, "Jimmy Carter and the End of the Politics of Productivity," in Gary M. Fink and Hugh Davis Graham, eds., *The Carter Presidency: Policy Choices in the Post-New Deal Era* (Lawrence: University Press of Kansas, 1998), 100; *National Journal* (April 30, 1977), 682.

53. Carter had originally not wanted to add the 3,000 jobs entailed by the YACC to the federal payroll. However, DPS felt the bill's political future would be smoother if the YACC, dear to several key congressional hearts, could be included. See Jeffrey Weinberg to Jim Frye, "Outline of Administration Proposal on Youth Employment," memo of 3/4/77, RG 51, Legislative Reference Division: Legislative Records, 1976–1980, Box 32, [R2–2/77.6, Youth Employment and Training Act of 1977], NA-II.

54. Eizenstat to President, "Youth Employment Legislation," memo of 3/3/77, WHSF: Staff Secretary, Handwriting Files, box 11, [3/7/77 [1]]; see also *Congressional Quarterly Almanac, 1977*, 116.

55. See the Youth Employment and Training Act of 1977 file referenced above, notably the comments on the draft bill; Naomi Sweeney, "Labor Draft Bill 'Youth Employment and Training Act of 1977,'" note to the file of 4/5/77; and Jim Frey to Secretary Ray Marshall, letter of 4/14/77, noting that the bill is cleared "in accord," after "discussions between our staffs and an interagency meeting resulted in agreement to make changes in the draft bill and transmittal letter."

56. Schnoor to Rommel, Revenue Sharing Act of 1969, memo of 8/15/69. RG 51, Records of the [BoB/ OMB] Government Organization Branch: Program Records, 1969–72 (series 69.5), Box 32, [G3-1 Revenue Sharing], NA-II. Note that the term "manpower," as a synonym for jobs and job training, was widely

used into the 1970s. On the development of the 1971 plan, see A. James Reichley, *Conservatives in a Time of Change* (Washington, D.C.: Brookings Institution, 1981), 158f.; H. R. Haldeman, *The Haldeman Diaries* (Sony/Imagesoft CD-ROM edition, 1994), entry of January 19, 1971.

57. See Ray Waldmann to Ken Cole, "Secretary Hodgson's memo to John Ehrlichman on a New Manpower Bill," memo of 1/27/71; Richard Nathan to Ed Harper, no title, 2/2/71, attaching Hodgson memo to Shultz on the topic; Nathan to Harper, "Special Revenue Sharing for Manpower," 2/9/71. All in WHCF: Office files of Edwin L. Harper, Box 32, [Revenue Sharing — Manpower], NPMP. See also Nathan to Harper, "Status Report on Special Revenue Sharing Programs," memo of 2/5/71, WHCF: Office files of Edwin L. Harper, Box 26, [Revenue Sharing Feb. 1971 [2 of 2]].

58. Dwight Ink to Richard Nathan, "Comments on MSRS Draft Legislation," memo of 2/20/71; Nathan to John Ehrlichman, "Status of MSRS," memo of 2/20/71 and attaching Ink's memo; Ehrlichman to Secretary Hodgson, letter of 3/1/71. All in WHCF: Office files of Edwin L. Harper, Box 32, [Revenue Sharing — Manpower], NPMP.

59. Charles Culhane, "Labor Report: Differences over Public Service Jobs Complicate Manpower Revenue-Sharing Plan," *National Journal* (March 27, 1971): 648.

60. Bureau of the Budget Staff, "Transfer of Functions of the Regional Agricultural Credit Corporation," memorandum of 12/12/47; Acting Secretary of Agriculture N. E. Dodd to James Webb, letter of 2/27/48; Arnold Miles to Director Webb, "Legislation to Effect Reorganization of RACC," memo of 3/31/48. All in RG 51, General Legislation: Main Series, 80th to 82nd Congress (series 47.1), Box 148, [T2–4/47.2], NA-II.

61. Lyndon B. Johnson, *The Vantage Point: Perspectives on the Presidency, 1963–69*, paperback ed. (New York: Popular Library, 1971), 343. Johnson was literally right: the statute governing the District dated from 1878.

62. See Schuyler Lowe (director of D.C. General Administration) to Horsky, 11/30/64 draft of suggested message on home rule; Horsky to Richard Lyon (president of the Washington Home Rule Committee, Inc.), letter of 12/7/64; Irving Bryan, assistant corporation counsel for D.C, 12/11/64 memo to file; testimony of Elmer Staats (deputy director of BoB) before the Senate Committee on the District of Columbia on S. 1118, 3/9/65. All in WHSF: Charles A. Horsky, Box 66, [Home Rule — 89th Congress], LBJL.

63. Horsky to President, "Proposed D.C. Home Rule Bill," memo of 12/18/64; Horsky to Bill Moyers, "Edits to Home Rule Message," memo of 1/26/65. WHSF: Charles A. Horsky, Box 66, [Home Rule — 89th Congress], LBJL.

64. Terry M. Moe, "The Politicized Presidency," in John Chubb and Paul E. Peterson, *New Directions in American Politics* (Washington, D.C.: Brookings Institution, 1985), 269.

65. Table 4.4 collapses categories four and five (EOP and White House). This is in part for ease of presentation, but mainly because, as argued in Chapter Three, the EOP and WHO staffs are largely indistinguishable from the point of view of centralization. This is confirmed in Chapter Five using cutpoint analysis. However, the full five-point scale is presented in like form in the Appendix, table A.3.

66. This puts codes 0 and 1 in the first category and 2, 3, and 4 in the second.

CHAPTER FIVE. PUTTING CENTRALIZATION TO THE TEST

1. As discussed in more detail below, since the formulation process matters for legislative success, what I am describing here is in some sense a system of equations that could be estimated simultaneously. Whether the president has enough information to make realistic calculations along these lines is open to question, however, and the temporal sequence matters in and of itself. In any case I have chosen for ease of exposition to analyze each stage separately and report the analysis that way. However, all the key results hold if this is estimated as a two- or three-stage least-squares model instead of the ordered probit models presented below.

2. These reports are most often found in the enacted and unenacted bill files kept by BoB/OMB on each measure in the president's program (and on a good many congressional items besides). These are available in the National Archives in College Park, Maryland (NA-II), for the 81st through 94th Congresses (the 95th and 96th Congresses are not yet indexed). Bills that became law are filed in a series entitled the "Legislative History of the Public Laws of the xth Congress"; those that did not are in a series called "General Legislation, xth to yth Congress."

3. With the exception of the two agencies discussed in Chapter Two as examples of constituent-based agencies that are not truly "presidential outfits," the Office of Economic Opportunity and the United States Trade Representative.

4. See the materials in folder [R10–8/49.1], FG 51, General Legislation: Main Series, 80th to 82nd Congress (Series 47.1), Box 135, NA-II. The Federal Security Agency, created in 1939 to house several New Deal agencies, is the predecessor to the Cabinet-level Department of Health, Education, and Welfare (HEW) created in 1953.

5. See Richard S. Williamson, *Reagan's Federalism* (Lanham, Md.: University Press of America, 1989), 159n38.

6. Although the true number of interested parties is likely undercounted (after 500 pages of EOP and departmental listings, the *U.S. Government Manual* devotes 225 pages to "independent establishments and government corporations" and another 20 to "quasi-official" agencies), any undercount should be consistent across time. Another possible concern is that this analysis disguises a secular trend: if issues are simply getting bigger over time, and this causes centralization, then contingent centralization and linear centralization might be observationally equivalent. However, while the weighted mean of the number of agency jurisdictions per message has risen over time (from 3.14 for the first six years of the sample [1949–1954] to 3.61 for the last [1991–1996]), this is not a substantively — or statistically — significant difference.

7. Again, with the exception of OEO and USTR employees. As noted in Chapter Three, consistent staff size figures are hard to obtain. This figure was developed from Harold W. Stanley and Richard G. Niemi, *Vital Statistics on American Politics*, 4th ed. (Washington, D.C.: CQ Press, 1994), table 8.7, up-

dated from the Office of Personnel Management's bimonthly publication *Employment and Trends*. Using EOP staff proved a stronger predictor than the White House Office figures defined in the production of figure 3.4; the two correlate at $r = .70$.

8. For another example of an analysis using White House staff size as a dependent variable, see Matthew J. Dickinson, "Staffing the White House, 1937–1996: A Theory and Test," in Robert Y. Shapiro, Martha Joynt Kumar, and Lawrence R. Jacobs, eds., *Presidential Power: Forging the Presidency for the 21st Century* (New York: Columbia University Press, 2000). John Hart stresses that it is the qualitative use of staff that matters, not a raw count; see *The Presidential Branch*, 2d ed. (Chatham, N.J.: Chatham House, 1995), 202–4. Interestingly, the correlation between total staff size and the size of the program as measured by annual messages is minimal ($r = .02$).

9. This index is not perfectly spaced and thus is not a pure linear measure. But using a simple dichotomous variable, or multiple dichotomous variables representing each category, gives nearly identical substantive results.

10. See Paul C. Light, *The President's Agenda: Domestic Policy Choice from Kennedy to Clinton*, 3d ed. (Baltimore: Johns Hopkins University Press, 1999), 285ff.; the example is from p. 122. See also Light, "Presidential Policy Making," in George C. Edwards III, John H. Kessel, and Bert A. Rockman, eds., *Researching the Presidency: Vital Questions, New Approaches* (Pittsburgh: University of Pittsburgh Press, 1993).

11. Or, in the two cases (Johnson, Ford) in which a new president finished the uncompleted term of his predecessor, if the former president offered it before.

12. John W. Kingdon, *Agendas, Alternatives, and Public Policies*, 2d ed. (New York: Harper Collins, 1995), 141–42; the biblical reference is to Ecclesiastes 1:9.

13. By my definition, about 70 percent of program items are considered new.

14. Light, *The President's Agenda*, 119f.

15. As described in Chapter Four, with 1993–1996 added by the author. See Michael J. Malbin, "Presidential Proposals to Congress and Related Roll Call Votes, 1789–1993," in Elaine K. Swift et al., *Database of Congressional Historical Statistics 1789–1988* (Ann Arbor, Mich.: Inter-University Consortium for Political and Social Research, 2001).

16. An advantage of this measure of complexity is that it teases out this difference: it is not co-linear with the cross-cut measure laid out above ($r = .168$). Like the reorganizational case it is not purely linear; however, using separate dichotomous variables for each point on the index produced no substantive differences.

17. Quoted in Thomas Weko, *The Politicizing Presidency: The White House Personnel Office, 1948–1994.* (Lawrence: University Press of Kansas, 1995), 124.

18. Gabriel Hauge to Sherman Adams, no title, memorandum of 11/23/53. WHSF: Gabriel Hauge Papers, Box 1, [Carbon Copies of Memoranda and Letters to Members of the White House Staff, 1952–56], DDEL.

19. Richard Nathan, *The Administrative Presidency* (New York: Wiley,

1983); Terry Moe, "The Politicized Presidency," in John Chubb and Paul E. Peterson, eds., *New Directions in American Politics* (Washington, D.C.: Brookings Institution, 1985).

20. This figure was developed from Stanley and Niemi, *Vital Statistics on American Politics*, table 8-8, updated through 1996 using the bimonthly figures of the U.S. Office of Personnel Management's *Federal Civilian Workplace Statistics: Employment and Trends*; many thanks to British Morrison of OPM for assistance. Figures are as of June of each year, except 1989 (which is as of May). Unfortunately, agency-by-agency figures were not available across the entire time period. Note that in 1972, the Postal Reorganization Act of 1970 shifted U.S. Postal Service employees from competitive to excepted service, resulting in a sizable (20–25 percentage point) drop-off in the percentage of the executive branch employed under the merit civil service. Given the nature of the newly independent, "quasi-corporate" USPS, this shift did not result in a more politicized executive branch; thus I have adjusted figures for 1949–1971 to exclude post office employees.

21. See table A.4. The list is quite conservative. Only former staff (either in prepresidential life or in the EOP) or longtime personal associates were included. Former congressional colleagues were not, unless they qualified under another category.

22. Figures refer to civilian, nonpostal employees and are drawn from Office of Personnel Management figures: the "Fact Book" of Federal Civilian Workforce Statistics (2000 edition), and "Political Appointments by Type and Work Schedule: December 1999," calculated from the Office of Workforce Information Central Personnel Data File. Obtained from *http://www.opm.gov/* on May 5, 2001. All told, there were 2,841 full-time political employees in place at the start of 2000. Non-PAS appointees (that is, political appointees not needing Senate confirmation) include noncareer members of the Senior Executive Service (660) and Schedule C (1,331) personnel. Schedule C employees are a special class of political appointment within the middle to upper ranks of the federal system (grades GS-9 through GS-15), generally performing confidential but not policy making tasks. See Judith Michaels, *The President's Call: Executive Leadership from FDR to George Bush* (Pittsburgh: University of Pittsburgh Press, 1997), 3; G. Calvin Mackenzie, ed., *The In-and-Outers: Presidential Appointees and Transient Government in Washington* (Baltimore: Johns Hopkins University Press, 1987).

23. Thomas E. Cronin, *The State of the Presidency* (Boston: Little, Brown, 1975); Jeffrey E. Cohen, *The Politics of the U.S. Cabinet* (Pittsburgh: University of Pittsburgh Press, 1988).

24. Richard Nathan, *The Plot That Failed: Nixon and the Administrative Presidency* (New York: Wiley, 1975); Weko, *The Politicizing Presidency*, 124.

25. The presidential desire for larger majorities is more explicit, of course, in the context of Chapter Six, which discusses the success of the program in Congress. For a broad treatment of the importance of legislative supermajorities to lawmaking, see Keith Krehbiel, *Pivotal Politics: A Theory of U.S. Lawmaking* (Chicago: University of Chicago Press, 1998); Barry R. Weingast, "A Rational

Choice Perspective on Congressional Norms," *American Journal of Political Science* 23 (May 1979): 245–62.

26. Keith Krehbiel, "Where's the Party?" *British Journal of Political Science* 23 (1993): 235–66. But this is hardly uncontested: see, for example, John H. Aldrich and David Rohde, "The Consequences of Party Organization in the House: The Role of the Majority and Minority Parties in Conditional Party Government," in Jon R. Bond and Richard Fleisher, eds., *Polarized Politics: Congress and the President in a Partisan Era* (Washington, D.C.: CQ Press, 2000).

27. An alternate measure is the magisterial set of NOMINATE scores calculated by Keith Poole and Howard Rosenthal, which extracts a scaled ideology code for each member of Congress from his or her votes in each session. Poole and Rosenthal calculate "common space coordinates" for the first dimension of the NOMINATE score of each member of each Congress. This process may be utilized to calculate scores for presidents as well. See Keith T. Poole and Howard Rosenthal, *Congress: A Political-Economic History of Roll Call Voting* (New York: Oxford University Press, 1997); Poole and Rosenthal, "Estimating a Basic Space from a Set of Issue Scales," *American Journal of Political Science* 42 (1998): 954–93; and with regard to the presidential scores, Poole, Rosenthal, and Nolan M. McCarty, "Veto Power and Legislation: An Empirical Analysis of Executive and Legislative Bargaining from 1961–1986," *Journal of Law, Economics, and Organization* 11 (1995): 282–312. One downside to this measure is that each score is a constant: that is, a president (or member of Congress, for that matter) is not given an ideology score for each Congress but is assumed to have the same ideology throughout his term. This assumption is not completely unrealistic but should be extended with some caution. Also, presidential NOMINATE scores were calculated on the basis of presidential positions on Congressional Quarterly's "key votes." Because these were first published for the 1953 session, using NOMINATE scores drops the four years of the second Truman administration from the analysis.

In fact the two measures are highly correlated. Presidents' scores across the real ADA and common space coordinates correlate at −.94; House medians at −.82; and Senate medians at −.87. (These correlations are negative because liberals are scored on the positive end of the −1-to-1 axis for the ADA, and on the negative end for Poole-Rosenthal.) Because the NOMINATE data are more tractable with regard to the effort to explore committee data discussed below, they are employed in models that use the committee variable. In those cases, President Truman is assigned the common space coordinate value that he earned in the U.S. Senate during his ten years of service there.

28. Because the set of roll-call votes used each year varies widely (depending, in large part, on what issues arise each year and whether they come to a vote), it is difficult to compare annual scores across years or chambers. For instance, an 80 is a "liberal" score (100, on a 0–100 scale, represents a perfect match with the ADA's preferred positions). But it is far from clear that a legislator who receives an 80 one year can be considered ideologically equivalent to a legislator receiving an 80 some years later—when the basis for judgment may have

changed completely—or even to a colleague that very same year in the other chamber, which itself had a different set of votes. See Tim Groseclose, Steven D. Levitt, and James M. Snyder, Jr., "Comparing Interest Group Scores across Time and Chambers: Adjusted ADA Scores for the U.S. Congress," *American Political Science Review* 93 (1999): 33–50. Note that since the ADA did not score legislators in 1962, no "real" scores exist either. I have followed the convention of using the 1961 scores for 1962.

For presidential scores, I have relied on the series of presidential equivalents calculated by George Krause and extended through 1996 by Dan Ponder. I am grateful to Professors Krause and Ponder for making these data available.

29. Garrison Nelson, *Committees in the U.S. Congress, 1947–1992*, 2 vols. (Washington, D.C.: Congressional Quarterly, 1993); Charles Stewart and Jonathan Woon, "Congressional Committee Assignments Data, 1993–1998," codebook and dataset, Massachusetts Institute of Technology. On the Rules Committee, see Forrest Maltzman, *Competing Principals: Committees, Parties, and the Organization of Congress* (Ann Arbor: University of Michigan Press, 1997), 169–72.

30. One is that there may be some endogeneity in the relationship between formulation and referral, if presidents tweak bill language to gain referral to a given committee. Beyond this, the effort to calculate the president's ideological distance from a given committee is complicated by the difficulty in knowing which committee is the correct reference point, given multiple referrals, sequential referrals, and the reality of bicameralism. Not only that, the congressional literature suggests that committees may act differently toward the bureaucracy (prompting, perhaps, different relationships with the president), depending on whether their jurisdiction hinges on control over distributive goods. See, inter alia, Maltzman, *Competing Principals*; David C. King, *Turf Wars* (Chicago: University of Chicago Press, 1997), Walter J. Oleszek, *Congressional Procedures and the Policy Process*, 4th ed. (Washington, D.C.: CQ Press, 1996).

31. Lisa Bordeaux, a member of the Carter congressional liaison office, makes the point: "In domestic initiatives there is usually one convenient vehicle for implementing strategies—legislation. . . . In Congress, the bill is the center of attention with Members lining up, according to their political interests, to kill it, modify it, or push it through. [But] even putting aside the vast problems of diplomatic negotiations and military security considerations, foreign policy initiatives are much more complex than domestic initiatives. As can be seen by the South Korea chronology [regarding troop withdrawals], there is no one central vehicle occupying congressional attention. . . . With respect to congressional liaison, on domestic policy initiatives our clear job is to help push the legislation through, kill, or modify it. On foreign policy initiatives (other than funding levels which have the legislative vehicle) we find ourselves, for the most part, trying to put out fires." Typescript and handwritten notes, no date [summer 1977]. WH Staff Offices: Congressional Liaison: Lisa Bordeaux, Box 112, [South Korea, 1/9/77–8/5/77], JCL. The notes seem to be for a memo signed by Ann Dye to Hamilton Jordan, "South Korea Policy—Case Study," 8/5/77, which is in the same folder.

32. The following table presents the proportion, and specific examples, of

policy at each point on the scale. Examples are all drawn from the Reagan administration for ease of comparison (weighted mean = −.81; S.E. = .08):

−2   (52.3%)   Conversion of CETA program to block grant (2/6/82)
−1   (15.1%)   Agricultural Adjustment Act (2/23/85)
0   (7.4%)   Amend Foreign Corrupt Practices Act (1/27/87)
1   (12.2%)   Defense modernization program (MX, et al) (4/19/83)
2   (13.0%)   Improve security at U.S. embassies (9/27/84)

Another useful division of policy issues is found in Steven A. Shull, *Presidential-Congressional Relations: Policy and Time Approaches* (Ann Arbor: University of Michigan Press, 1997), table A.1, who expands an early typology devised by Gary King and Lyn Ragsdale to classify roll calls into seven mutually exclusive categories: foreign trade, foreign aid, defense, social welfare, government/economic management, resources (including everything from energy to transportation to crime to housing), and agriculture.

33. Light, *The President's Agenda*, 126.

34. The variable is defined in David R. Mayhew, *Divided We Govern* (New Haven: Yale University Press, 1992), 177. I calculated it from Council of Economic Advisers, *Economic Report of the President, January 2001* (Washington, D.C.: U.S. Government Printing Office, 2001), table B-78, 367. Similar measures (for example, a simple measure of the budget deficit or surplus as a percentage of GDP) were tested as well, but tended to be highly correlated. Another specification included a measure of "fiscal impact," which hypothesized via an interaction term that only the formulation of spending items was affected by the budget situation. This does prove to be the case, as noted below, but the overall budget situation is a stronger predictor.

35. Robert B. Reich to author, e-mail communication of October 28, 1999.

36. Work on presidential "must" legislation has been limited to the Kennedy and Johnson administrations as the most consistent keepers of records on this score. See Cary R. Covington, "Congressional Support for the President," *Journal of Politics* 48 (1986): 717–28; Terry Sullivan, "Headcounts, Expectations, and Presidential Coalitions in Congress," *American Journal of Political Science* 32 (1988): 567–89.

37. I am grateful to Sarah Binder for providing these data from her ongoing research on gridlock in government.

38. Or to "hit the ground running." See Light, *The President's Agenda*; James Pfiffner, *The Strategic Presidency*, 2d rev. ed. (Lawrence: University Press of Kansas, 1996).

39. Erwin Hargrove, "Presidential Personality and Leadership Style," in George C. Edwards III, John H. Kessel, and Bert A. Rockman, eds., *Researching the Presidency: Vital Questions, New Approaches* (Pittsburgh: University of Pittsburgh Press, 1993), 106.

40. Hugh Heclo, "The Changing Presidential Office," in James P. Pfiffner, ed., *The Managerial Presidency*, 2d ed. (College Station: Texas A&M Press, 1999), 24. See also the literature on the institutional presidency cited in Chapter One.

41. The historical review in Chapter Three suggested that EOP staff—most

prominently BoB/OMB and CEA—were not analytically separate from the White House staff. Further, comparative statistical results suggest that extending the index doesn't give much, if any, additional leverage. One would not expect much difference in the estimates of individual coefficients—the ordering remains the same, after all, merely compressed—and there is not. However, a quick examination of the "cutpoints" calculated by the ordered probit maximum likelihood function gives a sense of how far apart are each grouping of observations. (That is, how far are "zeroes" from "ones" from "twos," and so forth?) The answer is that the last cutpoint is nearly twice that of the others. When using a four-point index, the cutpoints are more evenly spaced, indicating that centralization values of three and four (EOP and WHO, respectively) are predicted by the same combinations of coefficients.

42. Unless otherwise noted, these models will be calculated using the "svyoprob" commands in StataCorp, *Stata Statistical Software: Release 6.0* (College Station, Tex.: Stata Corporation, 1999).

43. Tim Liao, *Interpreting Probability Models* (Thousand Oaks, Calif.: Sage, 1994), 37.

44. As would be expected from the cutpoint analysis above. Note that another methodological issue raised earlier should be kept in mind: namely, that since the formulation process matters for legislative success, success—or rather, president's estimates of future success—might be justifiably incorporated into the prior decision about the appropriate strategy of centralization. That is, in one sense, a theory of contingent centralization describes a system of equations that could be estimated simultaneously instead of sequentially. However, as a practical matter, these events and choices *are* temporally sequential; further, it seems wrong to assume (as using actual success to help solve the first model does) that the president knows exactly what will happen further down the legislative road. A systematic set of presidential ex ante estimates along these lines would be most desirable; unfortunately, it doesn't exist.

For this reason, and for ease of exposition, I have analyzed each stage separately and report the analysis that way. Still, as an additional check on the estimates below, the two models in this book (the causes of centralization and the sources of legislative success) were estimated simultaneously in a two-stage least-squares model, with success serving as an independent variable in the first equation and as the dependent variable in the second. All the results reported here in the ordered probit models—encompassing both the determinants of success and the determinants of centralization—were replicated there. For a description of simultaneous equations, see Peter Kennedy, *A Guide to Econometrics*, 3d ed. (Cambridge: MIT Press, 1992), chap. 10.

45. See William H. DuMouchel and Greg J. Duncan, "Using Sample Survey Weights in Multiple Regression Analysis," *Journal of the American Statistical Association* 78 (1983): 535–43; Christopher Winship and Larry Radbill, "Sampling Weights and Regression Analysis," *Sociological Methods and Research* 23 (1994): 230–57.

46. These figures are based on the first column of table 5.2. Given the consistency of coefficients and standard errors for the main variables of interest across specifications, this choice does not matter much; the impact of the variables not

included in this specification ("trusted secretary," foreign/domestic policy, president's distance from Rules Committee median) were estimated from other models but are presented here for convenience.

Transformations were calculated using Michael Tomz, Jason Wittenberg, and Gary King, *CLARIFY Software for Interpreting and Presenting Statistical Results, Version 1.2.2* (Cambridge: Harvard University, March 3, 2000). This program, which estimates probable impact based on one thousand simulations of the main model, is available for download at *http://gking.harvard.edu/*. See also Gary King, Michael Tomz, and Jason Wittenberg, "Making the Most of Statistical Analyses: Improving Interpretation and Presentation," *American Journal of Political Science* 44 (2000): 347–61.

47. Shifts from the 25th to the 75th percentile values were also calculated, to ensure that the findings are robust (that is, not springing entirely from extreme values of the variable); these are presented in figures 5.1 and 5.2 as a subset of the 10th to the 90th percentile shift.

48. To keep the chart readable, only variables found in one of the specifications in table 5.1 to be significant at $p < .10$ (two tailed test) are included.

49. Ralph L. Rosnow and Robert Rosenthal, quoted in Jeff Gill, "The Insignificance of Null Hypothesis Significance Testing," *Political Research Quarterly* 52 (1999): 659. See also Steven A. Shull and Thomas C. Shaw, *Explaining Presidential-Congressional Relations: A Multiple Perspective Approach* (Albany: State University of New York Press, 1999), 163–64.

50. Lyn Ragsdale and John Theis, "The Institutionalization of the American Presidency," *American Journal of Political Science* 41 (1997): 1316. Parallel reasoning, though differently purposed, may be found in George A. Krause and Jeffrey E. Cohen, "Opportunity, Constraints, and the Development of the Institutional Presidency: The Issuance of Executive Orders, 1939–1996," *Journal of Politics* 62 (February 2000): 88–114.

51. A variety of annual cutpoints in the 1970s were examined, but made little difference to the overall result.

52. Though of course, as discussed in Chapter Seven, it will matter a good deal to the prospects of presidential success in getting proposals through Congress.

53. The difference is statistically significant if centralization is linked to the ability to break a filibuster in the Senate (requiring a two-thirds vote before 1975 and three-fifths thereafter). But there are not enough observations, especially after 1975, to have real confidence in this finding.

54. One might think that since Republicans, generally, have distrusted the wider executive apparatus more than have Democrats, they will be more likely to centralize policy formulation in the EOP. A further refinement of partisan import splits the sample into instances of divided and unified government (I am grateful to an anonymous reviewer for this suggestion). This shows that the major managerial factors described above remain robust no matter the status of congressional partisanship: new, cross-cutting program items, especially those with reorganizational impact, are much more likely to be centralized than their older, narrower counterparts.

These two tests are discussed together here because they are linked, practically speaking: in the time period under consideration, most occurrences of divided government coincide with Republican presidencies.

55. The two variables, policy type and inner Cabinet status, are jointly significant at $p < .15$. The italicized figures in a quick cross-tabulation make the point even more strongly:

Policy type (2 = for.)	Inner/outer Cabinet (1 = inner)		Total
	0	1	
−2	159	38	197
−1	28	29	57
0	14	14	28
1	10	36	46
2	6	43	49
Total	217	160	377

56. Developing a department-by-department measure of politicization remains an important goal here; as noted earlier, extant data are insufficient for this task. Divided government may play a role in presidential attention to the politicization question. The only notable finding in the analysis splitting the sample into divided and unified government is that politicization, as measured by the merit-protection variable, matters much more in the former case. Recent research (for example, David Epstein and Sharyn O'Halloran, *Delegating Powers: A Transaction Cost Politics Approach to Policy Making under Separate Powers* [New York: Cambridge University Press, 1999]) indicates that Congress is less willing to delegate authority to agencies under divided government; it comes as no surprise that the president is equally wary. When government is unified, it may be less important to presidents that the bureaucracy is politicized, since congressional influence over bureaucratic decisions can be expected to be more congruent with presidential preferences.

CHAPTER SIX. CONGRESS IS A WHISKEY DRINKER

1. "From White House to Capitol . . . How Things Get Done," *U.S. News and World Report* (September 20, 1965): 68.

2. Program names seem to have been a particular obsession of the Nixon administration; Domestic Council staffer Ken Cole complained in late 1970 that "one of the things that we have talked about over the last two years but have done very little about is to come up with names for the President's legislative programs that have some degree of political pizzaz and sex appeal to them." Cole to Jim Keogh, memo of 10/9/70, no title. WHCF: Subject Files: LE, Box 2, [12 of 39, October 7–26, 1970], NPMP. For a commentary on Nixon's desire for a "good catchy name" for what became the Family Assistance Plan, see the entries of July 18, 1969, and August 7, 1969 in H. R. Haldeman, *The Haldeman Diaries* (Sony/Imagesoft CD-ROM, 1994).

3. Bryce Harlow, memo, "Public Statements by Administration Officials,"

2/11/69, copy in RG 51 (series 69.1), Director's Office and Central File: Subject Files of the Director, 1969–1976, Box 2, [E5–7/Executive Review of Proposed and Enrolled Legislation, 1969], NA-II.

4. Joseph A. Califano, Jr., *The Triumph and Tragedy of Lyndon Johnson: The White House Years* (New York: Simon & Schuster, 1991), 142.

5. Jon R. Bond and Richard Fleisher, *The President in the Legislative Arena* (Chicago: University of Chicago Press, 1990), 230. George Edwards comes to similar conclusions in *At the Margins: Presidential Leadership of Congress* (New Haven: Yale University Press, 1989); see also Mark A. Peterson, "The President and Congress," in Michael Nelson, ed., *The Presidency and the Political System*, 6th ed. (Washington, D.C.: CQ Press, 2000).

6. Paul Quirk, "What Do We Know?" in William Crotty, ed., *Political Science: Looking toward the Future*, Vol. 4 (Evanston, Ill.: Northwestern University Press, 1991), 47. See also Peterson, "President and Congress," 495.

7. Two partial exceptions build quantitatively on Theodore Lowi's insight that different policies can generate their own politics. See Steven A. Shull, *Domestic Policy Formation: Presidential-Congressional Partnership?* (Westport, Conn.: Greenwood Press, 1983), and Robert J. Spitzer, *The Presidency and Public Policy: The Four Arenas of Presidential Power* (University: University of Alabama Press, 1983). Following their example, I will utilize policy type (coded somewhat differently) as an independent variable in my analysis.

8. Jon R. Bond, Richard Fleisher, and Glen S. Krutz, "An Overview of the Empirical Findings on Presidential-Congressional Relations," in James Thurber, ed., *Rivals for Power: Presidential-Congressional Relations* (Washington, D.C.: CQ Press, 1996), 120.

9. Mark A. Peterson, *Legislating Together: The White House and Capitol Hill from Eisenhower to Reagan* (Cambridge: Harvard University Press, 1990); see also Peterson, "President and Congress," 488, and Steven A. Shull and Thomas C. Shaw, *Explaining Presidential-Congressional Relations: A Multiple Perspective Approach* (Albany: State University of New York Press, 1999), 12–13, 42–45, for a good review of various measures of success and support.

10. Michael J. Malbin, "Rhetoric and Leadership: A Look Backward at the Carter Energy Plan," in Anthony King, ed., *Both Ends of the Avenue* (Washington, D.C.: American Enterprise Institute, 1983), 215–16.

11. See Keith Krehbiel, *Information and Legislative Organization* (Ann Arbor: University of Michigan Press, 1991), for this informational argument, which receives empirical support in David Whiteman, *Communication in Congress: Members, Staff, and the Search for Information* (Lawrence: University Press of Kansas, 1995), 43ff. Other scholars have interpreted committee power in terms of "institutionalized log-rolling" across issues of importance to different members' districts. The variation may be by committee, with some distributional in this latter sense and others informational; for a good review of the debate see Forrest Maltzman, *Competing Principals: Committees, Parties, and the Organization of Congress* (Ann Arbor: University of Michigan Press, 1997).

12. Or subcommittee. Unless specifically noted, I will use the parent body to refer to its subdivisions as well.

13. Kenneth E. Collier, *Between the Branches: The White House Office of*

Legislative Affairs (Pittsburgh: University of Pittsburgh Press, 1997), chap. 9; see also Whiteman, *Communication in Congress*, 46–48.

14. Quoted in Whiteman, *Communication in Congress*, 47.

15. Quoted in Dana Milbank, "A Loyalist Calls White House to Order," *Washington Post* (February 20, 2001): A1.

16. Quoted in Peterson, *Legislating Together*, 56.

17. House leadership aide, quoted in ibid., 55.

18. Moore, via Rick Hutcheson, to "Wednesday Meeting Participants," no title, memo of 6/7/78. WHSF: Legislation, Box LE-2, [6/1/78–9/30/78], JCL. See, in a similar vein, Steve Simmons to Stuart Eizenstat, "1979 Legislative Agenda and Procedure," memo of 10/19/78, WHSF: Legislation, Box LE-2, [10/1/78–10/31/78], JCL.

19. Quoted in Doris Kearns Goodwin, *Lyndon Johnson and the American Dream* (1976; reprint, New York: St. Martin's Press, 1991), 222.

20. See Chapter Three.

21. And thus, most fundamentally, the program is rightly called presidential. On this point, see Peterson, *Legislating Together*, 49–60, and chap. 2 generally.

22. See Bob Woodward, *The Agenda* (New York: Simon and Schuster, 1994).

23. Quoted in Peterson, *Legislating Together*, 51.

24. See the materials in WHCF: Official Files, Box 640, [124–G Taft Hartley Act 1953], DDEL, and in WHCF: Confidential Files, Box 82, [Taft Hartley (Working Papers of Proposed Changes in Bill)], DDEL. The leak produced a near hysterical response from business.

25. A more complete discussion of this point can be found in John B. Gilmour, *Strategic Disagreement: Stalemate in American Politics* (Pittsburgh: University of Pittsburgh Press, 1995).

26. For a discussion of the Nixon administration's problems in this regard, see Stephen Hess, *Organizing the Presidency*, 2d ed. (Washington, D.C.: Brookings Institution, 1988), 124–25.

27. For approaches widely separated in time and methodology, but reaching the same conclusion, see E. Pendleton Herring, *Presidential Leadership: Political Relations of Congress and the Chief Executive* (New York: Farrar and Rinehart, 1940); Terry Moe and Scott A. Wilson, "Presidents and the Politics of Structure," *Law and Contemporary Problems* 57 (Summer 1994): 1–44.

28. Morris Fiorina, *Congress: Keystone of the Washington Establishment*, 2d ed. (New Haven: Yale University Press, 1989), 127. Emphasis in original.

29. David Halberstam, *The Best and the Brightest* (New York: Random House, 1972), 53.

30. Kenneth O'Donnell, oral history of July 23, 1969 (AC 82–19), LBJL, 25.

31. Quoted in Haynes Johnson and David S. Broder, *The System*, paperbacked. (Boston: Little, Brown, 1997), 172. Departmental staff are not elected either. But their relationship to Congress is, as discussed, quite different — which is not to say that legislators never feel the same way about bureaucrats, especially during policies' implementation.

32. "From White House to Capitol," 68.

33. Barbara Sinclair, "The President as Legislative Leader," in Colin Campbell and Bert A. Rockman, eds., *The Clinton Presidency: First Appraisals* (Chatham, N.J.: Chatham House, 1996), 87–88.

34. Interview with Dan Rather for CBS's *60 Minutes,* August 10, 1980, in Don Richardson, ed., *Conversations with Carter* (Boulder, Colo.: Lynne Rienner, 1998), 203–4. It is, of course, not clear that voters agreed.

35. "Carter Energy Plan Fails to Clear," *Congressional Quarterly Almanac, 1977* (Washington, D.C.: CQ Press, 1978), 709. For additional background, see John C. Barrow, "An Age of Limits: Jimmy Carter and the Quest for a National Energy Policy," in Gary M. Fink and Hugh Davis Graham, eds., *The Carter Presidency: Policy Choices in the Post-New Deal Era* (Lawrence: University Press of Kansas, 1998); Jimmy Carter, *Keeping Faith: Memoirs of a President,* paperback ed. (New York: Bantam Books, 1982), 93–97; Charles O. Jones, *The Trusteeship Presidency: Jimmy Carter and the United States Congress* (Baton Rouge: Louisiana State University Press, 1988), 135ff. Carter's message to Congress describing the plan was delivered on April 20; the formal legislative language was sent April 29.

36. The quoted phrase is from Jones, *The Trusteeship Presidency,* 138. For a description of Schlesinger's team, see James L. Cochrane, "Carter Energy Policy and the 95th Congress," in Craufurd D. Goodwin, ed., *Energy Policy in Perspective* (Washington, D.C.: Brookings Institution, 1981), 551–56. The group worked out of second-floor offices in the Old Executive Office Building.

37. Sources are unanimous on this point. See the above, along with Peter G. Bourne, *Jimmy Carter* (New York: Lisa Drew/Scribner, 1997), 376. Bourne served in the Carter White House as a domestic policy adviser.

38. Interview with Stuart Eizenstat, head of Carter's Domestic Policy Staff (Miller Center Interviews, Carter Presidency Project, Volume XIII, January 1982, JCL), 28.

39. Erwin C. Hargrove, *Jimmy Carter as President: Leadership and the Politics of the Public Good* (Baton Rouge: Louisiana State University Press, 1988), 50; Carter, *Keeping Faith,* 96; Eizenstat, Miller Center interview, 27–29.

40. *Congressional Quarterly Almanac, 1977,* 709; Hargrove, *Jimmy Carter as President,* 50.

41. *Congressional Quarterly Almanac, 1977,* 709.

42. See Malbin, "Rhetoric and Leadership," 222.

43. Frank Potter, staff director of the House Commerce Subcommittee on Energy and Power, quoted in *Congressional Quarterly Almanac, 1977,* 709.

44. The Senate also created a new Energy Committee, though it did not have sole jurisdiction over the bill (Senate Finance also worked on it). See Mary Russell and Warren Brown, "Fate of Program Rests with Key Congressional Leaders; Both Houses Prepared for Complex Task," *Washington Post* (April 23, 1977): A1; Barbara Kellerman, *The Political Presidency: Practice of Leadership from Kennedy through Reagan* (New York: Oxford University Press, 1984), chap. 10; Bruce Oppenheimer, "Policy Effects of U.S. House Reform: Decentralization and the Capacity to Resolve Energy Issues," *Legislative Studies Quarterly* (February 1980): 5–30.

45. *Congressional Quarterly Almanac, 1977,* 709.

46. "Energy Bill: The End of an Odyssey," *Congressional Quarterly Almanac, 1978,* 639ff. For a description of the 1978 session, see Pietro Nivola, "Energy Policy and the Congress: The Politics of the Natural Gas Policy Act of 1978," *Public Policy* 28 (1980): 491–543.

47. Jones, *The Trusteeship Presidency*, 137.
48. Quoted in ibid., 135.
49. Ibid., 137.
50. Hargrove, *Jimmy Carter as President*, 52.
51. Eizenstat, Miller Center interview, 31.
52. Barrow, "An Age of Limits," 168ff.; Larry Light, "Case Study: Creation of an Energy Plan," *Congressional Quarterly Weekly Report* (October 6, 1979): 2203; Daniel E. Ponder, "Presidential Agents and Policy Responsiveness: Information, Control, and Delegation in the Presidency" (Ph.D. dissertation, Vanderbilt University, May 1994), 139–57; Joseph Yager, "The Energy Battles of 1979," in Craufurd D. Goodwin, ed., *Energy Policy in Perspective* (Washington, D.C.: Brookings Institution, 1981).
53. Eizenstat, Miller Center interview, 77–78. Jim Wright (D-Tex.) was then House majority leader; "Scoop" refers to Senator Henry Jackson (D-Wash.), chair of the Senate Energy Committee.
54. To which Carter penciled in "wow!" A title, in this context, is a sizable division of a large bill, often one sufficiently distinct in its substance that it could stand alone as separate legislation. See Eizenstat to President, "Energy Program — Status Report No. 1," memo of 4/21/79. WHSF: Handwriting file, Box 127, [4/24/79], JCL.
55. Eizenstat, "Energy Program — Status Report No. 1." See also Ponder, "Presidential Agents and Policy Responsiveness," 149–51.
56. It did not help that the energy issue was folded into the aftermath of the infamous "malaise" speech of July 15, 1979, or that Senator Edward Kennedy (D-Mass.) was gearing up to run against Carter. See Barrow, "An Age of Limits," 171; Carter, *Keeping Faith*, 114–24.
57. Quoted in Kellerman, *The Political Presidency*, 201.
58. George Goodwin, Jr., *The Little Legislatures: Committees of Congress* (Amherst: University of Massachusetts Press, 1970), 3.
59. Roger H. Davidson, "Building the Republican Regime: Leaders and Committees," in Nicol C. Rae and Colton C. Campbell, eds., *New Majority or Old Minority? The Impact of Republicans on Congress* (Lanham, Md.: Rowman and Littlefield, 1999), 70.
60. Woodrow Wilson, *Congressional Government* (1885; reprint, New York: Meridian Books, 1956), 82. A current summary is Tim Groseclose and David C. King, "Little Theatre: Committees in Congress," in Herbert F. Weisberg and Samuel C. Patterson, eds., *Great Theatre: The American Congress in the 1990s* (New York: Cambridge University Press, 1998). For background on the proliferation of subcommittees, see the cites in Kenneth Shepsle, "The Changing Textbook Congress," in John Chubb and Paul E. Peterson, eds., *Can the Government Govern?* (Washington, D.C.: Brookings Institution, 1989).
61. Samuel Kernell, *Going Public: New Strategies of Presidential Leadership*, 3d ed. (Washington, D.C.: CQ Press, 1997), chap. 2.
62. David C. King, *Turf Wars* (Chicago: University of Chicago Press, 1997), 9.
63. Barbara Sinclair, *Unorthodox Lawmaking: New Legislative Processes in the U.S. Congress* (Washington, D.C.: CQ Press, 1997).

64. Walter J. Oleszek, *Congressional Procedures and the Policy Process*, 4th ed. (Washington, D.C.: CQ Press, 1996), 17.

65. Quoted in Cabinet Meeting Minutes, 8/27/75, WHSF: James E. Connor Files, Box 5, GRFL.

66. James L. Sundquist, *Politics and Policy* (Washington, D.C.: Brookings Institution, 1968), 206. This reflected a careful thought process within the administration that concluded, in light of the failure of administration policy in the 87th Congress, that a "fresh approach to new Federal programs in education" was needed in order to stress the wider role of education as a part of social welfare and economic growth. Bureau of the Budget staff memorandum of 11/7/62, "A New Federal Program in Education," WHSF: Sorensen, Box 33, [Education 8/3/62–11/8/62], JFKL. For the resulting referrals, see Bureau of the Budget, "Legislative Recommendations of the President, 88th Congress, 1st Session," 10/4/63, RG 51, Office of Legislative Reference Subject Files (series 39.39), Box 6, [Legislative Program Material—1963], NA-II, and the complaints of HEW's Wilbur Cohen on the topic to Ted Sorensen and Larry O'Brien. Memo of 7/11/63, "Next Steps in Education Legislation," WHSF: Sorensen, Box 33, [Education 4/22/63–7/25/63], JFKL.

67. Sinclair, *Unorthodox Lawmaking*, 11. For the raw material see Office of Management and Budget, "Cleared Administration-Sponsored Legislation, 103d Congress, 2d Session," 12/30/94.

68. Kennedy to Rep. Howard W. Smith, correspondence covered by letter of 4/4/63, WHCF: Subject Files, Box 472, [LE/FA 2 3/21/62–], JFKL.

69. King, *Turf Wars*, 100–104. Note though that a presidential proposal does not need, necessarily, to be sent to more than one committee for the fragmented process described here to have an impact—the division of the proposals into separate bills within one committee might well have the same effect. As Eisenhower CEA chair Raymond Saulnier noted with regard to the 1956 farm program, "Because it was a set of mutually dependent parts the program would work only if it were taken as a whole. But what Congress did, as [Agriculture staffer] Don Paarlberg . . . put it, was to 'untie the package'. . . . It was not an unprecedented handling of a multisided legislative proposal, but the treatment was in this case particularly damaging." See Saulnier, *Constructive Years: The U.S. Economy under Eisenhower* (Lanham, Md.: University Press of America, 1991), 148.

70. Sinclair, *Unorthodox Lawmaking*, 218 and chap. 6 generally.

71. Oppenheimer, "Policy Effects of U.S. House Reform."

72. Johnson and Broder, *The System*, 305.

73. Interview with Nick Littlefield, former staff director and chief counsel to Senate Committee on Labor and Human Resources, October 23, 1999.

Presidents seeking to overcome congressional fragmentation have also tried to use the budget process to their advantage, most notably in 1981, when President Reagan was able to force an up-or-down roll call on a wide array of budget cuts that would likely not have survived individual votes. In some ways the Reagan experience is the exception that proves the rule. While omnibus legislation has become a more frequent vehicle for passing discrete measures that may be less than wholly germane and even unpopular on their own merits, these packages tend to be congressionally constructed (in part because the package is often designed to allow its less savory parts to avoid veto by their inclusion in a "must" measure). Reconciliation has been less vulnerable to surprise attack since the Reagan success. In the mid-1980s the Senate adopted the "Byrd Rule" (after the West Virginian Democrat) to prevent extraneous additions to reconciliation bills. In 1993 Senator Byrd himself warned President Clinton that he would scuttle any effort to attach health care reform to the budget. For the Reagan case, see (among many other accounts), Kernell, *Going Public*, chap. 5; James P. Pfiffner, "The Reagan Budget Juggernaut," in Pfiffner, ed., *The Presidency and Economic Policy* (Philadelphia: Institute for the Study of Human Issues, 1986); and David A. Stockman, *The Triumph of Politics* (New York: Harper and Row, 1986). On the Byrd rule, see Oleszek, *Congressional Procedures*, 74–75; Johnson and Broder, *The System*, 125–27.

74. James Q. Wilson, *Bureaucracy* (New York: Basic Books, 1989), 268.

75. For a good account, see Peri Arnold, *Making the Managerial Presidency*, 2d ed. (Lawrence: University Press of Kansas, 1998), 18–20.

76. Fiorina, *Keystone*.

77. See Arnold, *Making the Managerial Presidency*, 295.

78. Shepsle, "The Changing Textbook Congress."

79. See, for example, Terry Moe's argument about the politics of bureaucratic structure. As he puts it, "the congressional bureaucracy is not supposed to function as a coherent whole. Only the pieces are important." Moe, "Presidents, Institutions, and Theory," in George C. Edwards, III, John H. Kessel, and Bert A. Rockman, eds., *Researching the Presidency: Vital Questions, New Approaches* (Pittsburgh: University of Pittsburgh Press, 1993), 363.

For example, President Nixon complained in his memoirs that in 1972 "it took seventy-one different signatures to buy one piece of construction equipment. . . . Nine federal departments and twenty agencies all had responsibilities for educational programs." However, Congress reacted to Nixon's lengthy effort to create functionally based "superdepartments" with a certain lack of outrage at these facts. The Nixon efforts at lobbying aimed to educate members of Congress about the proposals' inherent rationality; yet, as Peri Arnold notes, "it was exactly those characteristics of such agencies as the Corps of Engineers and the Bureau of Reclamation that made it so desirable to place them within one department that made the move so politically unlikely." See Richard M. Nixon, *RN: The Memoirs of Richard Nixon* (1978; reprint, New York: Simon & Schuster/Touchstone, 1990), 767; Arnold, *Making the Managerial Presidency*, chap. 9. The proposals never got out of committee.

80. See, for example, Barry R. Weingast, "A Rational Choice Perspective on Congressional Norms," *American Journal of Political Science* 23 (1979): 245–62.

81. Schultze, oral history of April 10, 1969, (AC 83–18), LBJL, 30.

82. For a useful discussion of the distinction, see Deborah Stone, *Policy Paradox and Political Reason* (Glenview, Ill.: Scott, Foresman, 1988).

83. John Kingdon, *Agendas, Alternatives, and Public Policies*, 2d ed. (New York: HarperCollins, 1995), chap. 6.

84. As noted in Chapter Two, as many as two-thirds of committee staff are hired by the majority members, regardless of how close the partisan balance is

on the committee. This imbalance is usually more pronounced in the House, according to Groseclose and King, "Little Theatre," 138. But at least some committees in the Senate also have a ⅔–⅓ split in favor of majority staff (Littlefield, interview of October 23, 1999).

85. It should be noted that, as in Chapter Five, an item's complexity and its jurisdictional scope (that is, its cross-cutting nature) are distinct concepts. Complexity refers to the technical knowledge required to draft an effective legislative proposal. A proposal to cut the budget across the board by x percent would affect many departments, but not be complicated to formulate.

86. Data from the *Congressional Record* of January 30, 2001, D45. To compare the 91st through 107th Congresses, see *http://thomas.loc.gov/home/resume/resume.html*

87. Cary Covington, J. Mark Wrighton, and Rhonda Kinney, "A 'Presidency-Augmented' Model of Presidential Success on House Roll Call Votes," *American Journal of Political Science* 39 (1995): 1001–24. (See cites below in chapter seven, note 10, for more detail.)

88. McCurry, White House press corps briefing of May 14, 1997, Office of the White House Press Secretary.

89. Press conference of December 10, 1977, *PPP.*

90. O'Neill noted not only that Congress could not work fast enough to keep up, but that "each new controversial proposal increases his chance of losing." Mary Russell, "Tip O'Neill, the Great Accommodator; Boston Pol Is Teaching Carter the First Lesson of a Ward Heeler — Compromise," *Washington Post* (June 19, 1977): A18. Warned by Treasury Secretary Michael Blumenthal that the timing of his welfare proposal might undermine his tax plan, Carter responded, "I have no preferences; my preference is to move ahead with everything at once" (quoted in Laurence E. Lynn, Jr., and David DeF. Whitman, *The President as Policymaker: Jimmy Carter and Welfare Reform* [Philadelphia: Temple University Press, 1981], 271).

91. George C. Edwards III, *Presidential Influence in Congress* (San Francisco: W. H. Freeman, 1980), 119.

92. See James P. Pfiffner, *The Strategic Presidency*, 2d rev. ed. (Lawrence: University Press of Kansas, 1996), 125 and chap. 6 generally; Paul C. Light, *The President's Agenda: Domestic Policy Choice from Kennedy to Clinton*, 3d ed. (Baltimore: Johns Hopkins University Press, 1999), 237.

93. Jack Nelson and Robert J. Donovan, "The Education of a President," *Los Angeles Times Magazine* (August 1, 1993): 12. Johnson aide Harry McPherson defended LBJ's efforts to push a wide agenda in similar terms: "If you said, 'all right, my concern is going to be with housing,' education had so much to do with housing and employment had so much to do with housing and mass transportation had to do with housing. There was no [single] place you could stand to get a fix on it." McPherson oral history of March 24, 1969 (AC 74–210), LBJL, 7.

94. Though most of it is either dated or preliminary. See, for example, Richard F. Fenno, Jr., *Congressmen in Committees* (Boston: Little, Brown and Co., 1973); Cary R. Covington and Jon Frericks, "The Role of Presidents in the Legislative Process: The Case of the Ways and Means Committee" (paper pre-

sented at the annual meeting of the Midwest Political Science Association, Chicago, April 1997).

95. See, respectively, Edwards, *Presidential Influence in Congress* and *At the Margins*, and Bond and Fleisher, *The President in the Legislative Arena*. The latter is updated by Fleisher and Bond, "Partisanship and the President's Quest for Votes on the Floor of Congress," in Jon R. Bond and Richard Fleisher, eds., *Polarized Politics: Congress and the President in a Partisan Era* (Washington, D.C.: CQ Press, 2000). Shull and Shaw, *Explaining Presidential-Congressional Relations*, provide a useful review and original data.

96. See Edwards, *At the Margins*; Bond and Fleisher, *The President in the Legislative Arena*.

97. Peterson, "President and Congress," 490. See also Edwards, *At the Margins*, chap. 11; Bond and Fleisher, *The President in the Legislative Arena*, 29–41, 230–34.

98. George C. Edwards III, "Aligning Tests with Theory: Presidential Approval as a Source of Influence in Congress," *Congress and the Presidency* 24 (1997): 113. See also Kernell, *Going Public*.

99. Bond and Fleisher, *The President in the Legislative Arena*; Bond, Fleisher, and Krutz, "Overview of the Empirical Findings"; Kenneth E. Collier and Terry Sullivan, "New Evidence Undercutting the Linkage of Approval with Presidential Support and Influence," *Journal of Politics* 57 (1995): 197–209; Edwards, "Aligning Tests with Theory"; Douglas Rivers and Nancy L. Rose, "Passing the President's Program: Public Opinion and Presidential Influence in Congress," *American Journal of Political Science* 29 (1985): 183–96.

100. The debate was originally sparked by Aaron Wildavsky in 1966. See "The Two Presidencies," in Wildavsky, ed., *The Presidency* (Boston: Little, Brown, 1969). For a good summary of work in the field, see Stephen Shull, ed., *The Two Presidencies: A Quarter-Century Assessment* (Chicago: Nelson-Hall, 1991). More recent research includes Richard S. Conley, "Unified Government, the Two Presidencies Thesis, and Presidential Support in the Senate: An Analysis of President Clinton's First Two Years," *Presidential Studies Quarterly* 27 (1997): 229–50; James M. Lindsay and Wayne P. Steger, "The 'Two Presidencies' in Future Research: Moving beyond Roll-Call Analysis," *Congress and the Presidency* 20 (1993): 103–17. Note that the divergent levels of support do not guarantee a very high absolute level of support in either arena, which goes against Wildavsky's original predictions: see Richard Fleisher et al., "The Demise of the Two Presidencies," *American Politics Quarterly* 28 (2000): 3–25.

101. "'Some would say, "well, if you do this you are supporting the President . . . ,"' Dole said on the Senate floor. 'I say that is all right with me. We have one President at a time.'" See Bob Woodward, *The Choice* (New York: Simon and Schuster, 1996), 332. More generally, see Charles W. Ostrom, Jr., and Brian L. Job, "The President and the Political Use of Force," *American Political Science Review* 80 (1986): 541–66.

102. Kingdon, *Agendas, Alternatives, and Public Policies*.

103. See the *Congressional Quarterly Almanac*, 1977, 668, and the materials in the White House Central Files: Subject Files, Box HE-17, [HE 7–3 (Water pollution, 1/20/77–3/31/77)], JCL.

104. O'Donnell oral history of July 23, 1969, AC 82–19, LBJL, 91.

105. See Bond, Fleisher, and Krutz, "Overview of the Empirical Findings," 124–25; David Rohde, "Parties and Committees in the House," *Legislative Studies Quarterly* 19 (1994): 341–59; and Keith T. Poole and Howard Rosenthal's magisterial *Congress: A Political-Economic History of Roll Call Voting* (New York: Oxford University Press, 1997).

106. Light, *The President's Agenda*, 281.

107. Robert Dahl, "Myth of the Presidential Mandate," *Political Science Quarterly* 105 (1990): 355–72.

CHAPTER SEVEN. THE ODDS ARE WITH THE HOUSE

1. See Jim Fallows to Jerry Rafshoon, memo of 9/18/78, no title, WHSF: Office of Staff Secretary, Presidential Handwriting Files, Box 102, [9/20/78 [2]], JCL. Carter failed to use the joke in the speech, however; see the *PPP*, September 20, 1978, 1542–55.

2. Another method of testing this would be to provide a dummy variable for each of the points on the centralization index (for example, four dummies overall, with three in any given equation). The index is preferable, though, especially given the cutpoint calculations noted in Chapter Five which show that its spacing is basically linear. This maintains a larger effective n and retains the theoretic notion of centralization strategies as presidential choices along a continuum of choice.

3. Mark A. Peterson, *Legislating Together: The White House and Capitol Hill from Eisenhower to Reagan* (Cambridge: Harvard University Press, 1990). Keep in mind that Peterson's data differ somewhat from mine. As described in Chapter Four, the unit of analysis here — "the message" — is the larger presidential message, which contains anywhere from one to forty or more individual parts. Peterson's "proposals" are those discrete parts.

4. *PPP*, August 22, 1996. Prior to signing this bill — which became the Personal Responsibility and Work Opportunity Reconciliation Act — President Clinton had vetoed two earlier versions he liked even less. On presidential veto strategies generally, see Charles M. Cameron, *Veto Bargaining: Presidents and the Politics of Negative Power* (New York: Cambridge University Press, 2000).

5. See Peterson, *Legislating Together*, chaps. 3, 6, and app. D, esp. pp. 189ff.

6. To be even more specific: a zero meant that no bill reached the president's desk; a one, that less than half of the presidentially proposed provisions were included in the law as passed; a two, that more than half of those provisions were included; a three, that the president's message was adopted essentially as sent. It is important to stress, though, that the nature of the data does not always make this level of specificity possible, for three reasons. First, it can be difficult to track each part of a bill across time. Even congressional sources tend to evaluate a measure in the way my own narrative does — as some, most, or all of what the president wanted. Second, and critically, the manner in which messages are sent does not always give the researcher an accurate sense of the number of proposals that were included therein. See Chapters Four and Five for additional discussion of this point. Third, some proposals within a single mes-

sage are more important than others—achieving the passage of 60 percent of the proposals made, but none of the really critical ones, might not warrant the conclusion that the president got "most" of what he wanted. Therefore the coding is also guided by close observers' assessments of how much of the president's original programmatic proposal was enacted, especially by Congressional Quarterly's *Weekly Reports* and annual *Almanacs*, the *New York Times*, and the *Washington Post*.

7. See Jon R. Bond, Richard Fleisher, and Glen S. Krutz, "An Overview of the Empirical Findings on Presidential-Congressional Relations," in James Thurber, ed., *Rivals for Power: Presidential-Congressional Relations* (Washington, D.C.: CQ Press, 1996); Paul Light, *The President's Agenda: Domestic Policy Choice from Kennedy to Clinton*, 3d ed. (Baltimore: Johns Hopkins University Press, 1999); Peterson, *Legislating Together*, 306f.

8. These reports, though not always consistent across different presidencies, provide an excellent snapshot of the status of the president's program at the end of a given session of Congress. As detailed in Chapter Four, reports covering 1949–1979 are, with some gaps, available in the OMB subject files (Record Group 51) in the National Archives, and in the various presidential libraries, usually in the "LE" subject series files. Special thanks to James Murr and James Jukes at OMB for providing clearance records for 1989–2000.

9. Peterson, *Legislating Together*, table 3.1; George C. Edwards III and Andrew Barrett, "Presidential Agenda Setting in Congress," in Jon R. Bond and Richard Fleisher, eds., *Polarized Politics: Congress and the President in a Partisan Era* (Washington, D.C.: CQ Press, 2000).

10. Edwards and Barrett, "Presidential Agenda Setting in Congress," 114; Peterson, *Legislating Together*, 96, and more generally, chap. 5. Other work in this area includes Frank R. Baumgartner and Bryan D. Jones, *Agendas and Instability in American Politics* (Chicago: University of Chicago Press, 1993), 241; Cary R. Covington, Mark Wrighton, and Rhonda Kinney, "A 'Presidency-Augmented' Model of Presidential Success on House Roll Call Votes," *American Journal of Political Science* 39 (1995): 1001–24; Patrick Fett, "Presidential Legislative Priorities and Legislators' Voting Decisions: An Exploratory Analysis," *Journal of Politics* 56 (1994): 502–12; Wayne P. Steger, "Presidential Policy Initiation and the Politics of Agenda Control," *Congress and the Presidency* 24 (1997): 17–36.

11. [Clyde A.] Wheeler to Secretary [of Agriculture] Benson, memo of 11/13/58, "Suggested Plan of Operations for the Next Two Years," WHSF: Jack Z. Anderson, Box 1, [Agriculture], DDEL.

12. Cohen finds that presidents are unlikely to simply mirror public opinion on substantive issues, though they do on symbolic matters. See Jeffrey E. Cohen, *Presidential Responsiveness and Public Policy-Making* (Ann Arbor: University of Michigan Press, 1997).

13. Peterson, *Legislating Together*, table 7.1 and 234f. For a useful comparison of the varying measures of success and support, see Mark A. Peterson, "The President and Congress," in Michael Nelson, ed., *The Presidency and the Political System*, 6th ed. (Washington, D.C.: CQ Press, 2000), table 17.1.

14. See Peterson, "The President and Congress," table 17.1.

15. From a mean of 1.89 in 1993–94 to a lowly 1.19 in 1995–96.

16. Data from Harold W. Stanley and Richard G. Niemi, eds., *Vital Statistics on American Politics*, 4th ed. (Washington, D.C.: CQ Press, 1994), table 7-12, and updated from the resumés on legislative activity at *http://thomas.loc.gov/home/resume*. Simple and concurrent resolutions are excluded.

17. It is not clear from models of congressional decision making that salient measures should be less likely to pass. Arguments concerning the role of visibility and traceability in legislative choice would conclude the reverse, at least under certain circumstances. This measure may work better as a gauge of importance (as in Chapter Five) than of contentiousness per se, with any negative impact thus muted. See R. Douglas Arnold, *The Logic of Congressional Action* (New Haven: Yale University Press, 1990). The measure was, however, used in alternate specifications — both as substitute for and as complement to the priority variable — and proved insignificant.

18. George Edwards has argued that this is a matter of poor model specification — or rather, of models specifying an implausible process of influence. Edwards, "Aligning Tests with Theory: Presidential Approval as a Source of Influence in Congress," *Congress and the Presidency* 24 (1997): 113–30. See also Jon R. Bond and Richard Fleisher, *The President in the Legislative Arena* (Chicago: University of Chicago Press, 1990); Kenneth E. Collier and Terry Sullivan, "New Evidence Undercutting the Linkage of Approval with Presidential Support and Influence," *Journal of Politics* 57 (1995): 197–209.

19. Compiled from Lyn Ragsdale, *Vital Statistics on the Presidency: Washington to Clinton*, rev. ed. (Washington, D.C.: CQ Press, 1998), table 5.3.

20. In the main these are bilateral agreements governing fishing, required by the Fishery Conservation and Management Act of 1976 (P.L. 94-265), and the exchange of nonmilitary nuclear technology pursuant to 42 U.S.C. 2153. For descriptions of these statutes, see Chapter Three.

21. Arnold, *Logic of Congressional Action*; John W. Kingdon, *Agendas, Alternatives, and Public Policies*, 2d ed. (New York: HarperCollins, 1995).

22. See Light, *The President's Agenda*; quantitative studies include Steven A. Shull, *Presidential-Congressional Relations: Policy and Time Approaches* (Ann Arbor: University of Michigan Press, 1997), 89ff., and Steven A. Shull and Thomas C. Shaw, *Explaining Presidential-Congressional Relations: A Multiple Perspective Approach* (Albany: State University of New York Press, 1999), 88f. However, the latter studies do not find significant difference in legislative support for presidents across the years of their terms.

23. A variety of alternate specifications were also considered to try to clarify the impact of the honeymoon and lame duck concepts. For example, items considered by Congress in the last two years of a president's second term, or after an eligible president has announced he will not run again (that is, after March 1952 or 1968), were marked with a dichotomous variable. This did not prove to be a better predictor than the simple month-of-term figure; this is not surprising given the results of the Shull, and Shull and Shaw, studies cited in note 22. Efforts to specify presidential mandates, which are said to affect the scope of the president's honeymoon, also yielded little. The coattails that elections produce presumably vary; some presidents have them, or are perceived to, while others

don't. The president's share of the two-party vote in the prior election was thus utilized as an independent variable, but did not prove significant. This may be in part because the theory of the "mandate" is itself faulty, given our separated system (see Robert Dahl, "Myth of the Presidential Mandate," *Political Science Quarterly* 105 [1990]: 355–72; George C. Edwards III, *At the Margins: Presidential Leadership of Congress* [New Haven: Yale University Press, 1989], chap. 8; Wayne P. Steger, "The Occurrence and Consequences of Electoral Mandates in Historical Context," *Congress and the Presidency* 27 [2000]: 121–48). Further, a president can have coattails (a honeymoon period) without having a coat (an election), a fact to which the two unelected presidents who served during this period bear varying witness. After all, the theory of the mandate is that members of Congress judge that ignoring the president will hurt them in their own constituencies; on that score Lyndon Johnson, especially, had the ability of moral suasion even before the 1964 election.

In one variant, then, a variable marking the year of the president's term was combined with dummy variables representing items sent to Congress after the Kennedy assassination (and before LBJ's own election) and those sent after Watergate. This proved negative and statistically significant — legislative success declined over time — and the JFK aftermath variable was positive and significant (Watergate was not, perhaps because Gerald Ford's honeymoon period ended abruptly with his pardon of Richard Nixon in September 1974). Still, the month-of-term variable was also able to account for these dynamics, and in a more parsimonious manner.

24. For an in-depth analysis of presidents and the OLA (known as the Office of Congressional Relations in some administrations), see Kenneth E. Collier, *Between the Branches: The White House Office of Legislative Affairs* (Pittsburgh: University of Pittsburgh Press, 1997).

25. Interestingly, this confounding impact seems to be much greater for measurements of the distance between the president and the House Rules Committee than for measurements from the president to the floor median, perhaps because the latter is more or less captured in the party measure. As noted below, the predictive power of the party measurement increases greatly when the floor median variable is removed, and vice versa.

26. Again, these calculations were made using Clarify simulations in Stata 6. See Chapter Five for details. Only variables with a statistical significance of $p < .10$ (two-tailed test) were included.

27. Utilizing the Poole-Rosenthal common space coordinates instead of "real ADA" scores gives much stronger results for the ideological distance measure, even when the partisan variable is included in the equation — though neither measure, in the specifications reported here at least, reach standard levels of statistical significance. It is not clear why the common space and ADA measures should diverge here, but it suggests that careful specification of (especially) presidential ideology remains an important task.

28. James M. Lindsay and Wayne P. Steger, "The 'Two Presidencies' in Future Research: Moving beyond Roll-Call Analysis," *Congress and the Presidency* 20 (1993): 103–17.

29. The latter's reversal of the burden of action, such that Congress must act

to *dis*-approve it, results in a whopping 64 percentage point increase in the likelihood of passage ($p < .001$) and a large decrease in the likelihood of any other outcome.

30. Although I do not adopt his definitions exactly, see Daniel Ponder's *Good Advice: Information and Policymaking in the White House* (College Station: Texas A&M Press, 2000) for a useful discussion of the White House staff as "director," "facilitator," and "coordinator."

31. An interesting topic for future research entails examining the wrong predictions: that is, are there any commonalities between the proposals that the model predicts will fail but that actually pass in some form?

32. Collier, *Between the Branches*, 280.

CHAPTER EIGHT. HARD CHOICES

1. Laurence E. Lynn, Jr., and David DeF. Whitman, *The President as Policymaker: Jimmy Carter and Welfare Reform* (Philadelphia: Temple University Press, 1981), 3.

2. The "investment" metaphor is borrowed from Daniel E. Ponder, *Good Advice: Information and Policy Making in the White House* (College Station: Texas A&M Press, 2000), 29–31.

3. See especially Terry M. Moe, "The Politicized Presidency," in John Chubb and Paul Peterson, eds., *New Directions in American Politics* (Washington, D.C.: Brookings Institution, 1985).

4. Richard Neustadt's discussion of presidential transitions stresses this point. See *Presidential Power and the Modern Presidents* (New York: Free Press, 1990), chap. 11.

5. Joseph A. Pika, "Moving beyond the Oval Office: Problems in Studying the Presidency," *Congress and the Presidency* 9 (1982): 27.

6. Charles M. Cameron's discussion of the kinds of questions amenable to formal analysis is a useful analogue. See Cameron, *Veto Bargaining: Presidents and the Politics of Negative Power* (New York: Cambridge University Press, 2000), chap. 3. In any case, whatever evidence scholars use to test their ideas, it is important they be clear about their assumptions and hypotheses.

7. As economist Josiah Stamp complained in 1929, "the Government are very keen on amassing statistics — they collect them, add them, raise them to the nth power, take the cube root, and prepare wonderful diagrams. But what you must never forget is that every one of those figures comes in the first instance from the village watchman, who just puts down what he damn pleases." Quoted in Peter Kennedy, *A Guide to Econometrics*, 3d ed. (Cambridge: MIT Press, 1992), 137.

8. A useful compilation of extant data is Lyn Ragsdale, *Vital Statistics on the Presidency: Washington to Clinton*, rev. ed. (Washington, D.C.: CQ Press, 1998). This highlights both the range of accurate information that is available and how much is not.

9. See, inter alia, William G. Howell, "Presidential Power and the Politics of Unilateral Action" (Ph.D. diss., Stanford University, 2000); Kenneth R. Mayer, *With the Stroke of a Pen: Executive Orders and Presidential Power* (Princeton:

Princeton University Press, 2001); Terry M. Moe and William G. Howell, "The Presidential Power of Unilateral Action," *Journal of Law, Economics, and Organization* 15 (1999): 132–79. Alexander Hamilton's *Federalist* no. 70 recognized early on the structural advantages of a unitary president vis-à-vis a plural Congress.

10. *PPP, 1995,* September 25, 1995, 1475.

11. See, for example, Charles Babington and Joby Warrick, "White House Seeks Legacy," *Washington Post* (August 25, 2000): A1; Dan Morgan, "Clinton's Last Regulatory Rush," *Washington Post* (December 6, 2000): A1.

12. Cited by Mark Rozell in Kenneth W. Thompson, ed., *Portraits of American Presidents,* vol. XI: *The Bush Presidency,* pt. 2 (Lanham, Md.: University Press of America, 1998), 115–16.

13. On this point see Howell, *Presidential Power*; Mayer, *Stroke of a Pen.*

14. Richard Fleisher and Jon R. Bond, "Partisanship and the President's Quest for Votes on the Floor of Congress," in Bond and Fleisher, eds., *Polarized Politics: Congress and the President in a Partisan Era* (Washington, D.C.: CQ Press, 2000), 155. They also quote Anthony King, who noted that as president, "all you really need from Congress is votes, but you need those votes very badly."

15. William Carey to Lawrence O'Brien, "Congressional Liaison, Bureau of the Budget," memo of 3/10/61. RG 51, Legislative Reference Division Subject Files, 1939–70 (series 39.39), Box 10, [White House Correspondence—1961], NA-II. Carey gave two examples: "the recent order affecting discrimination in employment on Federal contracts," and "the Food-for-Peace order."

16. "Little systematic evidence has emerged that executive orders are used to circumvent a hostile Congress," note Christopher J. Deering and Forrest Maltzman, in "The Politics of Executive Orders: Legislative Constraints on Presidential Power," *Political Research Quarterly* 52 (1999): 768. Several recent studies have found instead that the number of executive orders issued rises during unified government, perhaps owing to presidents' use of such orders to reinforce legislative victories administratively (see especially Steven A. Shull, *Presidential-Congressional Relations: Policy and Time Approaches* [Ann Arbor: University of Michigan Press, 1997], chap. 7). Deering and Maltzman provide an excellent review of the recent literature on executive orders; the quoted statement does not summarize their own view, which argues that presidents act rather strategically in anticipating the likely consequences of issuing executive orders. See also George A. Krause and Jeffrey E. Cohen, "Opportunity, Constraints, and the Development of the Institutional Presidency: The Issuance of Executive Orders, 1939–1996," *Journal of Politics* 62 (2000): 88–114; Howell, "Presidential Power"; Mayer, *Stroke of a Pen.*

17. Louis Fisher, *The Politics of Shared Power: Congress and the Executive,* 4th ed. (College Station: Texas A&M Press, 1998), 35–36. This is true with regards to policy changes, but even affects presidential staff use. A memo from White House counsel John Dean in November 1972 warned President Nixon that the "counsellor" system to be installed in 1973, in which White House staff would oversee related departments, must not be called a reorganization but "a redirecting of the President's supervisory and management powers." The announcement, Dean cautioned, could not say that Nixon was doing indirectly

"what Congress won't let him do directly"; the president had to emphasize instead that he was "not changing the organizational structure per se." John Dean, memo of 11/21/72, "Redirecting Executive Branch Management," WHSF: John W. Dean III, Box 63, [Reorganization 1972/73 (1 of 5)], NPMP.

18. Mike Allen, "Bush Reverses Abortion Aid: U.S. Funds Are Denied to Groups That Promote Procedure Abroad," *Washington Post* (January 23, 2001): A1.

19. Elizabeth Drew, *On the Edge: The Clinton Presidency*, paperback ed. (New York: Touchstone, 1994).

20. As part of the Small Business Regulatory Enforcement Fairness Act of 1996 (P.L. 104–121), Congress provided for a sixty-day window during which it could veto, by joint resolution, "major" rules (defined as having a $100 million annual effect on the economy, requiring a "major" increase in costs or prices, or having "significant adverse effects of competition, employment, investment, productivity, innovation, or on the ability of United States–based enterprises to compete with foreign-based enterprises in domestic and export markets" (§804)). Juliet Eilperin, "Republicans Target 45 Regulations to Overturn: Clinton Rules Involved Energy, Environment, Abortion Issues," *Washington Post* (April 8, 2001): A1.

21. The order would have applied to any housing bought or financed through a bank loan (and thus insured through the FDIC).

22. Harry McPherson, oral history of April 9, 1969 (AC 74–210), LBJL, 3. In a similar instance, McPherson summarized a 1967 conversation in a memo to the president: "The union wanted you to consider issuing an Executive Order prohibiting [contracting with violators of labor laws]. You said you had grave doubts about the wisdom of acting in this manner, particularly when the main argument for issuing an executive order was the difficulty of getting Congress to pass a law." Quoted in Harry McPherson, *A Political Education: A Washington Memoir* (1972; reprint, Boston: Houghton Mifflin, 1988), 288.

23. Quoted in Paul C. Light, *The President's Agenda: Domestic Policy Choice from Kennedy to Clinton*, 3d ed. (Baltimore: Johns Hopkins University Press, 1999), 59. Light adds: "Thus, Nixon's 'administrative Presidency' was more a reaction to political circumstance than presidential ideology."

24. Quoted in Alexis Simendinger, "The Paper Wars," *National Journal* (July 25, 1998), 1737.

25. See, for example, Moe and Howell, "The Presidential Power of Unilateral Action."

26. Doris Kearns Goodwin, *Lyndon Johnson and the American Dream* (1976; reprint, New York: St. Martin's Press, 1991), 222.

27. Cameron, *Veto Bargaining*; David Epstein and Sharyn O'Halloran, *Delegating Powers: A Transaction Cost Politics Approach to Policy Making under Separate Powers* (New York: Cambridge University Press, 1999); Charles O. Jones, *The Presidency in a Separated System* (Washington, D.C.: Brookings Institution, 1994).

28. Mark A. Peterson, *Legislating Together: The White House and Capitol Hill from Eisenhower to Reagan* (Cambridge: Harvard University Press, 1990), 2.

29. Quoted in John P. Burke and Fred I. Greenstein, with Larry Berman and

Richard Immerman, *How Presidents Test Reality* (New York: Russell Sage Foundation, 1989), 265.

30. Quoted in Alistair Horne, *How Far from Austerlitz?* (London: Papermac, 1997), 100.

31. See Burke and Greenstein, *How Presidents Test Reality*; Alexander L. George, *Presidential Decisionmaking in Foreign Policy: The Effective Use of Information and Advice* (Boulder, Colo.: Westview, 1980). Walcott and Hult address the flip side of the question in some detail, asking how uncertainty affects organizational structure. See Charles E. Walcott and Karen M. Hult, "Organizing the White House: Structure, Environment, and Organizational Governance," *American Journal of Political Science* 31 (1987): 109–25, and *Governing the White House: From Hoover through LBJ* (Lawrence: University Press of Kansas, 1995).

32. Kenneth A. Shepsle, "Studying Institutions: Some Lessons from the Rational Choice Approach," *Journal of Theoretical Politics* 1 (1989): 131–47.

33. Douglass C. North, "The New Institutional Economics," *Journal of Institutional and Theoretical Economics* 142 (1986): 230.

34. Jonathan Bendor and Thomas Hammond, "Rethinking Allison's Models," *American Political Science Review* 86 (1992): 317. See also Thomas Hammond, "Toward a General Theory of Hierarchy," *Journal of Public Administration Research and Theory* 3 (1993): 120–45.

35. Gary J. Miller, *Managerial Dilemmas: The Political Economy of Hierarchy* (New York: Cambridge University Press, 1992), 79.

36. Walter Williams, "George Bush and Executive Branch Domestic Policymaking Competence," *Policy Studies Journal* 21 (1993): 706. Moe himself, of course, is an exception to this: his "Politicized Presidency" is partly motivated as a defense of such presidential actions as reasonable, given the institutional environment they inhabit.

37. John Hart, *The Presidential Branch*, 2d ed. (Chatham, N.J.: Chatham House, 1995), 216.

38. See Thomas Weko's similar findings with regard to the political appointments process in *The Politicizing Presidency: The White House Personnel Office, 1948–1994* (Lawrence: University Press of Kansas, 1995).

REFERENCES

Aberbach, Joel. "The President and the Executive Branch." In *The Bush Presidency: First Appraisals*, edited by Colin Campbell and Bert A. Rockman. Chatham, N.J.: Chatham House, 1991.

Aberbach, Joel, and Bert A. Rockman. "The Political Views of U.S. Senior Federal Executives, 1970–92." *Journal of Politics* 57 (1995): 838–52.

———. *Inside the Web of Politics*. Washington, D.C.: Brookings Institution, 2000.

Adams, Sherman. *Firsthand Report: The Story of the Eisenhower Administration*. New York: Harper and Brothers, 1961.

Aldrich, John H., and David Rohde. "The Consequences of Party Organization in the House: The Role of the Majority and Minority Parties in Conditional Party Government." In *Polarized Politics: Congress and the President in a Partisan Era*, edited by Jon R. Bond and Richard Fleisher. Washington, D.C.: CQ Press, 2000.

Allen, Mike. "Bush Reverses Abortion Aid: U.S. Funds Are Denied to Groups That Promote Procedure Abroad." *Washington Post* (January 23, 2001): A1.

Allison, Graham T. *Essence of Decision*. Boston: Little, Brown, 1971.

Alt, James E., and Kenneth A. Shepsle, eds. *Perspectives on Positive Political Economy*. New York: Cambridge University Press, 1990.

Ambrose, Stephen E. *Eisenhower*. Volume 2: *The President*. New York: Simon and Schuster, 1984.

Anderson, Jack. "Kissinger: One-Man State Department." *Washington Post* (October 18, 1974): D19.

Anderson, Patrick. *The Presidents' Men*. Paperback ed. Garden City, N.Y.: Anchor Books, 1969.

Arnold, Peri E. *Making the Managerial Presidency: Comprehensive Reorganization Planning, 1905–1996*. 2d rev. ed. Lawrence: University Press of Kansas, 1998.

Arnold, R. Douglas. *Congress and the Bureaucracy: A Theory of Influence*. New Haven: Yale University Press, 1979.

———. *The Logic of Congressional Action*. New Haven: Yale University Press, 1990.

Arrow, Kenneth. *Information and Economic Behavior*. Technical Report 14SNR. Harvard Project on Efficiency in Decision Making, Cambridge, Mass., 1973.

Babington, Charles, and Joby Warrick. "White House Seeks Legacy." *Washington Post* (August 25, 2000): A1.

Bardach, Eugene. *Getting Agencies to Work Together: The Practice and Theory of Managerial Craftsmanship*. Washington, D.C.: Brookings Institution, 1998.

Barrow, John C. "An Age of Limits: Jimmy Carter and the Quest for a National Energy Policy." In *The Carter Presidency: Policy Choices in the Post-New Deal Era*, edited by Gary M. Fink and Hugh Davis Graham. Lawrence: University Press of Kansas, 1998.

Baumgartner, Frank R., and Bryan D. Jones. *Agendas and Instability in American Politics*. Chicago: University of Chicago Press, 1993.

Benda, Peter M., and Charles Levine. "Reagan and the Bureaucracy." In *The Reagan Legacy: Promise and Performance*, edited by Charles O. Jones. Chatham, N.J.: Chatham House, 1988.

Bendor, Jonathan, and Thomas Hammond. "Rethinking Allison's Models." *American Political Science Review* 86 (1992): 301–22.

Bendor, Jonathan, Serge Taylor, and Roland Van Gaalen. "Stacking the Deck: Bureaucratic Missions and Policy Design." *American Political Science Review* 81 (1987): 873–96.

Bennett, Anthony J. *The American President's Cabinet*. New York: St. Martin's, 1996.

Berke, Richard L. "Bush Is Providing Corporate Model for White House." *New York Times* (March 11, 2001): A1.

Berkowitz, Edward D. *Mr. Social Security: The Life of Wilbur J. Cohen*. Lawrence: University Press of Kansas, 1995.

Berlin, Isaiah. *Four Essays on Liberty*. New York: Oxford University Press, 1969.

Berman, Larry. *The Office of Management and Budget and the Presidency, 1921–1979*. Princeton: Princeton University Press, 1979.

Berry, Jeffrey M. *The Interest Group Society*. 3d ed. New York: Longman, 1997.

Bianco, William T. *Trust: Representatives and Constituents*. Ann Arbor: University of Michigan Press, 1994.

Binkley, Wilfred E. *President and Congress*. 3d rev. ed. New York: Vintage Books, 1962.

Birnbaum, Jeffrey H., and Alan Murray. *Showdown at Gucci Gulch*. New York: Random House, 1987.

Bonafede, Dom, and John K. Iglehart. "White House Report: End of Counselor System Enlarges Policy-Forming Role of Cabinet." *National Journal* (May 19, 1973): 726–29.

Bond, Jon R., and Richard Fleisher. *The President in the Legislative Arena*. Chicago: University of Chicago Press, 1990.

Bond, Jon R., and Richard Fleisher, eds. *Polarized Politics: Congress and the President in a Partisan Era*. Washington, D.C.: CQ Press, 2000.

Bond, Jon R., Richard Fleisher, and Glen S. Krutz. "An Overview of the Empirical Findings on Presidential-Congressional Relations." In *Rivals for Power: Presidential-Congressional Relations*, edited by James Thurber. Washington, D.C.: CQ Press, 1996.

Bourne, Peter G. *Jimmy Carter*. New York: Lisa Drew/Scribner, 1997.

Branch, Taylor. *Parting the Waters: America in the King Years, 1954–63*. New York: Touchstone, 1988.

Brehm, John, and Scott Gates. *Working, Shirking, and Sabotage: Bureaucratic*

Response to a Democratic Public. Ann Arbor: University of Michigan Press, 1997.

Burke, John P. *The Institutional Presidency*. Baltimore: Johns Hopkins University Press, 1992.

———. "The Institutional Presidency." In *The Presidency and the Political System*, edited by Michael Nelson. 6th ed. Washington, D.C.: CQ Press, 2000.

Burke, John P., and Fred I. Greenstein, with Larry Berman and Richard Immerman. *How Presidents Test Reality*. New York: Russell Sage Foundation, 1989.

Burns, James MacGregor. *Roosevelt: The Lion and the Fox*. New York: Harcourt, Brace and World, 1956.

———. *Presidential Government: The Crucible of Leadership*. Boston: Houghton Mifflin, 1965.

Califano, Joseph A., Jr. *Governing America*. New York: Simon and Schuster, 1981.

———. *The Triumph and Tragedy of Lyndon Johnson: The White House Years*. New York: Simon and Schuster, 1991.

Calvert, Randall. "The Value of Biased Information." *Journal of Politics* 47 (1985): 530–55.

Cameron, Charles M. *Veto Bargaining: Presidents and the Politics of Negative Power*. New York: Cambridge University Press, 2000.

Campbell, Colin. *Managing the Presidency: Carter, Reagan, and the Search for Executive Harmony*. Pittsburgh: University of Pittsburgh Press, 1986.

———. "The White House and Presidency under the 'Let's Deal' President." In *The Bush Presidency: First Appraisals*, edited by Colin Campbell and Bert A. Rockman. Chatham, N.J.: Chatham House, 1991.

Campbell, Colin, and Bert A. Rockman, eds. *The Bush Presidency: First Appraisals*. Chatham, N.J.: Chatham House, 1991.

———. *The Clinton Presidency: First Appraisals*. Chatham, N.J.: Chatham House, 1996.

Carter, Jimmy. *Keeping Faith: Memoirs of a President*. Paperback ed. New York: Bantam, 1982.

Chamberlain, Lawrence. *The President, Congress, and Legislation*. New York: Columbia University Press, 1946.

Chubb, John, and Paul E. Peterson, eds. *New Directions in American Politics*. Washington, D.C.: Brookings Institution, 1985.

———. *Can the Government Govern?* Washington, D.C.: Brookings Institution, 1989.

Clifford, Clark, with Richard Holbrooke. *Counsel to the President*. New York: Random House, 1991.

Coase, Ronald. "The Nature of the Firm." *Economica* 4 (1937): 386–405.

Cochran, William G. *Sampling Techniques*. 3d ed. New York: Wiley, 1977.

Cochrane, James L. "Carter Energy Policy and the 95th Congress." In *Energy Policy in Perspective*, edited by Craufurd D. Goodwin. Washington, D.C.: Brookings Institution, 1981.

Cohen, Jeffrey E. *The Politics of the U.S. Cabinet*. Pittsburgh: University of Pittsburgh Press, 1988.

———. *Presidential Responsiveness and Public Policy-Making.* Ann Arbor: University of Michigan Press, 1997.

Cohen, Richard E. *Washington at Work: Back Rooms and Clean Air.* New York: Macmillan, 1992.

Collier, Kenneth E. "Behind the Bully Pulpit: The Reagan Administration and Congress." *Presidential Studies Quarterly* 26 (1996): 805–15.

———. *Between the Branches: The White House Office of Legislative Affairs.* Pittsburgh: University of Pittsburgh Press, 1997.

Collier, Kenneth E., and Terry Sullivan. "New Evidence Undercutting the Linkage of Approval with Presidential Support and Influence." *Journal of Politics* 57 (1995): 197–209.

Congressional Quarterly. *Congressional Quarterly Almanac.* Washington, D.C.: CQ Press, 1949–1996.

Conley, Richard S. "Unified Government, the Two Presidencies Thesis, and Presidential Support in the Senate: An Analysis of President Clinton's First Two Years." *Presidential Studies Quarterly* 27 (1997): 229–50.

Corwin, Edward S. *The President: Office and Powers.* 5th rev. ed., updated by Randall W. Bland, Theodore T. Hindson, and Jack W. Peltason. New York: New York University Press, 1984.

Council of Economic Advisers. *Economic Report of the President, January 2001.* Washington, D.C.: U.S. Government Printing Office, 2001.

Covington, Cary R. "Congressional Support for the President: The View from the Kennedy/Johnson White House." *Journal of Politics* 48 (1986): 717–28.

Covington, Cary R., and Jon Frericks. "The Role of Presidents in the Legislative Process: The Case of the Ways and Means Committee." Paper presented at the annual meeting of the Midwest Political Science Association, Chicago, April 1997.

Covington, Cary R., J. Mark Wrighton, and Rhonda Kinney. "A 'Presidency-Augmented' Model of Presidential Success on House Roll Call Votes." *American Journal of Political Science* 39 (1995): 1001–24.

Cronin, Thomas E. *The State of the Presidency.* Boston: Little, Brown, 1975.

Cronin, Thomas E., and Sanford D. Greenberg, eds. *The Presidential Advisory System.* New York: Harper and Row, 1969.

Crotty, William, ed. *Political Science: Looking toward the Future.* Vol. 4. Evanston, Ill.: Northwestern University Press, 1991.

Culhane, Charles. "Labor Report: Differences over Public Service Jobs Complicate Manpower Revenue-Sharing Plan." *National Journal* (March 27, 1971): 647–56.

Dahl, Robert. "Myth of the Presidential Mandate." *Political Science Quarterly* 105 (1990): 355–72.

Davidson, Roger H. "Building the Republican Regime: Leaders and Committees." In *New Majority or Old Minority? The Impact of Republicans on Congress,* edited by Nicol C. Rae and Colton C. Campbell. Lanham, Md.: Rowman and Littlefield, 1999.

Deering, Christopher J., and Forrest Maltzman. "The Politics of Executive Orders: Legislative Constraints on Presidential Power." *Political Research Quarterly* 52 (1999): 767–83.

Demsetz, Harold. "The Theory of the Firm Revisited." *Journal of Law, Economics, and Organization* 4 (1988): 141–61.

Destler, I. M. "National Security II: The Rise of the Assistant 1961–1981." In *The Illusion of Presidential Government*, edited by Hugh Heclo and Lester M. Salamon. Boulder, Colo.: Westview, 1981.

———. *American Trade Politics*. 2d ed. Washington, D.C.: Institute for International Economics, 1992.

———. *The National Economic Council: A Work in Progress*. Policy Analyses in International Economics, vol. 46. Washington, D.C.: Institute for International Economics, 1996.

Dickinson, Matthew J. *Bitter Harvest: FDR, Presidential Power, and the Growth of the Presidential Branch*. New York: Cambridge University Press, 1997.

———. "Staffing the White House, 1937–1996: A Theory and Test." In *Presidential Power: Forging the Presidency for the 21st Century*, edited by Robert Y. Shapiro, Martha Joynt Kumar, and Lawrence R. Jacobs. New York: Columbia University Press, 2000.

Dickinson, Matthew J., and Andrew Rudalevige. "Revisiting the Golden Age: Responsiveness and Competence at the Bureau of the Budget, 1945–1952." Paper presented at the annual meeting of the American Political Science Association, San Francisco, August 2001.

Dodd, Lawrence, and Richard L. Schott. *Congress and the Administrative State*. New York: Macmillan, 1986.

Donovan, Robert J. *Eisenhower: The Inside Story*. New York: Harper, 1956.

Drew, Elizabeth. *On the Edge: The Clinton Presidency*. Paperback ed. New York: Touchstone, 1994.

Dubofsky, Melvyn. "Jimmy Carter and the End of the Politics of Productivity." In *The Carter Presidency: Policy Choices in the Post–New Deal Era*, edited by Gary M. Fink and Hugh Davis Graham. Lawrence: University Press of Kansas, 1998.

DuMouchel, William H., and Greg J. Duncan. "Using Sample Survey Weights in Multiple Regression Analysis." *Journal of the American Statistical Association* 78 (1983): 535–43.

Durant, Robert. *The Administrative Presidency Revisited*. Albany: State University of New York Press, 1992.

Edwards, George C., III. *Presidential Influence in Congress*. San Francisco: W. H. Freeman, 1980.

———. *At the Margins: Presidential Leadership of Congress*. New Haven: Yale University Press, 1989.

———. "Aligning Tests with Theory: Presidential Approval as a Source of Influence in Congress." *Congress and the Presidency* 24 (1997): 113–30.

Edwards, George C., III, and Andrew Barrett. "Presidential Agenda Setting in Congress." In *Polarized Politics: Congress and the President in a Partisan Era*, edited by Jon R. Bond and Richard Fleisher. Washington, D.C.: CQ Press, 2000.

Edwards, George C., III, John H. Kessel, and Bert A. Rockman, eds. *Researching the Presidency: Vital Questions, New Approaches*. Pittsburgh: University of Pittsburgh Press, 1993.

Edwards, George C., III, and Stephen J. Wayne, eds. *Studying the Presidency.* Knoxville: University of Tennessee Press, 1983.

Ehrlichman, John. *Witness to Power: The Nixon Years.* New York: Simon and Schuster, 1982.

Eilperin, Juliet. "Republicans Target 45 Regulations to Overturn: Clinton Rules Involved Energy, Environment, Abortion Issues." *Washington Post* (April 8, 2001): A1.

Eisenhower, Milton. *The President Is Calling.* Garden City, N.Y.: Doubleday, 1974.

Epstein, David, and Sharyn O'Halloran. *Delegating Powers: A Transaction Cost Politics Approach to Policy Making under Separate Powers.* New York: Cambridge University Press, 1999.

Fay, Bernard. *Roosevelt and His America.* Boston: Little, Brown, 1933.

Fenno, Richard F., Jr. *The President's Cabinet.* Cambridge: Harvard University Press, 1959.

————. *Congressmen in Committees.* Boston: Little, Brown and Co., 1973.

Fett, Patrick. "Presidential Legislative Priorities and Legislators' Voting Decisions: An Exploratory Analysis." *Journal of Politics* 56 (1994): 502–12.

Fink, Gary M., and Hugh Davis Graham, eds. *The Carter Presidency: Policy Choices in the Post–New Deal Era.* Lawrence: University Press of Kansas, 1998.

Fiorina, Morris P. *Congress: Keystone of the Washington Establishment.* 2d ed. New Haven: Yale University Press, 1989.

Fisher, Louis. *The Politics of Shared Power: Congress and the Executive.* 4th ed. College Station: Texas A&M Press, 1998.

Flash, Edward S., Jr. *Economic Advice and Presidential Leadership.* New York: Columbia University Press, 1965.

Fleisher, Richard, and Jon R. Bond. "Partisanship and the President's Quest for Votes on the Floor of Congress." In *Polarized Politics: Congress and the President in a Partisan Era*, edited by Jon R. Bond and Richard Fleisher. Washington, D.C.: CQ Press, 2000.

Fleisher, Richard, Jon R. Bond, Glen S. Krutz, and Stephen Hanna. "The Demise of the Two Presidencies." *American Politics Quarterly* 28 (2000): 3–25.

Follett, Mary Parker. *The Speaker of the House of Representatives.* New York: Longmans, Green, 1896.

Freidel, Frank. *Franklin D. Roosevelt: A Rendezvous with Destiny.* Boston: Little, Brown, 1990.

Gelb, Leslie. "Muskie and Brzezinski: The Struggle over Foreign Policy." *New York Times Magazine* (July 20, 1980).

George, Alexander L. *Presidential Decisionmaking in Foreign Policy: The Effective Use of Information and Advice.* Boulder, Colo.: Westview, 1980.

Gill, Jeff. "The Insignificance of Null Hypothesis Significance Testing." *Political Research Quarterly* 52 (1999): 647–74.

Gilmour, John B. *Strategic Disagreement: Stalemate in American Politics.* Pittsburgh: University of Pittsburgh Press, 1995.

Gilmour, Robert S. "Central Legislative Clearance: A Revised Perspective." *Public Administration Review* 31 (1971): 150–58.

Goodin, Robert E. "Institutions and Their Design." In *The Theory of Institutional Design*, edited by Robert E. Goodin. New York: Cambridge University Press, 1996.

Goodwin, Craufurd D., ed. *Energy Policy in Perspective*. Washington, D.C.: Brookings Institution, 1981.

Goodwin, Doris Kearns. *Lyndon Johnson and the American Dream*. 1976. Reprint, New York: St. Martin's Press, 1991.

Goodwin, George, Jr. *The Little Legislatures: Committees of Congress*. Amherst: University of Massachusetts Press, 1970.

Gosselin, Peter G. "Clinton Makes Pitch, Delivers Health Plan." *Boston Globe* (October 28, 1993): A1.

Graham, Hugh Davis. "Short Circuiting the Bureaucracy in the Great Society: Policy Origins in Education." *Presidential Studies Quarterly* 12 (1982): 407–20.

Greenstein, Fred I. "Change and Continuity in the Modern Presidency." In *The New American Political System*, edited by Anthony King. Washington, D.C.: American Enterprise Institute, 1978.

Groseclose, Tim, and David C. King. "Little Theatre: Committees in Congress." In *Great Theatre: The American Congress in the 1990s*, edited by Herbert F. Weisberg and Samuel C. Patterson. New York: Cambridge University Press, 1998.

Groseclose, Tim, Steven D. Levitt, and James M. Snyder, Jr. "Comparing Interest Group Scores across Time and Chambers: Adjusted ADA Scores for the U.S. Congress." *American Political Science Review* 93 (1999): 33–50.

Halberstam, David. *The Best and the Brightest*. New York: Random House, 1972.

Haldeman, H. R. *The Haldeman Diaries*. Sony/Imagesoft CD-ROM edition, 1994.

Hall, Peter A., and Rosemary C. R. Taylor. "Political Science and the Three New Institutionalisms." *Political Studies* 44 (1996): 936–57.

Hammond, Thomas. "Toward a General Theory of Hierarchy." *Journal of Public Administration Research and Theory* 3 (1993): 120–45.

———. "Structure, Strategy, and the Agenda of the Firm." In *Fundamental Issues in Strategy: A Research Agenda*, edited by Richard P. Rumelt, Dan E. Schendel, and David J. Teece. Boston: Harvard Business School Press, 1994.

Hansen, John Mark. *Gaining Access: Congress and the Farm Lobby, 1919–1981*. Chicago: University of Chicago Press, 1991.

Hargrove, Erwin C. *Jimmy Carter as President: Leadership and the Politics of the Public Good*. Baton Rouge: Louisiana State University Press, 1988.

———. "Presidential Personality and Leadership Style." In *Researching the Presidency: Vital Questions, New Approaches*, edited by George C. Edwards III, John H. Kessel, and Bert A. Rockman. Pittsburgh: University of Pittsburgh Press, 1993.

Hargrove, Erwin C., and Samuel A. Morley, eds. *The President and the Council of Economic Advisers: Interviews with CEA Chairmen*. Boulder, Colo.: Westview Press, 1984.

Hart, John. *The Presidential Branch*. 2d ed. Chatham, N.J.: Chatham House, 1995.

Hart, Oliver. "An Economist's Perspective on the Theory of the Firm." In *Organization Theory: From Chester Barnard to the Present and Beyond*, edited by Oliver Williamson. Expanded ed. New York: Oxford University Press, 1995.

Havemann, Joel. "White House Report: OMB's Legislative Role Is Growing More Powerful and More Political." *National Journal* (October 27, 1973): 1589–98.

Heclo, Hugh. "The Office of Management and Budget and the Presidency: The Problem of Neutral Competence." *Public Interest* 38 (1975): 80–98.

———. "The Changing Presidential Office." In *The Managerial Presidency*, edited by James P. Pfiffner. 2d ed. College Station: Texas A&M Press, 1999.

Heclo, Hugh, and Lester M. Salamon, eds. *The Illusion of Presidential Government*. Boulder, Colo.: Westview Press, 1981.

Heller, Francis H., ed. *The Truman White House: The Administration of the Presidency, 1945–1953*. Lawrence: Regents Press of Kansas, 1980.

Henderson, Phillip G. *Managing the Presidency: The Eisenhower Legacy, from Kennedy to Reagan*. Boulder, Colo.: Westview Press, 1988.

Henry, Gary T. *Practical Sampling*. Newbury Park, Calif.: Sage Publications, 1990.

Herring, E. Pendleton. *Presidential Leadership: Political Relations of Congress and the Chief Executive*. New York: Farrar and Rinehart, 1940.

Hershey, Robert D., Jr. "Reagan Said to Consider Saving Energy Dept." *New York Times* (December 16, 1981): A22.

Hess, Stephen. *Organizing the Presidency*. 2d ed. Washington, D.C.: Brookings Institution, 1988.

Hoff, Joan. *Nixon Reconsidered*. New York: Basic Books, 1994.

Hoffman, David. "Bush Outlines Housing Initiative but Leaves Funding Unclear." *Washington Post* (November 11, 1989): A14.

Hogan, Joseph, ed. *The Reagan Years: The Record in Presidential Leadership*. New York: Manchester University Press, 1990.

Horn, Murray. *The Political Economy of Public Administration: Institutional Choice in the Public Sector*. New York: Cambridge University Press, 1995.

Horne, Alistair. *How Far from Austerlitz?* London: Papermac, 1997.

Howell, William. "Presidential Power and the Politics of Unilateral Action." Ph.D. dissertation, Stanford University, 2000.

Hoxie, R. Gordon. "Staffing the Ford and Carter Presidencies." In *Organizing and Staffing the Presidency*, edited by Bradley D. Nash, Milton S. Eisenhower, R. Gordon Hoxie, and William C. Spragens. New York: Center for the Study of the Presidency, 1980.

Huber, John D., Charles R. Shipan, and Madelaine Pfahler. "Legislatures and Statutory Control of Bureaucracy." *American Journal of Political Science* 45 (2001): 330–45.

Hult, Karen M. "Advising the President." In *Researching the Presidency: Vital Questions, New Approaches*, edited by George C. Edwards III, John H. Kessel, and Bert A. Rockman. Pittsburgh: University of Pittsburgh Press, 1993.

Ifill, Gwen. "Bush Housing Proposals Reflect Kemp Philosophy." *Washington Post* (November 12, 1989): A9.

Jackson, Henry M., ed. *The National Security Council: Jackson Subcommittee Papers on Policy-Making at the Presidential Level.* New York: Praeger, 1965.

Jacobs, Lawrence R., and Robert Y. Shapiro. *Politicians Don't Pander: Political Manipulation and the Loss of Democratic Responsiveness.* Chicago: University of Chicago Press, 2000.

———. "Presidential Power, Institutions, and Democracy." In *Presidential Power: Forging the Presidency for the 21st Century,* edited by Robert Y. Shapiro, Martha Joynt Kumar, and Lawrence R. Jacobs. New York: Columbia University Press, 2000.

Johnson, Haynes, and David S. Broder. *The System.* Paperback ed. Boston: Little, Brown, 1997.

Johnson, Lyndon Baines. *The Vantage Point: Perspectives on the Presidency, 1963–69.* Paperback ed. New York: Popular Library, 1971.

Jones, Charles O. *The Trusteeship Presidency: Jimmy Carter and the United States Congress.* Baton Rouge: Louisiana State University Press, 1988.

———. *The Presidency in a Separated System.* Washington, D.C.: Brookings Institution, 1994.

———. *Passages to the Presidency: From Campaigning to Governing.* Washington, D.C.: Brookings Institution, 1998.

Karl, Barry D. *Executive Reorganization and Reform in the New Deal: The Genesis of Administrative Management, 1900–1939.* Cambridge: Harvard University Press, 1963.

Katz, James Everett. *Presidential Politics and Science Policy.* New York: Praeger, 1978.

Kaufman, Herbert. *The Administrative Behavior of Federal Bureau Chiefs.* Washington, D.C.: Brookings Institution, 1981.

Kellerman, Barbara. *The Political Presidency: Practice of Leadership from Kennedy through Reagan.* New York: Oxford University Press, 1984.

Kennedy, Peter. *A Guide to Econometrics.* 3d ed. Cambridge: MIT Press, 1992.

Kernell, Samuel. *Going Public: New Strategies of Presidential Leadership.* 3d ed. Washington, D.C.: CQ Press, 1997.

Kernell, Samuel, and Samuel L. Popkin, eds. *Chief of Staff.* Berkeley: University of California Press, 1986.

Kessel, John H. *The Domestic Presidency.* Scituate, Mass.: Duxbury Press, 1975.

———. "The Structures of the Carter White House." *American Journal of Political Science* 27 (1983): 431–63.

———. "The Structures of the Reagan White House." *American Journal of Political Science* 28 (1984): 231–58.

Kessler, Glenn, and Dana Milbank. "'Review Board' Rules the Funding Process." *Washington Post* (March 1, 2001): A1.

Kettl, Donald F. *Deficit Politics.* New York: Macmillan, 1992.

Kiefer, Francine, and Abraham McLaughlin. "Bush Starts on Clear, Simple Plan." *Christian Science Monitor* (January 22, 2001): 1.

Kiewiet, D. Roderick, and Mathew D. McCubbins. *The Logic of Delegation.* Chicago: University of Chicago Press, 1991.

King, Anthony, ed. *The New American Political System*. Washington, D.C.: American Enterprise Institute, 1978.

———. *Both Ends of the Avenue*. Washington, D.C.: American Enterprise Institute, 1983.

King, David C. *Turf Wars*. Chicago: University of Chicago Press, 1997.

King, Gary. "The Methodology of Presidential Research." In *Researching the Presidency: Vital Questions, New Approaches*, edited by George C. Edwards III, John H. Kessel, and Bert A. Rockman. Pittsburgh: University of Pittsburgh Press, 1993.

King, Gary, Michael Tomz, and Jason Wittenberg. "Making the Most of Statistical Analyses: Improving Interpretation and Presentation." *American Journal of Political Science* 44 (2000): 347–61.

Kingdon, John W. *Agendas, Alternatives, and Public Policies*. 2d ed. New York: HarperCollins, 1995.

Kirschten, Dick. "Decision Making in the White House: How Well Does It Serve the President?" *National Journal* (April 3, 1982): 584–89.

Kissinger, Henry A. *A World Restored*. Boston: Houghton Mifflin, 1957.

———. *White House Years*. Boston: Little, Brown, 1979.

Koenig, Louis. *The Chief Executive*. Rev. ed. New York: Harcourt, Brace, and World, 1968.

Krause, George A., and Jeffrey E. Cohen. "Opportunity, Constraints, and the Development of the Institutional Presidency: The Issuance of Executive Orders, 1939–1996." *Journal of Politics* 62 (February 2000): 88–114.

Krehbiel, Keith. *Information and Legislative Organization*. Ann Arbor: University of Michigan Press, 1991.

———. "Where's the Party?" *British Journal of Political Science* 23 (1993): 235–66.

———. *Pivotal Politics: A Theory of U.S. Lawmaking*. Chicago: University of Chicago Press, 1998.

Laffin, Martin. "The President and the Subcontractors: The Role of Top Level Policy Entrepreneurs in the Bush Administration." *Presidential Studies Quarterly* 26 (Spring 1996): 550–66.

Lakoff, Sanford A., ed. *Knowledge and Power*. New York: Free Press, 1966.

Liao, Tim Futing. *Interpreting Probability Models*. Thousand Oaks, Calif.: Sage, 1994.

Light, Larry. "White House Domestic Policy Staff Plays Important Role in Formulating Legislation." *Congressional Quarterly Weekly Report* (October 6, 1979): 2199–2204.

———. "Case Study: Creation of an Energy Plan." *Congressional Quarterly Weekly Report* (October 6, 1979): 2203.

Light, Paul C. "Presidential Policy Making." In *Researching the Presidency: Vital Questions, New Approaches*, edited by George C. Edwards III, John H. Kessel, and Bert A. Rockman. Pittsburgh: University of Pittsburgh Press, 1993.

———. *Thickening Government*. Washington, D.C.: Brookings Institution, 1995.

———. *The Tides of Reform*. New Haven: Yale University Press, 1997.

————. *The President's Agenda: Domestic Policy Choice from Kennedy to Clinton*. 3d ed. Baltimore: Johns Hopkins University Press, 1999.

Lindsay, James M., and Wayne P. Steger. "The 'Two Presidencies' in Future Research: Moving beyond Roll-Call Analysis." *Congress and the Presidency* 20 (1993): 103–17.

Lowery, David. "The Presidency, the Bureaucracy, and Reinvention: A Gentle Plea for Chaos." *Presidential Studies Quarterly* 30 (2000): 79–108.

Lowi, Theodore J. *The Personal Presidency*. Ithaca, N.Y.: Cornell University Press, 1985.

Lynn, Laurence E., Jr., and David DeF. Whitman. *The President as Policymaker: Jimmy Carter and Welfare Reform*. Philadelphia: Temple University Press, 1981.

Maass, Arthur. "In Accord with the Program of the President? An Essay on Staffing the Presidency." *Public Policy* 9 (1953): 77–93.

Mackenzie, G. Calvin, ed. *The In-and-Outers: Presidential Appointees and Transient Government in Washington*. Baltimore: Johns Hopkins University Press, 1987.

Maitland, Leslie. "Plan For Homeless Is Called Modest." *New York Times* (November 26, 1989): I-35.

Malbin, Michael J. "Rhetoric and Leadership: A Look Backward at the Carter Energy Plan." In *Both Ends of the Avenue*, edited by Anthony King. Washington, D.C.: American Enterprise Institute, 1983.

————. "Presidential Proposals to Congress and Related Roll Call Votes, 1789–1993." In Elaine K. Swift, Robert G. Brookshire, David T. Canon, Evelyn C. Fink, John R. Hibbing, Brian D. Humes, Michael J. Malbin, and Kenneth C. Martis, *Database of Congressional Historical Statistics, 1789–1988* [computer file]. Ann Arbor, Mich.: Inter-University Consortium for Political and Social Research, 2001.

Maltzman, Forrest. *Competing Principals: Committees, Parties, and the Organization of Congress*. Ann Arbor: University of Michigan Press, 1997.

Mansfield, Harvey C., Sr., ed. *Congress against the President*. New York: Praeger, 1975.

Markun, Rachel. "Prospects for Pension Legislation in 1997." *Defined Contribution Plan Investing* (December 24, 1996): 2.

Mayer, Kenneth R. *With the Stroke of a Pen: Executive Orders and Presidential Power*. Princeton: Princeton University Press, 2001.

Mayhew, David R. *Divided We Govern*. New Haven: Yale University Press, 1992.

Mazmanian, Daniel A., and Paul A. Sabatier. *Implementation and Public Policy*. Glenview, Ill.: Scott, Foresman, 1983.

McPherson, Harry. *A Political Education: A Washington Memoir*. 1972. Reprint, Boston: Houghton Mifflin, 1988.

Merriam, Robert E. "The Bureau of the Budget as Part of the President's Staff." *Annals of the American Academy of Political and Social Science* 307 (1956): 15–23.

Mezey, Michael L. *Congress, the President, and Public Policy*. Boulder, Colo.: Westview Press, 1989.

Michaels, Judith. *The President's Call: Executive Leadership from FDR to George Bush*. Pittsburgh: University of Pittsburgh Press, 1997.

Milbank, Dana. "A Loyalist Calls White House to Order." *Washington Post* (February 20, 2001): A1.

Milgrom, Paul, and John Roberts. "Bargaining Costs, Influence Costs, and the Organization of Economic Activity." In *Perspectives on Positive Political Economy*, edited by James E. Alt and Kenneth A. Shepsle. New York: Cambridge University Press, 1990.

Milkis, Sidney, and Michael Nelson. *The American Presidency: Origins and Development, 1776–1998*. 3d ed. Washington, D.C.: CQ Press, 1999.

Miller, Gary J. *Managerial Dilemmas: The Political Economy of Hierarchy*. New York: Cambridge University Press, 1992.

Mitchell, Alison. "Winning: Now He Must Persuade the Voters." *New York Times* (December 17, 2000): IV-1.

Moe, Ronald C. "The Domestic Council in Perspective." *The Bureaucrat* 5 (1976): 251–72.

———. *The Hoover Commissions Revisited*. Boulder, Colo.: Westview Press, 1982.

Moe, Ronald C. and Steven C. Teel. "Congress as Policy-Maker: A Necessary Reappraisal." *Political Science Quarterly* 85 (1970): 443–70.

Moe, Terry M. "The New Economics of Organization." *American Journal of Political Science* 28 (November 1984): 739–77.

———. "The Politicized Presidency." In *New Directions in American Politics*, edited by John Chubb and Paul E. Peterson. Washington, D.C.: Brookings Institution, 1985.

———. "The Politics of Bureaucratic Structure." In *Can the Government Govern?* edited by John Chubb and Paul E. Peterson. Washington, D.C.: Brookings Institution, 1989.

———. "Presidents, Institutions, and Theory." In *Researching the Presidency: Vital Questions, New Approaches*, edited by George C. Edwards III, John H. Kessel, and Bert A. Rockman. Pittsburgh: University of Pittsburgh Press, 1993.

Moe, Terry M., and William G. Howell. "The Presidential Power of Unilateral Action." *Journal of Law, Economics, and Organization* 15 (1999): 132–79.

Moe, Terry M., and Scott A. Wilson. "Presidents and the Politics of Structure." *Law and Contemporary Problems* 57 (Summer 1994): 1–44.

Morgan, Dan. "Clinton's Last Regulatory Rush." *Washington Post* (December 6, 2000): A1.

Morris, Dick. *Behind the Oval Office*. New York: Random House, 1997.

Mosher, Frederick C. *A Tale of Two Agencies*. Baton Rouge: Louisiana State University Press, 1984.

Moynihan, Daniel P. *The Politics of a Guaranteed Income: The Nixon Administration and the Family Assistance Plan*. New York: Random House, 1972.

———. *Coping*. New York: Random House, 1973.

Nash, Bradley D., Milton S. Eisenhower, R. Gordon Hoxie, and William C. Spragens, eds. *Organizing and Staffing the Presidency*. New York: Center for the Study of the Presidency, 1980.

Nathan, Richard. *The Plot That Failed: Nixon and the Administrative Presidency*. New York: Wiley, 1975.

———. *The Administrative Presidency*. New York: Wiley, 1983.

Nelson, Garrison. *Committees in the U.S. Congress, 1947–1992*. 2 vols. Washington, D.C.: Congressional Quarterly, 1993.

Nelson, Jack, and Robert J. Donovan. "The Education of a President." *Los Angeles Times Magazine* (August 1, 1993).

Nelson, Michael, ed. *The Presidency and the Political System*. 6th ed. Washington, D.C.: CQ Press, 2000.

Neustadt, Richard E. "Presidency and Legislation: The Growth of Central Clearance," *American Political Science Review* 48 (1954): 641–71.

———. "Presidency and Legislation: Planning the President's Program." *American Political Science Review* 49 (1955): 980–1021.

———. 1965. "Statement before the Subcommittee on National Security Staffing and Operations of the Senate Committee on Government Operations, March 25, 1963." In *The National Security Council: Jackson Subcommittee Papers on Policy-Making at the Presidential Level*, edited by Henry M. Jackson. New York: Praeger, 1965.

———. *Presidential Power and the Modern Presidents*. New York: Free Press, 1990.

Newland, Chester. "Executive Office Policy Apparatus: Enforcing the Reagan Agenda." In *The Reagan Presidency and the Governing of America*, edited by Lester Salamon and Michael S. Lund. Washington, D.C.: Urban Institute Press, 1984.

Niskanen, William A. *Reaganomics*. New York: Oxford University Press, 1988.

Nivola, Pietro S. "Energy Policy and the Congress: The Politics of the Natural Gas Policy Act of 1978." *Public Policy* 28 (1980): 491–543.

Nixon, Richard M. *RN: The Memoirs of Richard Nixon*. 1978. Reprint, New York: Simon and Schuster/Touchstone, 1990.

North, Douglass C. "The New Institutional Economics." *Journal of Institutional and Theoretical Economics* 142 (1986): 230–37.

Office of Management and Budget. *Budget of the United States, Fiscal Year 2002*. Washington, D.C.: Government Printing Office, 2001.

Oleszek, Walter J. *Congressional Procedures and the Policy Process*. 4th ed. Washington, D.C.: CQ Press, 1996.

Oppenheimer, Bruce. "Policy Effects of U.S. House Reform: Decentralization and the Capacity to Resolve Energy Issues." *Legislative Studies Quarterly* (February 1980): 5–30.

Osborne, John. *White House Watch: The Ford Years*. Washington, D.C.: New Republic Books, 1977.

Ostrom, Charles W., Jr., and Brian L. Job. "The President and the Political Use of Force." *American Political Science Review* 80 (1986): 541–66.

Patterson, Bradley H., Jr. *Ring of Power: The White House Staff and Its Expanding Role in Government*. New York: Basic Books, 1988.

———. "Team and Staff: Dwight Eisenhower's Innovations in the Structure and Operations of the Modern White House." *Presidential Studies Quarterly* 24 (1994): 277–98.

———. *The White House Staff: Inside the West Wing and Beyond*. Washington, D.C.: Brookings Institution, 2000.

Pear, Robert. "Meese Playing Central Role in Domestic Policy Now." *New York Times* (September 17, 1986): B8.

Pemberton, William E. *Bureaucratic Politics*. Columbia: University of Missouri Press, 1979.

Peterson, Mark A. *Legislating Together: The White House and Capitol Hill from Eisenhower to Reagan*. Cambridge: Harvard University Press, 1990.

———. "The President and Congress." In *The Presidency and the Political System*, edited by Michael Nelson. 6th ed. Washington, D.C.: CQ Press, 2000.

Pfeffer, Jeffrey. *Managing with Power: Politics and Influence in Organizations*. Boston: Harvard Business School Press, 1992.

Pfiffner, James P. "The Reagan Budget Juggernaut." In *The Presidency and Economic Policy*, edited by James P. Pfiffner. Philadelphia: Institute for the Study of Human Issues, 1986.

———. *The Strategic Presidency*. 2d rev. ed. Lawrence: University Press of Kansas, 1996.

———. "Presidential Constraints and Transitions." In *Presidential Policymaking: An End-of-Century Assessment*, edited by Steven A. Shull. Armonk, N.Y.: M. E. Sharpe, 1999.

Pfiffner, James P., ed. *The Managerial Presidency*. 2d ed. College Station: Texas A&M University Press, 1999.

Pika, Joseph A. "Moving beyond the Oval Office: Problems in Studying the Presidency." *Congress and the Presidency* 9 (1982): 17–36.

———. "White House Boundary Roles: Marginal Men amidst the Palace Guard." *Presidential Studies Quarterly* 16 (1986): 700–15.

Pious, Richard M. "Sources of Domestic Policy Initiatives." In *Congress against the President*, edited by Harvey C. Mansfield, Sr. New York: Praeger, 1975.

Podhoretz, John. *Hell of a Ride: Backstage at the White House Follies, 1989–1993*. New York: Simon and Schuster, 1993.

Ponder, Daniel E. "Presidential Agents and Policy Responsiveness: Information, Control, and Delegation in the Presidency." Ph.D. dissertation, Vanderbilt University, 1994.

———. *Good Advice: Information and Policy Making in the White House*. College Station: Texas A&M University Press, 2000.

Poole, Keith T., and Howard Rosenthal. *Congress: A Political-Economic History of Roll Call Voting*. New York: Oxford University Press, 1997.

———. "Estimating a Basic Space from a Set of Issue Scales." *American Journal of Political Science* 42 (1998): 954–93.

Poole, Keith T., Howard Rosenthal, and Nolan M. McCarty. "Veto Power and Legislation: An Empirical Analysis of Executive and Legislative Bargaining from 1961–1986." *Journal of Law, Economics, and Organization* 11 (1995): 282–312.

Porter, Roger B. *Presidential Decision Making: The Economic Policy Board*. New York: Cambridge University Press, 1980.

Prados, John. *Keepers of the Keys: A History of the National Security Council from Truman to Bush*. New York: Morrow, 1991.

Public Papers of the Presidents of the United States. Washington, D.C.: U.S. Government Printing Office, 1949–1996.

Quirk, Paul. "What Do We Know?" In *Political Science: Looking toward the Future*, edited by William Crotty. Vol. 4. Evanston, Ill.: Northwestern University Press, 1991.

Rae, Nicol C., and Colton C. Campbell, eds. *New Majority or Old Minority? The Impact of Republicans on Congress*. Lanham, Md.: Rowman and Littlefield, 1999.

Ragsdale, Lyn, ed. *Vital Statistics on the Presidency: Washington to Clinton*. Rev. ed. Washington, D.C.: CQ Press, 1998.

Ragsdale, Lyn, and John Theis. "The Institutionalization of the American Presidency." *American Journal of Political Science* 41 (1997): 1280–1318.

Raines, Howell. "Reagan Adopts Plan to End Energy Department and Shift Its Duties," *New York Times* (December 17, 1981): A1.

Redford, Emmette S., and Richard T. McCulley. *White House Operations: The Johnson Presidency*. Austin: University of Texas Press, 1986.

Reeves, Richard. *President Kennedy: Profile of Power*. New York: Touchstone, 1993.

Reich, Robert B. *Locked in the Cabinet*. New York: Knopf, 1997.

Reichley, A. James. *Conservatives in an Age of Change*. Washington, D.C.: Brookings Institution, 1981.

Richardson, Don, ed. *Conversations with Carter*. Boulder, Colo.: Lynne Rienner, 1998.

Rivers, Douglas, and Nancy L. Rose. "Passing the President's Program: Public Opinion and Presidential Influence in Congress." *American Journal of Political Science* 29 (1985): 183–96.

Roberts, Charles, ed. *Has the President Too Much Power?* New York: Harper's Magazine Press, 1974.

Rockman, Bert A. *The Leadership Question*. New York: Praeger, 1984.

Rohde, David. "Parties and Committees in the House." *Legislative Studies Quarterly* 19 (1994): 341–59.

Roosevelt, Theodore. *An Autobiography*. 1913. Reprint, New York: Da Capo Press, 1985.

Rosenbaum, Herbert, and Alexej Ugrinsky, eds. *The Presidency and Domestic Policies of Jimmy Carter*. Westport, Conn.: Greenwood Press, 1994.

Rudalevige, Andrew. "The Institutional Perspective and the Presidency: The Organization of Information and the Structure of Leadership." Paper presented at the annual meeting of the American Political Science Association, Washington, D.C., August 1997.

Rumelt, Richard P., Dan E. Schendel, and David J. Teece, eds. *Fundamental Issues in Strategy: A Research Agenda*. Boston: Harvard Business School Press, 1994.

Russell, Mary. "Tip O'Neill, the Great Accommodator; Boston Pol Is Teaching Carter the First Lesson of a Ward Heeler — Compromise." *Washington Post* (June 19, 1977): A18.

Russell, Mary, and Warren Brown. "Fate of Program Rests with Key Congressional Leaders; Both Houses Prepared for Complex Task." *Washington Post* (April 23, 1977): A1.

Salamon, Lester M. "The Presidency and Domestic Policy Formation." In *The Illusion of Presidential Government*, edited by Hugh Heclo and Lester M. Salamon. Boulder, Colo.: Westview, 1981.

Salamon, Lester M., and Michael S. Lund, eds. *The Reagan Presidency and the Governing of America*. Washington, D.C.: Urban Institute Press, 1984.

Sander, Alfred Dick. *A Staff for the President: The Executive Office, 1921–1952*. New York: Greenwood, 1989.

———. *Eisenhower's Executive Office*. Westport, Conn.: Greenwood, 1999.

Saulnier, Raymond J. *Constructive Years: The U.S. Economy under Eisenhower*. Lanham, Md.: University Press of America, 1991.

Schlesinger, Arthur M., Jr. *A Thousand Days: John F. Kennedy in the White House*. Paperback ed. New York: Fawcett, 1965.

———. *Robert Kennedy and His Times*. Paperback ed. New York: Ballantine, 1979.

Schneier, Edward V., and Bertram Gross. *Legislative Strategy: Shaping Public Policy*. New York: St. Martin's, 1993.

Schoettle, Enid. "The Establishment of NASA." In *Knowledge and Power*, edited by Sanford A. Lakoff. New York: Free Press, 1966.

Seidman, Harold, and Robert Gilmour. *Politics, Position, and Power*. 4th ed. New York: Oxford University Press, 1986.

Shapiro, Robert Y., Martha Joynt Kumar, and Lawrence R. Jacobs, eds. *Presidential Power: Forging the Presidency for the 21st Century*. New York: Columbia University Press, 2000.

Shepsle, Kenneth A. "The Changing Textbook Congress." In *Can the Government Govern?* edited by John Chubb and Paul E. Peterson. Washington, D.C.: Brookings Institution, 1989.

———. "Studying Institutions: Some Lessons from the Rational Choice Approach." *Journal of Theoretical Politics* 1 (1989): 131–47.

Shoemaker, Christopher C. *The NSC Staff: Counseling the Council*. Boulder, Colo.: Westview, 1991.

Shull, Steven A. *Domestic Policy Formation: Presidential-Congressional Partnership?* Westport, Conn.: Greenwood Press, 1983.

———. *Presidential-Congressional Relations: Policy and Time Approaches*. Ann Arbor: University of Michigan Press, 1997.

Shull, Steven A., ed. *The Two Presidencies: A Quarter-Century Assessment*. Chicago: Nelson-Hall, 1991.

———. *Presidential Policymaking: An End-of-Century Assessment*. Armonk, N.Y.: M. E. Sharpe, 1999.

Shull, Steven A., and Thomas C. Shaw. *Explaining Presidential-Congressional Relations: A Multiple Perspective Approach*. Albany: State University of New York Press, 1999.

Shultz, George P., and Kenneth Dam. *Economic Policy beyond the Headlines*. New York: W. W. Norton, 1977.

Simendinger, Alexis. "The Paper Wars." *National Journal* (July 25, 1998): 1732–39.

Sinclair, Barbara. "The President as Legislative Leader." In *The Clinton Presi-*

dency: First Appraisals, edited by Colin Campbell and Bert A. Rockman. Chatham, N.J.: Chatham House, 1996.

———. *Unorthodox Lawmaking: New Legislative Processes in the U.S. Congress*. Washington, D.C.: CQ Press, 1997.

Skocpol, Theda. *Boomerang: Clinton's Health Security Effort and the Turn against Government in U.S. Politics*. New York: W. W. Norton and Company, 1996.

Skowronek, Stephen. *The Politics Presidents Make*. Cambridge: Harvard University Press, 1994.

Smith, Hedrick. *The Power Game*. Paperback ed. New York: Ballantine Books, 1988.

Smith, Nancy Kegan. "Presidential Task Force Operation during the Johnson Administration." *Presidential Studies Quarterly* 15 (1985): 320–29.

Sorensen, Theodore C. *Kennedy*. New York: Harper and Row, 1965.

Solomon, Burt. "Send in the Clones." *National Journal* 24 (March 21, 1992): 678–83.

———. "Drawn and Redrawn, the Lines in the West Wing Get Blurrier." *National Journal* 26 (January 15, 1994): 134.

Sperlich, Peter W. "Bargaining and Overload: An Essay on *Presidential Power*." In *The Presidency*, edited by Aaron Wildavsky. Boston: Little, Brown, 1969.

Spitzer, Robert J. *The Presidency and Public Policy: The Four Arenas of Presidential Power*. University: University of Alabama Press, 1983.

Stanley, Harold W., and Richard G. Niemi, eds. *Vital Statistics on American Politics*. 4th ed. Washington, D.C.: CQ Press, 1994.

Starobin, Paul. "The Broker." *National Journal* 26 (April 16, 1994): 878–83.

Starr, Paul. *The Logic of Health Care Reform*. Rev. ed. New York: Whittle Books/Penguin Books, 1994.

StataCorp. *Stata Statistical Software: Release 6.0*. College Station, Tex.: Stata Corporation, 1999.

Steger, Wayne P. "Presidential Policy Initiation and the Politics of Agenda Control." *Congress and the Presidency* 24 (1997): 17–36.

———. "The Occurrence and Consequences of Electoral Mandates in Historical Context." *Congress and the Presidency* 27 (2000): 121–48.

Stephanopoulos, George. *All Too Human: A Political Education*. Boston: Little, Brown, 1999.

Stewart, Charles, and Jonathan Woon. "Congressional Committee Assignments Data, 1993–1998." Dataset and codebook. Massachusetts Institute of Technology.

Stockman, David A. *The Triumph of Politics*. New York: Harper and Row, 1986.

Stone, Deborah. *Policy Paradox and Political Reason*. Glenview, Ill.: Scott, Foresman, 1988.

Sullivan, Terry. "Headcounts, Expectations, and Presidential Coalitions in Congress." *American Journal of Political Science* 32 (1988): 567–89.

Sundquist, James L. *Politics and Policy*. Washington, D.C.: Brookings Institution, 1968.

———. *The Decline and Resurgence of Congress*. Washington, D.C.: Brookings Institution, 1981.

Taylor, Andrew J. "Domestic Agenda Setting, 1947–1994." *Legislative Studies Quarterly* 23 (1998): 373–97.

Taylor, Paul. "Regan, as Promised, Will Ask Congress to Dismantle Energy Department," *Washington Post* (December 18, 1981): A16.

Tenpas, Kathryn Dunn, and Matthew J. Dickinson. "Governing, Campaigning, and Organizing the Presidency: An Electoral Connection?" *Political Science Quarterly* 112 (Spring 1997): 51–66.

Thomas, Norman C. "Presidential Advice and Information: Policy and Program Formulation." *Law and Contemporary Problems* 35 (1970): 540–72.

Thomas, Norman C., and Joseph A. Pika. *The Politics of the Presidency*. Rev. 4th ed. Washington, D.C.: CQ Press, 1997.

Thomas, Norman C., and Harold L. Wolman. "Policy Formulation in the Institutionalized Presidency: The Johnson Task Forces." In *The Presidential Advisory System*, edited by Thomas E. Cronin and Sanford D. Greenberg. New York: Harper and Row, 1969.

Thompson, Kenneth W., ed. *Portraits of American Presidents*. Vol. 2: The Truman Presidency. Lanham, Md.: University Press of America, 1984.

——— -. *Portraits of American Presidents*. Vol. 5: *The Johnson Presidency*. Lanham, Md.: University Press of America, 1986.

———. *Portraits of American Presidents*. Vol. 8: *The Carter Presidency*. Lanham, Md.: University Press of America, 1990.

———. *Portraits of American Presidents*. Vol. 9: *The Reagan Presidency*. Lanham, Md.: University Press of America, 1992.

———. *Portraits of American Presidents*. Vol. 11: *The Bush Presidency*, pt. 2. Lanham, Md.: University Press of America, 1998.

Thurber, James, ed. *Rivals for Power: Presidential-Congressional Relations*. Washington, D.C.: CQ Press, 1996.

Tomkin, Shelley Lynne. *Inside OMB: Politics and Process in the President's Budget Office*. Armonk, N.Y.: M. E. Sharpe, 1998.

Tomz, Michael, Jason Wittenberg, and Gary King. *CLARIFY: Software for Interpreting and Presenting Statistical Results, Version 1.2.2*. Harvard University, March 3, 2000. <*http://gking.harvard.edu/*>

Tulis, Jeffrey K. *The Rhetorical Presidency*. Princeton: Princeton University Press, 1987.

Verba, Sidney, Kay Schlozman, and Henry Brady. *Voice and Equality*. Cambridge: Harvard University Press, 1995.

Walcott, Charles E., and Karen M. Hult. "Organizing the White House: Structure, Environment, and Organizational Governance." *American Journal of Political Science* 31 (1987): 109–25.

———. *Governing the White House: From Hoover through LBJ*. Lawrence: University Press of Kansas, 1995.

Waldman, Steven. 1996. *The Bill*. Rev. paperback ed. New York: Penguin, 1996.

Waldmann, Raymond J. "The Domestic Council: Innovation in Presidential Government." *Public Administration Review* 36 (1976): 260–68.

Waldstein, Fredric A. "Cabinet Government: The Reagan Management Model." In *The Reagan Years: The Record in Presidential Leadership*, edited by Joseph Hogan. New York: Manchester University Press, 1990.

Warshaw, Shirley Anne. "The Carter Experience with Cabinet Government." In *The Presidency and Domestic Policies of Jimmy Carter*, edited by Herbert Rosenbaum and Alexej Ugrinsky. Westport, Conn.: Greenwood Press, 1994.

———. "White House Control of Domestic Policymaking: The Reagan Years." *Public Administration Review* 55 (1995): 247–53.

———. *Powersharing: White House–Cabinet Relations in the Modern Presidency*. Albany: State University of New York Press, 1996.

———. *The Domestic Presidency: Policy Making in the White House*. Boston: Allyn and Bacon, 1997.

Warshaw, Shirley Anne, ed. *The Eisenhower Legacy: Discussions of Presidential Leadership*. Silver Spring, Md.: Bartleby Press, 1992.

Waterman, Richard W. *Presidential Influence and the Administrative State*. Knoxville: University of Tennessee Press, 1989.

Wayne, Stephen J. *The Legislative Presidency*. New York: Harper and Row, 1978.

———. "Comments: Politics instead of Policy." In *The Reagan Presidency and the Governing of America*, edited by Lester Salamon and Michael S. Lund. Washington, D.C.: Urban Institute Press, 1984.

Weingast, Barry R. "A Rational Choice Perspective on Congressional Norms." *American Journal of Political Science* 23 (1979): 245–62.

Weisberg, Herbert F., and Samuel C. Patterson, eds. *Great Theatre: The American Congress in the 1990s*. New York: Cambridge University Press, 1998.

Weko, Thomas J. *The Politicizing Presidency: The White House Personnel Office, 1948–1994*. Lawrence: University Press of Kansas, 1995.

White, Leonard. *Introduction to the Study of Public Administration*. 3d ed. New York: Macmillan, 1948.

Whiteman, David. *Communication in Congress: Members, Staff, and the Search for Information*. Lawrence: University Press of Kansas, 1995.

Wildavsky, Aaron. "The Two Presidencies." In *The Presidency*, edited by Aaron Wildavsky. Boston: Little, Brown, 1969.

———. *The New Politics of the Budgetary Process*. 2d ed. New York: Harper-Collins, 1992.

Wildavsky, Aaron, ed. *The Presidency*. Boston: Little, Brown, 1969.

Williams, Walter. "George Bush and Executive Branch Domestic Policymaking Competence." *Policy Studies Journal* 21 (1993): 700–719.

Williamson, Oliver. *Markets and Hierarchies*. New York: Free Press, 1975.

———. *The Economic Institutions of Capitalism*. New York: Free Press, 1985.

———. *The Mechanisms of Governance*. New York: Oxford University Press, 1996.

Williamson, Oliver, ed. *Organization Theory: From Chester Barnard to the Present and Beyond*. Expanded ed. New York: Oxford University Press, 1995.

Williamson, Richard S. *Reagan's Federalism*. Lanham, Md.: University Press of America, 1989.

Wilson, James Q. *Bureaucracy*. New York: Basic Books, 1989.

Wilson, Woodrow. *Congressional Government*. 1885. Reprint, New York: Meridian Books, 1956.

Winship, Christopher, and Larry Radbill. "Sampling Weights and Regression Analysis." *Sociological Methods and Research* 23 (November 1994): 230–57.

Wolanin, Thomas R. *Presidential Advisory Commissions: Truman to Nixon*. Madison: University of Wisconsin Press, 1975.

Wolman, Harold L., and Astrid E. Merget. "The Presidency and Policy Formulation: President Carter and the Urban Policy." *Presidential Studies Quarterly* 10 (1980): 402–15.

Wood, B. Dan, and Richard W. Waterman. *Bureaucratic Dynamics: The Role of Bureaucracy in a Democracy*. Boulder, Colo.: Westview, 1994.

Woodward, Bob. *The Agenda*. New York: Simon and Schuster, 1994.

———. *The Choice*. New York: Simon and Schuster, 1996.

———. *Shadow: Five Presidents and the Legacy of Watergate*. Paperback ed. New York: Simon & Schuster/Touchstone, 2000.

Yager, Joseph. "The Energy Battles of 1979." In *Energy Policy in Perspective*, edited by Craufurd D. Goodwin. Washington, D.C.: Brookings Institution, 1981.

INDEX

Ackley, Gardner, 22–23
ADA (Americans for Democratic Action), 94. *See also* "real" ADA scores
Adams, Brock, 199n.79
Adams, Sherman, 55, 56, 74–75
Americans for Democratic Action. *See* ADA
Anderson, Clinton, 75
approval, presidential, 130–32, 140, 239n.18
Argo (tanker) wreck, 132
Arms Control and Disarmament Agency, 212n.104
Arnold, Peri, 35, 234n.79
Article II (Constitution), 41, 64–65
Ash, Roy, 3, 31, 114, 210n.87
Aviation Act (1975), 36, 91

Baker, Bobby, 188n.2
Baker, James, 38, 211n.98
Baldridge, Malcolm, 34–35
Barrett, Andrew, 136, 188n.9
Bell, David, 53
Berlin, Isaiah, 1
Blumenthal, Michael, 120, 235n.90
BoB. *See* Bureau of the Budget
Bond, Jon, 113, 138, 159
Bordeaux, Lisa, 224n.31
Boxscore listings (Congressional Quarterly), 13, 14, 64, 66–67, 68, 70
Brademas, John, 123
Brzezinski, Zbigniew, 33, 50, 198n.64
Budget and Accounting Act (1921), 45, 60
budgetary/deficit issues: conventional wisdom on, 60, 211n.99; as determining contingent centralization, 96–97, 110, 225n.34; and limits of centralization, 141; and the OMB, 60, 211n.102; under Reagan, 60, 233–34n.73
Budget Bureau. *See* Bureau of the Budget (BoB)

Budget Circular A-19 (OMB), 46–47, 50, 73
Budget Message, 71
Bundy, McGeorge, 50
bureaucracy: and contingent centralization, 36; definition of, 193n.5; Nixon on, 19; politics of, 127, 234n.79; and responsiveness, 32–33, 198n.63
Bureau of the Budget (BoB), 43, 45–47, 49, 203nn.22–23; clearance records of, 87, 220n.2; and Dwight Eisenhower, 55; and John Kennedy, 56–57, 209n.74; on the RACC, 79; and Franklin Roosevelt, 46; and Harry Truman, 53–54, 207–8n.62
Burns, James MacGregor, 20
Bush, George H. W.: agenda size of, 130; "to Congress and the Nation," 214n.13; HOPE proposed by, 76–77, 218n.49; program development under, 51; savings and loan rescue proposed by, 89; staff of, 61, 212n.106; on wilderness areas, 90
Bush, George W.: "Address to the Joint Session of Congress," 214n.13; on election reform, 68; on foreign policy, 159; legislative successes needed by, 188–89n.10; and the September 11 attacks, xii, 132, 159–60; unilateral action by, 159–60, 161
Byrd Rule, 234n.73

Cabinet: as decentralized, 19; government by, 50, 58–59, 153, 205n.46; growth of, 7; inner vs. outer, 39, 93, 110, 228n.55; vs. White House, 19–23, 194n.13, 194n.16, 195n.18
Cabinet Councils, 50, 59, 195n.18, 211nn.97–98
Califano, Joe, 33, 36, 49; on the Department of Justice, 217–18n.46; on task forces, 57–58, 209n.81

Calio, Nicholas, 116
Cameron, Charles, 5
Cannon, Jim, 210–11n.91
Carey, William, 34, 242n.15
Carter, Jimmy: on Brzezinski, 33,
198n.64; on Cabinet governance, 50,
59; on cargo ship safety and oil spills,
132; on congressional workload, 129,
235n.90; decentralization by, 93; energy
legislation proposed by, 119–23,
231n.44, 232n.54, 232n.56; gambling
joke of, 134, 237n.1; Hospital Cost
Containment Act of, 90; on Humphrey-
Hawkins legislation, 68; legislative success of, 137–38; malaise speech of,
232n.56; rescission messages from, 60,
212n.103; staffing techniques of, 13; on
the State Department, 33; State of the
Union addresses of, 65; town meetings
of, 69; on welfare reform, 35, 36;
Youth Employment and Demonstration
Projects Act proposed by, 77–78,
218n.53
Cater, Doug, 209n.78
centralization: costs of, xii, 11–12, 24–25;
definition of, 6, 19; and institutionalism, 24–25, 27–28; limits of (see centralization's limits); and management
environment, 25–28, 196–97n.41; success of (see legislative success); and
White House/departmental divide, 19–
23, 194n.13, 194n.16, 195n.18. See
also contingent centralization; contingent centralization, factors determining;
linear centralization
centralization's limits, 134–51, 156; and
budgetary/deficit issues, 141; and complexity, 140; and crises, 140; and cross-
cutting jurisdictions, 139; defining
centralization and success, 134–38,
237–38n.6, 237nn.2–4, 238n.12; and
expertise, 150; independent variables,
138–43, 239–40n.23, 239n.20,
239nn.17–18, 240n.25; models of,
141–50, 240–41n.29, 240nn.26–27,
241n.31; and novelty, 139; and political
parties/ideology, 139–40; and presidential approval, 140, 239n.18; and
priority/salience, 140, 239n.17; and reorganization, 139; and staff size, 141;
and timing within a president's term,

141, 239–40n.23; and the "two presi-
dencies" thesis, 140, 239n.20; and
workload, 139
Chamberlain, Lawrence, 14–15, 43, 75
Cheney, Dick, 205n.46
choice. See presidential choices
Circular A-19 (OMB), 46–47, 50, 73
Civil Rights Act (1967), 161, 243n.21
Civil Service Commission, 92
CLARIFY (software), 227n.46
Clark, Ramsey, 217n.39
Clifford, Clark, 53, 200n.81
Clinton, Bill: "Administration Goals,"
214n.13; affirmative action policy developed by, 32; agenda size of, 130; Bos-
nian proposal of, 132; Cabinet retreat
at Camp David with, 195n.18; Cabinet
selection by, 62; campaign finance commission proposed by, 91; on decentralization, 93; deficit reduction proposed
by, 117; on ERISA, 9–10; health care
program proposed by, 97, 126,
215n.24; health care task forces/teams,
8, 191n.30; Health Security Act proposed by, 8, 191n.30, 207n.57; legislative success of, 3, 63, 138; National
Economic Council established by, 51;
NPR package of, 125; Office of Environmental Policy established by,
206n.51; rescission power of, 211n.102;
Ryan White CARE Act of, 90; staff of,
35, 61; talk show appearances of, 69;
transition report of, 20; unilateral action by, 158–59, 161; welfare reform
proposal of, 135, 237n.4
Clinton, Hillary Rodham, 8, 61
Coase, Ronald, 30
Cohen, Jeffrey, 66, 238n.12
Cohen, Wilbur, 36
Cole, Ken, 228n.2
Collier, Kenneth, 151
Committee on Economic Security, 207n.57
committees and subcommittees, 116, 125,
196n.29
complexity: and contingent centralization,
35, 36, 39, 91, 111–12, 199n.69,
221n.16; and limits of centralization,
140
Congress: committees of, as informational
institutions, 196n.29; decentralization
as strengthened by, 60–61; and fishing

rights agreements, 61; leaks to press by, 117–18, 230n.24; and nuclear export agreements, 61, 212n.104; and rescissions, 60, 211n.102; vs. White House, 114, 118–19, 230n.31. *See also* legislative success

Congressional Quarterly (CQ), 13, 14, 64, 66–67, 68, 70

contingent centralization, 5–13, 15–16, 28–40, 154; and bureaucracy, 36; and centrality of information, 26, 28–29, 197n.48; and expertise/technical Knowledge, 35–36, 198n.58, 199n.79, 200n.81; limits of (*see* centralization's limits); and policy complexity, 35, 36, 39, 91, 111–12, 199n.69, 221n.16; and policy scope, 33–34, 39; and politicization, 37–39, 58, 201nn.90–91, 210n.88; and principal congruence, 36–39, 200nn.85–86; and reorganization, 34–35, 39, 199n.74; and responsiveness, 32–33, 198n.63; and staff size, 34, 199n.70; testing of (*see* centralization's limits; contingent centralization, factors determining); and transaction costs in decision making, 29–32, 197n.50

contingent centralization, factors determining, 86–112, 155, 182–83, 220n.1; alternate hypotheses/controls, 110–11; bureau proximity to president, 92–93, 179–80, 222nn.20–22; causes of centralization, 102–4, 105–7, 226–27nn.46–48; centralization, conditions favoring, 87–90, 220–21nn.6–9, 220nn.2–3, 221n.11, 221n.13; centralizing strategies, 108–9; congressional proximity to president, 93–95, 181–82, 223–24nn.27–28, 224n.30; decentralization, conditions favoring, 90–95, 221n.16, 222nn.20–22, 223–24nn.27–28, 224n.30; decentralizing strategies, 109–10, 227–28nn.52–56; and mixed strategies, 111–12; presidential style, 98–99; priority/salience, 97–98, 111; summary of variables, 99–101; timing within a president's term, 98; and weighting, 101–2

conventional wisdom. *See* history and conventional wisdom

Council of Economic Advisers, 49, 54

Council on International Economic Policy, 59

CQ. *See* Congressional Quarterly

crises, 66, 89, 140

Cronin, Thomas, 39, 93

cross-cutting jurisdictions, 87–88, 220n.6, 220nn.2–4; and legislative success, 124–26, 233–34n.73, 233n.66, 233n.69, 235n.85; and limits of centralization, 139

Cutter, W. Bowman, 35

Darman, Richard, 51

data. *See* contingent centralization, factors determining; empirical overview of president's program

Dean, John, 242–43n.17

decision making. *See* presidential choices

deep structure, 98

Deering, Christopher J., 242n.16

deficit issues. *See* budgetary/deficit issues

Demarest, David, 65

Democrats, centralization by, 227–28n.54

Department of Agriculture, 55–56, 79, 88, 208n.72

Department of Defense, 8–9, 88

Department of Energy, 34–35, 122

Department of Health, Education, and Welfare (HEW), 89, 90, 220n.4

Department of Housing and Urban Development (HUD), 77, 218n.49

Department of the Interior, 88

Department of Justice, 38, 217–18n.46

Department of Labor, 77–78, 161, 218n.53, 218n.55

Department of State, 61

Department of Transportation, 36

Department of the Treasury, 77, 78

Depression. *See* Great Depression

derivative presidency, 89

Dickinson, Matthew, 12–13

Dirksen, Everett, 1, 188n.2

District of Columbia, home rule by, 79–80, 219n.61

Division of Coordination, 203n.24

Dodd, N. E., 79

Dodge, Joseph, 55–56, 208n.72

Dole, Bob, 132, 236n.101

Domestic Council: establishment of, 49–50, 58, 205n.38; and Ford, 59; and the OMB, 59, 210n.87; policymaking effec-

Domestic Council (*cont.*)
  tiveness of, 58, 59, 210–11n.91,
  210n.87; revenue-sharing proposal
  of, 78–79; Rockefeller as head of,
  59
domestic policy. *See* policies, types of
Domestic Policy Staff (DPS), 59, 77–78,
  120
Donahue, John, 217n.45
"Do-Nothing" 80th Congress, 118
DPS (Domestic Policy Staff), 59, 77–78,
  120

Economic Policy Board (EPB), 59
Economic Report, 43, 71
Edley, Christopher, 32
Education Professions Development Act
  (1967), 57, 209n.78
Edwards, George C., III, 136, 188n.9,
  239n.18
Ehrlichman, John, 21, 78–79
Eisenhower, Dwight D.: and the BoB, 55;
  Budget Message of, 65; bureau proximity to, 92; commissions used by, 74–
  75; EOP/staff expanded by, 49, 54–55;
  on Hawaiian statehood, 136; on leadership, 163; legislative success of, 63,
  137–38, 212–13n.1; on NASA, 8–9,
  191n.31, 191n.33; and the NSC, 55; on
  OASI, 7; president's program demanded
  by Congress, 45; State of the Union addresses of, 65, 214n.10; Taft-Hartley
  amendment proposed by, 118; vetoes
  by, 75
Eisenhower, Milton, 55
Eizenstat, Stuart, 50, 77–78, 120, 122–23
Elsey, George, 53
Emanuel, Rahm, 161
empirical overview of president's program,
  63–85, 212–13n.1; centralization in the
  EOP, 79; centralization in the WHO,
  79–80, 219n.61; comparative statics,
  80–84, 179, 219–20nn.65–66; Congressional Quarterly Boxscore listings,
  64, 66–67, 68, 70; the data, 71–72,
  165–66, 215–16nn.28–30; the decentralized process, 76–77, 218n.49; Labor
  Department leadership, 77–78,
  218n.53, 218n.55; prehistory of president's program, 73–80, 217n.45,
  217nn.38–39, 217nn.45–46, 218n.48;

presidential legislative proposals, 1949–
  1996, 64–73, 213nn.5–6; *Public Papers
  of the President*, 66, 67–71, 71–72,
  215nn.23–24; the sample, 72–73, 166–
  79, 216n.33, 216nn.30–31; State of the
  Union addresses, 64–66, 214n.13,
  214nn.9–10; White House leadership,
  78–79, 218–19n.56
Employee Retirement Income Security Act
  (ERISA) Enforcement Improvement Act,
  9–10
Employment Act (1946), 43
Energy Committee, 231n.44
energy legislation (1977 and 1979), 119–
  23, 231n.44, 232n.54, 232n.56
EOP (Executive Office of the President):
  BoB as part of, 46; as centralized, 19,
  219n.65; growth of, 7, 51; informational function of, 197n.51; prehistory
  of centralization in, 79; staff of, vs.
  WHO staff, 99, 225–26n.41
EPB (Economic Policy Board), 59
ERISA (Employee Retirement Income Security Act) Enforcement Improvement
  Act, 9–10
executive action. *See* unilateral action
Executive Office of the President. *See* EOP
expertise/technical knowledge, 35–36,
  111, 128–29, 150, 198n.58, 199n.79,
  200n.81

Fay, Bernard, 202n.8
Federal Executive Service, 89
Federal Register, 47, 48
Federal Security Agency, 88, 220n.4
Fenno, Richard, 21
filibuster, 227n.53
Fiorina, Morris, 118
Fishery Conservation and Management
  Act (1976), 61, 239n.20
fishing rights agreements, 61, 239n.20
Fleisher, Richard, 113, 138, 159
focusing events. *See* crises
Ford, Gerald, 191n.33; Aviation Act of,
  36, 91; on block vs. categorical grants,
  38; on Cabinet governance, 50, 58–59,
  205n.46; counsellors appointed by, 58–
  59; decision-making style of, 31; and
  the Domestic Council, 59; energy bill
  proposed by, 70; legislative success of,
  137; Nixon pardoned by, 240n.23; re-

scission messages from, 60, 212n.103; State of the Union addresses of, 65
foreign policy. *See* policies, types of
Frey, Jim, 218n.55

Gaither, Jim, 34
Gardner, John, 57
Gelb, Leslie, 20
General Services Administration, 88
Gephardt, Dick, 126
Gilmour, Robert, 32, 58
Gingrich, Newt, 91, 126
Great Depression, 42
Great Society, 49, 57
Greenstein, Fred, 2
Groseclose, Tim, 94, 235n.84

Haldeman, H. R., 38, 201n.91
Hall, Peter, 29
Hamilton, Alexander, 242n.9
Hargrove, Erwin, 98, 122
Harlow, Bryce, 113
Hart, John, 164, 221n.8
Hauge, Gabriel, 74–75, 92
Head Start, 96
Health Security Act, 8, 191n.30, 207n.57
Heclo, Hugh, 98
HEW (Department of Health, Education, and Welfare), 89, 90, 220n.4
history and conventional wisdom, 41–64, 157–58, 206n.51; Article II of the Constitution, 41; budgetary/deficit issues, 60, 211n.99; early centralization, 53, 56, 207n.57; early coordinating mechanisms, 45–47, 203nn.22–26; *Federal Register* as measure of government growth, 47, 48; institutionalization of president's program, 42–45, 201–2nn.7–8, 202n.13; novelty in policymaking, focus on, 57; and organizational untidiness, 62; special presidential programs vs. administration proposals, 44, 202n.15; staff size, as shifting over time, 52–62, 207–8n.62, 207n.57, 208–9n.72; tracking conventional wisdom, 47–52; World War II's end, 44, 46
Hobby, Oveta, 7
Hodgson, James, 78–79
Homeownership and Opportunity for People Everywhere (HOPE), 76–77, 218n.49

Hoover Commission, 53
HOPE (Homeownership and Opportunity for People Everywhere), 76–77, 218n.49
Horsky, Charles, 80
Hospital Cost Containment Act (1979), 90
House Rules Committee, 147, 240n.25
Howe, Harold, 57
HUD (Department of Housing and Urban Development), 77, 218n.49
Hughes, P. S. ("Sam"), 202n.13, 202n.15
Humbert, Thomas, 218n.49
"Hundred Days," 42, 117

ideology. *See* political parties/ideology
independent agencies, as decentralized, 19
influence, iron triangle model of, 22
information: centrality of, 26, 28–29, 197n.48; cost of, 154; legislators', and legislative success, 116–18, 229n.11, 230n.24; and presidential leadership, 162–64, 244n.36; studies of, 23, 196n.29
institutionalism, 4–5, 11, 24–25, 27–28, 153, 157–58, 189n.16
"Intensive Care Unit" (1993–94 health care reform), 191n.30
interest groups, 127
intermestic policy, 96
International Development and Humanitarian Assistance Act, 215n.23
International Security Assistance Act, 215n.23
Iran-*contra* affair, 51, 199n.70

Jackson, Henry ("Scoop"), 122–23, 232n.53
Johnson, Lyndon: agenda size of, 129–30, 235n.93; Califano on, 33, 49; on the Civil Rights Act, 161, 243n.21; on congressional consultation, 117; on congressional workload, 129–30; on District of Columbia home rule, 79–80, 219n.61; Great Society agenda of, 49, 57; on leadership, 162; on legislative success, 113; legislative successes of, 63; legislative success of, 137–38; moral suasion of, 240n.23; on NASA, 9; and the Office of Legal Counsel, 217n.46; omnibus messages of, 71; staff, his ex-

Johnson, Lyndon (*cont.*)
  pectations of, 49, 53; task forces of,
  57–58, 209nn.78, 81; on unilateral action, 161, 243n.22
Jordan, Hamilton, 50

Karl, Barry, 29
Katzenbach, Nicholas, 200n.81
Kaufman, Herbert, 22
Kemp, Jack, 77
Kennedy, Edward, 232n.56
Kennedy, John F.: assassination of,
  240n.23; and the BoB, 56–57, 209n.74;
  civil rights legislation proposed by, 1,
  152, 188n.2; on elected officers, 119;
  familiarity of program of, 75; legislative
  successes of, measuring, 13, 63, 212–
  13n.1; omnibus proposals of, 71, 125;
  on the president's program as a respon-
  sibility, 2; staff, his expectations of, 49;
  State of the Union addresses of, 65; task
  forces of, 57; tax package proposed by,
  70; treaties proposed by, 69; unilateral
  action by, 160
Keogh, Jim, 63
Kernell, Samuel, 124–25
Killian, James R., 9, 55
King, Anthony, 242n.14
King, David C., 235n.84
King, Gary, 225n.32, 227n.46
Kingdon, John, 3, 89, 90
Kissinger, Henry, 50, 194n.13
Koenig, Louis, 42
Kondratas, Anna, 218n.49
Korea, policy on, 43
Krehbiel, Keith, 29, 94
Krutz, Glen, 113

leadership, 131, 162–64, 244n.36; by the
  Department of Labor, 77–78, 218n.53,
  218n.55; by the White House, 78–79,
  218–19n.56
legislative agenda. *See* president's program
Legislative Reference Division (LRD; *later
  called* Office of Legislative Reference),
  46, 47, 64, 203nn.24–25. *See also* Office of Legislative Reference (OLR)
Legislative Strategy Group, 50
legislative success, 113–33; and contingent
  centralization/congressional decentralization, 123–30, 155–56; definition of,

115; empirical factors in, 130–33; importance of, 114; presentation as beginning of process, 113, 228n.2; and
  presidential choice, 117, 230n.21; presidential rates of, 184–85. *See also* centralization's limits
Levitt, Steven, 94
Light, Paul, 4, 13; on the derivative presidency, 89; on large vs. small agenda
  proposals, 91; on Nixon's administrative presidency, 243n.23; on political
  parties, 133; on presidential draft bills
  considered by OMB, 64, 213nn.5–6; on
  president's agenda vs. program, 66; on
  thickening government, 47–48
linear centralization, 24–28, 39, 62, 82–
  83, 196–97n.41; plausibility of, 153;
  tests of, 95, 104; and time periods, 104,
  106–8, 227n.51
Line Item Veto Act (1996), 211n.102
Long, Russell, 121
Lowi, Theodore, 229n.7
LRD. *See* Legislative Reference Division
Lynn, Laurence, 35, 152

Magaziner, Ira, 8, 119, 191n.30
"make or buy" analogy, 29–32, 197n.50
Malbin, Michael, 115
Maltzman, Forrest, 242n.16
management environment, 25–28, 196–
  97n.41
mandate theory, 240n.23
"manpower," use of term, 218–19n.56
Manpower Revenue Sharing Act (1971),
  78
Mansfield, Mike, 1, 45, 57, 188n.2
Marsh, Jack, 58–59, 125
Marshall, Ray, 77
Marshall Plan, 43, 188n.2
maximum likelihood models, 99, 101
Mayhew, David, 97
Mazmanian, Daniel A., 196–97n.41
McClaughry, John, 59
McCurry, Mike, 129
McDermott, Jim, 119
McGroarty, Dan, 159
McKinley, William, 42
McPherson, Harry, 235n.93, 243n.22
Meese, Edwin, 59, 211n.98
Merget, Astrid, 74
messages, by year, 165–66

methodology. *See* contingent centralization, factors determining; empirical overview of president's program; OLS (ordinary least-squares) models; ordered probit models

Moe, Terry: on bureaucracy, 234n.79; on institutionalism, 4; on politicization, 37, 92, 190n.25; on responsive competence, 24, 92, 244n.36; on structures and incentives, 25, 26, 28

Moore, Frank, 117

Morris, Dick, 35, 61

Morse, True, 21, 56

Moyers, Bill, 24

Moynihan, Daniel Patrick, xii

Murphy, Charlie, 43, 53

Mutual Security Administration, 96

NACA (National Advisory Committee for Aeronautics), 8–9

names of programs, 228n.2

Napoleon Bonaparte, 163

NASA (National Aeronautics and Space Administration), 8–9, 191n.31, 191n.33

Nathan, Richard, 78–79, 92, 210n.88

National Advisory Committee for Aeronautics (NACA), 8–9

National Aeronautics and Space Administration (NASA), 8–9, 191n.31, 191n.33

National Economic Council, 51

National Emergency Council, 46

National Energy Plan (1977), 121

National Performance Review (NPR), 70, 125

National Science Foundation, 9

National Security Council (NSC), 49, 50–51, 55, 96

Nelson, Garrison, 95

Neustadt, Richard: on the BoB, 54; on crises, 66; on demands on the president, 17; on legislative proposals and policy decisions, 5; on the OLR, 207–8n.62; on a persuading, bargaining president, 28–29; on the uniqueness of a president's program, 43–44

neutral competence, 24

New Deal, 24, 42

New Frontier, 57, 63

Newland, Chester, 50

Niskanen, William A., 211nn.97–98

Nixon, Richard: appointment politicization of, 58, 93; on bureaucracy, 19, 234n.79; bureau proximity to, 92; counsellor system of, 23, 242–43n.17; Domestic Council established by, 49–50, 58, 205n.38; Ford's pardon of, 240n.23; on the International Development and Humanitarian Assistance Act, 215n.23; on the International Security Assistance Act, 215n.23; legislative successes of, measuring, 13, 63; Manpower Revenue Sharing Act proposed by, 78; on names of programs, 228n.2; OMB established by, 49–50, 205n.38; on reorganization, 34; staff, expertise of, 35; State of the Union addresses of, 65, 214n.10; unilateral action by, 161, 242–43n.17, 243n.23

NOMINATE scores, 223n.27

novelty: conventional wisdom on, 57; as a factor in contingent centralization, 89–90, 221n.11, 221n.13; and legislative success, 127–28; and limits of centralization, 139

NPR (National Performance Review), 70, 125

NSC (National Security Council), 49, 50–51, 55, 96

Nuclear Nonproliferation Act (1978), 61, 212n.104

OASI (Old Age and Survivors Insurance), 7

O'Brien, Larry, 113, 119

O'Donnell, Ken, 119, 132–33

OEO (Office of Economic Opportunity), 19, 20, 21, 220–21n.7, 220n.3

Office of Environmental Policy, 206n.51

Office of Homeland Security, 159, 160

Office of Legal Counsel, 217n.46

Office of Legislative Reference (OLR; *formerly* Legislative Reference Division), 207–8n.62. *See also* Legislative Reference Division (LRD)

Office of Management and Budget. *See* OMB

Office of Personnel Management, 92

Office of Policy Development (OPD), 50, 59, 61–62

Okun, Art, 36

Old Age and Survivors Insurance (OASI), 7

OLR. *See* Office of Legislative Reference

OLS (ordinary least-squares) models, 99, 226n.44

OMB (Office of Management and Budget): and budgetary/deficit issues, 60, 211n.102; Budget Circular A-19, 46–47, 50, 73; clearance records of, 87, 220n.2; and the Domestic Council, 59, 210n.87; establishment of, 49–50, 205n.38; HOPE opposed by, 77; presidential draft bills considered by, 64, 213nn.5–6; and rescissions, 60, 211n.102; on the Youth Employment and Demonstration Projects Act, 78

omnibus legislation, 125–26, 233–34n.73

O'Neill, Thomas P. ("Tip"), 121, 122, 126, 129, 235n.90

OPD (Office of Policy Development), 50, 59, 61–62

ordered probit models, 99, 101, 104, 225–26n.41, 226n.44

ordinary least-squares (OLS) models, 99, 226n.44

Outdoor Recreation Resources Review Commission (ORRRC), 75

overview, empirical. See empirical overview of president's program

Paarlberg, Don, 233n.69

Pace, Frank, Jr., 203n.26

Panetta, Leon, 62

Patterson, Bradley, 195n.18

Pension and Welfare Benefits Administration and ERISA Advisory Council, 9

Pension Benefit Guaranty Corporation, 9

Personal Responsibility and Work Reconciliation Act, 135, 237n.4

Peterson, Mark A., 135, 136, 137, 138, 237n.3

Pious, Richard, 58, 210n.87

pluralism, 124–25

Point IV, 43, 91

policies: complexity of (see complexity); scope of, 33–34, 39; types of, 26–27, 72, 196–97n.41; types of, as determining contingent centralization, 96, 111, 224–25nn.31–32, 228n.55; types of, and legislative success, 130, 132, 229n.7, 236nn.100–101; types of, and limits of centralization, 140, 239n.20

political parties/ideology, 94, 109, 227–28n.54; and legislative success, 128–29, 130, 132–33, 234–35n.84; and limits of centralization, 139–40

politicization, 39, 201n.90, 210n.88; and decentralization, 93; Haldeman on, 38, 201n.91; measurement of, 228n.56; Moe on, 37, 92, 190n.25; of Nixon's appointments, 58; and presidential choices, 154, 155

Polsby, Nelson, 75

Ponder, Daniel, 13, 74

Poole, Keith, 223n.27

Poole-Rosenthal common space coordinates, 240n.27

popularity, presidential, 130–32, 140, 239n.18

Postal Reorganization Act (1970), 222n.20

PPP. See Public Papers of the President

preferenceship, 94

preponderant source of legislation, 14–15, 75

presidential choices, 152–64; limits and extensions, 157–58, 241nn.6–7; old questions, new findings on, 153–57; qualitative/quantitative research on, need for, 158, 241nn.6–7

presidential preferences, 196n.40

presidential style, 155

President's Advisory Commission on Government Organization, 55

president's program, 1–17, 188n.2; contingent centralization of, 5–13, 15–16; definition/origins of, 2; importance of, 2–5, 114, 188–89nn.9–10; institutionalism of, 4–5, 11, 153, 157–58, 189n.16; legislative success vs. executive ability, 3–4; limits of, as test of centralization, 16–17; measurement of (see empirical overview of president's program); new data and systematic analysis of, 13–16; policy types/issues within, 26–27, 196–97n.41; politicization of, 190n.25; as a responsibility, 2. See also history and conventional wisdom

President's Task Force on Health Care Reform, 8

press, leaks to, 117–18, 230n.24

principal congruence, 36–39, 200nn.85–86

priority/salience, 97–98, 111, 140, 239n.17

programmatic capacity, 88, 220–21nn.7–8
proposals, tables of, 165–66, 179
Public Papers of the President (PPP): data from, 14, 66, 67–71, 71–72, 215nn.23–24; treaties in, 69, 215–16n.29

Quirk, Paul, 4, 113

RACC (Regional Agricultural Credit Corporation), 79
Ragsdale, Lyn, 106, 215–16n.29, 225n.32
Rayburn, Sam, 119
Reagan, Ronald: agenda size of, 130; budgetary/deficit issues under, 60, 233–34n.73; bureau proximity to, 92; Cabinet Councils of, 50, 59, 195n.18, 211nn.97–98; data gaps under, 64, 213n.6; on the Department of Energy, 34–35; and Iran-*contra* affair, 51, 199n.70; Legislative Strategy Group established by, 50; OPD established by, 50, 59; on port modernization, 136; radio addresses of, 69; rescission messages from, 60; State of the Union addresses of, 65, 214n.10, 214n.13; on student loan programs, 91; Technical Working Group established by, 88
"real" ADA scores, 94, 181–82, 223–24nn.27–28, 240n.27
Regional Agricultural Credit Corporation (RACC), 79
Reich, Robert, 9–10, 33, 97
reorganization, 34–35, 39, 88–89, 199n.74, 221n.9; and legislative success, 126–27, 234n.79; and limits of centralization, 139
Reorganization Act (1949), 68–69, 139, 199n.74
Republicans, centralization by, 227–28n.54
rescissions, 60, 211n.102
responsive competence, 17, 24, 92, 163–64, 244n.36
responsiveness, 32–33, 198n.63
revenue sharing, 78–79
Ridge, Tom, 159
Rockefeller, Jay, 126
Rockefeller, Laurance, 75
Rockefeller, Nelson, 7, 59, 191n.33
roll-call votes, 130

Roosevelt, Franklin: bargaining by, 202n.8; and the BoB, 46; "Hundred Days" of, 42, 117; and the National Emergency Council, 46; New Deal bills of, 42; Social Security legislation proposed by, 207n.57; staffing techniques of, 12–13
Roosevelt, Theodore, 42
Rosenthal, Howard, 223n.27
Rostow, Walt, 50
Rubin, Robert, 38
Rumsfeld, Donald, 34, 193n.4
Ryan White CARE Act, 90

Sabatier, Paul A., 196–97n.41
salience. *See* priority/salience
Saulnier, Raymond, 233n.69
Schedule C employees, 222n.22
Schlesinger, James, 120, 122
Schultze, Charles L., 19, 24, 57, 127, 217n.38
Science Advisory Council, 9
secretaries, 92–93, 110, 179–80, 222nn.20–22
Seidman, Bill, 59
Seidman, Harold, 32
separation of powers, 162
September 11 terrorist attacks, xii, 132, 159–60
Shanley, Bernard, 118
Shaw, Thomas C., 239n.23
Shull, Steven A., 225n.32, 239n.23
Shultz, George, 38, 78–79, 210n.87
Simon, Paul, 9–10
Simon, William, 210–11n.91
Sinclair, Barbara, 119
Skocpol, Theda, 207n.57
Skowronek, Stephen, 27
Small Business Regulatory Enforcement Fairness Act (1996), 243n.20
Smith, Adam, 26
Smith, Harold, 203n.24
Snow, John, 36
Snyder, James, 94
Social Security legislation, 207n.57
Sorensen, Ted, 1, 194n.16
Special Counsel, 54
staff size, 51–62, 141, 207–8n.62, 207n.57, 208–9n.72
Stamp, Josiah, 241n.7
Stans, Maurice, 44

State of the Union addresses: of Carter, 65; and centrality of information, 197n.48; data from, 13, 64–66, 214n.13, 214nn.9–10; of Dwight Eisenhower, 65, 214n.10; of Gerald Ford, 65; of John Kennedy, 65; of Richard Nixon, 65, 214n.10; and presidential priorities, 97; of Ronald Reagan, 65, 214n.10, 214n.13
Stephanopoulos, George, 8, 20
Stewart, Charles, 95
Stockman, David, 50, 59
strategic disagreement, 118
Sununu, John, 51, 212n.106
Sweeney, Naomi, 78

Taft, William Howard: and Congress, 42
Taft-Hartley Act (1953), 118, 230n.24
task forces/commissions, 57–58, 74, 209n.78, 209n.81, 217nn.38–39
Taylor, Rosemary, 29
technical knowledge. See expertise/technical knowledge
Technical Working Group, 88
temporal pressures, 89
Theis, John, 106
thickening government, 47–48
Thomas, Norman, 30
Three Mile Island accident, 122
timing within a president's term, 98, 141, 239–40n.23
Toley, Tom, 126
Tomz, Michael, 227n.46
transaction costs in decision making, 29–32, 197n.50
treaties, 69, 215–16n.29
Truman, Harry: and the BoB, 53–54, 207–8n.62; on budgeting, 60, 211n.99; "Do-Nothing," 80th Congress called by, 118; education program consolidation proposed by, 88; and the Hoover Commission, 53; legislative strategy of, 43, 46, 203n.25; legislative successes of, measuring, 63; Marshall Plan of, 188n.2; Point Four message of, 91; on the RACC, 79; staff of, 49, 53–54; on tax policy, 68; on Treasury bonds, 91
trusted secretaries. See secretaries
"two presidencies" thesis, 140, 239n.20

Two-Stage Least Squares regression, 220n.1, 226n.44

unilateral action, 158–62, 242n.9, 242–43nn.14–17, 243nn.20–23
U.S. Postal Service (USPS), 222n.20
U.S. Trade Representative (USTR), 19, 220nn.3, 7

Valenti, Jack, 53
Vandenberg, Arthur, 1, 188n.2

Warshaw, Shirley Anne, 52
Washington Home Rule Committee, 80
Watergate affair, 240n.23
Watt, James, 34–35
Wayne, Stephen, 4, 13, 45
Webb, James, 46, 54, 208n.62
Weko, Thomas J., 93
Whitaker, John, 35, 210n.87
White, Leonard, 197n.51
White House, leadership by, 78–79, 218–19n.56
White House Office. See WHO
White House staff size, 51–52
Whitman, David, 35, 152
WHO (White House Office): as centralized, 19, 219n.65; vs. Congress, 114, 118–19, 230n.31; prehistory of centralization in, 79–80, 219n.61; staff of, vs. EOP staff, 99, 225–26n.41
Wildavsky, Aaron, 60, 132, 236n.100
Williams, Walter, 19, 163
Williamson, Oliver, 26
Wilson, James Q., 20, 126
Wilson, Woodrow, 42, 124
Wittenberg, Jason, 227n.46
Wolman, Harold, 74
Wood, Robert C., 55
Woon, Jonathan, 95
workload, 129–30, 139, 235nn.90, 93
Wright, Jim, 122–23, 232n.53

Young Adult Conservation Corps (YACC), 77–78, 218n.53
Youth Employment and Demonstration Projects Act, 77–78, 218n.53
Youth Employment and Training Act (1977), 218n.55

PRINCETON STUDIES IN AMERICAN POLITICS:
HISTORICAL, INTERNATIONAL, AND COMPARATIVE PERSPECTIVES

Labor Visions and State Power: The Origins of Business Unionism in the United States by Victoria C. Hattam

The Lincoln Persuasion: Remaking American Liberalism by J. David Greenstone

Politics and Industrialization: Early Railroads in the United States and Prussia by Colleen A. Dunlavy

Political Parties and the State: The American Historical Experience by Martin Shefter

Prisoners of Myth: The Leadership of the Tennessee Valley Authority, 1933–1990 by Erwin C. Hargrove

Bound by Our Constitution: Women, Workers, and the Minimum Wage by Vivien Hart

Experts and Politicians: Reform Challenges to Machine Politics in New York, Cleveland, and Chicago by Kenneth Finegold

Social Policy in the United States: Future Possibilities in Historical Perspective by Theda Skocpol

Political Organizations by James Q. Wilson

Facing Up to the American Dream: Race, Class, and the Soul of the Nation by Jennifer L. Hochschild

Classifying by Race edited by Paul E. Peterson

From the Outside In: World War II and the American State by Bartholomew H. Sparrow

Kindred Strangers: The Uneasy Relationship between Politics and Business in America by David Vogel

Why Movements Succeed or Fail: Opportunity, Culture, and the Struggle for Woman Suffrage by Lee Ann Banaszak

The Power of Separation: American Constitutionalism and the Myth of the Legislative Veto by Jessica Korn

Party Decline in America: Policy, Politics, and the Fiscal State by John J. Coleman

The Origins of the Urban Crisis: Race and Inequality in Postwar Detroit by Thomas J. Sugrue

The Road to Nowhere: The Genesis of President Clinton's Plan for Health Security by Jacob Hacker

Imperiled Innocents: Anthony Comstock and Family Reproduction in Victorian America by Nicola Beisel

Morning Glories: Municipal Reform in the Southwest by Amy Bridges

The Hidden Welfare State: Tax Expenditures and Social Policy in the United States by Christopher Howard

Bold Relief: Institutional Politics and the Origins of Modern American Social Policy by Edwin Amenta

Parting at the Crossroads: The Emergence of Health Insurance in the United States and Canada by Antonia Maioni

Forged Consensus: Science, Technology, and Economic Policy in the United States, 1921–1953 by David M. Hart

Faithful and Fearless: Moving Feminist Protest inside the Church and Military by Mary Fainsod Katzenstein

Uneasy Alliances: Race and Party Competition in America by Paul Frymer

Stuck in Neutral: Business and the Politics of Human Capital Investment Policy by Cathie Jo Martin

In the Shadow of the Garrison State: America's Anti-Statism and Its Cold War Grand Strategy by Aaron L. Friedberg

The Rise of the Agricultural Welfare State: Institutions and Interest Group Power in the United States, France, and Japan by Adam D. Sheingate

Disjointed Pluralism: Institutional Innovation and the Development of the U.S. Congress by Eric Schickler

The Forging of Bureaucratic Autonomy: Reputations, Networks, and Policy Innovation in Executive Agencies, 1862–1928 by Daniel P. Carpenter

Dry Bones Rattling: Community Building to Revitalize American Democracy by Mark R. Warren

Managing the President's Program: Presidential Leadership and Legislative Policy Formulation by Andrew Rudalevige